Commercial Property Insurance and Risk Management

Volume I

Commercial Property Insurance and Risk Management

Volume I

James S. Trieschmann, D.B.A., CPCU, CLU
Associate Dean, Terry College of Business
and Dudley L. Moore, Jr., Chair of Insurance
The University of Georgia

Eric A. Wiening, CPCU, ARM, AU
Assistant Vice President
American Institute for CPCU

Bob A. Hedges, Ph.D., CPCU, CLU
Professor Emeritus
Department of Risk Management and Insurance
Temple University

Jerome Trupin, CPCU, CLU, ChFC
Partner
Trupin Insurance Services

Arthur L. Flitner, CPCU, ARM
Director of Curriculum
American Institute for CPCU

Fourth Edition • 1994

American Institute for CPCU
720 Providence Road, Malvern, Pennsylvania 19355-0770

Fourth Edition • August 1994

Library of Congress Catalog Number 94-71921
International Standard Book Number 0-89463-068-7

Printed in the United States of America

Dedication

The American Institute for Chartered Property Casualty Underwriters dedicates this edition of *Commercial Property Insurance and Risk Management* to the memory of William H. Rodda, CPCU.

Born in 1903, Mr. Rodda graduated from Rutgers University in 1925, earning a bachelor of arts degree in economics. He began his career working for various regional insurance rating bureaus, quickly rising to the position of manager in 1930.

From 1940 to 1968, Mr. Rodda served as manager of the Mutual Marine Conference, later named the Transportation Insurance Rating Bureau. TIRB, a predecessor to the American Association of Insurance Services, specialized in inland marine ratemaking and policy drafting.

In 1949, Mr. Rodda published his first book, *Inland Marine and Transportation Insurance*. It received the Elizur Wright Insurance Literature Award in 1951. The book was assigned as study material for CPCU candidates beginning in 1950, the same year that Mr. Rodda received his CPCU designation. Subsequently, the Institute assigned the 1958 second edition and, later, the 1970 third edition of that text, renamed *Marine Insurance—Ocean and Inland.*

In 1978, the American Institute restructured the CPCU program and replaced many of the previously assigned texts with books published by the Institute. Among the new publications was the CPCU 3 textbook, *Commercial Property Risk Management and Insurance*, by William H. Rodda, James S. Trieschmann, and Bob A. Hedges. Mr. Rodda was a coauthor of the second and third editions of that text, which remained in use until 1994. Thus, for forty-four consecutive years, one or another of Mr. Rodda's books was assigned reading for CPCU students.

From 1968 until his death in 1989, Mr. Rodda was president of Marine Insurance Handbook, Inc. He also served as editor of *Best's Underwriting Newsletter*.

A modest and personable man, Mr. Rodda eagerly shared his immense store of insurance knowledge and understanding with insurance people at all levels. His legacy to insurance education will survive him for many years.

Foreword

The American Institute for Chartered Property Casualty Underwriters and the Insurance Institute of America are independent, nonprofit, educational organizations serving the needs of the property and liability insurance business. The Institutes develop a wide range of programs—curricula, study materials, and examinations—in response to the educational requirements of various elements of the business.

The American Institute confers the Chartered Property Casualty Underwriter (CPCU®) professional designation on those who meet the Institute's experience, ethics, and examination requirements.

The Insurance Institute of America offers associate designations and certificate programs in the following technical and managerial disciplines:

Accredited Adviser in Insurance (AAI®)
Associate in Claims (AIC)
Associate in Underwriting (AU)
Associate in Risk Management (ARM)
Associate in Loss Control Management (ALCM®)
Associate in Premium Auditing (APA®)
Associate in Management (AIM)
Associate in Research and Planning (ARP®)
Associate in Insurance Accounting and Finance (AIAF)
Associate in Automation Management (AAM®)
Associate in Marine Insurance Management (AMIM®)
Associate in Reinsurance (ARe)
Associate in Fidelity and Surety Bonding (AFSB)
Associate in Insurance Services (AIS)
Certificate in General Insurance
Certificate in Supervisory Management

Certificate in Introduction to Claims
Certificate in Introduction to Property and Liability Insurance
Certificate in Business Writing

The Institutes began publishing textbooks in 1976 to help students meet the national examination standards. Since that time, we have produced more than eighty individual textbook volumes. Despite the vast differences in the subjects and purposes of these volumes, they all have much in common. First, each book is specifically designed to increase knowledge and develop skills that can improve job performance and help students achieve the educational objectives of the course for which it is assigned. Second, all of the manuscripts of our texts are widely reviewed before publication, by both insurance business practitioners and members of the academic community. In addition, all of our texts and course guides reflect the work of Institute staff members. These writing or editing duties are seen as an integral part of their professional responsibilities, and no one earns a royalty based on the sale of our texts. We have proceeded in this way to avoid even the appearance of any conflict of interests. Finally, the revisions of our texts often incorporate improvements suggested by students and course leaders.

We welcome criticisms of and suggestions for improving our publications. It is only with such constructive comments that we can hope to improve the quality of our study materials. Please direct any comments you may have on this text to the Curriculum Department of the Institutes.

Norman A. Baglini, Ph.D., CPCU, CLU
President and Chief Executive Officer

Preface

This text contains the principal study material for CPCU 3, one of the courses in the curriculum leading to the Chartered Property Casualty Underwriter designation. Other required study material for CPCU 3 is contained in the CPCU 3 Course Guide and *The CPCU Handbook of Insurance Policies*, both of which are published by the American Institute for CPCU.

The contents of the text can be summarized as follows:

- Chapter 1 gives an overview of risk management, providing a conceptual framework for the more intensive study of insurance as a tool of risk management in later chapters.
- Chapter 2 examines the noninsurance technique of risk control, with emphasis on controlling fire and theft losses.
- Chapters 3 through 14 are an in-depth study of the various types of insurance available for insuring businesses and other organizations against property loss.
- Chapter 15 brings the various insurance coverages and noninsurance techniques together in several case studies. These case studies analyze the loss exposures of representative organizations and demonstrate appropriate risk management treatments.

The text is the retitled fourth edition of *Commercial Property Risk Management and Insurance*, first published in 1978. The subtle change in the new title, *Commercial Property Insurance and Risk Management*, acknowledges that insurance—viewed within the larger context of risk management—is the principal subject of the text. Examining commercial property insurance in the context of risk management was the primary purpose of all previous editions as well.

Many people participated in revising and updating the current text. In addition to the principal authors shown on the title page, several contributing authors provided material for one or more chapters. These contributing authors are more fully acknowledged on the page that follows this preface.

Professionals in the appropriate fields reviewed the manuscript to verify that the material was correct, complete, and at an appropriate level of difficulty for CPCU studies. The authors owe a great debt of thanks to the reviewers for their many corrections and adjustments. Those who reviewed one or more chapters of the manuscript are recognized below.

Joseph M. Boslet, PE, CPCU, ARM, ALCM, APA
Vice President—Safety Management Services
Inservco Insurance Services, Inc.

James E. Brennan, CPCU, CLU, CIC
Academic Advisor for the Professional Insurance Program
Lecturer, Finance and Insurance
University of Connecticut

Walter G. Butterworth, CPCU
Vice President
Cohen-Seltzer, Inc.

Chris Campos, CPA
Campos & Stratis

Patricia A. Connors, CPCU
Senior Underwriting Manager, Utilities
The Hartford Steam Boiler Inspection and Insurance Company

Robert B. Edgar
Vice President
Chubb & Son, Inc.

Michael W. Elliott, CPCU, AIAF
Assistant Vice President
American Institute for CPCU

Robert J. Gibbons, Ph.D., CPCU, CLU
Vice President
American Institute for CPCU

Peter C. Imbs, CPCU, AMIM
Vice President
Fireman's Fund Insurance Companies

Donald S. Malecki, CPCU
President
Donald S. Malecki and Associates, Inc.

James E. Mooney, CPCU, ARM, AMIM, AIM
President
Inland Marine Underwriters Association

Sharon L. Rader, CPCU, AMIM
Assistant Vice President, Inland Marine
Great American Insurance Company

Colin J. Rose, CPCU
Royal Insurance (Retired)

Lawton Swan III, CPCU, CLU, ARM
President
Interisk Corporation

Joyce M. Tignino
Vice President—Marketing and Industry Relations
American Association of Insurance Services

S. Joel Vonderscher, CPCU, ARM
Senior Underwriter
Financial Pacific Insurance Company

Robin V. Weldy, J.D.
Director and Counsel
The Surety Association of America

The reviewers listed below are all staff members of Insurance Services Office, Inc. Having their input was especially apt because many of the forms described in this text are ISO products. Paul Edgcomb, CPCU, Assistant Vice President—Customer Service, of ISO's Industry Relations Department, coordinated their efforts.

Lawrence E. Brown, Jr.
Manager—Commercial Property and Package

George M. Burris, CPCU
Specialist—Insurance Lines

Alfred L. Chin, CPCU
Assistant Manager—Insurance Lines

Lisa Eimbinder, CPCU
Assistant Manager—Insurance Lines

Tammy Foster
Intermediate Insurance Lines Analyst

Loretta F. Newman, CPCU
Manager—Commercial Property and Package

Robert P. Ruess
Specialist—Insurance Lines

Maurice E. Southwell, CPCU, CLU, ChFC, ARM, AMIM
Manager—Commercial Property and Package

Haratia J. Pitts Trahan
Senior Analyst—Insurance Lines

In addition to the reviewers recognized above, CPCU course leaders and students too numerous to list here played an essential role in shaping this edition of the text by sending us their questions and comments on the previous edition. We invite *you* to help shape the next edition of the text by sending us your comments regarding the current edition. Please address your comments to the Curriculum Department of the Institutes.

James S. Trieschmann

Eric A. Wiening

Bob A. Hedges

Jerome Trupin

Arthur L. Flitner

Contributing Authors

The American Institute for CPCU and the authors of this text acknowledge, with deep appreciation, the work of the following contributing authors:

Paul O. Dudey, CPCU
Editor
Malecki on Insurance

C. Raymond Ford
Technical Services Manager
Zurich-American Insurance Group

George L. Head, Ph.D., CPCU, ARM, CSP, CLU
Vice President
American Institute for CPCU

Donald S. Malecki, CPCU
President
Donald S. Malecki & Associates, Inc.

Samuel L. Rosenthal, CPCU, ARM
Rosenthal Insurance Consulting, Inc.

Paul W. Watson, CPCU
Farm Team Leader
ITT Hartford

Contents

1 Property Risk Management 1

The Risk Management Process 2

Step 1: Identify and Analyze Loss Exposures 3

Step 2: Examine the Feasibility of Alternative Risk Management Techniques 25

Step 3: Select the Best Risk Management Techniques 35

Step 4: Implement the Techniques 38

Step 5: Monitor the Program 39

The Risk Management Process at Work 39

Summary 45

2 Property Risk Control 49

Controlling Fire Losses 49

Controlling Theft Losses 80

Controlling Other Losses 97

Summary 100

3 Building and Personal Property Coverage 103

Overview of Commercial Property Insurance 103

Building and Personal Property Coverage Form 109

Summary 143

4 Building and Personal Property Coverage Options 145

Optional Valuation Methods 146

Alternatives to Coinsurance 152

Blanket Insurance 156

Options for Insuring Fluctuating Personal Property Values 161

Other Coverage Options 169

Summary 171

5 Covered Causes of Loss 173

Evolution of Causes-of-Loss Forms 173

Concurrent Causation 175

Basic and Broad Causes-of-Loss Forms 176

Causes of Loss—Special Form 197

Optional Coverages 207

Summary 215

6 Other "Commercial Property" Forms 217

Condominiums 217

Builders Risk Insurance 229

Standard Property Policy 237

Legal Liability Coverage Form 240

Glass Coverage Form 242

Leasehold Interest Coverage Form 246

Tenants' Improvements and Betterments 248

Summary 251

7 Business Income Loss Exposures 253

Financial Elements of Business Income Loss 254

Analyzing Business Income Exposures 258

The Business Income Worksheet 273

Summary 296

8 Business Income Insurance 299

Business Income Coverage Form 299

BIC Coverage Options 315

Extra Expense Coverage Form 327

Other Types of Business Income Insurance 331

Case Study 334

Summary 341

Index 343

Chapter 1

Property Risk Management

Every organization is exposed to the possibility of accidental loss. Regardless of whether the organization is a business trying to make a profit or a charitable institution trying to carry out its mission, accidental loss can hinder the organization from achieving its objectives or even totally destroy it. Accordingly, most organizations seek to control their exposures to accidental loss by preventing accidents, by taking measures to limit the size of losses that occur, and by using insurance or some other method to pay for losses that cannot be avoided, prevented, or limited.

In this text, you will study the various methods used by businesses and other organizations (such as governmental or nonprofit entities) to control the effects of property losses. A **property loss** is any loss that a person or organization sustains as a result of the damaging, destruction, taking, or loss of use of property in which that person or organization has a financial interest. Examples of property loss include the destruction of a factory by fire and the theft of public funds by a governmental official.

Another major category of loss that businesses must deal with is liability loss. A **liability loss** is any loss that a person or organization sustains as a result of a claim made against that person or organization by someone seeking monetary damages or some other legal remedy. An example of a liability loss is a court judgment that a building contractor becomes legally liable to pay to a member of the public who was injured when the contractor's scaffolding collapsed. The measures that can be taken to handle liability losses are the subjects covered in CPCU 4.

Although the bulk of this text describes insurance methods used to handle property losses, insurance is best understood within the larger context of risk management. Accordingly, this chapter examines risk management in order to provide a framework for studying property insurance in later chapters.

The Risk Management Process

Ancient commerce included certain insurance-like practices, but true insurance came into being in the late Middle Ages, when it provided indemnity for loss to ships and their cargoes. Since then, insurance has evolved into the principal means of indemnifying individuals and organizations for most types of accidental property loss. In the latter half of the twentieth century, insurance has begun to be viewed in the larger framework of **risk management.** Risk management takes a broad-based, systematic approach to preventing accidental losses, reducing the cost of losses that occur, and finding the most efficient way to pay for whatever losses remain. In the context of risk management, insurance is only one of several possible techniques that can be used to handle "loss exposures."

A **loss exposure** is a *possibility* of loss. In other words, if an organization has a particular loss exposure, an actual loss may or may not occur. The phrase "loss exposure" is frequently used in risk management because a major concern of risk management is how to prevent or plan for losses before they occur. The word "risk" also is used to mean a possibility of loss. (Hence the term "risk management.") However, "risk" has so many other shades of meaning that "loss exposure" will be used throughout this text to mean a possibility of loss.

Central to the discipline of risk management is the **risk management process.** A convenient way of summarizing the process is to list the steps shown below.

1. Identify and analyze loss exposures
2. Examine the feasibility of alternative risk management techniques
3. Select the best risk management techniques
4. Implement the techniques
5. Monitor the program

The basic purpose of the risk management process is to enable an organization to meet its objectives, given the possibility of accidental losses. Thus, in order to use the risk management process successfully, an organization must first establish objectives. Two simple examples illustrate the need for setting objectives.

- Joe has invested some of his money in a self-service storage facility; what he expects from the facility is preservation of his principal and a reasonable return on it. Should the facility be destroyed, he would still want those things out of it. A good insurance program could meet that goal.
- In a hospital operating room, both the patient and the hospital staff have the objective of successful completion of the operation. Insurance cannot attain that goal; an adequate program of loss prevention could do so.

Assuming that objectives are understood, the risk management process attempts to determine the best techniques for treating a particular entity's loss exposures. As steps 1 and 2 above indicate, the decision maker must, before selecting techniques, be familiar with the loss exposures that need to be treated and understand the various risk management techniques available. Risk management techniques include not only insurance but also avoidance, loss control, noninsurance transfers, and retention. After risk management techniques are chosen, they must be implemented—that is, put into action. Once implemented, the risk management program must be monitored to make sure that it is meeting whatever standards have been established by the organization. The steps in the risk management process are described in more detail in the sections that follow.

Step 1: Identify and Analyze Loss Exposures

Identifying loss exposures is somewhat like searching for objects that have been misplaced or hidden. That is, we can spot loss exposures more readily if we know what we are looking for. This section examines the general characteristics of property loss exposures and then reviews some of the methods commonly used to identify and analyze them. (Identifying liability loss exposures is also part of the risk management process, but that subject is discussed in CPCU 4, not here.)

Property Loss Exposures

To give you a better understanding of property loss exposures—that is, the property losses that a business or other organization could suffer—we will consider three important aspects of property losses:

1. The item exposed to loss
2. The cause of loss
3. The effects of loss

Item Exposed to Loss

Property is either real property or personal property. **Real property** consists of land and all structures permanently attached to the land. Some examples of real property are buildings, driveways, sidewalks, underground piping, and radio transmitting towers. **Personal property** consists of all other property and so its primary characteristic is that it is not permanently attached to real property. Some examples of personal property are vehicles, merchandise, furniture, tools, clothing, and oil being transported through an underground pipeline.

The same piece of property can be either real or personal property depending on whether it is permanently attached to real property. Plumbing supplies, for example, are personal property while being manufactured and delivered to a work site. As soon as they are physically attached to the building in which they are to remain, they become real property. A modular home while being transported on a highway is personal property but becomes real property when it has been delivered and secured to a foundation.

The distinction between real and personal property is often significant for risk management purposes. For example, it is usually impossible to move real property out of the path of rising flood waters or an approaching fire. Personal property, in contrast, can usually be moved if sufficient time and resources are available. Moreover, some personal property, such as vehicles and merchandise, spends some or all of its life in transit, thus exposing it to causes of loss that do not ordinarily affect real property, such as collision, overturn, rough handling, or misdelivery.

Exhibit 1-1 shows a useful approach to classifying real and personal property for risk management purposes. It is based on the standard balance sheet, a financial statement commonly used to show an organization's assets, liabilities, and owners' equities.

In balance sheets, assets are commonly divided into "current assets" (those assets commonly turned over in less than a year) and "property, plant, and equipment" (relatively long-lived assets). Although current assets are normally listed before property, plant, and equipment in balance sheets, reversing that order—placing the most obvious property first—is probably better for risk management purposes.

Balance sheets, however, do not include all types of property. Two common omissions are (1) materials and supplies and (2) valuable information of various kinds. When materials and supplies do appear they may be labeled "prepaid expenses." Information includes such things as mailing lists; em-

Exhibit 1-1
Classification of Property for Risk Management Purposes

Property, Plant, and Equipment

- Real Property
  - Land
  - Buildings
  - Other structures
- Personal Property
  - Machinery and equipment, including
    - Data processing equipment
    - Vehicles
    - Other
  - Office and store furnishings and fixtures

Current Assets

- Personal Property
  - Accounts receivable
  - Inventory, including raw materials and stock in process
  - Securities
  - Cash

ployee records, tax records, inventory records, and various other records; research reports; plans for many things such as advertising and market development; and computer programs.

Careful categorization helps you to become aware of the various items of property exposed to loss and to analyze the loss characteristics of each class. For example, money is highly attractive to thieves and therefore calls for greater protection against thieves than, say, office furniture and supplies. Another example can be seen in records of accounts receivable. These records, which may be the only proof a business has of what its customers owe the business, can be difficult or even impossible to reconstruct following a loss. However, unlike most other property, they can be duplicated inexpensively before a loss occurs. If the duplicates are kept current and at a separate location, the loss exposure can be greatly reduced, since it is unlikely that both locations would suffer a loss at the same time, particularly if the two locations were far apart.

Cause of Loss

Risk management professionals seek to identify all important causes of loss to property with which they are concerned. A cause of loss is important if it can produce losses that would keep the organization from achieving its objectives. Causes of loss are also called **perils**. The two terms will be used interchangeably in this text.

As shown in Exhibit 1-2, a multitude of perils can damage or destroy property and so interfere with reaching objectives whose achievement depends on the existence or use of that property. As the multitude of items in the exhibit suggests, identifying perils individually is a never-ending task and therefore cannot be expected actually to be accomplished. Risk management professionals know that "the unknown perils" always exist.

An examination of the perils that can damage a particular item or category of property is necessary when deciding which risk management techniques are most appropriate for that property. For example, if a common cause of physical damage losses to River City's automobiles has been collisions in which River City employees were at fault, River City's risk manager may decide to focus company resources on driver screening and training rather than building a garage to protect the vehicles from hailstorms and vandalism, which may be expected to cause much less loss.

Risk management is also concerned with **hazards**, which may be defined as conditions that create or increase the probability or likely size of loss. Outdated electrical wiring and the storage of gasoline in open containers are examples of fire hazards. A common goal of risk management programs is to eliminate as many hazards as is economically and practically feasible.

Effects of Loss

The third aspect of property loss exposures consists of the effects of loss. The effects of loss can be categorized as physical, operational, and financial. Physical effects consist of what happens to the property itself: in a fire, for example, the extent and nature of the damage by burning, smoke, and fire fighting are the physical effects. When property is damaged or lost it cannot be used, and this affects operations: production halts because essential machinery is broken; sales stop because flood water blocks entrance to the store; and so on. Achievement of objectives after loss requires money—money for repair and replacement, money to protect or rebuild market position, and money for people to manage the repair and replacement of the property and the protection and rebuilding of market position. The amount of money so needed represents the financial effect. The more common types of financial effects are described below.

Exhibit 1-2
Examples of Property Perils

- Aircraft
- Animals
- Barnacles, marine life
- Burglary
- Breakage
- Centrifugal force
- Civil commotion
- Collapse
- Collision or upset
- Computer fraud
- Computer virus
- Condemnation
- Confiscation
- Contamination, pollution
- Corrosion
- Decay
- Delay
- Drought
- Dust
- Earthquake
- Electrical overload, arcing
- Embezzlement
- Evaporation
- Erosion
- Expansive soil
- Explosion
- Expropriation
- Extortion
- Falling objects
- Faulty design, workmanship
- Fire
- Flood and runoff
- Forgery
- Fraud
- Fungus
- Governmental seizure
- Hail
- Human error
- Humidity extremes
- Hurricane
- Insects
- Jettison
- Labor disturbance
- Latent defect, inherent vice
- Landslide
- Lightning
- Malicious mischief
- Mechanical break-down
- Mildew, mold
- Misdelivery
- Mudslide
- Neglect
- Perils of the sea
- Power outage
- Radioactive contami-nation
- Rain
- Riot
- Robbery
- Rot
- Rust
- Sabotage
- Shoplifting
- Shrinkage
- Sinkhole collapse
- Smoke
- Sonic boom
- Spoilage
- Sprinkler leakage
- Static electricity
- Strikes
- Subsidence
- Temperature extremes
- Terrorism
- Theft
- Tides
- Tidal wave
- Tornado
- Trickery
- Vandalism
- Vehicles
- Vibration
- Volcanic action
- Water
- Weight of ice, snow, sleet
- War, military action
- Windstorm

Reduction in Value

When property having value is damaged, destroyed, taken, or lost, the organization suffers a corresponding reduction in the value of its assets. In some cases the property can be replaced for an amount that is the same as the reduction in asset value. For example, if a retailer's merchandise is destroyed in a fire, the retailer may be able to buy replacement merchandise for the same price that was paid for the destroyed merchandise.

Increased Cost To Repair or Replace

In many cases, the cost of replacing damaged or destroyed property is unavoidably greater than the decrease in value of the property. For example, a roof surface that is twenty-five years old is nearing the end of its "useful life" and therefore has an "actual cash value" (commonly defined as replacement cost minus accumulated depreciation) that is well below the amount required to replace the roof. If the roof surface is torn off by high winds, the owner cannot buy a "used roof surface" equal in value to the old one. The roof can be replaced only by rebuilding with new materials. Therefore, the cost of replacing the roof surface will be considerably more than the decrease in value that resulted from the windstorm damage. A similar situation can occur when building codes require a damaged structure to be rebuilt using methods or materials that are more expensive than those used for the original structure.

Loss of Revenue

Revenue is money that an organization makes by selling goods, renting space to tenants, providing services, collecting taxes or tolls, soliciting donations, or performing other operations. When an organization's property is damaged, an important and sometimes overlooked possibility is that the property damage will curtail or hamper the organization's ability to produce revenue. For example, if fire damage to a shoe store requires that the store be closed for three weeks to make repairs, the store will lose all revenue from shoe sales that would have been made during those three weeks. This type of loss is often referred to as **business interruption** or **business income loss**.

Even if its own property is not damaged, an organization can suffer what is called a **contingent business interruption loss** if certain other property is damaged. If, for example, a manufacturer's major supplier of raw materials has to suspend its operations because of a property loss on its premises, the manufacturer's output (and ultimately its revenue) can be reduced. A similar contingent business interruption exposure exists for (1) a supplier or manufacturer that depends on a key customer or (2) a smaller retail store that depends on a "leader property" (such as a department store) in the immediate vicinity to attract customers.

A firm located in a multi-tenant building, even if the firm has no business dealings with other tenants in the building, can suffer a loss of revenue if accidental loss on a lower floor prevents access to the floor on which the firm is located.

Extra Expense

The term **extra expense** is used to describe extraordinary expenses incurred to continue operations following an occurrence that would otherwise cause a suspension of operations. In the shoe store example above, if the time required for repairs had been a longer period, say six months, the store might have been able to rent temporary space in a nearby location in order to continue operations. Even if the store had thereby avoided a revenue loss, it still would have incurred an extra expense loss: the additional cost of renting the second location plus any other additional costs such as the expense of moving to and from the temporary location, furniture rental, installation of telephones, and so on.

Understanding the financial consequences of loss is essential to identifying the loss exposures one faces. For example, Judy may be fully aware that her store and its contents are subject to loss by fire and several other perils. But if Judy is aware of only one financial consequence of loss—reduction in value—she will not be able to implement risk management measures to deal specifically with revenue loss and other possible consequences. As a result, Judy may suffer an unanticipated, and perhaps devastating, business interruption loss.

Direct Loss and Indirect Loss

The terms **direct loss** and **indirect loss** are often used in insurance to describe two basic categories of loss. Direct loss can generally be equated with decrease in value and perhaps increased cost to repair or replace. Indirect loss is generally used to mean revenue loss and extra expense.

The term **consequential loss** is sometimes used as a synonym for indirect loss. However, the term is also used in a more limited sense to describe either (1) loss resulting from spoilage of perishable items or (2) loss of value of undamaged property because property with which it is used has been damaged or destroyed. An example of the latter type of consequential loss can occur when one part of a pair or set of jewelry, clothing, or furniture is destroyed.

Methods for Identifying Property Loss Exposures

Mismanagement is much less likely for loss exposures that have been identified than for exposures that have been overlooked. Consequently, risk management professionals place considerable emphasis on identifying the types of losses that can affect an organization. Several methods serve to reveal loss exposures. The best approach to exposure identification is a combination of many or all of these methods. Using any one method by itself is likely to result in a failure to recognize some exposures.

Common methods of exposure identification include the following:

1. Inspections
2. Interviews

3. Questionnaires
4. Financial statements
5. Flow charts
6. Loss records

In general terms, inspections are a method in which you "look for yourself," whereas interviews require you to "learn from others." Questionnaires might fall into either of those categories, depending on whether you fill out the questionnaire yourself or give it to someone else to fill out. Financial statements, flow charts, and loss records can be categorized as "analyzing records." These three general categories—"look for yourself," "learn from others," and "analyze records"—may help you to remember the specific methods listed above and to think of other possible methods within each category.

Inspections

An **inspection** of an organization's premises and activities has a great deal of intuitive appeal as a means of discovering and understanding many of the organization's loss exposures. By being present where losses may occur, the risk management professional can use his or her own senses and impressions to spot loss exposures. The value of this approach is confirmed by the fact that insurance companies have long used on-site inspections to evaluate the loss exposures of both insurance applicants and currently insured businesses for purposes of gathering underwriting information and making loss control recommendations.

For example, by visiting a prospective customer's premises, an insurance agent or broker can get a precise measurement of the number of buildings, the square footage of each building (which may be useful in confirming property values), the types of contents in each building, the quality of the customer's housekeeping and industrial hygiene, the types of property kept in the open, and the fire protection provided, if any.

Of course, inspections have their limitations. Some organizations' premises and activities may be so extensive that it is impossible—or at least impractical—to inspect everything. In this case a sampling of several premises and activities might determine if further inspection would be justified.

In many cases, inspections serve to supplement other methods to be discussed below. For example, an inspection can confirm the existence of exposures identified by the other methods, and it can reveal some exposures that would not otherwise be identified. For example, the inspection may reveal that the "old factory building" shown on a list of properties is no longer a manufacturing plant but has been converted to a retail outlet. Inspection might also show that a firm's auto maintenance garage is much more than a small repair shop; it includes a body shop with a haphazard spray-painting operation that presents significant fire and pollution exposures.

Interviews

Interviews are closely related to inspections and are often conducted during the course of an inspection. Worthwhile interviews may be conducted with anyone in the organization, ranging from the organization's president to its janitors. Typically, the persons interviewed are not trained in risk management but usually know more about their departments than any outsider could. The proper questions can elicit extremely useful risk management information that may not be available otherwise.

Questionnaires

Written questionnaires are commonly used to discover loss exposures. Using a questionnaire to reveal and analyze loss exposures is like conducting an interview, since in both cases the objective is to obtain useful information from the person being interviewed or completing the questionnaire. Questionnaires fall into two general categories: insurance survey questionnaires and risk management questionnaires.

Insurance Survey Questionnaire

Insurance survey questionnaire forms are supplied by many insurance companies as an aid to their producers. Most **insurance survey questionnaires** are designed to reveal the insurable loss exposures of the prospect or client and to provide the information needed to underwrite and rate the policies that would cover these loss exposures.

When combined with the knowledge, skill, and experience of an insurance professional, the insurance survey can develop the information needed to design an insurance program that treats the exposures of the organization surveyed. However, because they are insurance-oriented, insurance surveys may lead to the use of insurance when other techniques should be used in addition—or even instead—to meet an organization's risk management objectives. This is a major deficiency of insurance surveys.

To develop the information shown in an insurance survey, typically it is necessary for the surveyor to tour the premises, at least in part, and to interview personnel who are capable of providing the necessary information. Throughout the information-gathering process, the surveyor assimilates the information received and combines it with his or her knowledge of insurance coverages. To discover *uninsurable* loss exposures, the results of the insurance survey must be supplemented with information obtained from other sources.

Risk Management Survey Questionnaire

Risk management survey questionnaires, unlike insurance survey questionnaires, ask questions that are helpful in discovering both insurable and uninsurable loss exposures. Because risk management questionnaires address both insurable and uninsurable loss exposures, they overcome the major limitation of insurance survey questionnaires. However, a risk management survey questionnaire has its own limitations. The questionnaire can be completed only with considerable expense of time and effort. Interviews with a number of different people are required, as well as extensive research to develop much of the detailed information. Consequently, it may be impractical to complete the questionnaire more frequently than once every several years.

Although some survey questions can be answered with simple fact information, the questionnaire is most effectively used by a trained risk management professional who recognizes the implications of each item. The answers to certain questions prompt the knowledgeable user to probe further in order to pin down some of the more unusual exposures. The amount of detail in the form may lull a less knowledgeable user into thinking that all possible exposures have been recognized once the questionnaire is complete.

Most risk management survey questionnaires are standardized in the sense that virtually all the questions are meaningful for most organizations. This is both a strength and a weakness—a strength in that their basic relevance is universal, and a weakness in that no standardized questionnaire can be expected to uncover the exposures particularly characteristic of a given industry, let alone those unique to a given organization.

Financial Statement Analysis

Various documents can be useful in revealing loss exposures. An organization's **financial statements** are one category of such documents. Two financial statements that may be especially useful for risk management purposes are the balance sheet and the income statement.

Balance Sheet

The **balance sheet** reports most of the organization's assets, its liabilities, and the owners' equity as of a specific date. Assets are usually listed on the left side of the statement, and liabilities and owners' equity on the right side. The balance sheet derives its name from the fact that both sides are equal, or in balance. In other words, the accounting value of assets is equal to the accounting value of liabilities plus owners' equity.

- Assets include all property with any accounting value that is owned by the organization, such as cash, buildings, and machinery.

- Liabilities include all debts and financial obligations of the organization, other than owners' equity. Examples of liabilities are accounts payable, income tax payable, and unpaid wages of employees.
- Owners' equity is the net accounting value of the organization to its owners, representing the current worth of their investment.

The left side of a simplified balance sheet, which is more pertinent to exposure recognition than the right side, is shown in Exhibit 1-3.

Exhibit 1-3
Left Side of a Balance Sheet

December 31, 1994 Assets		
Current Assets		
Cash	$ 30,000	
Marketable securities	40,000	
Accounts receivable	140,000	
Inventories	250,000	
Total current assets		$460,000
Property, Plant, and Equipment		
Land	$ 90,000	
Buildings	150,000	
Machinery	200,000	
Vehicles and equipment	27,000	
Total property, plant, and equipment		$467,000
Total Assets		$927,000

The balance sheet provides a starting point for identifying exposures; each line in the balance sheet may suggest further inquiries. For example, the entries "land" and "buildings" raise the questions of where and what kind. With "money" the questions are, again, where (on hand, in a bank, or in transit?) and in what form (currency or checks?).

As noted above, the balance sheet does not list all assets of importance to the company that is the subject of the balance sheet. For example, the balance sheet omits materials and supplies and various types of information owned by the company. The balance sheet also omits property not owned by the company. Nonowned property includes property leased by the company, such as premises, vehicles, or office equipment. Nonowned property also includes property of customers being worked on by the company.

Moreover, the balance sheet reports the situation as of a particular date. Various assets will have been acquired or disposed of since that date. At the very least, inventory will have changed.

The values shown in balance sheets are essentially worthless for risk management. They are accounting values, which means they are based on historical cost from which deductions (for depreciation and sales) have been made according to standard accounting practices.

Income Statement

The "bottom line" of the **income statement** is the organization's net income for the year (as determined by accounting procedures). The net income is the difference between items recognized as "income" and those recognized as "expenses." An income statement is shown in Exhibit 1-4.

Exhibit 1-4
Income Statement

EFG COMPANY
Income Statement
For Year Ended December 31, 1994

Sales		$195,000
Expenses:		
Salaries	$90,000	
Advertising	5,000	
Utilities	9,000	
Rent	15,000	
Payroll taxes expense	7,000	
Insurance	3,000	
Supplies	9,000	
Depreciation—equipment	5,000	
Depreciation—fixtures	3,000	
Interest	2,000	
Miscellaneous	1,000	
Federal income taxes	5,000	
Total expenses		154,000
Net income		$ 41,000

The income statement, like the balance sheet, is a starting point for identifying property loss exposures. What property was involved in producing the sales? What premises or other property does the "rent" item represent? What "fixtures" does the company own or use?

The monetary amounts in the income statement are subject to accounting conventions, just as the balance sheet is. (In fact, the two statements are interrelated.) Nevertheless, the income and expense figures are more useful than the balance sheet figures. If, for example, the worst possible instance of property damage would cause a one-year shutdown, a business could estimate its income loss as last year's net income (adjusted for inflation and any anticipated changes in income or expenses) plus any expenses that would be incurred during the shutdown.

Flow Chart Analysis

A **flow chart** is a diagram of an organization's operations. For example, a flow chart of a manufacturer's operations could show the flow of goods from suppliers in the form of raw materials to final customers in the form of finished products. For many operations, a flow chart will be quite complex. For some organizations, several flow charts will be needed. There may be a different one for each product line and separate ones for flows of services (such as electric power) and information (such as sales orders and billing data).

Flow charts are especially helpful in identifying business income loss exposures. For example, see Exhibit 1-5, which shows the movement of goods into and out of a plant, and Exhibit 1-6, which shows the flow of goods within a plant. Exhibit 1-5 reveals that severe damage at the raw materials warehouse might require a slowdown in activity at stages three through six because of lack of raw materials to process. Similarly, Exhibit 1-6 reveals that minor damage to process AB might make it necessary to shut down the entire plant. Both of these possibilities could be further investigated to evaluate the extent of the loss exposure. The key role played by the raw materials warehouse and "process AB" might not be revealed by any of the other methods for recognizing loss exposures.

Flow charts can also be useful in identifying and understanding an organization's loss exposures involving property in transit to and from the organization's premises. Similarly, a flow chart showing the movement of cash within an organization can help to pinpoint exposures to loss of money by employee dishonesty, robbery, and burglary.

Exhibit 1-5
Flow Chart Covering External Flow

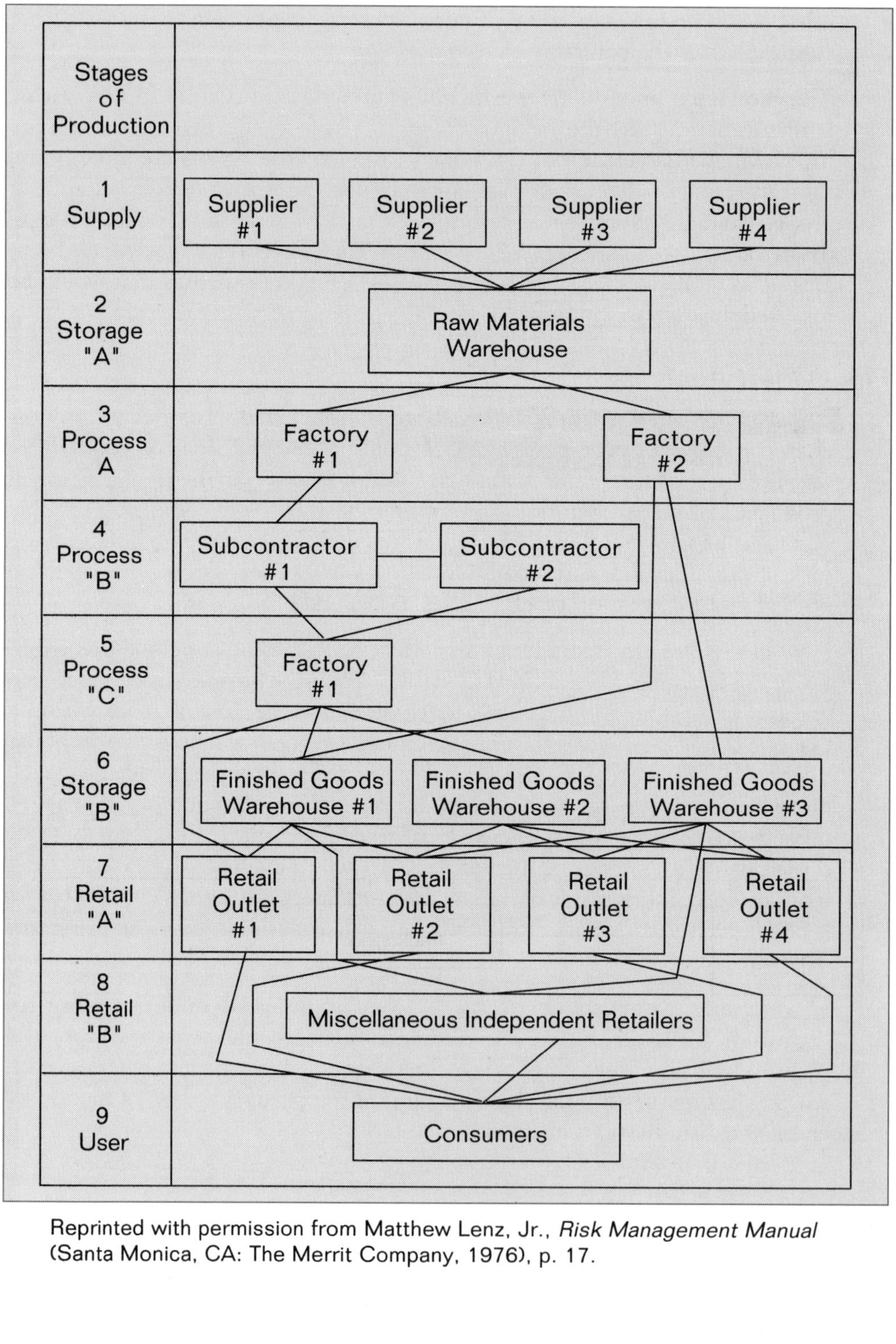

Reprinted with permission from Matthew Lenz, Jr., *Risk Management Manual* (Santa Monica, CA: The Merrit Company, 1976), p. 17.

Exhibit 1-6
Flow Chart Covering Internal Flow

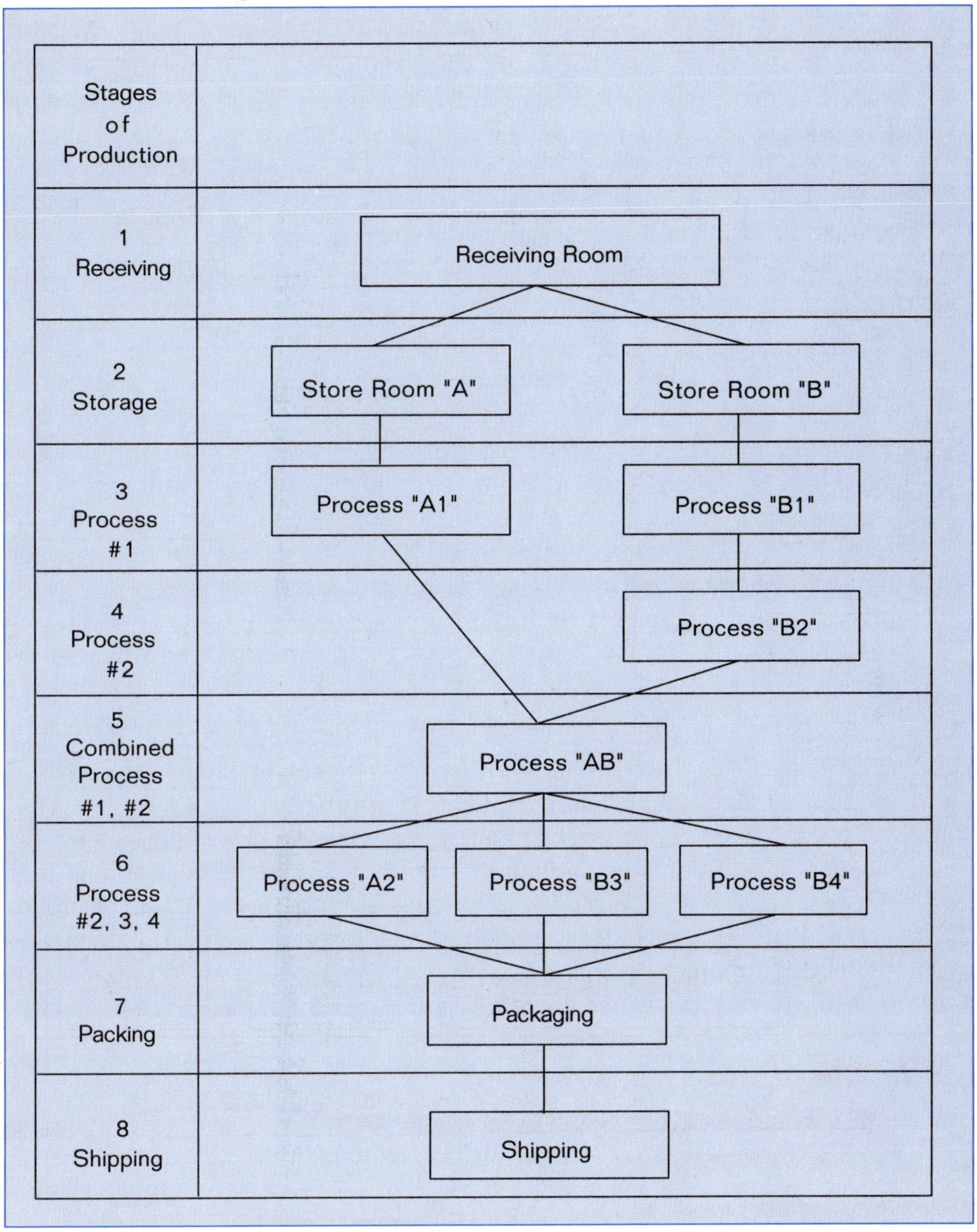

Reprinted with permission from Matthew Lenz, Jr., *Risk Management Manual* (Santa Monica, CA: The Merrit Company, 1976), p. 17.

Loss Analysis

Information on past losses is useful in identifying loss exposures, because history often does repeat itself. Clearly, the exposure analyst should study past losses to determine whether they or any similar losses might happen again. However, many types of loss an organization will incur in the future may never have affected the organization before. The larger the organization, the more useful the information on past losses is likely to be, since the organization is more likely to have already experienced many types of losses. A small firm, in contrast, may never have experienced some common types of losses.

Additional Considerations

The methods described above are by no means the only ways in which loss exposures can be identified. Through a variety of formal and informal communications with persons inside the organization, a risk manager can develop an information network that builds a continuing awareness of new and changing exposures. Through interaction with outsiders, and even through regular reading of general insurance and risk management publications, as well as the trade press of the industry in question, one can learn of risk management problems encountered by similar organizations. For example, none of the preceding methods may alert the risk management professional to the loss exposures implicit in new legislation such as the Americans with Disabilities Act.

The need for identifying loss exposures is ongoing. As time passes, an organization's activities, assets, and environment change, and so, therefore, do its loss exposures. Important developments during the year must be carefully considered from a risk management perspective. For example, a firm that acquires an additional building or introduces a new product line should try to discover all new or changed loss exposures that the new building or product line will entail. So although identification of loss exposures is the first step in the risk management process, it is also part of the last step in the process—monitoring the risk management program to see if adjustments are needed.

Analysis of Loss Exposures

The first step in the risk management process involves both identifying and analyzing loss exposures. Identifying loss exposures entails an awareness that a particular loss can happen and under what circumstances. Analysis of loss exposures entails an understanding of how often a particular type of loss could occur (potential frequency), how large the loss could be (potential severity), and how much confidence, or credibility, can be placed in the risk management professional's predictions of loss severity and frequency.

Analysis of loss exposures is important because it enables the risk management professional to judge the relative significance of loss exposures and prioritize them for risk management treatment. Of most interest are (1) those exposures that have potential for serious effects and (2) those that produce the highest loss frequency. The former are important in assuring ongoing achievement of objectives, whereas the latter are most likely to produce savings by application of risk control. Analysis of loss exposures is also essential to selecting appropriate limits of insurance for exposures that will be insured.

Potential Loss Frequency

Potential loss frequency is the number of events—fires, thefts, or earthquakes, for example—that are expected to occur within some time interval such as a century, a decade, or a year. An estimate of loss frequency for theft losses at a particular building might be one every two years, whereas the estimated loss frequency for fire losses at the same location may be one every hundred years.

It is perhaps confusing to speak of the "frequency" of something that happens so infrequently as a fire to a given building. Many buildings in the United States have stood for 200 years or more without suffering a fire. To suggest that a certain loss prevention measure would "reduce fire frequency" for a 200-year-old building seems contrary to the normal use of this term. However, there is some "frequency" of the fire losses in *buildings of this type*. Thus, frequency can be considered as referring to experience, on the average, over many cases.

As a general rule, loss frequency is more predictable than loss severity. In fact, loss frequency can be predicted with a fairly high degree of confidence for some exposures for large organizations. For example, an organization with 1,000 motor vehicles probably would be quite confident of its ability to predict accurately the number of accidents involving physical damage during a given time period. Similarly, a mail-order house that ships hundreds of parcels each day can predict accurately the number of transit losses it will sustain in a given year. Some companies may even be able to make satisfactory projections of the number of fire losses to be expected each year. An example would be a fast food chain with, say, 2,000 stores throughout the country.

Significant property losses occur infrequently, and most organizations do not have a sufficiently large number of exposure units to permit accurate prediction of loss frequency. However, an estimate with a substantial margin for error is better than no estimate at all, as long as the risk manager recognizes its limitations.

Potential Loss Severity

Potential loss severity refers to how serious a loss occurrence may be. Loss severity is measured first in physical effect: How much territory will be involved in a single windstorm? How many units will be stolen in a single night? After physical effects are measured, operational effects and, finally, financial effects can be measured.

In most cases, severity varies a great deal from loss to loss. For example, windstorms vary a great deal in severity, and earthquakes can range from below 1.0 to more than 7.0 on the Richter scale. In addition, severity often depends on many local conditions that vary from time to time. For example, fires that start at night, when most businesses are closed, commonly cause more damage than fires that start in the daytime when they are likely to be promptly detected and extinguished.

Knowing the size of loss most likely to occur is useful. However, there is little comfort or value in knowing that the most probable amount of loss was $25,000 if a $1 million loss has actually occurred. In measuring loss exposures, then, it is particularly important to know the size of the largest loss that could occur, or **maximum possible loss.** It is also helpful to determine the largest loss *likely* to occur, or **maximum probable loss.**

Maximum Possible Loss

The first important consideration in estimating property loss from fire or other perils is the maximum possible loss, sometimes called the **amount subject.** The maximum possible loss is the total value exposed to loss at any one location or from any one event. In the case of fire damage to a building and its contents, the maximum possible loss is usually the total building and contents values exposed to loss within any one building or fire division. (A fire division is a portion of a building that is separated from the rest of the building by fire walls, which prevent or slow the advance of fire.) It is the maximum possible loss that should usually be considered by the business owner or risk manager when choosing among risk financing alternatives and in establishing insurance limits if insurance is chosen.

Fire is not always the most serious peril, in terms of severity, to which buildings and contents are exposed. If a building is fire resistive and well divided by fire walls, fire damage may be relatively minor, even in the worst conceivable situation. However, the fire resistive construction may offer little protection against damage by earthquake, windstorm, landslide, explosion, or flood.

The maximum possible loss must be considered with regard to other property also, not just for buildings and contents. For example, what is the maximum possible physical damage loss for a fleet of motor vehicles? Is it the value of the most expensive unit? Are several vehicles stored in the same building at night? What are the chances of flood or tornado damage at the company's parking area?

At first glance, the amount to which goods in transit are subject in a single loss would seem to be the value of the largest shipment. However, one must also consider the possibility that several shipments might be in a terminal, warehouse, or vessel at the same time.

Maximum Probable Loss

The largest loss *likely* to occur may involve less value than the maximum possible loss. The probable fire loss will be limited by the fire protection available—such as automatic sprinklers, public fire departments, and so forth. This smaller estimate might be termed probable maximum loss, or maximum probable loss.

The diagram in Exhibit 1-7 illustrates the concepts described above. The premises consist of two buildings: Building A and Building B. Building A is subdivided into three areas by two fire walls. The values of buildings and contents in Area 1 of Building A are $1 million, $2 million in Area 2, and $3 million in Area 3.

The other building, Building B, is separated from Building A by 300 feet, including a river 200 feet wide, and contains total values of $10 million. In determining the maximum possible loss and maximum probable loss, it might be determined whether the fire walls and the separation distance between buildings will be recognized as effective fire separation. This sometimes calls for a fire protection engineer's evaluation of the premises, considering the combustibility of the materials and the effectiveness of the separations. Assuming the engineer reports that all separations are standard and effective, then the maximum possible fire loss would be $10 million (the value of Building B). Building A and Building B would not be deemed subject to a single fire loss. If, however, all buildings are equipped with an adequate sprinkler system, the maximum probable loss might be judged some fraction of the values exposed, say 40 percent. The maximum possible loss would stay at $10 million, because automatic sprinklers can be rendered ineffective.

If Building A by itself were considered and the two fire walls met all necessary standards (thus forming separate fire divisions), then both the maximum possible fire loss and the maximum probable fire loss might be considered $3 million. However, if the building is of fire-resistive construction and combustibility of the contents is low, or if automatic sprinklers have been installed, the maximum probable loss might be considered less than $3 million.

Exhibit 1-7
Maximum Probable Loss and Maximum Possible Loss Illustration

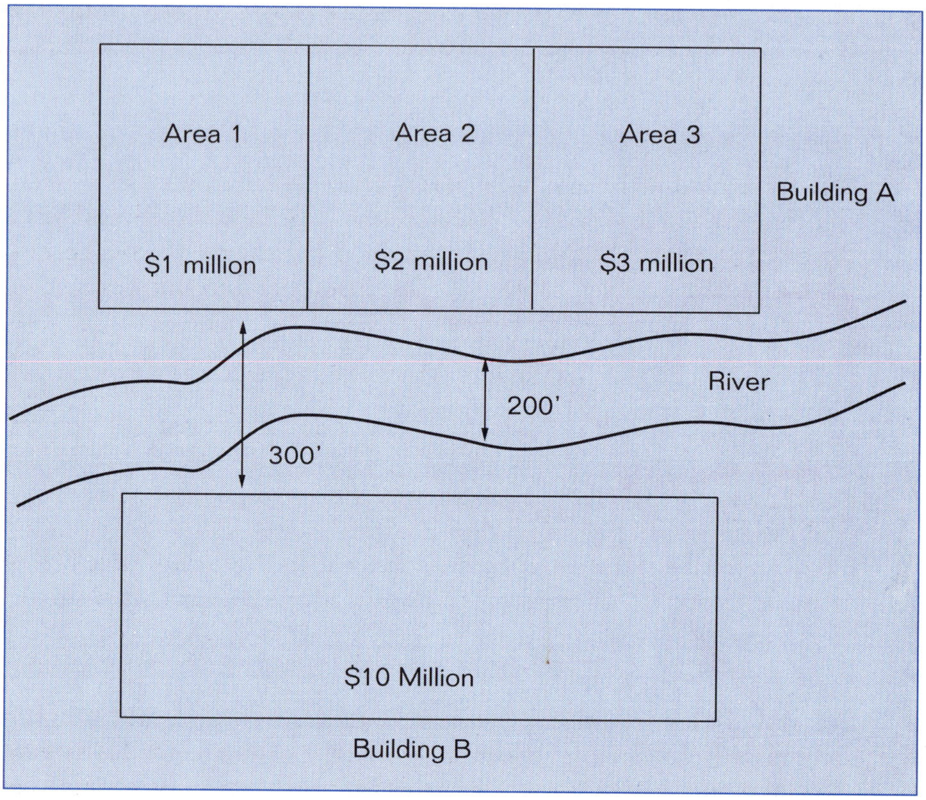

A similar analysis might be made of a multi-story building, estimating the probable maximum number of floors to be damaged.

We have determined that the maximum possible loss in any one fire is $10 million because it is virtually impossible for a single fire to damage both buildings simultaneously. Such a conclusion must be tempered with the realization that perils other than fire must also be considered. Because Buildings A and B are located alongside a river, it is possible that flooding of the river would result in simultaneous damage to both buildings. The likelihood of a flood at this location must be considered, as well as the degree of damage a flood might inflict. There is also the possibility that a windstorm could destroy both buildings.

The concepts of maximum possible loss and maximum probable loss are of value to risk managers and underwriters, who can use the concepts to establish the severity of exposures that must be treated. The maximum probable loss concept is of particular use in underwriting, since underwriters are concerned with the averaging effect of a large number of exposure units. Note, however, that the definitions used above and the conclusions reached represent only one approach, used by some underwriters and risk managers. Other approaches are possible.

Total Loss Concept

When calculating the maximum loss potential, attention must be given to the fact that a major loss can involve more than one peril and several loss effects. An earthquake can be followed by fires and explosions. Hurricane and flooding may come together, as may hurricane and fire. Many losses involve more than one type of loss effect. For example, a severe fire ordinarily results in not only decrease in value of the affected property but also business interruption and extra expense. Hence, the important figure to consider in measuring loss exposures is the maximum loss that could occur, considering all aspects of the loss.

Credibility

The term **credibility** is often used to mean the level of confidence that one can properly have in available data's being an accurate indicator of future losses. Credibility plays a large role in determining what insurance or noninsurance techniques will be used.

Suppose, for example, that losses can be predicted within a range as shown in Exhibit 1-8. The risk manager might predict that average losses would fall along the line labeled "expected," and that the maximum probable loss would lie along the line labeled "maximum." Minimum probable loss levels might also be predicted as shown by the "minimum" line. If such predictions can be made with a high degree of confidence, actual losses will be expected to follow a pattern something like the "actual" line on the graph, deviating from the average from one year to the next but in no case exceeding the maximum or falling below the minimum.

The pattern shown in Exhibit 1-8 might be expected for the transportation claims of a large shipper with ten years in business and a steadily increasing volume. In such a case, there is little uncertainty and the losses really represent current expenses, so are unlikely to be an appropriate subject for insurance.

A more common situation is illustrated in Exhibit 1-9. This exhibit might represent fire losses actually experienced by a large organization with a number of locations. A few losses usually occurred each year. In year 4, however, there were no losses, while in year 8, at least one major fire occurred. These losses

Exhibit 1-8
Predicted Losses Versus Actual Losses—Case 1

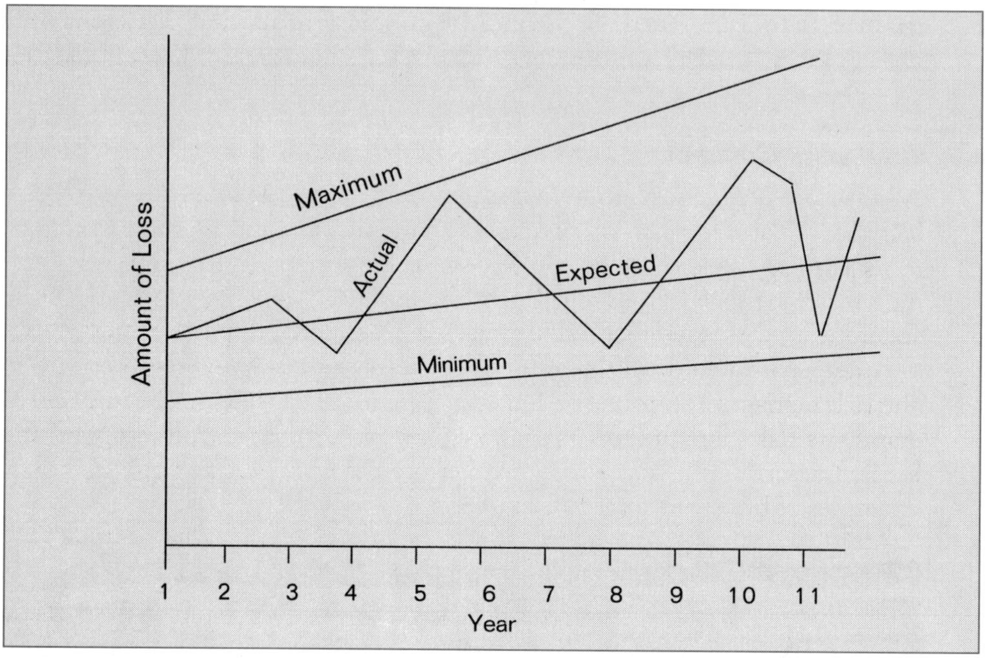

Exhibit 1-9
Predicted Losses Versus Actual Losses—Case 2

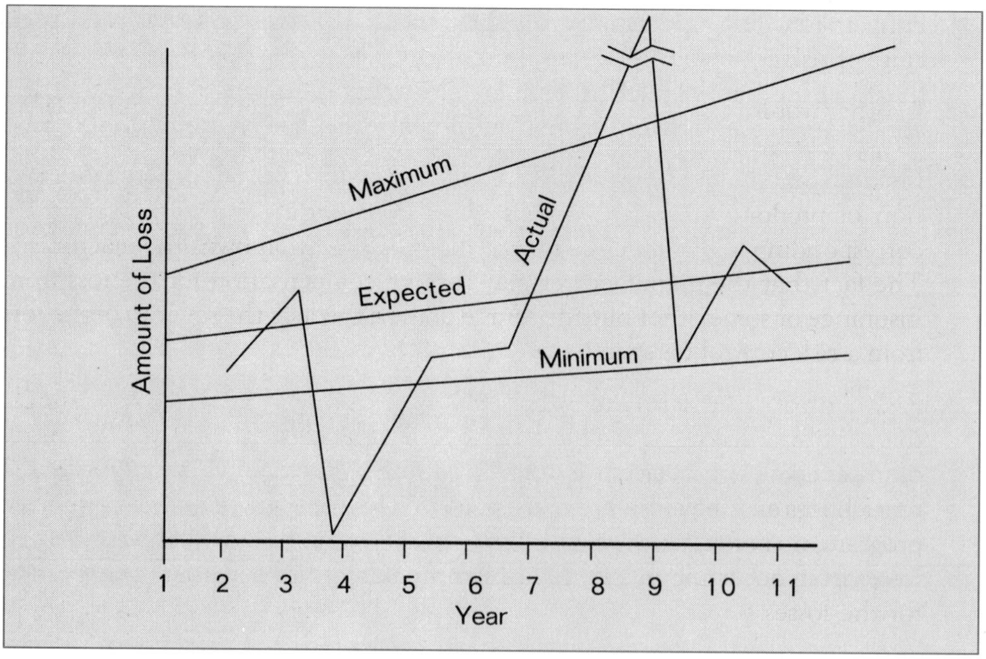

may have been predictable to a certain extent at lower levels, but possibilities existed for substantial losses above the normal loss levels. To attempt to finance such losses out of the organization's operating budget might be disastrous.

Step 2: Examine the Feasibility of Alternative Risk Management Techniques

Examining the feasibility of alternative risk management techniques for treating a particular loss exposure or set of loss exposures is the second step in the risk management process. In order to perform this step, one must understand the risk management techniques that are available. Accordingly, this section describes the various risk management techniques and provides some examples of how they might be applied.

Risk Control[1]

All risk management techniques can be classified as either risk control or risk financing. **Risk control**—also widely known as **loss control**—may be defined as any conscious action (or decision not to act) intended to reduce the frequency or severity of accidental losses. **Risk financing**, in contrast, is concerned with raising funds to pay for losses that actually occur—perhaps in spite of risk control efforts.

In other words, risk control focuses on actual harm, not on amounts of money paid to compensate for, or otherwise finance recovery from, this harm. Such financing matters are the concern of risk financing. For instance, the destruction of production machinery can result in both a loss of an asset and a corresponding loss of revenue for the manufacturer that owns the machinery. The fact that the manufacturer may receive compensation for the loss from insurance or some other outside source does not reduce the severity of the loss from a risk control perspective.

Risk control and risk financing are often used in combination to treat a single loss exposure. Taking cost-effective steps to reduce the frequency and severity of losses is of course desirable from the viewpoint of the organization exposed to such loss and may also benefit society as a whole. However, no risk control program, no matter how well designed and administered, is able to prevent all losses from occurring; hence the need for efficient risk financing plans to pay for the losses that do occur. In most cases, an efficient risk control program reduces the cost of an allied risk financing plan. For example, the cost of insurance (risk financing) against theft of money and securities is reduced considerably when the insured property is kept in a burglar-resistant safe (risk control).

An almost infinite number of specific risk control measures can be applied to various loss exposures. For purposes of this text, a risk control *measure* is any specific action taken to reduce loss frequency or severity—such as hiring armed guards or installing a burglar alarm. A risk control *technique* is a category of related risk control measures. Risk control techniques include the following:

- Exposure avoidance
- Loss prevention
- Loss reduction
- Segregation of loss exposure units

Exposure Avoidance

Exposure avoidance makes loss from a specified exposure impossible. It reduces the probability of such a loss to zero by either eliminating or deciding not to undertake a specified asset or activity. However, exposure avoidance has limited applications. A business organization cannot avoid an exposure without forgoing a corresponding source of revenue. However, some business organizations have decided not to manufacture particular products or not to use certain processes because of the hazards involved.

Loss Prevention

Loss prevention is any measure that reduces the *probability or frequency* of a particular loss but does not eliminate completely all possibility of that loss (as does exposure avoidance). Loss prevention is distinct in principle from loss reduction because loss reduction focuses on reducing the *severity* of losses, not their probability or frequency. In practice, a risk management action may combine elements of both loss prevention and loss reduction.

Most loss prevention measures go hand in hand with concepts of how losses are caused. In general, a loss prevention measure is an action taken before a loss occurs in order to break the sequence of circumstances that are thought to lead to the loss. Breaking the sequence is supposed to stop the loss from happening, or at least make it less likely. Because of the close link between loss causation and loss prevention, developing effective loss prevention measures usually requires a careful study of how particular losses are caused.

Some examples of loss prevention measures that could be used to reduce the frequency of fire losses are listed below.

1. Removing unnecessary flammables
2. Safe storage of necessary flammables
3. Elimination of open flames and other heat sources
4. Elimination of sources of spontaneous combustion
5. Enforcement of "no smoking" regulations

Loss Reduction

Loss reduction measures reduce the severity of those losses that do occur. Examples of loss reduction measures that Acme Company could take, before the outbreak of any fire, to reduce the likely severity of fire loss at its headquarters building include the following:

1. Erecting fire walls or otherwise establishing fire divisions so that the spread of any fire that did strike a portion of the building would be confined
2. Reducing fire intensity by removing or storing any flammable materials in fire-resistive containers
3. Cooperating with the fire department to establish pre-fire plans for the actions the fire department should take in a fire emergency
4. Installing and maintaining an appropriate fire detection/suppression system for the headquarters building (including any special fire protection needed for particular activities such as computer operations)

Examples of loss reduction measures that could be taken after the outbreak of a fire include the following:

1. Notifying public fire-fighting authorities (which may be a feature of the automatic fire detection/suppression system)
2. Providing temporary physical protection against other perils for property undamaged by the fire
3. Salvaging fire-damaged property

Segregation of Exposure Units

Segregation of exposure units encompasses two distinct but closely related risk management techniques—*separation* of exposure units and *duplication* of exposure units. Both techniques strive to reduce an organization's dependence on any particular asset or activity, thus tending to make individual losses smaller and more predictable. The basic logic of segregation of exposure units is exemplified in the maxim, "Don't put all your eggs in one basket."

Separation of exposure units involves dividing an organization's existing single asset or operation into two or more separate units. Two examples are dividing existing inventory between two warehouses or manufacturing a component part in two plants rather than in only one plant. Similarly, inventory or production might be divided among three or four different locations instead of two.

Duplication of exposure units involves complete reproduction of an organization's own asset or facility to be kept on standby or in reserve. This duplicate is not used unless the primary asset or activity is damaged or destroyed. Examples of duplication include the following:

1. Maintaining duplicates of accounting records and other valuable documents in a safe location to be used only if the original documents are damaged or otherwise unavailable
2. Keeping an inventory of spare machinery parts or even spare machines to be used when the primary ones are unusable for any reason
3. Entering into a mutual aid pact with similar organizations for use of one another's facilities—such as computers, printing presses, refrigerated storage, and the like—when one member's normal facilities are damaged or otherwise unavailable

Both separation and duplication tend to be expensive, sometimes impractical, risk management techniques. Separation, in particular, is seldom undertaken for its own sake but, instead, is often a by-product of another management decision. For example, few organizations build and use a second warehouse simply to reduce the severity of losses to the former single warehouse. However, if an organization is considering the construction of a second warehouse because of a need to expand production, the risk management implications of this new, separate, exposure unit may well be an additional argument in favor of the expansion.

In contrast, duplication—keeping a spare unit on standby, ready for emergency use—is often primarily prompted by risk management considerations. Senior management recognizes the crucial nature of a particular operation or asset and is willing to invest in duplicating it in order not to be without this essential element of its operations. Duplicate records, spare machinery parts, and cross-training employees to do several jobs within their departments are typical risk management safeguards.

Risk Financing[2]

The purpose of risk financing is to pay for those losses that do occur despite whatever is done for risk control. No risk financing arrangement can prevent losses from occurring or reduce the severity of the losses themselves. Good risk financing can, however, reduce the cost and ensure the success of raising the funds to pay for or recover from losses.

Each risk financing technique involves a planned source of funds with which an organization may finance recovery from accidental losses. *Unplanned* sources of funds—such as federal disaster relief or a settlement or court award paid by an outsider who is legally liable for having caused harm to the organization—are not reliable sources of funds. They may or may not be available after a loss.

All risk financing techniques can be broadly classified as (1) retention, (2) transfer, or (3) a technique that has elements of both retention and transfer. Retention techniques draw on funds originating within the organization or its economic family. In contrast, transfer techniques draw on sources of funds outside the organization whose losses are being financed. For example, paying for losses as current expenses is a basic form of retention, while purchasing guaranteed-cost insurance is a basic form of transfer. Risk financing techniques that combine elements of retention and transfer depend on funds originating both inside and outside the organization.

Retention

When an organization relies on **retention** to finance recovery from its losses, the cost of losses and of related administrative expenses (often called loss adjustment expenses) is borne entirely by the organization retaining the losses.

Loss exposures can be retained either consciously or unconsciously. An example of conscious retention is eliminating collision insurance on an older car because the value of the car has fallen so low that a total loss of the car could be paid by its owner without hardship. An example of unconscious retention occurs when an organization buys property insurance on its building but out of ignorance fails to obtain an adequate amount of insurance to cover a total loss. In this situation, the building owner will have retained the amount of the loss exposure in excess of what is payable under the policy.

Reasons for Using Retention

Retention can be well used, not just out of ignorance that a loss exposure exists. Sometimes no other risk financing technique is available, as in the case of war damage, which (with the exception of marine and aviation war loss exposures) is generally not covered by commercial insurers. In most cases, however, the reason for choosing retention is the organization's belief that retaining a loss exposure will be less expensive than insuring it. This is particularly true when a "hard market" exists and some forms of insurance are difficult to obtain or are obtainable only at premium levels that are prohibitive for many organizations.

In general, the premiums an insurance company collects from its policyholders have been calculated to pay the expected insured losses and loss adjustment expenses plus the insurer's operating expenses and, in some cases, a profit. By retaining its losses, an organization pays only its losses and loss adjusting expenses, and so, in theory, saves the part of the premium intended to pay the insurer's operating expenses and profit.

However, a firm's retained losses may be much higher than expected in a given year and therefore may end up costing the firm far more than what the insurance premium would have been, regardless of the fact that the premium contained a loading for insurer expenses and profit. The key to using retention effectively, then, is being able to hold the retained amount to an acceptable level. Doing so depends not only on limiting the amount retained in any one loss but also on limiting the total amount retained in multiple losses within a particular time period. In this regard, larger organizations have a double advantage: usually they can retain larger amounts, and often their larger number of exposure units allows better prediction of loss frequency.

One of the benefits of retention can be that an organization does not need to pay for retained losses before they occur. With insurance, the organization often must pay the policy premium at the beginning of the policy period, thus "tying up" funds that the firm could be using (to earn interest, for example) until losses are paid. Of course, any "cash flow" benefit derived from using retention instead of insurance can be quickly wiped out if actual losses exceed expected losses.

Methods of Paying Retained Losses

Any of three general methods can be used to pay for retained losses. These methods are pre-funding, current funding, and post-funding.

- With **pre-funding**, the money needed to pay for losses is set aside in advance of losses.
- With **current funding**, money is provided at the time of the loss or immediately after.
- With **post-funding**, the organization pays for its losses at some later time, using borrowing (or some other method of raising additional capital) in the meantime.

These methods are described in more detail below.

An important point about retention is that, under present income tax and financial accounting rules, loss costs cannot be deducted from income until the amount is certain—which is uniformly held to mean that no deduction can be made before the loss has actually occurred. This timing of the charge, which is known as "current expensing," applies no matter whether funding (the organization's provision of the money needed) takes place before, at the time of, or after the loss.

Pre-Funding The principal advantage of pre-funding is that it can allow the amount of retention to be as much money as can be saved over several budget periods. The principal disadvantage is that it ties up money that could otherwise be used to promote operations. This loss of productivity—represented by the difference between what funds fully employed in the organization can produce versus what can be earned on readily marketable securities—keeps pre-funding from being widely used except in one form: captive insurers.

A **captive insurer** is a subsidiary that the organization owns and uses to "insure" some of its own loss exposures. Since the financial results of the captive are passed on to its owner, using captives is a form of retention. And, since having a captive insurer requires first providing it with capital and then paying it premiums for the exposures it insures, use of a captive is a form of pre-funding. (Because captives commonly purchase reinsurance to cover a portion of the exposures they insure, using captives is also a means of risk transfer.)

Current Funding Current funding is the most popular and often the least expensive form of retention. Its big advantage is that it uses no funds before they are actually needed. Its principal disadvantage is that only as much money as can be spared from a single budget period can be devoted to it.

Post-Funding Suppose that a building is so badly damaged that most of it has to be rebuilt. The new structure will cost more than the value of the old building, and it will be worth more. So the owner may obtain a mortgage loan to fund the increased value—and thus engage in some post-funding of the loss. A clear advantage of post-loss funding is that the cost may be paid for over several years instead of all at once. Another advantage is that only the amount of money needed is used. An obvious disadvantage is the interest that must be paid on the debt. Another disadvantage is that the same loss event that produces the need to borrow may also reduce the organization's creditworthiness—its ability to borrow and repay.

"Self-Insurance"

The term **self-insurance** has not been used in this discussion of retention. In informal conversation and writing, "self-insurance" is commonly used to denote any form of retention. However, in other contexts self-insurance is more restrictively defined to include only those retention programs that possess one or more of the following characteristics:

- A sufficiently large number of independent loss exposures to make the organization's aggregate losses from these exposures highly predictable
- An established fund to which the organization makes regular contributions and from which losses are paid, much as they would be in a commercial insurance arrangement
- A formalized captive insurance program
- All of the features that the statutes of any state require of an organization that wishes to qualify as a self-insurer of workers compensation or other specified types of exposures in that state (and thus to be exempt from requirements to buy commercial insurance or to establish other financial responsibility acceptable to that state for these exposures)

Because it is sometimes difficult to determine how "self-insurance" is being defined, the term is used sparingly in this text and elsewhere in the CPCU curriculum.

Transfer

When transfer is used to finance loss exposures, one person or organization (the transferor) obtains a promise from another entity (the transferee) to pay for all or some part of losses that occur. Although the financial consequences of the loss exposure are transferred to the transferee, in reality they are transferred only to the extent that the transferee is financially able to honor its promise. If the transferee does not or cannot honor its promise, the transferor bears the loss.

Insurance

The most common example of transfer is insurance. **Insurance** works best when many loss exposures (more precisely, the financial effects of these loss exposures) in a particular class are transferred to an insurer and the losses arising out of the exposures are shared by all those in the insured class. Insurance also works when losses are divided among insurers (usually by reinsurance) in such a way that none of the insurers is called upon to pay more for any loss than it can afford. However, continuing success in such arrangements requires that each insurer collect in overall premiums enough money for it to be able to pay its overall claims.

Each insured person or organization enters into a written contract, called an insurance policy, with the insurance company. In the insurance policy the insured person or organization agrees to pay an insurance premium to the insurer, and the insurer agrees to pay for the type(s) of losses stipulated in the policy. The premium paid by each policyholder, in relation to the largest potential loss insured, is small.

Noninsurance Transfer for Risk Financing

In addition to insurance, **noninsurance transfer** is another form of risk financing transfer. In a noninsurance transfer, some entity other than an insurer agrees to pay certain losses incurred by another. The agreement is usually part of a larger contract, such as a lease, a construction agreement, or a maintenance agreement. Unlike insurance, noninsurance transfer for risk financing does not necessarily involve a spreading of risk among many people or organizations. In many noninsurance transfers, one party simply agrees to pay the losses of another.

Most noninsurance transfers involve liability, not property, loss exposures. For example, a construction contract might contain a "hold harmless" agreement that obligates the building contractor (transferee) to pay defense costs and damages on behalf of the property owner (transferor) if the property owner is sued for injury allegedly arising out of the work project. If the claimant wins the suit and the contractor is unable or unwilling to pay the damages, the owner will remain legally liable to pay damages despite the hold harmless agreement.

An example of a noninsurance transfer for financing *property* loss exposures is a clause in a building lease that obligates the lessee to pay for any fire loss that occurs to the building, even if the lessee would not otherwise be responsible. Similarly, a rental agreement for personal property, such as an automobile, might obligate the user to pay for any loss resulting from damage to the rented auto while in the user's custody. In both cases, the owner of the property has attempted to shift the burden of loss to another party. However, if the other party is unwilling or unable to honor its obligation, the loss will fall on the transferor.

In noninsurance transfers, the fact that the transferee is not an insurer can be important. From the standpoint of the transferor, the financial protection provided by a noninsurance transfer is often less reliable than commercial insurance coverage, for the following reasons:

- An insurer possesses greater financial resources, structured primarily for the purpose of indemnifying others for loss rather than for conducting some other business of the transferee. Also, information about the ability of an insurer to pay claims is usually easier to obtain.
- An insurer needs to maintain a reputation for fair dealing with policyholders (customers).

- Most insurance contract wording is standardized and therefore less subject to problems of interpretation than individually drawn contracts. Moreover, these standard contracts are "contracts of adhesion," which means that any ambiguities they contain will be interpreted in favor of the insured.
- In the United States, government regulation requires that most insurance contracts be scrutinized by governmental insurance regulators, who try to avoid wording that misleads, or is otherwise detrimental to, insureds. Government regulation also prescribes standards for insurers to follow in settling claims for losses. These specific protections do not apply to noninsurance transfers.

Because of the advantages of insurance, particularly with regard to financial stability, transferors often require that a transferee's obligation be covered by insurance purchased by the transferee. And, in some cases, it is advantageous for the transferor to purchase insurance to cover losses for which a transferee cannot pay.

A risk financing transfer to a noninsurer may be more desirable to the transferor than insurance when the following conditions exist:

- The transferee is in a better position than the transferor to control losses.
- The transferee has almost complete control of the operation, such as a construction company that is doing work for an absentee owner.
- Some unusual loss exposure or operating characteristic puts the transferor's risk financing needs outside the scope of typical insurance policies.
- The transferee's degree of commitment to fulfilling all the terms of its general business contracts with the transferor motivates the transferee to provide full indemnity when a commercial insurer might question the indemnitee's rights to payment.
- The transferee can finance losses more economically than the transferor. This can happen when the transferee has more capacity for retention or can purchase insurance less expensively than the transferor can.

Techniques Combining Retention and Transfer

Retention and transfer are often used in combination. A property insurance policy with an each-occurrence deductible of $500 is a common example. Under that arrangement, the insured organization retains the full amount of any loss that falls below the deductible amount and retains only $500 of any loss greater than the deductible amount. The amount of loss above $500 is transferred to the insurance company, up to the limit of insurance. Larger deductibles are usually available in return for a premium credit. Some organizations are involved in "large-deductible plans" whereby they retain much larger amounts, perhaps in the hundreds of thousands of dollars, above which a commercial insurer provides insurance.

Another technique that combines retention and transfer is **retrospectively rated insurance.** With this technique, the insured pays a premium based, in part, on either losses incurred or losses paid during the policy period, subject to a minimum premium and a maximum premium. In other words, the premium increases with the insured's own loss experience during the policy period. However, individual losses in excess of an agreed specified amount, and total losses beyond a certain amount, do not increase the premium. The arrangement entails retention to the extent that the premium is increased by the insured's own loss experience during the policy period, and it entails insurance to the extent that it will cover losses beyond those that increase the premium.

As discussed above, captive insurers with single owners regularly operate as devices combining retention with transfer: they buy reinsurance for losses in excess of those their parent companies wish to retain. A captive insurer that has two or more owners (called a **multi-parent captive** or a **group captive**) represents a more complex combination of retention and transfer. The results for each owner of a multi-parent captive depend only in part on its own losses. When all losses are shared according to the amount of ownership, the amount of each owner's retention depends on both its relative share of total losses and its percentage of ownership. When either of these shares is extremely small, the existence of a bit of retention can and should be ignored.

Step 3: Select the Best Risk Management Techniques

The third step in the risk management process is selecting the best risk management technique or combination of techniques to treat the organization's various loss exposures. What is "best" will depend on several factors, including (but not limited to) the ability of the organization to absorb loss, the ability of the organization to forecast future losses accurately, and the willingness of the organization's owners and managers to accept risk. Some examples of risk management decisions to be made in this step of the risk management process are as follows:

- Should the firm install a fire suppression (sprinkler) system? Even if insurance is deemed necessary, the firm must decide whether a sprinkler system would be in the firm's best interest.

- Should the firm retain a particular loss exposure in whole, or should it retain only a portion of the exposure?
- If the firm cannot retain a loss exposure in whole, how much should it retain?

The selection of risk management techniques does not always involve a choice. In some cases, a particular risk management technique may be required to meet some objective. For example, a building contractor who wants a loan to buy a new bulldozer may find that lenders require evidence of insurance on equipment purchased with the borrowed funds. Or a local building code may require that a new office building be equipped with a fire suppression (sprinkler) system; building owners whose objectives include "operate legally" then need to have such systems. Of course, such requirements do not bar an organization from using additional risk management techniques. For example, the contractor who has bought (and insured) a bulldozer may also decide to implement risk control measures to reduce the likelihood of loss to the bulldozer, and the owner of the sprinklered office building may also buy fire insurance.

In some cases, an organization that only wants to obtain insurance is required, by the insurer, to implement risk control measures before the insurer will accept the risk. For example, a ladies apparel store that also sells jewelry may need to install a burglar alarm and safe and agree to place all jewelry in the safe during closed hours before the insurer will agree to provide theft coverage on the store's merchandise.

However, quite apart from any outside pressure, the statements in the first paragraph of this chapter apply:

> [A]ccidental loss can hinder the organization from achieving its objectives or even totally destroy it. Accordingly, most organizations seek to control their exposures to accidental loss by preventing accidents, by taking measures to limit the size of losses that occur [in other words, by using some risk control], and by using insurance or some other method to pay for losses that cannot be avoided, prevented, or limited [that is, also using some kind of loss financing, even if only by default].

Effect of Size on Risk Management Decisions

The size of an organization has a considerable effect on its risk management decision making. Typically, small organizations of the sort described as Main Street or mom and pop businesses do not have the ability to absorb any but the smallest of losses. A small business may fully retain some of its limited exposures, such as damage to an outdoor sign or a chain-link fence around its premises. However, a single retained loss of larger size might put the organization out of business. So it is likely to insure, with a small to moderate deductible, any exposures with greater potential. Unfortunately, many small organizations show little interest in risk control, increasing their costs of risk financing, including insurance.

At the other extreme, truly large organizations—such as those listed in the Fortune 500—use a variety of risk management techniques, with retentions of perhaps $1 million or more. These organizations have a sufficiently large number of losses to enable them to predict future losses accurately for many of their exposures, and they have the financial might to retain large layers of loss. Large organizations also typically have highly sophisticated risk control programs with substantial investments in physical systems (such as fire suppression systems), training programs, risk control personnel, and disaster planning.

Nevertheless, nearly all large organizations also want large amounts of insurance—coverage in amounts such as $10 million above a retention of $1 million, or $100 million above a retention of $10 million. Indeed, sometimes they want higher limits than the market is willing to supply. However, their ability to retain losses also means that there is a considerable range in which their choice between retention and the purchase of insurance depends on how much the insurance costs—on how much the premium asked seems to exceed expected loss costs.

Between the extremes of Main Street and the Fortune 500 exists a wide range of "medium-sized" organizations with differing approaches to risk management. The risk management characteristics of some organizations within this broad group may more closely resemble those of small businesses, while others may more closely resemble those of large businesses.

Selection Methods

Various methods are used to select risk management techniques. For large organizations and many medium-sized organizations, sophisticated quantitative methods (which are beyond the scope of this text) are used to forecast losses and compare the financial benefits of the alternative risk management techniques under consideration. Those approaches that will yield the greatest financial benefits to the organization are likely to be selected unless other constraints apply.

Smaller organizations usually do not have enough losses to enable accurate loss forecasting. Consequently, using quantitative methods to select risk management techniques is often not meaningful. Instead, smaller organizations are more likely to use common-sense approaches to selecting risk management techniques that are consistent with their financial resources.

Two basic guidelines that a smaller organization might use in determining an appropriate mix of insurance and retention are illustrated below.

1. *Don't risk more than you can afford to lose.* For example, the Little Company, which has a net income of approximately $100,000 per year, has never had a serious building damage loss in its ten years of existence. Its owner might reason that by retaining building losses completely, the company could save the annual building insurance premium of approximately $2,000, thus increasing its net income by 2 percent. However, the possibility remains that a single occurrence could destroy the building, resulting in a loss of approximately $200,000—double the annual net income of the business. Clearly, Little Company would be risking more than it could afford to lose if it retained the entire building exposure, and so this approach should be rejected. The applicable guideline has also been expressed as "Don't risk a lot to save a little."
2. *Don't spend a lot for a little protection.* At the other extreme, Little Company could purchase building insurance with a minimum deductible of $250. However, since Little Company could easily retain a higher deductible in the event of a building loss, it probably should increase its deductible to a higher level. Insurance premiums are higher for the lower levels of coverage, and so retaining some of the lower level may bring substantial premium savings. Assume, for example, that Little's insurer would give a 4 percent premium reduction if Little increased its deductible to $1,000. Thus, by retaining an additional amount equal to less than one-half of one percent of the total amount of insurance, Little would save 4 percent of the total premium charged for $250 deductible insurance. In other words, the first $750 of coverage that Little would have bought is very expensive insurance that Little can do without. Following similar logic, Little might decide to take a higher deductible, such as $2,500. At some point, however, Little will decide that the premium reduction for a higher deductible is either inappropriate or not worth the risk presented by the increased retention (especially in view of the possibility of multiple losses).

Step 4: Implement the Techniques

Once risk management techniques have been selected, they must be implemented. Failure to implement the techniques effectively can negate what would otherwise be a good decision. Implementation requires action and further decisions.

For example, if a firm has decided to use risk control to handle a particular exposure, the firm must decide whether to install and maintain the control program or devices itself, or whether outsiders should be hired to perform these services. If insiders are the choice, should they be from the risk management department or some other division of the firm? If other divisions are involved, how can they be motivated to support or conduct the necessary activities?

If insurance is the recommended technique, the risk manager must choose an agent or broker and an insurer (or a direct-writing insurance company), decide what coverage forms and endorsements are desirable, prepare for loss adjustment negotiations with the insurer, and check on whether the insurer (or broker or agent) has sent the necessary evidence of insurance to secured creditors or others requiring such proof.

Step 5: Monitor the Program

All risk management measures implemented need to be monitored to determine whether they are working as intended. Experience with the program may suggest that the best technique or combination of techniques was not selected originally or that the choices made were not properly implemented. Conditions may also change so much that, although the original decision and implementation were correct, a different solution is now required.

To monitor a program, the risk manager must establish standards, implement methods for checking compliance with those standards, and decide what degree of noncompliance calls for a correction. If a correction is needed, the risk manager should repeat as many steps of the risk management process as are needed to determine the appropriate correction.

The Risk Management Process at Work

This chapter has described risk management as a process consisting of certain well-defined steps. In reality, the steps in making risk management decisions are seldom as clearly defined and sequential as they may seem from this presentation. Sometimes one step will overlap another, and, out of commercial necessity, decisions may need to be made and implemented before a complete analysis of exposures has occurred.

Applying the risk management process can be simple or complex, depending to a large degree on how many loss exposures need to be handled. If the risk manager is applying the process to an isolated set of loss exposures that has arisen—perhaps those arising out of the purchase of a new piece of mobile equipment—the process may be fairly straightforward, consuming perhaps an hour or less. If, instead, the risk manager's organization has acquired a whole new factory or is reevaluating its entire risk management program, developing and implementing the new program will be a complex and lengthy task, taking weeks or even months to complete.

To illustrate practical application of the risk management process, we will focus on how the MNO Corporation, a medium-sized manufacturer, might use the risk management process to handle the property loss exposures arising out of its plans to obtain a new production machine for its factory. The MNO Corporation has a risk manager, Kathy Grey, who has already established a risk management program for MNO's existing loss exposures. In a smaller firm, Kathy might be the chief financial officer who handles insurance as just one of her duties—or she might be the insurance producer responsible for the MNO account.

In accordance with MNO's corporate policy, MNO's management involved Kathy in the process of selecting and procuring the machine in order to have the benefit of her risk management perspective. Thus, Kathy was aware of the possibility of having to handle some new loss exposures well before they began to exist. As soon as Kathy became aware of the plans, she was able to begin making risk management recommendations—even though the full extent of loss exposures was unknown.

First, in selecting a vendor from whom MNO would buy the machine, Kathy reviewed her records of machine breakdowns and employee injuries caused by other machines owned by MNO. Her research—and conversations with others, including workers, supervisors, and other risk managers—suggested that the machines of one manufacturer were more reliable, more durable, and perhaps even safer than those of other manufacturers. With Kathy's input, the management team decided to buy the new machine from the indicated manufacturer, located approximately 1,000 miles from MNO's location.

MNO's purchasing department consulted with Kathy as they negotiated the contract of sale with the chosen manufacturer. The price quoted by the manufacturer was $200,000—FOB Point of Origin. "FOB Point of Origin" means that title (ownership)—and, therefore, the direct burden of any physical loss to the machine—would pass to MNO as soon as the machine was accepted by the carrier (trucking firm) transporting the machine. Other terms of sale were possible, such as "FOB Destination," meaning that title and risk of loss would not pass to MNO until the machine was delivered to MNO's factory. Although these or other selling terms might have lessened MNO's exposure during transit, all additional costs incurred by the seller for freight and insurance would be added to the invoice. Kathy and the purchasing department also knew that MNO might be able to exercise some additional risk control if MNO, and not the seller, made the transportation arrangements.

In developing its current risk management program, MNO obtained commercial property insurance on its factory building and contents, covering both physical damage and loss of business income, subject to a moderate deductible. MNO supplemented this coverage with a separate boiler and machinery policy covering both physical damage and business income losses resulting from sudden and accidental breakdown of all production machinery in the factory. (Breakdown of machinery is a peril not covered under the building and contents coverage.) The building and contents coverage would automatically cover the new machine (for perils other than breakdown) from the time it was delivered to the insured premises; the boiler and machinery policy would cover accidental breakdown of the machine from the time it was "in use or connected ready for use" in MNO's factory. However, the boiler and machinery policy would not cover breakdowns occurring during *testing* of the new machine. Since MNO wanted the current risk management treatment to apply to the new machine, no changes in the building and contents insurance were needed, other than increasing the amount of insurance accordingly. In addition, Kathy knew from past experience that the boiler and machinery policy could be extended for an additional premium to cover breakdown occurring during the testing period. Thus, Kathy's main concern was considering how best to treat the loss exposure while the new machine would be in transit between the seller's factory and MNO's factory. An additional concern was whether any additional risk control measures would be desirable after the new machine was delivered to MNO's premises.

Step 1: Identifying and Analyzing the Exposure

Because Kathy was involved early in the purchasing of and making shipping arrangements for the new machine, the loss exposure was identified well before Kathy had to select risk management techniques. Kathy's analysis of the exposure became more detailed as the details of the purchase unfolded. In terms of severity, Kathy knew that the maximum possible loss during transit would be the purchase price ($200,000) plus transportation charges plus any loss of revenue or extra expenses that would result if the machine were destroyed in transit.

To gauge the loss of revenue and extra expense possibilities, Kathy spoke with production supervisors and learned that the new machine was being purchased to replace two older, less efficient machines. By speaking with sales representatives of the seller, Kathy learned that if the new machine were destroyed in transit and had to be reordered, it would take sixty additional days to get the replacement delivered. During those sixty days, running costs for the existing machines (mainly labor costs) would be approximately $400 greater per day than for the new machine. However, MNO could rely on the old machines to turn out the desired level of production. Thus, Kathy estimated the maximum potential extra expense loss at $400 per day times sixty days, or $24,000.

Although it was relatively easy for Kathy to estimate potential loss severity during transit, estimating potential loss frequency was another matter. As a manufacturer, MNO of course had a steady stream of incoming shipments of raw materials and outgoing shipments of finished goods. However, the commodities being shipped—raw steel inbound and steel products outbound—had few risk characteristics in common with the high-tech machine to be delivered to MNO. Thus, Kathy knew that the loss frequency data on MNO's regular shipments would not be a credible predictor of the probability of loss for the single shipment of the machine. Moreover, Kathy knew that MNO's management was resolutely opposed to "risking a lot to save a little." Even if the probability of loss were low, MNO would not want to "go bare" on an exposure totaling approximately one-quarter of a million dollars, a sum far greater than MNO's usual property loss retention levels.

Step 2: Considering Risk Management Alternatives

After identifying and analyzing the transit exposure, Kathy considered the risk management alternatives. These alternatives are summarized below.

Risk Control

Recall that risk control techniques include avoidance, loss prevention and reduction, and segregation of exposure units.

Avoidance, as is often the case, is not acceptable to MNO because the new machine will provide several benefits, including significantly reduced operating costs.

Loss prevention and reduction during transit are viable options. Although the machine would be in the exclusive control of the carrier during the course of transit, MNO could prevent or reduce a loss by selecting a carrier experienced in transporting heavy machinery and with a good safety record and adequate and valid motor truck cargo (carrier's liability) insurance to pay for any loss for which it might be held liable. MNO could also provide, in cooperation with the seller, technical information about the machine that would assist the carrier in handling the cargo. MNO may even be able to provide local routing information to the carrier that would lessen over-the-road hazards, such as low overpasses, two-lane highways, bumpy roads, or congested or crime-prone areas. MNO could also hire a cargo surveyor to approve the packaging and loading procedures before transit begins, in order to ascertain that they will be sufficient to protect the machine against moisture, handling damage, or the stresses of motion during transportation.

Segregation of exposures cannot be used, because the machine is sold in one piece. Disassembling the machine solely in order to transport it on two or more different trucks would be highly impractical with no real risk management benefit: losing half the machine would render the entire machine as inoperable as losing the whole machine (although it *might* reduce replacement time).

Risk Financing

The risk financing alternatives include retention, insurance, and noninsurance transfer.

MNO could of course *retain* its entire loss exposure. As discussed earlier, however, the maximum possible loss is sizable, in excess of $200,000. Partial retention could be achieved by way of insurance with a deductible, or by insuring physical damage but not business income or extra expense.

MNO's existing *insurance* program includes an annual transit policy that covers both incoming and outgoing shipments of all property used in MNO's business operations, subject to a $1,000 per shipment deductible. Unless MNO notifies its insurer otherwise, the machine shipment will be automatically covered and MNO will be obliged to pay a premium for the coverage, based on the invoice value of the machine. The annual transit policy, however, does not cover loss of revenue or extra expense. This type of coverage could be obtained to apply to the specific shipment.

MNO's hiring of a common carrier to transport the machine entails some *noninsurance transfer*. With only limited exceptions, a common carrier of goods in surface transit is responsible for all accidental loss that may occur to the cargo while in the course of transit. These exceptions—the situations when a common carrier is *not* held liable—are losses caused by acts of God (floods, windstorms, and other natural perils), acts of a public enemy (war perils), acts of a governmental authority (such as seizure or quarantine), faults of the shipper (such as bad packing), or inherent vice or latent defect. Thus, simply by employing a common carrier, MNO transfers several loss possibilities to the carrier—such as loss by mishandling of the cargo or collision or overturn of the vehicle.

Although the foregoing is the general rule, the monetary amount of a common carrier's liability can be reduced by contract—specifically, by agreement to a released bill of lading, if such a bill of lading (contract of carriage) is available. Kathy needs to (1) compare the extra cost of a full (that is, not released) bill of lading against the cost of transit insurance that could be used as a substitute, and (2) consider the extent to which use of a released bill might cause the carrier—that is, its driver and other employees—to be less careful with the cargo.

Another possibility is to use a contract carrier instead of a common carrier. Contract carriers (carriers who do not hold themselves out as carriers to the general public) are liable only for damage resulting from their own negligence unless they and the shipper agree otherwise. Thus, when a shipper uses a contract carrier, various degrees of transfer are possible. Presumably, the cost of carriage will vary with the amount of loss transfer in the contract.

Step 3: Selecting the Best Techniques

After considering the alternatives, Kathy made several decisions, which she presented to MNO's management team as recommendations. First, she recommended that all of the loss prevention and reduction measures discussed above be pursued with a carefully selected common carrier. Pursuing these measures would cost MNO very little but could go a long way in protecting the new machine during loading, transit, and unloading.

For risk financing, Kathy recommended that MNO rely on its usual transit insurance arrangements. After having MNO's insurance broker "shop" for business income coverage on the shipment, Kathy recommended that the $24,000 extra expense exposure be retained. Although one insurer was willing to write the coverage, the premium quoted was unacceptable to MNO. Moreover, the management team tended to view the retained loss as nothing more than a short delay in realizing the lower operating costs of the new machine. Management's principal concern was to avert the possibility of a much larger physical damage loss.

Kathy also recommended that a safety meeting be held for all operators of the new machine. At this meeting, a representative from the manufacturer would explain safe operating techniques and basic troubleshooting procedures. The recommendation also urged management to authorize the purchase of commonly needed repair parts for the machine (the duplication technique) in order to minimize machine down time.

Step 4: Implementing the Techniques

MNO's management team approved all of Kathy's recommendations and charged her with implementing them in cooperation with certain other departments at MNO. In cooperation with the purchasing department, Kathy selected an experienced common carrier and provided it with appropriate loss prevention information. Kathy then requested MNO's insurance broker to take the following actions:

1. Notify MNO's cargo insurer of the impending shipment
2. Notify MNO's building and contents insurer of the new machine and increase the applicable amount of insurance accordingly
3. Request MNO's boiler and machinery insurer to extend coverage to the new machine during testing

In cooperation with a production supervisor from MNO and the seller's representative, Kathy oversaw the design and conduct of a safety meeting for operators of the new machine. The seller's representative also provided a list of commonly needed replacement parts. Kathy forwarded this list to the purchasing department for further action.

Step 5: Monitoring

The risk management decisions implemented needed little monitoring. The shipment arrived on time and with no apparent damage. However, as an additional risk control measure, MNO mechanics inspected the machine as soon as it was unloaded. No irregularities were visible, but if they had been, they would have been noted on the carrier's bill of lading. This practice of "noting exceptions" on the bill of lading would have made it much easier for MNO to pursue a cargo claim against the carrier had damage been observable at the time of delivery. After being delivered, the new machine was installed and tested. It was then put into use, and operation of the machine was specially monitored for a few days to see that proper behavior was indeed being used. Thereafter the operation was monitored as usual in MNO's overall risk management program.

Summary

Although the main subject of this text is commercial property insurance, insurance is best understood in the context of risk management. Risk management is concerned with the treatment of loss exposures in order to prevent accidental losses from interfering with an organization's objectives. Insurance is one of several risk management techniques.

Three important aspects of property loss exposures are (1) the item exposed to loss, (2) the cause of loss, and (3) the effects of loss. The item exposed to loss is either real property (real estate or property attached to real estate) or personal property (all property that is not real property). Causes of loss include some well-known important perils such as fire, windstorm, and earthquake; many perils that may or may not be important, such as burglary and leakage of sprinklers; many that are often unimportant, such as mold and fungus; and still others that are totally unanticipated. The major financial effects of loss are reduction in value, increased cost to repair or replace, loss of revenue, and extra expense.

Assuming that an organization has first set objectives, risk management can be viewed as a five-step process:

1. Identify and analyze loss exposures
2. Examine the feasibility of alternative risk management techniques
3. Select the best risk management techniques
4. Implement the techniques
5. Monitor the program

Whether a risk management program is satisfactory is determined by its ability to help achieve the organization's objectives. Different objectives lead to different risk management programs.

Various methods can be used to help in identifying loss exposures. These methods include, but are not limited to, inspections, interviews, questionnaires, financial statement analysis, flow chart analysis, and loss analysis. A risk management professional often uses several of these methods in combination, since each method has its own limitations.

Analysis of loss exposures entails an understanding of how often a particular type of loss is likely to occur (loss frequency), how large the loss could be (loss severity), and how much confidence, or credibility, can be placed in the risk management professional's predictions of loss severity and frequency.

The actual number of losses often is different from that expected, and most losses are less than the maximum possible loss (largest loss that can occur). Because the severity of losses is usually much more variable than the frequency, experience tells more about frequency than about severity. Thus, prediction of the number of losses that will occur is almost always more accurate than prediction of their severity. To help in determination of the significance of an exposure, the maximum probable loss (largest loss *likely* to occur) is often estimated.

Risk management techniques can be classified as either risk control or risk financing. Risk control techniques (which reduce the frequency or severity of losses) include exposure avoidance, loss prevention, loss reduction, and segregation of exposure units. Risk financing techniques (which pay for those losses that actually occur) include retention, transfer (through either insurance or noninsurance contracts), and techniques that combine retention and transfer, such as insurance with a deductible or retrospectively rated insurance.

Decisions regarding the selection of risk management techniques depend on several factors, including the organization's goals, its ability to absorb loss, and its ability to predict future losses accurately. In some cases, an organization will be required by law, lenders, or other factors to obtain insurance or exercise certain risk control measures. Small organizations and large organizations often adopt different combinations of risk management techniques.

After risk management techniques are selected, they must be implemented effectively. Finally, the program must be monitored. When changes are needed, various steps in the risk management process may need to be repeated as necessary to achieve objectives.

Chapter Notes

1. Parts of this section are adapted from George L. Head, *Essentials of Risk Control*, vol. I, 2d ed. (Malvern, PA: Insurance Institute of America, 1989), pp. 1-9, 22-30; and from George L. Head and Stephen Horn II, *Essentials of Risk Management*, vol. I, 2d ed. (Malvern, PA: Insurance Institute of America, 1991), pp. 10, 14.
2. Parts of this section are adapted from George L. Head, Michael W. Elliott, and James D. Blinn, *Essentials of Risk Financing*, vol.I, 2d ed. (Malvern, PA: Insurance Institute of America, 1993), pp. 43-46.

Chapter 2

Property Risk Control

Loss exposures are often responsive to some type of risk control. Risk control measures should always be considered, even when losses are financed by insurance or by a funded retention program. Effective *loss prevention* measures lower the expected loss frequency. Effective *loss reduction* measures reduce loss severity. Thus, effective control measures serve to lower both expected losses and the cost of financing losses. In addition to their dollar benefits, risk control measures can serve to reduce uncertainty and to meet the specific risk management objectives of any organization. Moreover, since there are always some loss costs that are not covered by insurance (such as the value of employee time devoted to handling the paperwork), risk control reduces risk financing costs even with full insurance. Even if they do not directly affect insurance premium rates, risk control measures are likely to make it easier to get and keep insurance or other transfers.

This chapter examines risk control measures commonly used to prevent or reduce losses caused by six of the most serious property perils: fire, theft, explosion, windstorm, flooding, and earthquake.

Controlling Fire Losses

Fire losses, like most other losses, result from chains of events. The 1967 McCormick Place fire in Chicago is a good illustration of a sequence of events that led up to a major loss.

The loss and its severity resulted from a conjunction of unrelated things that went wrong. In the McCormick Place exhibition hall, the exhibitors' need for electrical outlets had not been anticipated. Available circuits were overloaded with extension cords. One exhibitor used a defective cord that ran among other exhibits made of light, combustible materials such as cardboard, light pressed panels, and paper. Since combustibility of contents had not been specifically considered during the design phase (despite the building's intended use) and the ceiling was extremely high, the exhibition area was not sprinklered. A fire began while the guard was in another part of the building, and the blaze had grown substantially before he saw it. It took three or four minutes for him to reach an alarm station. When firefighters arrived, they found that valves on the lines to the fire hydrants had been left partially closed, seriously reducing dynamic water pressure. The firefighters did not know where the valves were. This series of events resulted in a $227 million fire (1993 dollars) and one death.[1] Many unsafe acts and physical hazards combined to produce this result, and not all of them have been mentioned. (For example, the valve problem with the hydrants was itself caused by a chain of events.)

Risk control measures are designed to break vital links in the chain of events that leads to a serious loss. Naturally, the use of specific measures depends on the nature of the particular perils and hazards being addressed.

In general, risk control measures take one or both of two approaches. The **engineering approach** involves attack by design and location of properties and equipment to reduce the number of physical hazards. The **human behavior approach** attacks the problem by modifying the behavior of people to reduce the frequency of unsafe acts. Although losses are usually caused by unsafe acts (note the several "people" failures in the exhibition hall loss chain), engineering often can be used to limit the losses resulting from unsafe acts (for example, automatic sprinklers can successfully interrupt fire loss chains that people have started, and fences and locked gates can keep people from tampering with equipment).

Elements of Fire Loss

To break a chain of loss-causing events, it is necessary to know how the events proceed—how one thing leads to another. Fire losses proceed by chemical processes—heat causes rapid oxidation of fuel. Thus, three things are required to have a fire: (1) an initial source of heat; (2) oxygen; and (3) fuel—material that will burn, given the amount of heat and oxygen available. And, once started, the chain reaction must be uninterrupted.[2] As more fuel burns, the amount of heat present usually increases. Strong fires create their own air drafts, thus bringing more oxygen to the fuel. So fires grow, engulfing more and more fuel as the burning process literally feeds on itself.

It follows that most fire loss prevention and reduction efforts center on removal of one or more of the three common essentials (heat, oxygen, and fuel) from the scene.

Heat Sources

Four types of energy can create heat sufficient to cause a fire—electrical energy, chemical energy, mechanical (frictional) energy, and nuclear energy.

- *Electrical heat energy* may come from natural sources (such as lightning) or artificial ones (such as power generating plants). It may be dynamic (for example, power flowing through power lines and operating motors) or static (such as the temporarily quiescent static electricity in the air or the charge in a storage battery).
- *Chemical heat energy* is released as part of a chemical reaction. Examples include the ignition of a match, the burning of a welding torch, and spontaneous combustion of oily rags left in a closet.
- *Mechanical or frictional heat energy* is developed when objects rub together. The brakes on a car create heat, as does the friction of a grinding wheel on a piece of metal, a belt running through a pulley, or a defective bearing.
- *Nuclear heat energy* is released by nuclear fission or fusion. Controlled nuclear reaction creates a source of heat that is converted to electricity in nuclear power plants. Uncontrolled release in a nuclear accident, or the controlled or uncontrolled release of a nuclear weapon, can cause widespread damage.

It is important to identify all the important heat sources from which fire damage might arise in order to give each of them proper risk control treatment. The specifics of treatment differ according to whether the source is planned or unplanned, fixed or mobile.

Planned Versus Unplanned Sources of Heat

Some heat sources are deliberately installed because they are needed for the operations of the organization; these can be called "planned" sources. Others are present or brought in without the intention of the organization's management; they may be called "unplanned" sources. Standard examples of planned sources include a wide variety of heat-creating equipment, ranging from soldering irons to blast furnaces. Heating furnaces, boilers, and welding and cutting torches are planned heat sources.

The heat from planned sources is often an unwanted by-product. Machinery creates heat from friction; the machinery itself is planned, but the heat it creates is unwanted. All electrical energy generates heat; the presence of electric lights, electric lines, and electrical motors is planned, but the heat they generate is a by-product that is not wanted. Many natural fibers generate heat while in storage, and many chemical processes necessarily produce unwanted heat. Control of loss from fire needs to take into account unwanted as well as wanted heat from planned sources.

Unplanned heat sources consist primarily of those that management has not been able, or has not tried, to control. Examples include smoking by employees and visitors, the use of personal coffee pots in a work area, and off-premises elements such as lightning that no amount of planning can eliminate.

Fixed Versus Mobile Heat Sources

Some planned sources of heat are fixed, while others move around. Furnaces and boilers for heating buildings are fixed. Welding and cutting torches are common mobile sources of heat, as are forklift trucks and other vehicles.

Fuels

For a fire to start, continue, or spread, it must have fuel. Fuels vary greatly in the ease with which they can be ignited. Gasoline vapor is thus generally more hazardous than paper, paper more hazardous than lumber, lumber more hazardous than steel, and so on. The relative combustibility or flammability of a fuel depends on the amount of heat required to cause it to produce burnable vapors. In a practical situation, two characteristics of a fuel are important: the temperature at which it vaporizes (a function of its chemical composition) and the extent to which it holds heat rather than spreading it (a matter strongly affected by the size and shape of the item, as well as by its chemistry).

Temperature at Which Substances Vaporize

An important characteristic of solid substances is the **ignition temperature.** The ignition temperature of a substance may be defined as the "minimum temperature to which it must be heated for it to ignite."[3] A substance that has reached the ignition temperature will continue to release vapors that burn and will continue to burn until they are consumed or the fire is extinguished.

An important characteristic of liquids is the **flash point.** The flash point is "the minimum temperature at which a liquid gives off vapors that can be ignited by a spark or flame." Gasoline, for example, has a flash point of −45° F, compared to kerosene's flash point of 100°F.[4] At room temperature, gasoline releases vapors that can be readily ignited. Kerosene must be heated above room temperature before it releases ignitable vapors.

Form of the Material

Wood in a toothpick and the same kind of wood in a dry log both have the same ignition temperature. But, when the surface of a toothpick is heated, there is little place else for the heat to go and so the toothpick quickly ignites. In a log, however, some of the heat at the surface is dissipated into the interior. Hence, it takes a hotter or longer sustained supply of heat to get the log to burst into flame. And when external heat is removed, the cool interior of the log may absorb enough heat to bring the temperature below the ignition temperature.

Continuing fire represents an ongoing reaction. Thus, when one starts a wood fire in a fireplace, initial heat may be created by friction (striking a match). It is then continued by burning of the chemicals in the match head. When the fire so generated has burned long enough, the wood of the match flames. The temperature thus created is not extremely high, but the shape and material of the match cause it to be a self-sustaining chain reaction. In the fireplace, fire is ignited in paper and light wood materials with ignition temperatures below that produced by the match. As more fuel catches fire, a higher temperature is generated. If this temperature is sustained long enough, logs can be induced to flame because heat (from already burning materials) is being applied more rapidly than it can be dissipated into the air and into the logs' interior. Eventually, if enough heat is produced rapidly enough, logs can continue to burn on their own, without any continuing outside source of heat.

The process is the same with most hostile fires. (A **hostile fire** is one that burns outside of any receptacle normally intended for containing fires, such as a furnace or stove.) In severe cases, the buildup of heat from the fuels that have, one by one, been heated to flaming point increases with each additional bit of fuel consumption until the fire reaches such a point that it cannot be stopped until it has completely consumed all available fuel.

Building Contents as Fuel

The variety of building contents that may be exposed to fire is tremendous. Depending on type of operations and particular location, inventory may be paper or pig iron, alcohol or asbestos, sulfur or silicon. Equipment and furnishings may be readily combustible or almost noncombustible, oily or clean, light or heavy. Not only the inherent flammability of each type but also its spacing and arrangement determine its actual significance as fuel for fire. Each occupancy, and in many cases each part of a single occupancy, presents a different exposure. Each must be evaluated on its own merits, or at least according to its own particular class. Overall, the possibilities range from a well-arranged office with metal furniture and a minimum of paper, to a stockpile of sulfur.

The expected amount of combustibles available as fuel for a hostile fire in a given area is called the **fire load,** commonly expressed in terms of weight of combustibles per square foot. Heat to be expected in a fire is estimated on the basis of known calorific content of those combustibles present in a building's contents and structural components. (The "calorific content" of anything is the amount of heat—number of calories—produced when it burns.) Since physical arrangement of the material greatly affects the amount of heat produced in any given amount of time, estimation of fire load in specific cases requires expert judgment.

Most high fire loads do not result from materials recognized as especially hazardous; where possible, care is taken to limit the amount of such exposure in a building. Rather, the usual high load cases come from bulk storage or relatively low hazard materials packed together in great quantity in a minimum of space. Modern lifting equipment allows stacking to considerable height, which can create extreme fire loads. The very heaviest fire loads, however, occur in situations with large quantities of extraordinarily hazardous materials: highly flammable liquids such as light petroleum products, lacquers, or alcohols; materials that burn explosively, or nearly so, such as sulfur and some sulfides, many nitrates, some peroxides, many types of metallic or organic dusts; and so on.

Buildings as Fuel

Fire load includes the combustible parts of a building. Wooden buildings, of course, contribute more ready fuel for fire than do buildings of masonry, noncombustible, or fire-resistive materials. When building materials are combustible, the common result is more damage to the building itself and faster spread of the fire to other fuel inside or outside the building.

The following discussion of construction types is based on the construction definitions used by Insurance Services Office (ISO) in determining property insurance rates. The National Fire Protection Association, various building codes, appraisal guides, and some insurance publications use classifications different from those used by ISO. In each case, construction types are categorized according to the needs of those using the system. Any of these building classification systems can be useful in evaluating fire loss exposures and developing appropriate alternatives for controlling fire losses.

Frame Construction **Wood frame construction** is illustrated in Exhibit 2-1. This classification includes buildings with exterior walls classified as noncombustible or slow burning but with wall support and the floors and roof

Exhibit 2-1
Wood Frame Construction

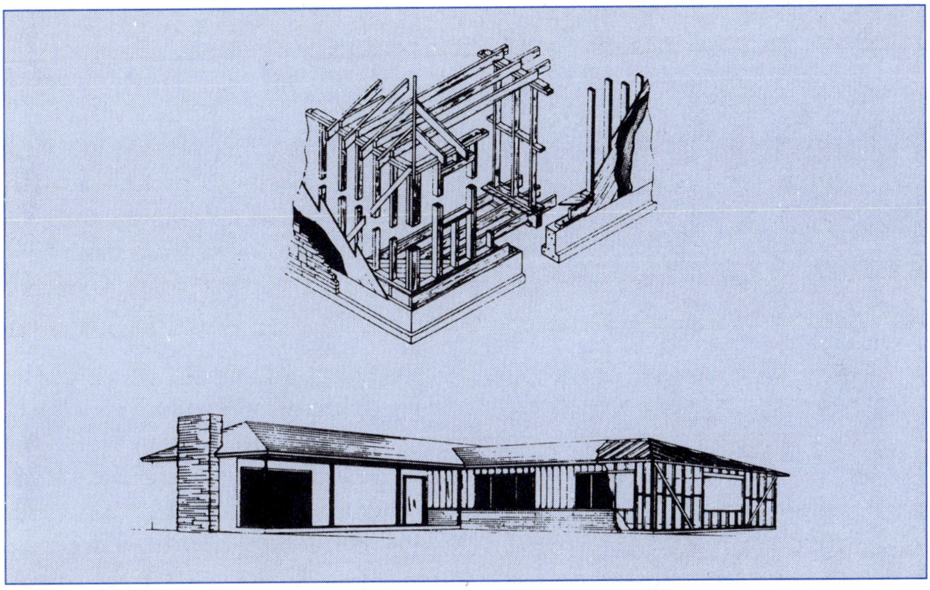

Reprinted with permission from *Stevens Valuation Quarterly* (Los Angeles: Marshall and Swift Publication Company, July 1973), p. A-12.

of combustible materials (such as wood). Thus, a building with a single thickness of brick (brick veneer) on the walls, with the combustible floors and roof supported by wood framing, is considered a frame building.

Many dwellings and small mercantile buildings are of frame construction, but the popularity of this type varies considerably by geographic region. The combustibility of wood makes frame buildings susceptible to fire damage. Everything is held up by wood in a frame structure. When the wood burns, the structure, or the involved part of it, is destroyed.

Joisted Masonry Construction In **joisted masonry construction,** also called "ordinary," "ordinary masonry," "brick," "brick joisted," or "wood joisted," the walls are self-supporting masonry—they stand without wood supports. Other supporting elements, however, are wood. Joists and beams supporting floors and roof are wood; so, usually, are the roof and floors themselves. Joisted masonry construction is illustrated in Exhibit 2-2.

In a fire of considerable intensity, only a shell will be left—the bare walls. In such a fire, some significant portion of the walls may even fall, be knocked down by fall of the roof, or be pulled and pushed down by collapsing wooden support beams. Even the bricks themselves can be damaged beyond use by heat when of sufficient intensity and duration.

Exhibit 2-2
Joisted Masonry Construction

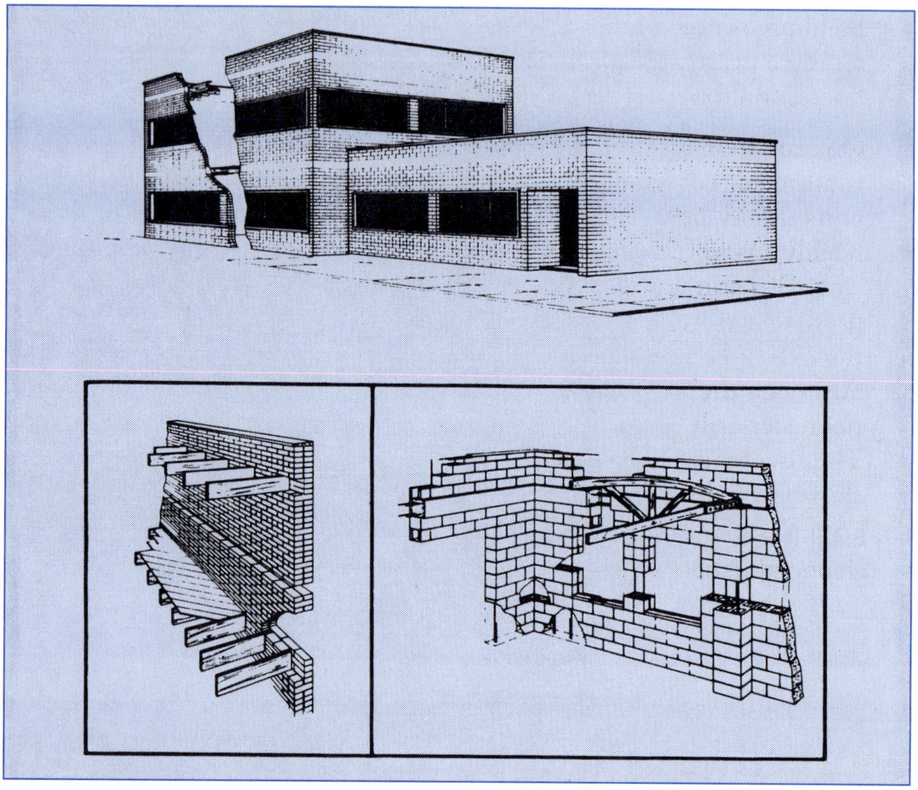

Reprinted with permission from *Stevens Valuation Quarterly* (Los Angeles: Marshall and Swift Publication Company, July 1973), p. A-11.

In the much more frequent, less intense fires, the exterior bearing walls usually remain in usable, or nearly usable, condition; they continue to support the roof, and walls and roof provide some degree of protection for the interior. Joisted masonry construction is usually preferable to frame construction when fire occurs.

There is a type of joisted masonry construction called **heavy timber** or **mill construction** that is considered more fire resistant than typical joisted masonry construction. Used mainly in older industrial buildings, heavy timber construction involves heavy timber structural supports and masonry wall construction. Large, solid pieces of wood are extremely difficult to burn. Thus, a bare wooden beam eight inches by ten inches in diameter ordinarily resists fire damage better than a bare steel beam with the same loadbearing capacity. Although the steel beam will not burn, it will warp and twist in a large fire and lose its strength.

Noncombustible Construction **Noncombustible construction** is a specialized term in fire protection and fire insurance. The term is *not* applied to all buildings of noncombustible materials—many such buildings fall into the fire-resistive category. A building is in the noncombustible class when its walls, floors, and roof are of materials that will contribute little if any fuel to a fire.

One common type of noncombustible construction, illustrated in Exhibit 2-3, is all metal construction—light metal walls and roof, with light metal supports. Many light noncombustible buildings do not add fuel to fires but are readily susceptible to heat resulting from fires involving building contents. Their structural members expand, twist, crack, and otherwise deteriorate in fires. Therefore, such structures often collapse in fires. This produces loss of the building, increased damage to contents, and increased threat to life safety. Although they do not contribute fuel to a fire, noncombustible buildings are not necessarily "safer" than buildings of frame or joisted masonry construction. The fire damage that can be sustained by a light noncombustible building is shown in Exhibit 2-4.

Exhibit 2-3
Noncombustible Construction

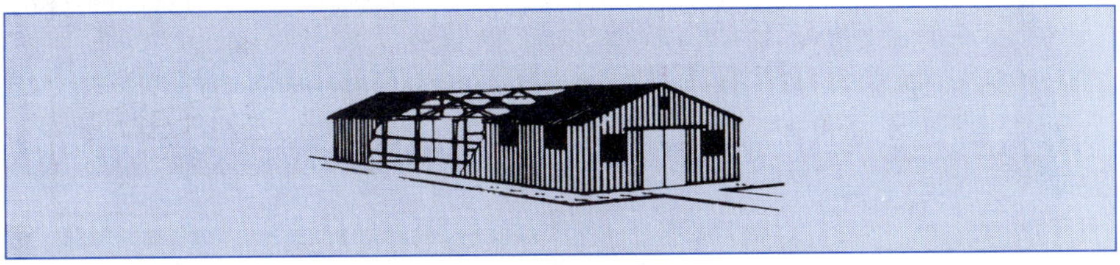

Reprinted with permission from *Stevens Valuation Quarterly* (Los Angeles: Marshall and Swift Publication Company, July 1973), pp. A-11 and A-12.

Exhibit 2-4
Noncombustible Building After Fire

Photo by Kim Holston.

Exhibit 2-5
Masonry Noncombustible Construction

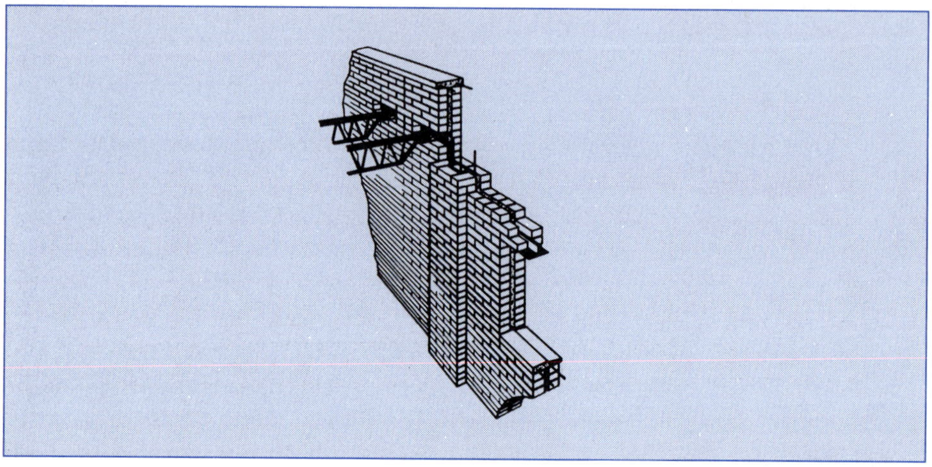

Reprinted with permission from *Stevens Valuation Quarterly* (Los Angeles: Marshall and Swift Publication Company, July 1973), pp. A-11 and A-12.

Masonry Noncombustible Like noncombustible construction, **masonry noncombustible construction** includes floor and roof of metal or some other noncombustible material. The walls are usually of masonry material but may be of fire-resistive construction. Masonry noncombustible buildings are, generally, more resistant to fire damage than any of the preceding types. Masonry noncombustible construction is illustrated in Exhibit 2-5.

Fire-Resistive Construction **Fire-resistive construction** provides more fire protection than all other types of construction. Building materials used in fire-resistive construction resist heat longer than materials required for protected ordinary or noncombustible construction, but they do not resist it forever, and they do not keep fires from happening. Fire-resistive buildings can be severely damaged, even totally destroyed, by fire.

There is also construction known as **modified fire resistive.** True fire-resistive construction requires certain thicknesses of masonry materials, and the fire resistance rating of structural assemblies must be at least two hours. Modified fire-resistive construction may include masonry materials slightly deficient in thickness or structural assemblies with a fire-resistive rating of at least one hour but less than two hours.

Fire resistance ratings of materials are determined by standard tests in laboratories. Fire resistance of building materials as typically assembled is commonly rated by testing in furnaces specially designed for exposing the assemblies to a standard fire. An assembly rated one-hour fire resistance would meet a furnace test under load without failure for approximately one hour. Two very important practical points about the resultant ratings are the following:

1. Standard fire tests take into consideration the capacity of materials and, in some cases, assemblies, to perform intended functions during fire exposure, and their subsequent load capacity. There is no reference to their suitability for further use (as in a repaired or reconstructed building).
2. There are many reasons why performance in a standard test and performance in an actual building fire may differ.[5]

Materials commonly used to meet fire-resistive requirements are reinforced concrete and protected structural steel for framing, reinforced concrete or masonry for bearing walls, and lighter noncombustible materials in other parts, such as curtain walls (walls that are enclosing but not load bearing).

Oxygen, Air Flow, and Related Factors

In addition to heat sources and fuels (in particular, buildings and contents as fuels for fire), the third element required for fire is oxygen.

Fires consist of fast oxidation of materials, a process that requires oxygen. The vast majority of fires obtain their necessary supply from ordinary air (about 20 percent of which is oxygen). When they cannot get enough oxygen, they die (are "smothered"). A hot fire tends to develop its own air supply by creating a draft: air heated by the fire rises, leaving a low-pressure area below into which fresh air flows.

The more favorable the arrangements for oxygen supply, the faster and better the fire burns, and when there is an abundance of oxygen, fuels flame at lower temperatures. Consequently, oxygen-rich atmospheres (used in oxygen tents in hospitals, for example, and in some industrial processes) increase the probability of a fire.

A few substances can burn without an outside oxygen supply. All of these are self-oxidants (such as nitrous oxide and nitrocellulose); their physical structure includes enough combined oxygen to support flame for a while. And a few special chemical combinations can produce fire without any free oxygen.

Pre-Loss Fire Control Measures

Fires can be extinguished by removal of heat, fuel, or oxygen, or by breaking the chemical chain reaction. Various methods are used to extinguish fires, and these will be discussed later in this chapter. Apart from extinguishing efforts after fires start, many measures can be taken before a fire breaks out either to prevent fires from occurring or to minimize the damage that an actual fire can cause before being extinguished.

Fires can be prevented by controlling heat sources and by separating fuel and heat. Fire severity can be reduced by various building design features that limit or slow the spread of fire and by reducing the damageability of property exposed to fire. Furthermore, steps can be taken to control arson losses.

Controlling Heat Sources

Much fire loss may be prevented by having no buildup of heat energy in heat sources not necessary to operations. For example, appropriate rules and procedures should be enforced in connection with smoking and with personal cooking and heating equipment.

Planned Heat Sources

The necessity of planned heat sources should be questioned. Are all the sources planned for energy actually required? With sources in which heat is an unwanted by-product, can storage of the heated material or use of the heat-producing process be avoided by practical alternative arrangements?

The second question is equally important: Where there must be energy, has care been taken not to have more than is necessary? Are electrical devices overheated? Are more furnaces, forges, kilns, or other heating devices in use than necessary? Are fires larger or hotter than necessary? Are there flames where something else (such as hot water) will do? The answers to these questions may identify planned heat sources that can be reduced or eliminated.

Heat as a By-Product

When heat is an unwanted by-product, a variety of options is often available. In lighting, fluorescent tubes are cooler than incandescent bulbs. Machines differ in the amount of friction heat they generate. Clearly, with self-heating materials and supplies, quantities stored should be controlled, and separation of such materials into smaller amounts at segregated locations is desirable.

The release of heat energy can be controlled by dissipating heat slowly through some kind of cooling. That the atmosphere around hot processes should be kept cool seem obvious, but only methodical, step-by-step analysis gives good assurance that such a move will not be overlooked.

Electrical Heat Energy

The rate and path of release of electrical energy can be controlled with proper fuses or automatic circuit breakers, and with adequate grounding. Grounding can be used both to protect power circuits and to control static electricity created by moving machinery, liquids, and dust. It also applies to the mightiest "unplanned" electrical source—lightning—which can be grounded by lightning protection systems consisting of air terminals (lightning rods), down conductors, and grounding rods.

Separation—Friendly Fires or Heat Sources

The measures that may be used to prevent friendly fires (fires contained within their intended receptacles) or heat sources from becoming a source of hostile fire vary, depending on whether the heat sources are planned or unplanned, fixed or mobile.

Fixed Location Planned Heat Sources

When fixed location planned heat sources have been identified, flammable or combustible materials must be kept away from them. The National Fire Protection Association (NFPA) and other organizations have developed standards that serve as a guide. Some involve only common sense. For example, the furnace room is not the place to keep trash, paper stocks, or janitors' materials. Other standards require more specific information. Building timbers and wood partitions should not be too close to furnaces and glues, but how close is too close? Here, recommendations are available from the NFPA and many insurers.

With cooking stoves, the major fuel hazard comes from cooking oils, greases, and fats in foods. Besides the immediate exposure, there is a buildup of greasy deposits in hoods and flues—a frequent factor in restaurant fires. Regular removal of the deposits is indicated as a standard fire protection measure.

With electrical equipment, the first and most important separation device is insulation of wiring, motor compartments, switches, and so on. Where there is or may be arcing—as there is in most electrical switches, motors, and generators, common sense again dictates separation from flammable materials. When they are in the presence of a heat source, finely divided particles of any kind, including lints, metal dusts and shavings, may provide fuel for a fire. Lubricating greases and oils are other obvious fuels.

Mobile Planned Heat Sources

Mobile planned heat sources are a significant problem in fire control. Welding and cutting torches are a frequent cause of fires, and portable heaters of various kinds are also significant.

With fixed planned sources, buildings, equipment, and operations can be designed to keep fuels away. Since the exposure does not change rapidly, the plans are relatively easy to manage effectively. With mobile equipment, the specific exposures keep changing. The equipment has to be taken where it is needed, and is not necessarily restricted to use in areas free of fuels. Furthermore, a major psychological difficulty exists because people are less impressed with the need to take elaborate precautions for an exposure that is going to last only a few minutes or even a few hours. If it takes, say, fifteen to thirty minutes to make an area thoroughly safe for a repair job that will last an hour and involve only several minutes of torch work, with another fifteen to thirty minutes to restore the area to operational condition, it can be difficult to get operators, and even supervisors, to take full care. Furthermore, under a variety of possible circumstances, it may be difficult to phrase rules and procedures that always define adequately what "full care" means.

Unplanned Heat Sources

With unplanned sources of heat, the obvious approaches are prohibition and restriction, as in having "no smoking" areas and possibly areas specifically reserved for "smoking breaks." Employees' hot plates or coffee makers may be prohibited or restricted in number or size, and there may be a supporting practice of providing convenient alternatives in planned lunchrooms or coffee nooks.

Separation—Hostile Fires

If friendly fires or heat sources are not adequately separated, the result may be a hostile fire. The severity of hostile fires may be reduced by effective building design. A building's design may incorporate features intended to limit the vertical or horizontal spread of fire or to create two or more "fire divisions" within the same building.

Limiting Vertical Fire Spread

Fire spread is encouraged by vertical openings that allow heat to rise past combustible property. The most frequent examples of such vertical openings are stairwells and elevator shafts, ducts and flues, and openings used to allow pipes and wiring to get from floor to floor. Windows can also contribute to the spread of fire from one floor to another as the fire shoots out of one window and into the next one. This action is called "looping."

Another major exposure involves high stacking in storage. In hundreds of warehouses (and in many stores), goods in cardboard containers are stacked up, row above row, for dozens of feet. Fires that start in lower rows are thus well supplied with fuel on which to grow.

Limiting vertical rise of fire is of prime importance in buildings designed for fire control. Of course, it is also important to maintain the integrity of fire barriers originally designed into a building. Although this principle should seem obvious, it is frequently violated in practice. Conveyor belts may be installed to deliver goods from one floor to another, piercing what was a fire-resistive floor. Electrical, plumbing, or heating equipment may be installed leaving a large rough-cut opening through which fire can spread. Fire doors originally installed in order to separate passageways between stories may be damaged or blocked or may suffer from improper maintenance.

Openings through which building service lines (pipes, wires, ducts) pass should be filled with an appropriate type of noncombustible material. Of course, air ducts are designed for movement of air through the building, and when a hostile fire occurs, its hot gases can move the same way. Providing isolation devices (fire dampers) to stop the spread of fire and smoke in all but the smallest ducts is recommended. These may be actuated by various fire-sensing devices.

Interior spaces in hollow walls and below floors (above ceilings) are other weak points. Finished walls in any type of construction may have open spaces. Open spaces between the floor of one story and the ceiling of the story below are standard features of frame and ordinary construction and are common in finished areas of other types. There are three reasons why such spaces contribute significantly to spread of fire:

1. Fire in these spaces can burn for a considerable time before it is noticed.
2. These spaces commonly contain some quantities of combustible debris, including dust.
3. With only a limited volume of air to heat, a fire in a small, contained space produces higher temperatures than it would in the open (like a fire in a stove, for example). For these reasons, structural **fire stops** should be inserted. These are solid pieces running from support to support of the wall or floor. In frame buildings, fire stops inside walls often are wooden two-by-fours, running horizontally from stud to stud. Although such stops are combustible, they do not burst into flame easily and they accomplish the purpose of delaying the flow of heat.

Attics are also hazardous for the same reasons. In addition, they are in the path of rising heat. In row buildings, for example, fires starting in one structure have bypassed brick walls by spreading through the common attic. Here again, while good fire-resistive materials are best in the dividers, lighter materials can delay spread until firefighters control the original fire.

Spread of heat through an attic or along the underside of any roof or ceiling can sometimes be reduced by venting, which protects by cooling (controlling the rate of release of fire energy) and by directing the flow of heat into the open, away from combustibles in the building (a form of separation of heat from fuel). Built-in venting can also prevent the problem of sudden flaming when firefighters vent the building after a fire in it has already heated the interior.

Looping of fire from one story to the next through exterior windows is less common but can be serious. The generally recommended controls are metal framing with wired glass or other installations that will not readily burn out, soften, or fall out in high heat. Staggering the lines of windows may help. Another device is installation of "fender walls" that extend out between in-line windows.

Limiting Horizontal Fire Spread

A fire may spread horizontally almost as easily as it spreads upward. In the presence of readily flammable materials, there is no significant difference. (In bowling alleys, for example, the alley surfaces have sometimes supported flash spread, so that within a few minutes the whole playing area has been involved.) Nearly all materials used to make walls, partitions, or doors in buildings have some value in slowing fire spread. (Unwired glass panels are a major exception.) Even a wooden stud partition with a half-inch of bare fir plywood on each side has a standard test rating of twenty minutes. Many plaster or wallboard partitions with wooden studs test at one hour. Even twenty minutes can make a large difference in the effectiveness of prompt fire fighting; in most fires, an hour's resistance means a contained fire. The problem, however, is that fires are not always noticed right away, and then the difference between combustible and fire-resistive barriers becomes important.

As with vertical separation, adequate horizontal separation calls for barriers with no holes for heat to get through. The ideal is an unbroken wall that extends from the floor at the lowest level through and beyond the roof, with no windows near it in the exterior walls. Next in desirability is a wall with openings properly protected with fire doors. When the doors are not as fire resistant as the wall, then the strength of the whole is limited by the strength of the doors. The doors should shut automatically whenever not actually in use **(self-closing doors)** or be arranged to close themselves in the presence of fire heat **(automatic fire doors).** Automatically closing equipment must not be blocked or rendered inoperable. Unfortunately, such blockage or interference is fairly common practice. A fire wall with an open door or other sizable opening is hardly more of a fire-stop than a wall of combustible materials, occasionally even less (depending on how long it takes the fire to find the opening—a process that may be shortened when the opening provides an exhaust channel for fire gases).

When equipment (such as a conveyor line) makes solid closure impossible, special water spray protection can be used. Special sprinklers are also needed where shafts cannot be fully enclosed (as with escalators, for example). Outside sprinkler heads may be used to help protect window openings in the event of a fire from outside the building.

Full Separation

When one space is sufficiently separated from another, the two are called separate **fire divisions.** A self-supporting solid wall the full width and height (including lowest basement) of the building plus adequate extensions (parapets) beyond any combustible roofs or walls, with appropriate fire resistance rating, is a **fire wall** that separates a building into fire divisions. Under most circumstances, a fire, even a very severe one, will not pass through or around a fire wall. (There is another type of divider, less strong, and usually not extending from basement to roof, called a **fire partition.** Although it can reduce the spread of fire, a fire partition does not create fire divisions.)

The other way to create a fire division or its equivalent is by outdoor open space separating two buildings. The amount of space necessary for reliable separation depends on the possible intensity of the exposing fire, the combustibility of the surfaces (walls and roofs), and the size and nature of windows and other openings in both buildings. The relative heights of two exposing buildings is also a factor. Common standards for adequacy of clear spaces regularly assume that firefighters will arrive and be able to help protect the exposed building. When this is not the case, the amount of clear space required is much greater. (More open space may be required than is often considered necessary. A fire in Massachusetts once spread 100 feet across a river and upwind to ignite another building.)[6]

In addition, the clear space needs to be *clear*. Too frequently, the value of open spaces has been compromised to the point where their effectiveness is all but destroyed by their being cluttered with combustible yard storage or by allowing grass and brush to grow between the structures.

Protected openings in a fire wall substantially reduce the reliability of the wall as a fire barrier, since there is no assurance that the protection will be properly in place when needed. Therefore, the possible spread of a fire from one side of the wall to the other (in other words, no actual fire division) must be taken into account.

Naturally, full separation is desirable between hazardous fire sources and less hazardous operations, such as between manufacturing and office occupancies, and between operations involving materials with low ignition temperatures and other materials.

A special type of full separation is provided by a fire-resistive vault. Valuable records, money, securities, jewelry, furs, or fine arts enclosed in a fire-resistive vault can often survive destruction of the rest of the building. Such fire protection also provides some protection against other perils. For full protection, the vault must not only resist entry of flame; it must also insulate the contents against increase of temperature within the vault to the point where contents can ignite or be damaged. It also must withstand rupture from collapse of the containing building. (Lesser degrees of protection, as in a fire-resistive file with, say, one-hour fire resistance are, of course, an improvement over ordinary cabinets or open filing with respect to fire damage.)

Physical separation between records and duplicates of them, at totally different locations, is often the most practical method of controlling fire loss from damage to an organization's valuable papers and records.

Reducing Damageability

A major method of fire control is substitution of noncombustible for combustible materials. With respect to the major components of buildings—as in the differences among wood frame, joisted masonry, noncombustible, and fire-resistive construction—this is obvious. It is also generally recognized in connection with special hazards, such as flammable and combustible liquids and gases. Combustibility is less frequently considered with ordinary property, such as desks and chairs. The use of steel instead of wood, or of heavy materials rather than light, can reduce damageability. Hotels and hospitals can use noncombustible bedding, rugs, drapery, and furnishings. Of course, the gain in resistance to fire (and other) damage, compared to the increase in cost of the safer equipment, is commonly much smaller in low hazard occupancies (such as offices) than in more hazardous ones. Combustibility of buildings and contents has actually increased in recent years with the growing use of plastic furnishings and structural components.

Controlling Loss From Arson

For risk control purposes, arson cases can be divided into crimes committed *against* the property owner and crimes committed *by* the property owner. Although insurers need to consider the possibility of both types, only crimes against the owner will be considered in this discussion.

The chance of an effective arson attempt is reduced when an arsonist's opportunity to enter the premises is made difficult and when the presence of an intruder will be quickly detected. Locks, guards, alarms, and other systems effective in protecting against forcible entry of a burglar can also serve to prevent entry by an arsonist. Of course, it is necessary that areas vulnerable to an arsonist be protected, as well as those areas attractive to a thief. Risk control measures for crime losses will be discussed in greater detail later in this chapter.

Sprinkler valves, fire alarm control devices, and similar protective devices can be protected so that any tampering by an arsonist will sound an alarm. Although alarms may not eliminate the arsonist's opportunity to set a fire, they can reduce the amount of time during which the arsonist can work undisturbed and may send firefighters to the scene even before the fire has been started. Any device that restricts entry or reduces the amount of time during which a would-be arsonist can work uninterrupted can reduce the chance of arson loss.

Extinguishment of Fires

Fire protection engineers categorize the facilities for extinguishing hostile fire into two principal groups—internal and external fire protection. Corresponding to what traditionally has been called "private" fire protection, **internal fire protection** consists of measures an organization can take to extinguish fires striking its own property. Corresponding to what traditionally has been called "public" fire protection, **external fire protection** consists of fire departments and other public facilities that the community makes available to safeguard the general public from the spread of hostile fire.[7]

Internal Fire Protection

The most common forms of internal fire protection are (1) automatic fire detection/suppression (sprinkler) systems, (2) portable fire extinguishers, (3) standpipe systems, (4) guard services, and (5) fire brigades.

Automatic Fire Detection/Suppression Systems

Automatic fire detection/suppression systems, also called **sprinkler systems,** may use water, dry or wet chemicals, carbon dioxide, foam, or Halon as extinguishants. These automatic systems rely on fire detection devices to sense the presence of a hostile fire and on signaling devices to alert personnel on or off the premises to the danger. Many organizations supplement these systems for detecting and suppressing fire with human resources in the form of guard services and fire brigades.

Every automatic sprinkler system consists of piping with discharging nozzles or heads, control valves for directing extinguishants within the system, gauges for monitoring pressure within the system, and alarm devices to signal when the system becomes operative. (Some systems also have other "monitoring" alarms that call attention to any malfunction or disabling of the system so that it can be repaired.) These automatic systems are classified by the types of extinguishants they use.

Water Systems Systems that rely on water are supplied from such sources as public water, gravity tanks, or—supported by an appropriate pump—in-ground tanks or natural bodies of water. The water is discharged from one or more sprinkler heads. Discharge occurs when a fire creates a sufficient level of heat to melt or break the sprinkler head operating mechanism (called a fusible link or frangible bulb) allowing the water to discharge. The water discharges either upward (through an upright sprinkler head) or downward (through a pendant sprinkler head), striking a deflector that is designed to break up the waterstream into water droplets. This spray pattern provides for a greater surface area to absorb the heat of the fire, cools the surrounding material and area, and confines, controls, and leads to extinguishment of the fire. To conserve water in the system and to minimize water damage to property not endangered by fire, many systems allow only the sprinkler heads that are directly affected by the heat of the fire to open; the entire system does not "go off."

The two basic types of water-based sprinkler systems are wet-pipe and dry-pipe systems. In a **wet-pipe system**, the piping is full of water and will immediately discharge that water when the sprinkler head opens as a result of the fusible link or frangible bulb melting or bursting. Since the piping is filled with water at all times, the system responds faster than a dry-pipe system. However, also because of the water in the piping, a building with this type of system must be continuously heated to prevent the water from freezing.

In a **dry-pipe system,** the piping is filled with air under pressure. This air holds back a greater amount of water pressure through the use of an air clapper. The advantage of this type of system is that it can be installed in unheated buildings. The only area where heat is needed is around the dry-pipe valve, and this can be provided by enclosing the dry-pipe valve(s) in a noncombustible enclosure and heating the area(s) around the valve(s) with electric space heaters.

However, the dry-pipe system has limitations. Because air is in its piping, any sprinkler head operations triggered by fire require the air to be released first. This action creates a delay that results in more heads operating than would be in operation with a wet-pipe system under similar conditions. Also, the dry-pipe system cannot protect as large a building area as can a wet-pipe system.

The sprinkler system must be properly designed to provide protection equal to the fire exposure. A system installed on a light hazard occupancy (such as an office) will not be adequate to provide the level of protection required, say, for a tire warehouse. The fact that a sprinkler system is present does not automatically guarantee that the system is adequate; it is essential to verify whether or not the protection available is acceptable for the exposure.

Although water-based sprinkler systems usually function effectively, there are a number of recognized reasons for some notable failures. The following are the most prevalent:

- Closed or inoperable valves, either the main control valve or a subcontrol valve
- Sprinkler protection for only a portion of a building
- Inadequate maintenance and testing of the system
- Painted or obstructed sprinkler heads
- Inadequate water supply and pressure
- Hazards of occupancy exceeding the system's design capabilities

A sound fire risk control program should include specific steps to eliminate all these reasons that water-based sprinkler systems sometimes fail.

In addition to basic wet and dry sprinkler systems, there are other types of water systems. One of them, the **deluge system,** is a sprinkler system in which all the heads remain permanently open; water is allowed into the system by a deluge valve, which in turn is activated by a separate detection system. Deluge systems are used to protect against fires that could spread faster than conventional sprinkler heads can open, as in spills of flammable liquids.

Another type of water-based system is a **preaction system.** This is the same as a deluge system except that the sprinkler heads normally are closed. Therefore, both the sprinkler heads and the detection components of a preaction system must operate before any water is released. Preaction systems are especially appropriate for occupancies that are unusually susceptible to water damage, such as computer rooms or small libraries, or for areas of limited water supply.

A third alternative, **water spray systems,** can have either open or closed nozzles. Instead of conventional sprinkler heads, these systems have directional nozzles specifically designed for the configuration of the space being protected and the hazards in that space. For example, water spray systems are used to safeguard aircraft in hangars, combustible cooling towers, and chemical plant reactors.

Dry Chemical Systems A **dry chemical system** contains finely divided powders stored in a cylinder. The cylinder is connected by pipes to nozzles positioned to allow for full distribution over the fire exposure area. Activation of the system can be by a heat detector, fusible link, or manual release.

The dry chemical type of system is listed by Underwriters Laboratories for use on Class B (flammable liquid) and Class C (electrical equipment) fires. Thus, it has applications for exposures involving dip tanks, cooking operations, flammable liquid storage, and spray painting. When discharged, however, the dry chemicals leave a residue and would not be suitable protection for areas housing computer operations or sensitive electronic testing equipment. Care must be exercised if a dry chemical system protects an area within the vicinity of computer or electronic equipment—the discharge of the system and air movement in the building may cause some of the dry chemical to settle on the equipment, thus interfering with its functions.

Carbon Dioxide Systems In a **carbon dioxide system,** carbon dioxide is stored as a liquid under pressure and discharged as a gas through the pipes of the system to the site of the fire. The system is activated by a heat or smoke detector, fusible link, or manual operation.

The carbon dioxide system is suited to the same types of Class B and Class C fires as is a dry chemical system. However, since the extinguishant changes into a gas when discharged, there has to be enough of the agent to extinguish the fire since the agent dissipates as it is released. For a total flooding system, such as for a flammable liquid storage room, all doors and vent openings to the area must be interconnected with the system so that when the system is activated, the openings will be closed off to contain the carbon dioxide concentration within the protected area.

Carbon dioxide displaces the oxygen in the air and so smothers a fire. This displacement of oxygen can be dangerous when the system is protecting a vault or other area that may be occupied by employees at one time or another. To protect personnel in such an area, a pre-alarm signal is necessary before the system's activation to allow time for personnel to evacuate the area. Signs should be posted by the entrance and in the protected area advising of the type of protection and the necessity to leave the area immediately if an alarm sounds.

Halon Systems The general term **Halon** refers to a series of ionized hydrocarbon gases and liquids (halogenated hydrocarbons) that have the ability to halt chemical reactions and thus extinguish fires rapidly.

Despite their excellent fire fighting qualities, however, some halogenated hydrocarbons have been identified as stratospheric ozone-depletion agents. Accordingly, the Environmental Protection Agency prohibited production of Halon 1301 (the Halon normally used in automatic fire extinguishment systems in the United States), as well as some other Halons, after January 1, 1994.

The rules do not, however, prohibit the *use or sale* of Halon 1301. Current supplies of Halon 1301, as well as supplies of recycled Halon 1301 after production of Halon 1301 ceased, should make existing Halon 1301 systems usable for years to come. Although alternative agents for Halon exist, none has been identified that can simply be charged into an existing Halon system. The main problem is that greater quantities of the new agents are usually needed, and so larger storage tanks, larger pipe sizing, and different nozzles may be needed to achieve adequate discharge within the recommended time period. Accordingly, many organizations with existing Halon 1301 systems may choose to continue using those systems as long they are able to obtain Halon 1301 at an affordable price.

The discussion that follows is equally descriptive of Halon 1301 systems and systems that use alternative agents.

Halogenated hydrocarbon extinguishants are effective on flammable liquids, electrical equipment, and surface fires in paper, wood, or other ordinary combustibles. These extinguishants put out fires very quickly, without water damage, and without contaminating the area as do other chemical extinguishants. Halon is frequently used in computer rooms, telephone equipment installations, and other electrical control rooms. Unlike carbon dioxide, which extinguishes fire by smothering, Halon extinguishes fire by breaking the combustion chain reaction. Therefore, much lower concentrations of Halon than of carbon dioxide may be used.

A drawback of halogenated hydrocarbons is that they can be toxic to humans and animals at certain concentrations. One of the reasons for the widespread use of Halon 1301 is that it can extinguish fires with as little as a 5 percent concentration of Halon in the air; it does not have harmful effects on humans until a 7 percent concentration is reached, and it does not have long-lasting adverse effects on people until a 10 percent concentration is reached. Other forms of Halon are harmful at lower concentrations. In fact, the manufacturers of some of the alternatives to Halon 1301 have recommended the alternatives for use only in nonoccupied areas. The possibly deleterious effects of a particular Halon extinguishant on people or animals must always be considered before any Halon system is installed.

In areas with moderate or high concentrations of combustibles, most authorities agree that Halon should not be considered as a substitute for more traditional, water-based sprinkler protection; rather, Halon should be considered a supplement to such protection. If a fire were to become sufficiently intense to open the sprinkler in a traditional wet-pipe or dry-pipe system, Halon probably could not extinguish such a blaze. Nonetheless, rooms with minimal combustibles can be protected by Halon alone.

Halon can be effective as an extinguishant only if it is released into an area engineered to prevent it from leaking—or to prevent leaking of air through doors, air ducts, pipes, windows, ceilings, drains, porous masonry, or other openings. Such a closed environment is critical for the proper use of Halon not only so that it can reach its required concentration to be effective, but also to maintain this concentration for at least ten minutes. Therefore, Halon should be installed only in areas that have been designed by knowledgeable engineers for its use.

Detection and Signaling Systems

Any extinguishant in an automatic suppression system is released only when that system is activated. Furthermore, these automatic systems usually need to be supplemented by human intervention from a public fire department or private fire brigade. Thus, two integral parts of every suppression system are (1) detectors to activate the system and (2) signals to alert an outside fire department or internal brigade.

Detection Devices Two integral parts of every fire suppression system are (1) detectors to activate the system and (2) signals to alert the organization's personnel and/or an outside fire department. To be effective, detectors must be properly located; must respond to hostile fire, but not to extraneous, nonhazardous conditions; and must be designed for the structure in which they operate. The following are some purposes for which detectors are particularly crucial:

- To activate shutdown of air handling systems in the event of smoke conditions
- To release magnetic door closures to zone off areas
- To activate an extinguishing system protecting specific hazards

Detectors may be set to respond to heat, rate of temperature increase, smoke, flame, or to a combination of these. The choice is designed to maximize efficiency: to assure response when danger truly exists yet generally avoid false alarms. Thus, firesafety engineers distinguish among the following types of detectors:

- **Fixed temperature heat detectors**—which can respond to a predetermined temperature level
- **Rate-of-rise heat detectors**—which respond to a present speed of temperature rise
- **Fixed temperature rate-of-rise detectors** (also called rate-of-rise compensated)—designed to respond to a fixed temperature determination or to an increase in that temperature that exceeds a predetermined level

- **Smoke detectors**—which can respond to visible as well as invisible products of combustion
- **Flame detectors**—designed to respond to the presence of flame in its very early stages
- **Combustible gas/vapor detectors**—which detect the presence of flammables or combustibles in the surrounding area

For the detection system to be effective, it must be properly maintained. It must also cover all building areas. If only partial protection is installed, then a gamble is being made that fire will start in the protected area(s) only or will occur in close proximity to a detector, which will respond and transmit the alarm.

Signaling Systems Adequate fire safety programs include action by people to put out the fire and to avoid further loss or damage. Therefore, one of the basic functions of virtually every automatic system is to emit a signal automatically to alert people to take appropriate actions. For such signaling, there are five basic categories of alarms, classified in terms of where the alarm signal is received. As shown in Exhibit 2-6, these alarms are **local alarms, auxiliary alarms, remote alarms** (sounding at either a police department or a fire department), **proprietary alarms,** and **central station alarms.**

Fire Extinguishers

Fire extinguishers are "first aid" devices to be used to control fire in its early stages. To be available for use, each extinguisher should be readily accessible, visible, properly inspected, and appropriate for the hazard. In many instances, the extinguisher may be used by an unskilled operator. Thus, education is an important element in the proper use of extinguishers. Education includes teaching personnel about the location of the extinguisher, its discharge range, its capabilities and limitations, the method of putting it into operation, and for some highly hazardous operations, the chance for "hands on" use of the extinguisher on training fires.

Fire extinguishers should be appropriate for the fire(s) likely to occur. As shown in Exhibit 2-7, there are four classes of extinguishers.

Another crucial management responsibility is thorough, periodic inspection and maintenance of fire extinguishers. The maintenance requirements vary in their specifics and intervals with the type of extinguishant, and different extinguishers even in the same class require different inspection procedures. Here, good risk management requires (1) determination of the maintenance and inspection requirements for each extinguisher, (2) assurance that an employee of the organization or a qualified outside specialist performs this

Exhibit 2-6
Basic Types of Fire Alarm Systems

Local Alarm	Rings only at the premises to notify occupants. If the alarm rings outside during hours when the building may not be occupied, action is required by a passing police officer or a "good Samaritan" to notify the fire department.
Auxiliary Alarm	Connected to an existing municipal alarm system on the same circuits that carry signals from the street fire alarm boxes. Any activation of this system causes the box alarm signal to be transmitted to the fire alarm dispatch.
Remote Alarm	Transmitted over leased phone lines from protected property to a fire department or police department. Before this type of system is chosen, the nature of the department's response should be determined. For example, it is vital that the police department's initial response to an alarm be dispatch of the fire department rather than a police dispatch for investigative purposes.
Proprietary Alarm	Rings to alert occupants (or "proprietors") on protected property or on another facility of the same organization and staffed with its personnel trained to handle alarms. This is a good arrangement for a large plant or one that has several buildings. Any alarm signal received permits the duty personnel to investigate and to take the necessary action, whether restoring the system for a needless alarm or initiating immediate notification of the fire department.
Central Station Alarm	Rings on the premises of a company that is in the business of handling alarms. The central station staff is trained in handling fire alarms and in notifying the proper fire department as well as notifying the individuals on the customer's call list.

Exhibit 2-7
Types of Fire Extinguishers

Type	Extinguishant	For Fires Involving
Class A	Pressurized water and multi-purpose dry chemical	Ordinary combustible materials, such as paper and wood
Class B	Ordinary dry chemical, multi-purpose dry chemical, foam, carbon dioxide, and Halon 1211	Flammable liquids and gases, such as gasoline, acetone, and propane
Class C	The same as for Class B with the important criterion that the extinguishant be a nonconductor of electricity	Energized electrical equipment
Class D	Dry powder agent specifically listed for use on the particular combustible metal that is on fire	Combustible metals, such as magnesium, sodium, and lithium

inspection and maintenance, and (3) maintenance and checking of extinguisher inspection and maintenance records.

Standpipe Systems

Combining elements of both automatic sprinkler systems and portable fire extinguishers are **standpipe systems,** which can be used by an organization's specially trained firefighting personnel or a public fire department. A standpipe system is a series of pipes running throughout a building through which water can be supplied to hoses that, in the event of an emergency, can be attached to valves in the standpipes. Standpipe systems increase the efficiency with which a human-operated system can distribute water. Standpipe protection plays an especially important role in getting hose lines into service on upper floors that are too distant to be reached by street level. Thus, installation and maintenance of a standpipe system is essential for fire protection in high-rise structures.

Guard Services

Guard services are another means of providing internal fire protection. Guard services may be provided either through a contract service or by employees of the facility. The watch personnel tour the property and preferably use a portable clock to verify that the guard has visited each station. The intent is for the guard to follow designated routes so that each area of the facility is checked on a definite frequency, building areas are secured, fire hazards are identified and reported, continuous production processes are monitored, fire protection equipment is checked, and the proper authorities can be notified if fire is discovered. Follow-up procedures by management of supervisory personnel should be used to verify that the clock stations are being visited at prescribed times and that the guards are performing their functions.

Fire Brigades

Every facility should have a fire emergency plan that includes some form of **fire brigade** activity. The brigade can range from three individuals responsible for notifying the fire department, initiating evacuation, securing areas, and removing important files that may be in the danger area, to an organization that has a fire chief with assistants and a crew capable of initiating and maintaining an effective attack on a fire.

To determine the size of a fire brigade appropriate for a specific facility, it is important to evaluate the potential for fire, existing on-site protection, the extent of critical operations, the potential magnitude of a fire, and the available public fire protection. Once these things have been evaluated, the organization's risk management staff can design a plan in cooperation with plant personnel and management to include the number of people on the team, designated crew leaders, and guidelines for the functions and duties of the crew. The plan should also outline the training required to make the brigade an effective part of the overall fire protection program.

External Fire Protection

External fire protection—the "fire department"—offers meaningful protection to a facility only when (1) adequate public fire hydrants are reasonably accessible and supplied with adequate water and pressure, and (2) fire department personnel are capable of responding to a fire at the facility.

For a facility to be "protected," hydrants are necessary. They must be available to the premises and must be within 500 to 1,000 feet road distance to the premises (not "as the crow flies"). Besides the hydrant locations, consideration also must be given to the underground water mains and the available water supply. Problems exist in older communities where a buildup of scale and sediment has developed in the water mains. This condition can significantly reduce the size of the water main's internal diameter and thus have a major impact on its waterflow capabilities. The facility also could be on a dead-end line, which will allow for waterflow in one direction only. In addition, any nearby development of properties with high water usage may result in a declining water supply.

For these reasons, it is important that water supplies be tested to verify the actual available supply and pressure before beginning new construction or making changes in existing operations. Such changes could increase the fire hazard potential, which might, in turn, have higher water supply and pressure requirements. Proper fact-finding procedures will reveal whether the water supply is stable, beginning to decline, or has deteriorated to the point that the present level may be inadequate. If inadequacies are discovered, supplemental supplies must be developed for adequate protection. It is better to identify problems before finalizing construction plans than to discover deficiencies after plans have been completed.

A problem that sometimes arises with large and special exposures is failure to acquaint public fire department personnel with plant layout, hazards, and firefighting resources ahead of time. This lack of preplanning can delay effective firefighting efforts (and sometimes even leads to ineffective or dangerous courses of action) when fire does occur. For example, firefighters may apply water to a substance that reacts violently with water. Or, they may get lost or trapped in an unfamiliar building.

Personnel responsible for firesafety can develop preplanning programs in cooperation with their local fire department. Among the items that should be considered in preplanning are informing the fire department of building floor plans, locations of exits, what hazardous materials are present and where they are located, and which valuable files should be removed from the burning building if at all possible. In many cases, the fire department will actually visit the site to inspect the premises and determine where water supplies are located.

Controlling Water Damage

Most firefighting is done with water, and occasionally the water causes more property damage than the fire. (Of course, if there were no water, the fire would do more damage—an elementary point that is sometimes overlooked.) Also, automatic sprinklers sometimes release water when there is no fire, with some resultant damage. (Plumbing systems sometimes break or overflow, resulting in the same type of damage.) Control of water damage is therefore of interest in property risk control.

Control starts with sources. With sprinkler systems, an obvious point is proper design, installation, and maintenance. There are various ways to design automatic sprinkler systems so they are less likely to respond to stimuli from sources other than hostile fires. For example, there are differing temperatures at which different sprinkler heads will open. Sprinkler heads should be chosen that will not respond to ambient temperatures produced by normal operations, and vulnerable sprinkler heads can have guards that reduce the probability of accidental damage.

Also important in reducing water damage loss severity is to provide means for water to move out of the building with minimum damage. Impermeable floors, and drains and scuppers to channel the water outside, are common means of control. Also, inexpensive skids or pallets that keep stock off the floor help to reduce water damage losses.

Most sprinkler systems have waterflow alarms that sound when water begins to flow through the system. Their primary purpose is to serve as a fire alarm. However, such alarms are also useful in providing prompt notification of an accidental discharge from a sprinkler system. In addition, sprinklers can be designed to withhold or interrupt water flow unless combinations of stimuli are received that confirm the presence of a hostile fire rather than something else. For example, one type of sprinkler head automatically shuts off when the temperature cools. This type of head could thus automatically extinguish a small fire and then cease spraying. Due to their expense, such heads are not frequently installed but are used in special applications.

When there is a fire and valuable property is exposed to water damage from fire hoses, crews trained and equipped to put waterproof covers in place can greatly reduce loss severity. Of course, it is ordinary wisdom to minimize the amount of water damageable property kept in basements or in lower floors below upper stories where there is serious fire exposure or other source of potential water damage.

Finally, where the possible loss from water damage is large, automatic extinguishing systems containing carbon dioxide, dry chemicals, or Halon may be used. Preaction systems, although they contain water, can also reduce (but not eliminate) the possibility of water damage.

Experience has shown that the danger of water damage from sprinklers has often been overestimated. Computer equipment, for example, is often assumed to be highly damageable by water from sprinklers. Experience has shown otherwise. Prompt drying and cleaning of computer equipment by restoration specialists can greatly minimize any water damage loss.

After the Fire Is Out

Loss control continues to be possible after a fire is out. Property losses can be minimized by good salvage techniques, and business interruption losses can be minimized by the use of alternate resources or by expediting repairs.

Fire salvage is a specialized skill. For anyone who rarely deals with fire losses, the services of an experienced salvor are needed. The salvor may be supplied by an insurer or hired directly.

Alternate resources may be arranged in advance by having standby or underutilized equipment and facilities at another location.

For some organizations, competitors' facilities may by available; occasionally there is even pre-loss understanding of mutual aid in this respect. More often, vacant facilities will have to be found, refurbished, and adapted to the organization's needs. Of course, temporary operation requires financing in addition to outlay for repair and reconstruction. Whether operations can be continued may depend on whether arrangements for risk financing have been adequate to cover all these expenditures.

Organized efforts to assure that the types of loss reduction measures described above will be taken at the time of and immediately following a severe fire or other catastrophe are known as **crisis management** or **disaster planning.** Effective crisis management requires extensive planning and practice *before* any crisis occurs.

Life Safety in Fires

Life safety engineers have developed extensive sets of firesafety standards for particular kinds of buildings. These standards have been codified in the *Life Safety Code*® published by the National Fire Protection Association and incorporated explicitly or by reference into the statutes and ordinances of most localities in the United States. Therefore, compliance with the applicable sections of the *Life Safety Code* usually is a legal requirement; failure to comply is not only a breach of an ordinance (bringing fines and other penalties) but also can be substantial evidence of negligence in failing to adequately safeguard others from injury or damage by fire. Consequently, not complying with the *Code* increases the likelihood not only of property and personnel losses, but also of liability losses.

Therefore, an important function of every organization's risk management department is to determine, and comply with, the provisions of the *Life Safety Code* (or local ordinances), which govern the life safety features of the building(s) the organization owns or occupies.[8] Although these provisions are quite detailed and vary significantly among types of occupancy and types of structure, the fundamental goals of the *Code* are summarized in Exhibit 2-8.

Exhibit 2-8
Goals of *Life Safety Code®*

1. To provide for adequate safety without dependence on any single safeguard
2. To ensure that construction is sufficient to provide structural integrity during a fire while occupants are exiting
3. To provide an appropriate degree of life safety considering the size, shape, and nature of the occupancy
4. To ensure that the exits are clear, unobstructed, and unlocked
5. To ensure that the exits and routes of escape are clearly marked so that there is no confusion in reaching an exit
6. To provide adequate lighting
7. To ensure prompt occupant response by providing early warning of fire
8. To provide for back-up or redundant exit arrangements
9. To ensure the suitable enclosure of vertical openings
10. To make allowances for those design criteria that go beyond the *Code* provisions and are tailored to the normal use and needs of the occupancy in question

Controlling Theft Losses

In its various forms, theft is one of the most severe and pervasive causes of property loss. The term "theft" is generally understood to include any act of stealing. Different types of theft are described by various labels, including burglary, robbery, employee dishonesty, extortion, fraud, forgery, alteration, looting, shoplifting, pilferage, and trickery.

Although money and securities are favorite commodities among thieves, any type of property that can be moved may be targeted for theft. However, thieves are most attracted to property that has high value and low weight and can be easily converted to cash. Cigarettes, liquor, drugs, food, and electronics are examples of "target commodities." The main loss consequence of theft is loss of value of the stolen property. Other consequences include property damage resulting from breaking and entering, vandalism during the commission of the theft, and reduction in revenue or increase in expenses.

The discussion of theft risk control that follows focuses on burglary, robbery, shoplifting, and employee dishonesty losses, four of the most common types of theft.

- **Burglary** is generally defined as theft by someone who forcibly enters the place where the property is kept.
- **Robbery**, or "hold-up," involves the use (or threat) of force against the person from whom the property is taken. (In crime insurance policies, "robbery" is defined more broadly, to also include theft *witnessed* by the person having custody of the property being stolen.)
- **Shoplifting** is not burglary, because shoplifters do not enter forcibly; nor is shoplifting robbery, since it does not involve threat of force. Instead, the shoplifter, posing as a normal shopper, attempts to steal merchandise from a store without being detected.
- **Employee dishonesty** is theft that an employee commits against his or her own employer.

Although these terms are defined more specifically in crime insurance policies, the general definitions given above are adequate for present purposes of examining control measures against common types of theft. Other forms of theft will be described in more detail in Chapter 10.

In most cases, the probable severity of a theft loss is less than that from other property exposures. A fire may destroy an entire building and its contents, but a thief is likely to steal only a small percentage of the total contents. Likewise, theft of cash in any one occurrence is limited to the amount of cash on hand. (This suggests some obvious avoidance or loss reduction measures: Eliminate or limit the cash!) Despite the lower severity of crime exposures, the overall frequency of crime loss may be greater than the frequency of fire losses (which suggests that loss prevention can be very useful).

Employee dishonesty can be an exception to the generality expressed above: trusted employees (particularly officers) have sometimes taken so much that sheer survival of the organization was threatened.

Controlling Burglary and Robbery Losses

Protective measures against burglary and robbery losses may be divided roughly into four groups:

1. Physical protection to premises in order to delay access by the criminal
2. Installation of alarm systems and other devices or the use of guards or security patrols that will indicate when access to the premises has been gained by an outsider

3. Use of automatic cameras or closed circuit television systems to help identify criminals in order to facilitate their arrest and conviction
4. Various protective procedures, including procedures for handling money and securities that will reduce the likelihood of theft or reduce the amount of property accessible to a thief

Physical Protection

Physical protection measures include passive restraints to entry of a building, safes, and vaults.

Restraints to Entry

A business owner can install passive restraints to entry. The type of lock used on doorways can make a difference of several minutes in the entry time needed by a thief. The ordinary snap lock can be manipulated in a matter of seconds. A deadbolt lock cannot be manipulated in the same way as a snap lock, but usually requires the picking of the tumblers or the use of force. Lockpicking requires tools and skills that many ordinary burglars do not possess.

The rear doors in a store or office can be barred from the inside so that access is difficult. Bars, gates, and grills can be put across windows or doorways. An "unbreakable" glazing material can be used for doors or windows where the proprietor wishes to maintain a clearly visible window display. (It is worth noting that any measure that impedes entry or exit by burglars may also serve to impede entry by firefighters or emergency exit by members of the public.)

Many thefts involve breaking a show window and grabbing valuable items. Ordinary plate glass is easily broken. Varieties of breakage-resistant glass and plastic materials often improve protection, particularly for smaller windows. In jewelry display windows, another device effectively impedes the access of a burglar to a show window display. This is a sheet of breakage-resistant glass suspended behind the show window glass. This second sheet is hung on chains from the top of the show window so that it swings backward when struck. The show window can be broken but this second sheet of glass is difficult to break—because of its composition and, particularly, because it swings. It is difficult for a thief to reach around such a glass when it is properly installed.

The installation of good locks, gates, bars, breakage-resistant glass, and similar devices may provide satisfactory protection for mercantile stocks of low value. This may be particularly true if the premises are under frequent surveillance by police and in a low crime area. However, such passive restraints merely delay the entrance of a burglar and do not guarantee that a burglary will not occur. The adequacy of such measures also must be considered in light of the values involved and whether small volume and low weight plus high value would make the merchandise attractive to a burglar.

Safes

Safes are another type of physical protective device. Safes vary in their vulnerability to burglary. Many safes are basically fire protection devices, referred to as **record safes,** and offer little resistance to the burglar. Designed to protect money and valuable records from fire damage, fire-resistive safes generally have square doors and are mounted on wheels.

Money safes are designed to be burglar resistive. Money safes generally have round doors and are not mounted on wheels. (However, some modern money safes have been designed with square doors to facilitate their use with cash register trays.)

Within each category, the safes offer degrees of resistance to fire and burglary. Exhibit 2-9 lists the classifications used in rating some crime policies and will give some idea of the different degrees of protection afforded by the various types of safes. Safes can be most readily classified by reference to the Underwriters Laboratories label found inside the door of most quality safes.

Vaults

Vaults are rooms or compartments designed to protect valuable property against theft, fire, and perhaps other causes of loss. Typically, the walls of the vault are constructed of steel, or concrete lined with steel, and the door to the vault is constructed of steel with a lock. Like safes, vaults provide varying degrees of protection depending on how thick their walls and doors are and the quality of their locks. Vaults, because they can be larger than safes, can be used to protect items such as furs, valuable rugs, fine arts, and other bulky items.

Safes and vaults, like other physical protective devices, do not eliminate the possibility of a loss. However, they reduce the likelihood of loss in proportion to the quality and management of the safe or vault and the skill of the thief.

Alarm Systems

Unlike some physical protection devices, alarm systems do not prevent burglars from entering. Except to the extent that they serve as a deterrent, the purpose of such systems is to indicate when an intruder has entered the premises.

A simple alarm system consists of electrical contact switches or metallic foil on each door, window, or other opening into the building. Usually, the system is wired so that an electrical current is passing through the system constantly.

Exhibit 2-9
Safe and Vault Classifications

Safe, Chest or Cabinet or Vault Classification	Construction		
		Walls	
	Doors	Safe, Chest or Cabinet	Vault
B (Fire-Resistive)	Steel less than 1" thick, or iron	Body of steel is less than 1/2" thick, or iron	Brick, concrete, stone, tile, iron or steel
	Any iron or steel safe or chest having a slot through which money can be deposited		Not Applicable
C (Burglar-Resistive)	Steel at least 1" thick	Body of steel at least 1/2" thick	Steel at least 1/2" thick; or reinforced concrete or stone at least 9" thick; or non-reinforced concrete or stone at least 12" thick
	Safe or chest bearing following label: "Underwriters Laboratories, Inc. Inspected Keylocked Safe KL Burglary"		Not Applicable
E (Burglar-Resistive)	Steel at least 1 1/2" thick	Body of steel at least 1" thick	Same as for C
ER (Burglar-Resistive)	Safe or chest bearing the following label: "Underwriters Laboratories, Inc. Inspected Tool Resisting Safe TL–15 Burglary"		Not Applicable
F (Burglar-Resistive)	Safe or chest bearing one of the following labels: 1. "Underwriters Laboratories, Inc. Inspected Tool Resisting Safe TL-30 Burglary" 2. "Underwriters Laboratories, Inc. Inspected Torch Resisting Safe TR–30 Burglary" 3. "Underwriters Laboratories, Inc. Inspected Explosive Resisting Safe with Relocking Device X–60 Burglary"		Not Applicable

G (Burglar-Resistive)	One or more steel doors (one in front of the other) each at least 1 1/2" thick and aggregating at least 3" thickness	Not Applicable	Steel at least 1/2" thick; or reinforced concrete or stone at least 12" thick; or non-reinforced concrete or stone at least 18" thick
H (Burglar-Resistive)	Safe or chest bearing one of the following labels: 1. "Underwriters Laboratories, Inc. Inspected Torch and Explosive Resisting Safe TX-60 Burglary" 2. "Underwriters Laboratories, Inc. Inspected Torch Resisting Safe TR–60 Burglary" 3. "Underwriters Laboratories, Inc. Inspected Torch and Tool Resisting Safe TRTL–30 Burglary"		Not Applicable
I (Burglar-Resistive)	Safe or chest bearing the following label: "Underwriters Laboratories, Inc. Inspected Torch and Tool Resisting Safe TRTL–15x6 Burglary		Not Applicable
J (Burglar Resistive)	Safe or chest bearing the follow label: "Underwriters Laboratories, Inc. Inspected Torch and Tool Resisting Safe TRTL–60 Burglary		Not Applicable
K (Burglar-Resistive)	Safe or chest bearing one of the following labels: 1. "Underwriters Laboratories, Inc. Inspected Torch and Tool Resisting Safe TRTL–60 Burglary 2. "Underwriters Laboratories, Inc. Inspected Torch Explosive and Tool Resisting Safe TXTL–60 Burglary"		Not Applicable

Reprinted with permission from *Commercial Lines Manual,* p. CR-SV-2, Copyright Insurance Services Office, Inc., 1985, 1987.

Opening a door or window interrupts the electrical current, which activates an alarm system. This is a **perimeter system**; the intent is to signal an alarm whenever unauthorized entry is made into the building.

In addition to contact switches and metallic foils, other detection devices used in perimeter systems include photoelectric detectors, vibration detectors, and glass breakage detectors. These and other types of detection devices are illustrated in Exhibit 2-10.

In addition to perimeter protection, some burglar alarm systems protect specific areas within a facility and are thus referred to as **area protection** or **space protection**. Detection devices used for area protection include photoelectric detectors, sound detectors, and motion detection devices, such as ultrasonic, microwave, or passive infrared motion detectors.

Burglar alarm systems can also be configured to protect specific objects that are likely to be targeted by burglars, such as safes, vaults, filing cabinets, display cases, and works of art. This type of protection, referred to as **object protection**, is usually provided in combination with perimeter or area protection. Detection devices commonly used for object protection include contact switches, vibration detectors, sound detectors, and smoke and heat detectors. (Smoke and heat are generated when a burglar tries to break into a safe or vault using a torch.)

In addition to detection devices, a burglar alarm system consists of a control unit and a reporting device. Upon receiving an alarm signal from a detection device, the control unit communicates with the reporting device to set off an alarm. Essentially the same options for setting off a fire alarm, discussed earlier in this chapter, are available for setting off a burglar alarm. These options are local alarms, remote alarms (sounding at a police department), proprietary alarms, and central station alarms. Of the two most commonly used types of alarms—local and central station—central station alarms are the more effective.[9]

Alarms are not limited to burglary prevention. Alarm systems may also be used to reduce the robbery exposure. Holdup buttons or foot pedals may be situated so they can be triggered by a bank teller or store clerk, sending a "silent alarm" to a central station company or to the police. (The "silent" alarm is silent at the location being robbed.) If rapid response is possible, the police may arrive while a robber is still on the premises. The value of holdup alarms should be weighed against the possibly increased danger of a robber doing harm to the employee(s) at the site if the police arrive while the robber is still there or if the robber detects that an employee has set off an alarm.

Exhibit 2-10
Burglar Alarm Detection Devices

Door Switches (Contacts) These devices are usually magnet-operated switches. They are affixed to a door or window in such a way that opening the door or window removes the magnetic field. This, in turn, activates the switch, causing an alarm.

These devices may be surface-mounted or recessed, exposed or concealed. A variety of switches exists for every kind of door or window and for all levels of security.

Metallic Foil (Window Tape) Metallic foil is the traditional means for detecting glass-breakage. Strips of thin foil are affixed to a glass surface. Breaking glass ruptures the foil and interrupts the detection circuit to signal an alarm.

Thin foil, however, is easily damaged by people or objects accidentally touching the glass surface. Also bonds at the corners and between multiple-foil strips deteriorate with time. Metallic foil, therefore, requires frequent maintenance, especially on glass doors.

Wooden Screens Openings such as air-duct passages and skylights can provide paths for an intruder. These can be secured by a cage-like frame of wooden rods. An intruder breaks the wire embedded within the frame, which triggers an alarm.

Wood screens are custom-built for each application. They can be mounted permanently or removed when the alarm system is turned off. Wooden screens require little maintenance. They are suitable for protecting openings where aesthetics are not important.

Continued on next page

Lacing (Paneling) Lacing can protect walls, doors and safes against penetration. Lacing is a closely woven pattern of metallic foil or fine brittle wire on the surface of the protected area. An intruder can enter only by breaking the foil or wire. This activates the alarm. A panel over the lacing protects it from accidental damage.

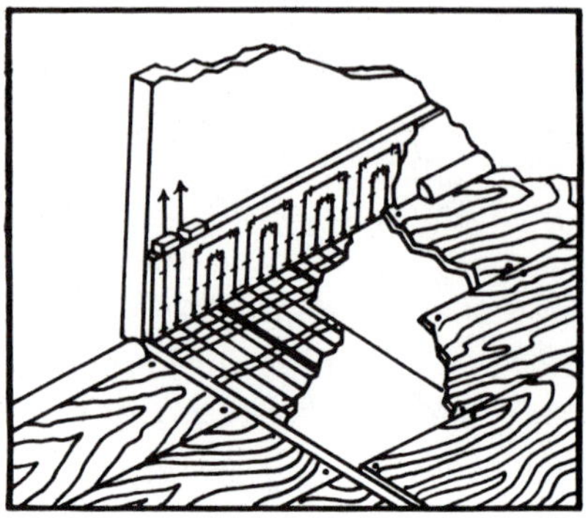

Photoelectric (Eyes, Beams) Photoelectric devices transmit a beam across a protected area. When an intruder interrupts this beam, the photoelectric circuit is disrupted. This starts an alarm.

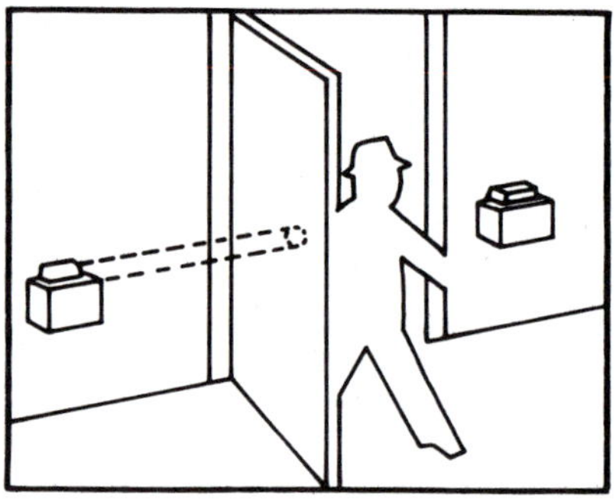

Modern photoelectric devices are a great improvement over their predecessors. Today's photoelectric devices use diodes that emit infrared light. These make the beam invisible to the naked eye. The beam usually pulses rapidly to prevent compromise by substitution.

Photoelectric devices are effective and reliable. Some have ranges of more than 1,000 feet for large buildings and hallways. These devices provide excellent protection for relatively low-risk areas.

Ultrasonic Detectors These devices also sense movement. Ultrasonic means "above the range of hearing." An intruder disrupting the ultrasonic wave pattern initiates the alarm.

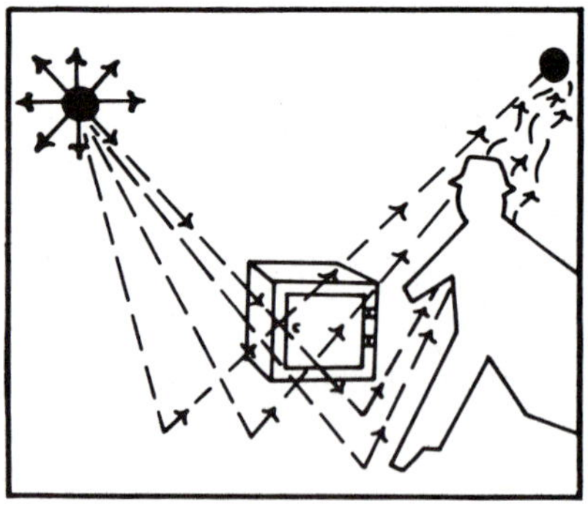

Ultrasonic devices can be mounted on the ceiling or wall. They protect three-dimensional areas with an invisible pattern. However, they are prone to false alarms, due to excessive air currents or ultrasonic noises from mechanical equipment. Again, proper application is important.

Infrared Detectors These devices are part of the motion-detection group. They sense the body heat of an intruder as he or she passes through the protected area. A change from the area's normal heat profile triggers an alarm. Infrared detectors are relatively free of false alarms. They provide relatively inexpensive protection for confined areas.

Microwave Detectors This kind of motion detector uses high-frequency radio waves, or microwaves, to detect movement. Microwave devices have greater range than ultrasonic. Since microwave devices do not use sound, or air, they are not prone to false alarms from air currents. However, they can cause false alarms, because they penetrate materials such as glass, and metal objects reflect them. This means microwaves can detect motion outside the protected area if the detectors are not properly installed.

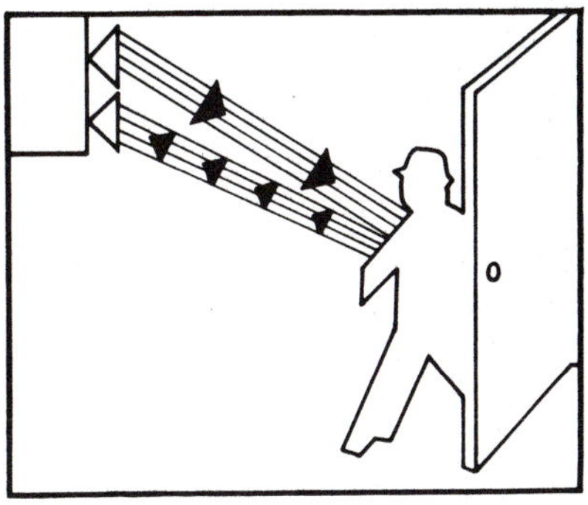

Object Protection Object protection provides direct security for individual items. It often is the final stage of an in-depth protection system with perimeter and area-protection devices. The objects most frequently protected are safes, filing cabinets, display cabinets, models, and expensive equipment.

Proximity (Capacitance or Electrostatic) With this system, the object itself becomes an antenna, electronically linked to the alarm control. When a person approaches or touches the object, its electrostatic field becomes unbalanced. This initiates the alarm. Only metal objects isolated from the ground can be protected this way.

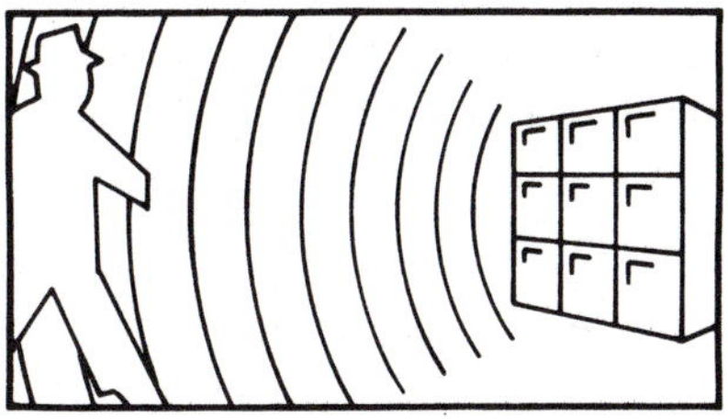

Continued on next page

Vibration Detectors (Seismic) These sensing devices use a highly sensitive piezoelectric crystal or microphone to detect the sound pattern that a hammer-like impact on a rigid surface would generate. These devices are attached directly to safes and filing cabinets or walls and floors.

The devices instantly detect a vibration an intruder makes. Some vibration detectors are adjustable. They can be adjusted to detect a sledgehammer attack on concrete or the delicate penetration of a glass surface.

This kind of protection generally is for securing the perimeter surfaces of a vault. The correct number, spacing and location of these sensors is important for suitable detection.

Reprinted with permission from *Alarm Handbook for the Security Manager,* Honeywell, Inc. 1984, pp. 8-11.

Selection of Alarm Systems

Alarm systems vary as to their quality and extent of protection. Insurance rate manuals generally give credits only for **approved alarm systems.** An approved system is one installed by an approved burglar alarm company named in the rating manual. Underwriters Laboratories, Inc., issues alarm certificates that indicate the grade, type, and extent of the alarm system, and these certificates are considered in granting insurance rate credits. No matter how expensive, an alarm system without an Underwriters Laboratories certificate may receive no premium reduction, a fact too often discovered only after money has been spent on an alarm.

Deficiencies of Alarm Systems

One of the most difficult problems with burglar alarms is false alarms caused by accidental triggering. Because of the high frequency of false alarms, police in some cities assign a low priority to calls that come in from burglar alarm systems. The services of a central station alarm company can greatly reduce this problem, since the alarm company can help verify whether an actual break-in has occurred.

Another deficiency is that an alarm system does not stop burglaries from occurring—it merely shortens the burglar's operating time. There is usually a delay of five to fifteen minutes or more from the time an alarm is given until a guard or police officer can reach the premises. This may be enough time for the burglars to complete their work. The expected response time is a vital consideration in determining whether the expense of a sophisticated burglary or robbery alarm system is worthwhile.

Another major problem is that telephone circuits generally are used to transmit signals from the premises to the central station or police department. A sophisticated burglar may be familiar enough with telephone lines in general that the security can be breached at some point where the lines are accessible. This may be in the basement of a multiple-occupancy building, in the overhead lines, or in a telephone line on a pole or box outside the building.

Watchman or Security Patrols

Many organizations find it worthwhile to maintain watchman service on the premises. A watchman goes through the building at periodic intervals (typically hourly) to see that everything is in good order. This, of course, protects against fire and, to a degree, against other perils such as burglary. The presence of the watchman is a deterrent as far as burglars are concerned, but it by no means eliminates loss possibilities.

Central station alarm companies also maintain a **supervised system** under which the watchman signals to the central station upon visiting each station throughout the premises. These systems are arranged so that a guard is sent to the premises by the central station alarm company if the watchman at the premises fails to signal as required. Sometimes burglars or robbers will force a watchman to continue making rounds while a theft is being carried out. Most signaling systems contain an arrangement whereby the watchman can secretly signal for help even while making rounds under the burglar's scrutiny.

Surveillance Cameras

Banks, twenty-four-hour convenience stores, and other firms with high robbery exposure frequently install automatic cameras to photograph criminals in the process of committing a crime. Such installations are effective in two ways:

1. They facilitate the identification and conviction of criminals after the offense has been committed, making the offenders unavailable for future offenses, at least for a short time.
2. The increased probability of identification and conviction discourages robbery.

Protective Procedures

A property owner can institute many procedures in addition to using the devices just described. One simple procedure used by many merchants is to have the safe or other particularly valuable property located where it can be observed by police patrols from outside the building. A light is installed to keep the inside of the premises illuminated.

Another common procedure is for some businesses to accept only credit cards or cash that does not exceed the purchase price by more than a small amount, thus not requiring a business to keep large amounts of "change" in the cash register. Incoming money is immediately deposited through a one-way slot or chute into a burglar-resistant safe. Robbers tend to "hit" isolated businesses with large amounts of money or "stealable" property and limited personnel. Steps that reduce isolation, reduce the amount of money or other attractive property on hand, and increase the number of people on duty tend to reduce the likelihood of a robbery.

Organizations that handle large quantities of money or securities may arrange for frequent deposits at a bank. This results in a smaller value on the premises at any one time and also means that messengers carrying property to the bank carry smaller quantities. Another procedure followed by many organizations is to transport money, securities, and other valuable property by an armored car messenger service.

Controlling Shoplifting Losses

According to statistics compiled by the National Retail Federation, approximately 34 percent of the $27 billion in inventory shortages (or "shrinkage") reported by U.S. retailers in 1992 can be attributed to shoplifting.[10]

Because shoplifting is so common, it generally does not fit the requirements for good usage of insurance: Insurers need to cover their own operating expenses as well as their claims cost. The charge for coverage against regular or constantly recurring events has to be greater than the cost of the events themselves. Insurance works well only when the losses covered are, for an individual insured, both random and individually significant. Therefore, most crime insurance policies (such as the one covering burglary and robbery only) do not include coverage for shoplifting losses. And those forms that do include some shoplifting losses ordinarily do not apply when the insured's only evidence of loss is an inventory shortage. Consequently, most shoplifting losses are retained by the business owner, and appropriate risk control measures may be the only way a retailer can minimize its shoplifting losses.

Surveillance

Many stores attempt to control shoplifting losses through surveillance of shoppers. Video surveillance of shoppers may not only alert store security personnel to a crime in progress, but also deter would-be shoplifters from acting. Security personnel, either uniformed or plain-clothed, may have a similar effect. Security personnel should always be adequately trained in their occupation. Blunders by security personnel when apprehending suspects can create unsafe conditions for other persons in the store and can cause the store to become legally liable for false arrest, false detention, or other injuries alleged by suspected shoplifters or by law-abiding customers.

Limiting Access

Limiting access to merchandise can also be effective against shoplifters. Small, high-priced items, such as jewelry, watches, silk ties, and handguns, can be placed in locked display cases and made subject to employee rules regarding removal and showing to customers. For example, a sales attendant at the jewelry counter may be allowed to remove no more than two items from the case for a single customer at one time, and then may not leave the customer unattended. Unfortunately, the average sales attendant is usually no match for a sleight-of-hand artist, who may be able to switch an authentic item with a bogus one while the attendant is watching. A similar method is to display certain merchandise that is especially attractive to shoplifters (such as cigarettes) within the restricted areas behind sales counters.

Another method of limiting access is to keep merchandise in secure warehouses, stock rooms, or vaults that do not permit entry of unauthorized persons. In the sales area of the store, floor models of the protected merchandise can be displayed, perhaps chained down or otherwise secured against theft. After a customer has selected and paid for a particular product, the product can be brought out of storage and delivered to the buyer. This approach might be used, for example, in a store selling computers, televisions, and other consumer electronics.

Anti-Theft Devices

Burglar alarms are not helpful in detecting shoplifting activity, since burglar alarms are aimed at detecting break-ins while the business is not open for business. However, some anti-theft devices are designed specifically for discouraging or detecting shoplifters. These devices include the following:

- Electronic tags ("hard tags"), which sound an alarm when tampered with or if someone tries to take the tagged item from the store before having the tag removed

- Dye tags, which permanently stain garments if removed improperly
- Electronic cables, which secure expensive garments, such as leather jackets, to a rack and trigger alarms if cut

Protective Procedures

Various store procedures can also be implemented to control shoplifting losses. For example, a clothing store may station an employee at the entrance to its dressing rooms to count the garments each customer takes in and out of the dressing area. Some stores require their shoppers to check all carrying cases such as backpacks and briefcases at the store entrance. Lockable compartments are usually provided for customers to secure their property while shopping. Although some customers are offended by such procedures, many recognize the seriousness of the shoplifting problem and are willing to cooperate. Unfortunately, however, many shoplifters are talented in their trade and escape detection despite the best efforts of storekeepers.

Controlling Employee Dishonesty Losses

Estimated at over $40 billion a year,[11] losses caused by employee dishonesty (or embezzlement) constitute the largest part of theft losses. Although many employees commit petty thefts of office supplies, long-distance personal telephone calls, and the like, the usual targets of serious embezzlement are money and merchandise.

Unfortunately for employers, many risk control activities that reduce outsiders' opportunities for taking property do not prevent most of the losses committed by employees. Employees are already present on the premises, and the employer's property is necessarily committed into their care. Also, employees have an understanding of the employer's procedures and vulnerabilities. And some employees are vested with a great deal of responsibility and authority in the organization, with accompanying knowledge of its procedures and vulnerabilities. Thus, different strategies and methods of risk control are needed.

Research has shown that the single most important factor affecting whether employees will take good care of their employer's interests, including property, is how they feel about their supervisors. Although good rapport between management and employees is the first line of defense, it is not foolproof. For this and other good management reasons, well-designed accounting and access controls should also be present.

Exhibit 2-11 presents one method of categorizing internal theft prevention systems. The top half of the chart depicts measures that increase the probability of quick discovery. Because these measures are based on the assumption

Exhibit 2-11
An Internal Theft Prevention System

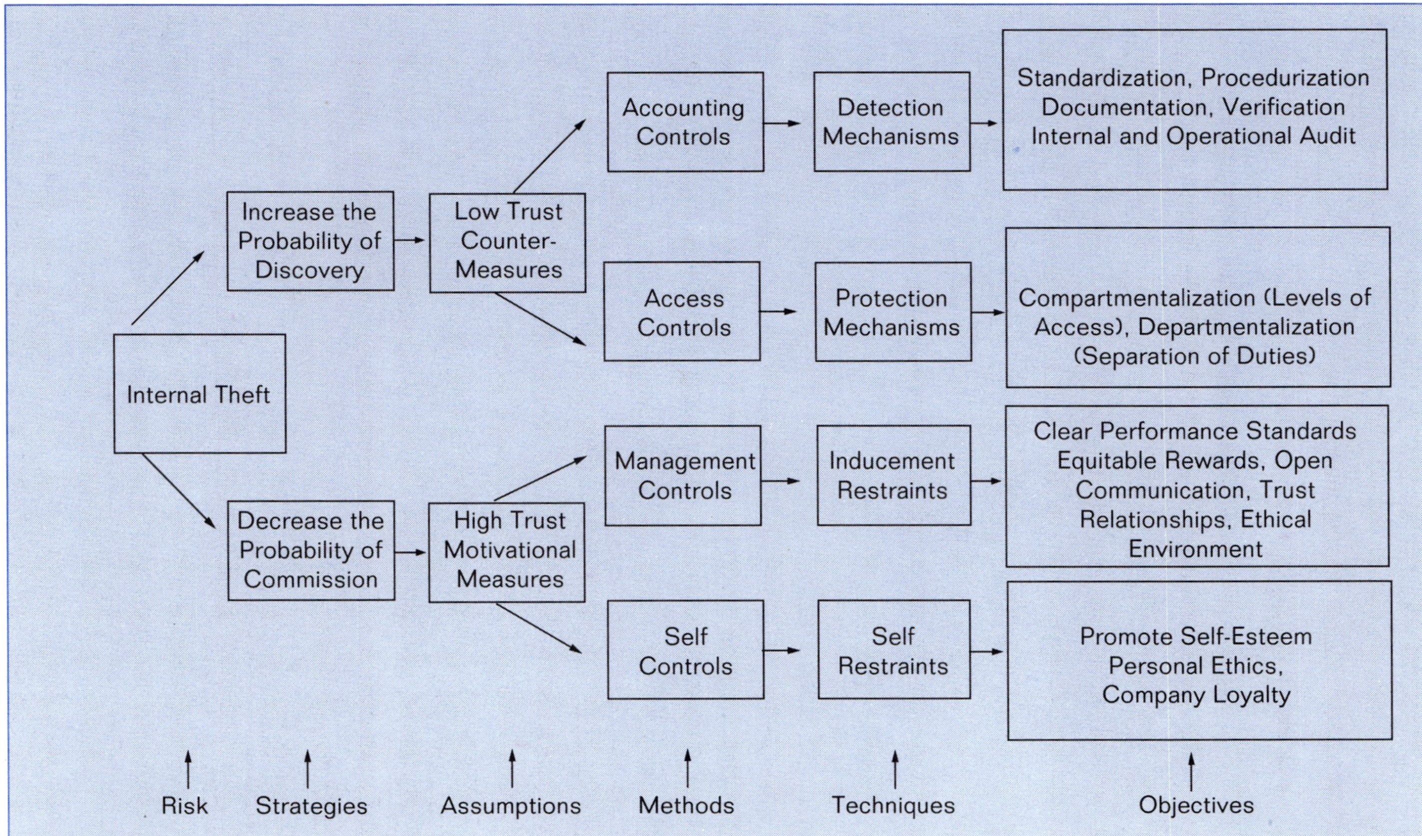

Adapted with permission from Jack Bologna, "A New Look at the Internal Theft Prevention Process," *Assets Protection,* Sept./Oct. 1980, p. 33.

that some thefts may happen despite good rapport between employees and management, they are labeled "low-trust measures. Low-trust measures include accounting controls and access controls.

- **Accounting controls,** to keep track of cash flows and detect any improprieties, limit loss caused by manipulating a firm's records. Examples of such controls include internal auditing, patrolling, observing, leaving audit trails, and enforcing the use of standardized procedures.
- **Access controls** reduce losses of merchandise and other property (including currency and coins, confidential documents, and trade secrets) by limiting access to target property to a limited number of key employees. For extremely valuable property and information, locked entrances, armed guards, and identification badges may be among the devices used to limit access. Keys and safe combinations are usually given to only a limited number of employees. Authority to sign checks, purchase orders, and contracts is given to only selected employees who cannot operate without this access.

Personnel Screening

Motivation, leadership, and management controls are dealt with in a much broader context in CPCU 7—Management. However, one management strategy that has particular application to controlling employee dishonesty will be emphasized here—proper personnel screening. One of the objectives of **personnel screening** is to prevent employee dishonesty losses by not employing dishonest people. A key ingredient in screening out dishonest people is gathering information about job applicants and checking references before hiring. In order to be effective, information regarding a prospective employee's background should be supplied by sources other than the applicant.

Separation of Duties

Separation of duties is another important strategy in many programs to control employee theft. The majority of employee thefts involve one employee acting alone. Proper separation of duties makes it difficult for any one employee to steal (or to steal a great deal) without the collaboration or cooperation of at least one other employee. Some basic approaches to using separation of duties are described below.

1. No individual should have total control over every phase of any significant transaction or sensitive job. (For example, those who maintain inventory records do not participate in physical counts of inventory.)
2. Work flows should proceed from one person to another so that, without duplication, the work of the second acts as a check upon that of the

first. (Merchandise for shipment is picked up by one employee, taken to the loading dock by another, and checked onto a truck by a third—all of whose tallies should agree.)

3. Those who authorize the use of assets should not also be responsible for their custody. (The inventory clerk releases materials only upon receipt of an authorization from a department head.)

4. Record keeping and bookkeeping activities should be separated from the handling and custody of assets. (The accounts receivable clerk should not also open mail containing incoming payments.)[12]

Controlling Other Losses

Risk control measures for some additional perils—explosion, windstorm, flood, and earth movement—are briefly described below.

Explosion Control

Many explosions have the chemistry of extremely rapid combustion. These explosions are, in essence, nearly instantaneous fire over the whole of a large quantity of material. Examples include explosions of flammable liquid vapors and gases, dust explosions (for example, grain elevator explosions), and the action of commercial explosives. The principles of explosion control are very similar to those for the slower combustion of fires. A major difference is the much shorter time available for explosion counteraction. There are, however, explosion suppressors that can act effectively the instant an explosion is initiated in order to suppress what would otherwise be a major explosion. Such suppression equipment detects a sudden abnormal increase in pressure and automatically floods the incipient explosion with a suppressing agent. This equipment resembles an automatic fire extinguishing system but differs in the type of detection and the extreme rapidity of response.

To prevent initial combustion that could lead to explosion, explosive materials should be properly handled. Sometimes, in addition, the material may be kept in a low-oxygen or oxygen-free atmosphere. (This is done by replacing much or all of the air in a chamber with inert gas, such as carbon dioxide or nitrogen.) Similar treatment may be provided for electrical equipment, or electrical equipment may be of explosion-proof design appropriate for the explosive environment.

For explosions that are not prevented or suppressed, venting is the standard method of control—directing the force toward open air and/or a solid barrier such as an earthen bank. Thus, for example, dynamite is stored in "igloos" with light roofs (so the explosive force is directed upwards); the "igloos" are surrounded by earth or concrete banks.

Explosion of pressure and vacuum vessels is the other major type of explosion. (Technically, vacuum vessels, which rupture inward rather than outward, suffer "implosion" rather than "explosion," but the difference is not important here.) Explosions occur in such equipment when the pressure exerted exceeds the capacity of the vessel to contain pressure. Such excess can occur from either an increase in the amount of pressure or a decrease in the strength of the vessel. Changes in strength or pressure must therefore be prevented or controlled. Proper operation, maintenance, and inspection are the keys to preventing explosions or other breakdowns of such equipment. This exposure will be dealt with in greater detail in Chapter 9.

Control of Windstorm Damage

Although the energy source in windstorms cannot be controlled, it is possible to locate away from areas with frequent severe storms, such as hurricanes and tornadoes. However, it is often impractical to select locations purely on the basis of windstorm exposure and no location above ground avoids windstorms completely. As has been demonstrated time after time, some buildings resist damage from wind better than others. Factors that affect probability of wind damage are always relevant. There is considerable correlation between ability to resist fire damage and ability to resist wind damage because stronger structures resist both types of damage.

Plate glass, attached exterior trim, and roofing are particularly susceptible to windstorm damage. Ordinarily glass is readily damaged by windblown objects. When the glass area is large, glass can be broken by the high wind itself; light trim can be torn off by winds; and high velocity wind passing over a building creates forces that tend to lift the roof. Inadequate anchorage of the roof assembly will result in loss of the roof, followed by more loss to exposed contents. When the roof itself holds, its surface can suffer considerable stress and there may be much damage to shingles, tiles, or other attached coverings. This possibility must be considered in selection and attachment of roof surfaces. Proper maintenance is necessary, as strength of materials and their fastenings can deteriorate over time.

Flood and High Water Losses

Water damage may be caused when the hazard of low ground is combined with the peril of high water. In major hurricanes there is often more damage from flooding than from force of wind. Natural flooding, whether from hurricanes or other storms, may be classified as three types:

1. Flooding from high tides
2. Riverine floods—from rising water in rivers, streams, and lakes
3. Floods from inadequate runoff of rain water (flash floods)

The best method of treating this exposure is to avoid areas known to have had flood experience. Since construction and rearrangement of the surface of the ground change runoff and flood patterns, consideration has to be given as to how these patterns may change. The consideration should, of course, be given before construction commences.

Where property is exposed to high water, design of grounds and buildings should take this into account, as should location of particular property in the building.

Many risk control measures are possible:

1. Placement of dams and other impoundments of water can cause, modify, or reduce energy buildup.
2. The rate and direction of release of water energy can be controlled by creating channels and impoundments to control direction and rate of runoff and by creation of open areas over which flooded waters can be spread out, reducing their depth and speed of flow.
3. Dikes and other barriers may be used to separate flood waters from property (and people) to be protected. Channels also effect such separation. Placing property at a high level (on high ground or in upper stories of a building) is another example of separation.
4. Property may be designed for strength against the pressure of flood waters and the effects of dampness. This can be done by making structures more solid and by giving them shapes that offer less direct impedance to water flow around and past them. Provision for runoff or pumping out water when the flood has subsided may also be necessary. (Dikes and levees sometimes increase loss by keeping water impounded longer.)
5. Buildings in flood prone areas can be constructed so that the bottom floor is above the 100-year flood level. On beachfront properties, construction on pilings serves not only to elevate the structure but also to withstand the pressure of waves.
6. Counteraction includes such activities as emergency sandbagging, moving property to higher levels, speeding draining by pumping, and promptly drying and cleaning damaged property to minimize adverse effects.

Losses Caused by Earth Movement

As a practical matter, little attention is paid to earthquake loss control except in geographic areas that have had a history of damaging earthquakes. Where a serious earthquake exposure exists, the effects of an earthquake can be reduced by careful attention to building design and construction, taking into consideration the conditions of the soil upon which the building will rest. Earthquake-resistant buildings are designed so that the structure as a whole will neutralize the forces of earth movement. Mortar between bricks is not strong enough to hold walls together during an earthquake without some type of reinforcing. In fact, ordinary masonry buildings have done poorly in resisting earthquakes. The most common method of designing an earthquake-resistant building is to build a rigid structure with walls, columns, and pillars tied securely to floors and roofs by horizontal, vertical, and cross members carried through to the foundations. Some modern high-rise buildings have been constructed to allow the building to sway with an earthquake, thereby absorbing the force exerted on the building during an earthquake.

Landslide, mudslides, subsidence (sinking), volcanic eruption, and expansive soil are other types of earth movement that may result in severe property damage. The major technique for controlling losses from these various earth movements is care in siting buildings.

Summary

Many losses can be prevented or reduced in severity through the use of appropriate risk control measures. This chapter examines risk control measures commonly used to treat property losses caused by fire, theft, explosion, windstorm, flooding, and earth movement.

A fire must have an initial source of heat, oxygen, and fuel. Fire prevention efforts focus on removing one or more of these three essentials from the scene. Heat sources may result from electrical, chemical, mechanical, or nuclear heat energy. Fuel for fires includes both building contents and construction materials used for buildings. The type of construction is thus an important factor in fire control. The main types of building construction include wood frame, joisted masonry, noncombustible, masonry noncombustible, and fire resistive. The source of oxygen for most fires is ordinary air—the better the supply of oxygen, the faster the fire burns.

Pre-loss measures for fire losses are focused on controlling heat sources and keeping them separated from fuels. Separation is also an important objective after a hostile fire breaks out. Various building design features can help prevent the spread of a hostile fire.

Fire extinguishment efforts can be classified as either internal or external fire protection. Internal protection includes (1) automatic fire detection/suppression (sprinkler) systems, (2) portable fire extinguishers, (3) standpipe systems, (4) guard services, and (5) fire brigades. External protection is the public fire department. External fire protection offers meaningful protection only when (1) public fire hydrants are accessible and adequately supplied with water, and (2) fire department personnel are capable of responding to a fire at the facility.

Theft—which may be loosely defined as any act of stealing—takes many different forms. Stealing may be by outsiders or by insiders. Theft by outsiders includes burglary, robbery, and shoplifting. Theft by insiders, known as employee dishonesty, commonly presents a much more serious threat.

Various means can be used to keep burglars out of a building or at least slow down their entry. Deadbolt locks, bars on windows, and breakage-resistant glass are examples. Once a burglar gains entry into the building, safes and vaults can keep burglars from getting their hands on valuable items or at least make it harder for the burglars to gain possession of the items. Burglar alarm systems do not prevent burglars from entering, but they can scare burglars away or increase the chances of apprehending them. Alarm systems can also be equipped with "holdup buttons" to alert a central station or the police that a robbery is occurring. Watchmen, security patrols, surveillance cameras, and various protective procedures can be used to provide further protection against burglary and robbery.

Shoplifting is a serious exposure for stores. The main techniques for combatting shoplifting losses include surveillance by video cameras or security personnel, limiting shoppers' access to merchandise, using various anti-theft devices on merchandise, and following protective procedures.

Employee dishonesty losses are difficult to control, since the dishonest employee may have access to the property, understands the employer's procedures, and may even be highly trusted by the employer. Risk control measures include accounting controls, access controls, personnel screening, and separation of duties.

Many explosions have the chemistry of extremely rapid combustion, and so the principles of explosion control are very similar to those for the slower combustion of fires. Controlling explosions of pressure vessels (such as steam boilers) involves proper operation, maintenance, and inspection of the equipment.

The best method of treating flood and high water losses is to avoid areas known to have flood experience. When flood exposure is unavoidable, many loss control measures are possible.

Where a serious earthquake exposure exists, the effects of an earthquake can be reduced by careful attention to building design and construction. The major technique for controlling losses caused by landslide, mudslides, subsidence, and expansive soil is care in siting buildings.

Chapter Notes

1. *Fire Protection Handbook*, 13th ed. (Boston, MA: National Fire Protection Association, 1969), pp. 1-69.
2. An "uninhibited chain reaction" is sometimes considered the fourth element necessary to have a fire. This element is of little importance in fire *prevention*. However, some chemicals used in fire extinguishers or extinguishing systems control or extinguish fires by breaking the chemical chain reaction.
3. *Fire Protection Handbook*, 16th ed. (Boston, MA: National Fire Protection Association, 1986), pp. 4-4 to 4-5.
4. NFPA *Inspection Manual*, 4th ed. (Boston, MA: National Fire Protection Association, 1976), pp. 146-148.
5. *Fire Protection Handbook*, 16th ed., pp. 7-83 to 7-84.
6. *Fire Protection Handbook*, 14th ed., pp. 6-14.
7. The majority of this section is adapted from George L. Head, ed., *Essentials of Risk Control*, 2nd. ed., vol. I (Malvern, PA: Insurance Institute of America, 1989), pp. 93-107.
8. The material in this section is adapted from *Essentials of Risk Control*, vol. I, pp. 70-73.
9. A source of further information on burglar alarms and safes is *An Insurance Guide to Selecting a Burglar Alarm System* (Bethesda, MD: Central Station Alarm Association, 1994).
10. David Dishneau, "Keeping a List of Who's Naughty," *The Philadelphia Inquirer*, December 18, 1993, p. D-1.
11. "Preventing Crime on the Job," *Nation's Business*, July 1990, p. 36.
12. *White Collar Crime* (Washington, DC: U.S. Chamber of Commerce, 1974), p. 60.

Chapter 3

Building and Personal Property Coverage

Many different forms of insurance are available for insuring commercial property loss exposures. This chapter begins with an overview of these forms and then examines one of the most common forms used to insure commercial buildings and their contents.

Overview of Commercial Property Insurance

Used as a general term, **commercial property insurance** includes all forms of insurance covering property loss exposures of both businesses and nonprofit organizations. The most common commercial property coverages are provided under standardized forms developed by Insurance Services Office, Inc. (ISO), or the American Association of Insurance Services (AAIS).

Role of Insurance Advisory Organizations

ISO and AAIS are national insurance advisory organizations that develop policy forms, manual rules, and loss costs for their member insurance companies. They also file these forms, rules, and loss costs on behalf of their members with regulatory authorities in the various states.

- Policy forms are the printed forms that make up insurance policies.
- Manual rules are the rules that insurers follow in providing policies to their

customers. Typical manual rules relate to eligibility, available limits of insurance, and policy rating (the calculation of premiums).

- Loss costs are the portion of an insurance rate representing projected losses and the costs of settling those losses. Insurers calculate insurance rates by adding other factors (such as the insurer's underwriting expenses) to the loss costs.

Most of the forms described in this text are those of ISO. AAIS forms, except for minor differences, are comparable in structure and coverage to the ISO forms. Some forms of crime insurance, which will be discussed in Chapter 10, are under the jurisdiction of the Surety Association of America (SAA), an advisory organization for insurance companies that underwrite surety bonds and employee dishonesty insurance. Insurance forms filed by ISO, AAIS, and SAA are commonly referred to as **standard forms**. They are sometimes called "bureau" forms, a phrase that dates back to the days when the functions performed by contemporary advisory organizations were handled by regional or state insurance rating bureaus.

For many classes of property insurance, there are no standard forms. Any insurer that underwrites these classes must develop its own forms, often referred to as **independent forms**. Some insurers use independent forms even though ISO or AAIS forms are available. This type of independent form may be essentially the standard form with a few coverage enhancements, or it may differ greatly from the standard form.

ISO Commercial Lines Program

In many cases, an organization's property insurance is provided in a package policy. A **package policy** ordinarily provides both property and liability insurance, usually for most of the insured's important loss exposures. A **monoline policy**, in contrast, provides only one line (or distinct type) of coverage. During the 1970s and 1980s, ISO had one set of forms for monoline policies and another set of forms for its "special multi-peril" (SMP) package policy. Working with two different sets of forms was not only an inconvenience for all concerned, but in some instances the coverage provided by a monoline form differed from the coverage provided by the corresponding SMP form.

In 1986, ISO introduced a simplified commercial lines program. This program, which is still in use today, includes a single set of modular **coverage parts** that can be used individually in a monoline policy or combined in a **commercial package policy (CPP)**. Rules and rating procedures for the ISO commercial lines program are contained in ISO's ***Commercial Lines Manual* (CLM)**.

The ISO coverage parts consist of the following:

- Commercial property
- Boiler and machinery
- Commercial crime
- Commercial inland marine
- Farm
- Commercial auto and various *liability* coverage parts (described in CPCU 4)

A coverage part consists of the following elements:

- One or more declarations forms (containing information about the insured and the particular exposures insured)
- A coverage form (containing most of the essential terms of coverage for one particular line of insurance)
- In some coverage parts, a general provisions form
- Any applicable endorsements (modifying the terms of the coverage form)

In addition to one or more coverage parts, every ISO commercial lines policy contains a common declarations page (often combined with the declarations for the various coverage forms included) and a one-page form called the **common policy conditions**. The common policy conditions address such matters as the rights of the insurer and the insured to cancel the policy, the insurer's right to examine the insured's books and records, and the insurer's right to make physical inspections of the insured's premises and operations. The various forms that might be included in a CPP are illustrated in Exhibit 3-1.

The coverage parts of the AAIS package policy, which are similar in structure to those of ISO, can be used as components in an ISO package policy.

The sections that follow describe the major types of commercial property insurance that can be included in a CPP.

"Commercial Property" Insurance

"Commercial property" insurance (which is set off by quotation marks in order to distinguish this particular line of insurance from commercial property insurance in general) can be described as insurance on buildings and their contents, or simply **building and contents insurance**. This is not an entirely accurate description, because "commercial property" insurance also covers certain structures that are not buildings. Moreover, it insures items of personal

Exhibit 3-1
Components of the Commercial Package Policy (CPP)

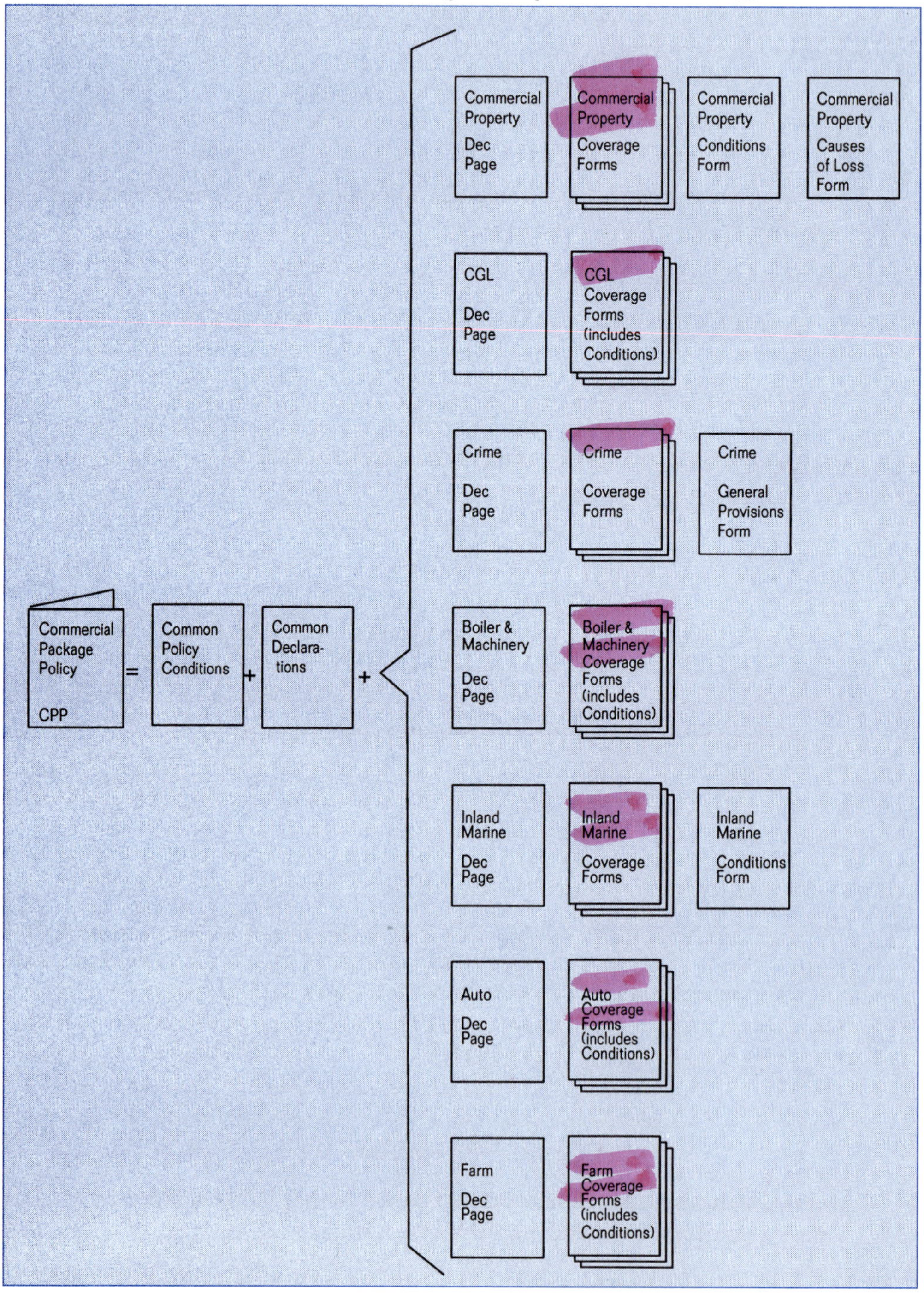

property other than those that are strictly contents of buildings, such as property kept in the open. However, with only limited exceptions, "commercial property" insurance is restricted to property on (or within 100 feet of) the insured location. Thus, most of the personal property insured is "contents," that is, personal property inside buildings. Organizations that wish to insure significant property values in transit or at other locations must supplement their "commercial property" insurance with other types of coverage.

"Commercial property" insurance also includes forms covering business income losses and extra expenses resulting from damage to buildings and personal property.

Several chapters of this text examine "commercial property" insurance:

- This chapter describes the building and personal property coverage form, used to provide building and contents coverage.
- Chapter 4 examines several optional coverages that can be added to the building and personal property coverage form to meet the coverage needs of various insureds.
- Chapter 5 describes the "commercial property" causes-of-loss forms, which are added to the "commercial property" coverage part to determine which causes of loss are covered.
- Chapter 6 describes "commercial property" coverage forms that can be used instead of, or in addition to, the BPP to handle special exposures, such as condominium buildings and units, buildings in the course of construction, and significant building glass exposures.
- Chapter 7 explores business income loss exposures, and Chapter 8 examines the "commercial property" forms and endorsements that can be used to insure business income loss exposures.

Boiler and Machinery Insurance

Boiler and machinery insurance meets coverage needs of organizations that have steam boilers, pressure vessels, and various types of machinery, such as air conditioning equipment, air compressors, turbines, and all types of production machines. Steam boilers and machinery are insured property under the building and personal property coverage form (BPP). However, they are susceptible to some causes of loss that are not covered by the "commercial property" causes-of-loss forms. These perils include steam boiler explosion, electrical disturbances (other than lightning), mechanical breakdown, and others.

Boiler and machinery insurance covers loss to boilers and machinery as well as loss to other property resulting from the "boiler and machinery" perils. For example, building and contents damage resulting from explosion of a steam boiler is not covered under the BPP but is covered under boiler and machinery insurance. Resulting business income loss can be covered by various boiler and machinery endorsements. Chapter 9 examines boiler and machinery insurance.

Commercial Crime Insurance

Like boiler and machinery insurance, commercial crime insurance covers causes of loss that are not covered in "commercial property" forms. These causes of loss include, but are not limited to, employee dishonesty, forgery, theft, burglary, robbery, and extortion.

Crime insurance also covers two important types of *property* excluded in "commercial property" forms: money and securities. Crime insurance on money and securities covers destruction or disappearance in addition to theft.

To cover the various combinations of property, perils, and special situations, eighteen different crime coverage forms and many endorsements are available under the joint ISO/SAA commercial crime program. These forms are discussed in Chapter 10.

Commercial Inland Marine Insurance

Inland marine insurance grew out of ocean marine cargo insurance to meet emerging coverage needs in the early twentieth century. Today the category covers a wide range of loss exposures whose initial common link was an element of transportation or communication. Examples of inland marine exposures are property in transit, mobile equipment, property being installed by a contractor, bridges, and radio towers.

Although ISO maintains some standard commercial inland marine forms, the great majority of commercial inland marine insurance is "nonfiled," meaning that many states do not require insurers to file their forms or rates with regulatory authorities. This freedom from filing requirements allows inland marine underwriters to tailor forms and rates to fit particular exposures.

AAIS provides a broader range of inland marine services to its member insurers than ISO. In addition to maintaining essentially the same "filed forms" as ISO, AAIS develops advisory forms and underwriting information for the "nonfiled" classes of inland marine. The various classes of inland marine insurance are surveyed in Chapter 11.

Farm Insurance

The ISO farm coverage part provides property and liability insurance needed by farmers and ranchers. Because farmers and ranchers usually live and work on their own land, farm insurance covers the farmer's residential loss exposures (dwelling and household personal property) and business loss exposures (farm buildings and farm personal property, including livestock) under one form. Farm coverage can also be used for a *business* that has farming exposures; in this case, the farm coverage part is simply added to the company's package policy. The ISO farm coverage part and some independent forms used to insure livestock and crops are discussed in Chapter 13.

Businessowners Policies

Many organizations are insured under businessowners package policies instead of the more cumbersome CPP. Typically, businessowners policies provide, in one form, most of the property coverages needed by small to medium-sized, uncomplicated risks such as stores, offices, and apartment buildings. A businessowners policy ordinarily provides building and contents coverage, business income coverage, and, for an additional premium, crime, boiler and machinery, and inland marine coverages. The ISO businessowners property form is discussed in Chapter 12.

In addition to ISO and AAIS forms, various types of property insurance are available to meet special coverage needs. Chapter 14 describes several such coverages.

Building and Personal Property Coverage Form

The remainder of this chapter describes the ISO **building and personal property coverage form (BPP)**. The BPP is commonly used to insure commercial buildings and contents. Although other forms, particularly the businessowners policy, have taken over some of the market once dominated by the BPP and its predecessor forms, the BPP remains the standard to which other forms can be compared.

As noted earlier, the BPP is not a completely self-contained policy. Covered perils for the BPP are listed in separate causes-of-loss forms discussed in Chapter 5. The BPP is also subject to several general provisions contained in the ISO **commercial property conditions**, a short form that is attached to any policy providing "commercial property" coverage. The commercial property conditions are discussed at the end of this chapter.

Covered Property

Rev Q #4

The BPP covers three broad categories of property:

1. Building
2. "Your" (that is, the named insured's) business personal property
3. Personal property of others

Coverage in any of these categories applies only when the declarations show a limit of insurance for that category. For example, if the declarations show no limit for building coverage, the policy provides no building coverage even though the BPP contains a section describing building coverage. Many insureds do not require coverage in every category, as in the following examples:

- The owner of a building rented to others might purchase coverage only for the building.
- A tenant might cover only its own personal property, or might also purchase coverage on the personal property of others.
- A building owner-occupant that takes custody of its customers' property (for example, a laundry) might purchase coverage for the building, its business personal property, and personal property of others.

Building

A description of each insured building is ordinarily entered in the declarations. This description includes each building's location, construction, and occupancy. Usually, the covered building is owned by the insured. However, a lessee might insure a leased building when required to do so by the terms of the lease.

In addition to the specific description of the insured building(s) inserted in the declarations, the BPP contains a general description of what property is included under the building coverage or, as it is often called, the "building item." This description is quoted in Exhibit 3-2.

The "building" definition is essential in defining covered property. The BPP covers real property other than a building or structure described in the declarations only to the extent that such property is included in the definition or listed elsewhere in the form. Coverage is not restricted to something with four walls and a roof. It can be any structure—for example, a sign—if it is described in the declarations. The definition clarifies that the building item includes permanently installed fixtures, machinery, and equipment. *Black's Law Dictionary* (5th ed.) defines **fixture** as follows:

Exhibit 3-2
BPP Building Description

Building, meaning the building or structure described in the Declarations, including:

(1) Completed additions;

(2) Permanently installed:

- **(a)** Fixtures;
- **(b)** Machinery; and
- **(c)** Equipment;

(3) Outdoor fixtures;

(4) Personal property owned by you that is used to maintain or service the building or structure or its premises, including:

- **(a)** Fire extinguishing equipment;
- **(b)** Outdoor furniture;
- **(c)** Floor coverings; and
- **(d)** Appliances used for refrigerating, ventilating, cooking, dishwashing or laundering

(5) If not covered by other insurance:

- **(a)** Additions under construction, alterations and repairs to the building or structure;
- **(b)** Materials, equipment, supplies and temporary structures, on or within 100 feet of the described premises, used for making additions, alterations or repairs to the building or structure.

> An article in the nature of personal property which has been so annexed to the realty that it is regarded as a part of the land . . . e.g., a furnace affixed to a house or other building; counters permanently affixed to the floor of a store; a sprinkler system installed in a building.

Certain types of property not ordinarily considered to be real property are included in the building item. Personal property owned by the insured and used to maintain or service the building or structure or premises is covered. Although this provision lists certain examples of such property—including outdoor furniture, floor coverings, and refrigerating, ventilating, cooking, dish washing, and laundering equipment—the provision does not limit coverage to these articles. It also covers unlisted articles such as window washing and floor cleaning equipment and materials, lawn mowers, and snow blowers.

This coverage eliminates the need for a landlord to purchase an additional amount of insurance under "your business personal property." However, furniture and other household personal property owned by a landlord and provided in a furnished apartment or room are not covered, since they are not used to service or maintain the building. A landlord can insure furnishings inside rooms or apartments under "your business personal property."

If a building is owner-occupied, coverage for personal property articles included in the definition of "building" overlaps with BPP personal property coverage. In the event of a covered loss to such articles, the insured could make claim under either coverage. For example, if the policy provides broader coverage on the building (perhaps the building is covered for replacement cost and the contents are covered only for actual cash value), the owner-occupant insured could make claim for these articles under the building item. Alternatively, if the damage to the building exceeded the limit of insurance on the building, some articles could be covered as personal property. The commercial property condition titled "insurance under two or more coverages" makes it clear that the insurer will not pay twice for the same loss.

Your Business Personal Property

The BPP description of "your business personal property" includes seven specific categories:

> (1) Furniture and fixtures;
>
> (2) Machinery and equipment;
>
> (3) "Stock";
>
> (4) All other personal property owned by you and used in your business;
>
> (5) Labor, materials or services furnished or arranged by you on personal property of others;
>
> (6) Your use interest as a tenant in improvements or betterments. . .;
>
> (7) Leased personal property for which you have a contractual responsibility to insure, unless otherwise provided for under Personal Property of Others.

Coverage can apply to all of these categories or be restricted to one or more of them by specifying the extent of coverage in the declarations or in an endorsement titled "your business personal property—separation of coverage." For example, if the declarations showed a limit of insurance for only "stock, furniture and fixtures," the policy would cover none of the other categories of personal property. However, the declarations of most policies simply show an amount of insurance for "your business personal property" and thus cover all seven categories of business personal property.

The seven categories of covered personal property can be informally subdivided along the following lines: categories 1 through 4 deal with property owned by the insured, and categories 5 through 7 involve certain types of property owned by others.

Property Owned by the Insured

Categories 1 through 4 encompass all personal property owned by the named insured and used in the named insured's business. Of the various words used in the first three categories of business personal property, only "stock" is defined in the policy. The definition states that **stock** means merchandise held in storage or for sale, raw materials, and in-process or finished goods. It also includes supplies used in packing or shipping stock.

The term "fixtures," for purposes of business personal property coverage, is generally interpreted to encompass not all fixtures (as under the building item) but only those fixtures that are removable by a tenant, generally called **trade fixtures**. Trade fixtures are therefore distinct from tenants' improvements and betterments (see below), which may not be removed by the tenants. Trade fixtures will be discussed in more detail in Chapter 6, along with improvements and betterments and other issues of special importance to commercial building tenants.

Category 4 clarifies that "your business personal property" includes all personal property owned by the named insured and used in the named insured's business, even though the property might not qualify under categories 1 through 3. For example, objects of art displayed in an office building, even if they were deemed not to qualify as "furniture" under category 1, would nevertheless be covered by category 4 if they were owned by the insured and used in the insured's business.

Property Owned by Others

It may seem strange that a coverage agreement titled "*your* business personal property" would cover some types of property belonging to *others*—especially since the BPP contains a separate agreement titled "personal property of others." Actually, this inconsistency is comparable to the *building* item's inclusion of some types of *personal* property. The purpose is to cover incidental exposures commonly associated with the main exposure insured.

Labor, Materials, or Services Furnished on Property of Others Category 5 includes the insured's work on personal property of others. This clarifies that the BPP will cover labor and materials the insured has put into customers' property, if the property is destroyed by an insured peril while still on the insured's premises. For example, a machinery repair and reconditioning shop has coverage for both the parts that have been placed in the customers' equipment and the labor expended in repairing it.

The coverage applies only to the extent of the insured's own costs; it does not cover any other part of the customers' property. Complete coverage for customers' property can be arranged under the "personal property of others" agreement. In addition, a coverage extension described below provides up to $2,500 for property of others at each insured location.

Category 5 also does not cover the insured's anticipated profit on the work performed. Coverage for lost profit can be provided under business income insurance, as discussed in Chapters 7 and 8.

Improvements and Betterments This category covers a tenant's use interest in improvements and betterments that the tenant has added to the landlord's building or has acquired at his or her own expense. **Improvements and betterments** are fixtures to real property that generally change the property and enhance its value—that is, they improve or better the property. Examples of tenants' improvements and betterments are the partitions, cabinets, and acoustic ceilings that a physician might have installed in his or her rented office.

Although a tenant may have made or paid for improvements and betterments, they ordinarily become the property of the landlord as soon as they are attached to the building. Nevertheless, the tenant has an insurable "use interest" in the improvements and betterments for the remainder of the rental period or lease. By including coverage for improvements and betterments in "your business personal property," the BPP enables a tenant who does not otherwise need building coverage to insure its use interest in such property under the same coverage agreement that covers the tenant's business personal property.

The improvements and betterments themselves are not personal property; they are real property. Accordingly, a landlord can insure its ownership interest in tenants' improvements and betterments through the BPP building item, since improvements and betterments are fixtures to the building. No special entry needs to be made in the declarations, but the limit of insurance should include the value of the improvements and betterments.

The insuring of tenants' improvements and betterments—from the points of view of both the landlord and the tenant—involves several important considerations, and the coverage is subject to special valuation provisions. In order not to disrupt the flow of the current discussion, these matters are treated separately in Chapter 6, along with leasehold interest insurance, another topic relevant to commercial building tenants.

Leased Personal Property Leased personal property that the insured is required by contract to insure is covered as part of "your business personal property" unless otherwise covered under "personal property of others." Computer and telephone systems, various types of specialized equipment, and many other kinds of property are commonly leased. In many cases, these leases are really financing agreements and, in accordance with generally accepted accounting principles (GAAP), are shown as assets in the insured's financial statements, with a corresponding liability for the unpaid balance.[1] Coverage is provided under "your business personal property" when the insured is obligated to insure the leased property even though the property is legally owned by others. Two requirements must be satisfied for coverage to apply:

1. The property must be leased
2. The lease must require the insured to insure the leased property

The leased personal property category does not include leased property that the insured is not required to insure. The category also does not include property of others held, but not leased, by the insured, even if the insured has agreed to insure the property.

Personal Property of Others

As discussed above, the BPP provides coverage, through "your business personal property," for some types of property of others. Moreover, a coverage extension automatically provides up to $2,500 for property of others in the insured's care, custody, or control. If the insured wants a higher limit of BPP insurance on personal property of others, it can be provided through the **personal property of others** agreement. Payment for "personal property of others" is made to the owner of the property, not to the insured. The coverage pays irrespective of whether the insured is legally liable for the loss.

Personal property of others coverage is ordinarily bought by organizations with commercial bailment exposures. A **commercial bailment** exists when one party (the **bailee**) holds the property of another (the **bailor**) for some purpose beneficial to both of them. Cleaners and shoe repairers are obvious examples of commercial bailees. In addition, many manufacturing and processing firms work, at least some of the time, on property that belongs to their customers.

Other firms, such as furriers and warehouses, store property of others either as an accommodation or for a fee. Some bailees assume that the bailor insures its own property and that this insurance will also protect the bailee if held legally liable for damage to the property. A subrogation claim by the property owner's insurance company proves the error of this assumption and often evokes bitter complaints from an unprepared bailee. Depending on the circumstances, liability may be imposed on the bailee even if no charge was made for holding the bailed property.

The BPP is not the only source of coverage for property of others. Some insureds may want to cover only their legal liability for property of others. In that event, the legal liability coverage form, discussed in Chapter 6, provides a less expensive alternative. Other businesses may find broader coverage under various inland marine forms tailored to particular kinds of bailees. These forms of insurance, as well as the bailment exposure itself, will be discussed in more detail in Chapter 11.

Property Not Covered

The BPP contains an extensive list of property not covered. Property not covered can be loosely grouped in three categories:

1. Buildings and other real property
2. Plants and outdoor property
3. Other personal property

This division of property not covered is for convenience of discussion. All "property not covered" items apply to all three categories of covered property.

Buildings and Other Real Property

Although the BPP does not separate property not covered into a "building" category, many excluded items are primarily building items or certain types of real property. These exclusions reaffirm that coverage applies only to buildings as defined and extended in the form. The items not covered are:

- Land
- Water
- Bridges
- Roadways, walks, patios, or other paved surfaces
- Retaining walls that are not a part of the described building
- Piers, wharves, or docks
- Cost of excavations, grading, back fillings, or filling

- Pilings
- Foundations below the lowest basement floor or, if there is no basement, the surface of the ground
- Underground pipes, flues, or drains

Land and water would not appear to be covered in the first place as they do not seem to be included in the definition of building. However, some court decisions in pollution claims have granted coverage for the cost of restoring polluted land and water under building policies. To prevent similar decisions, insurers now specifically exclude land and water.

According to the *Commercial Lines Manual*, any of the items listed as property not covered, other than land and water, can be insured. They are excluded either to reduce the amount of insurance needed to satisfy the coinsurance clause (such as the exclusion of foundations or pilings and underground pipes and flues) or because the exposures require careful underwriting (such as bridges, piers, wharves, or docks).

Automatically including coverage for the excluded items would increase the amount of insurance needed by as much as 10 percent.[2] However, the policy can be amended to provide coverage for these items and the insured should weigh the need for coverage carefully. Even though the probability of loss to items such as excavations, foundations below ground, and underground pipes is very low, some risk managers, consultants, and producers feel that this coverage should almost always be added back. A loss from such perils as explosion, water damage, and earthquake is possible, and can be serious.

Even without an endorsement, foundations are covered, *except* for those that are below the basement or, if there is no basement, below the surface of the ground. Likewise, pipes, flues, and drains are covered property, except when they are underground.

Plants and Outdoor Property

A second category of excluded property can be loosely classified as plants and other outdoor property. Specifically, this category includes the following:

- Growing crops and lawns
- Outdoor grain, hay, straw, or other harvested crops
- Outdoor trees, shrubs, and plants
- Outdoor fences, radio, and television antennas or towers
- Outdoor signs, except signs attached to buildings

Some of these items would generally not be considered part of a building but are excluded to reaffirm that real property is not covered unless included in the definition of building. Other items are so susceptible to some causes of loss that coverage would cost more than most insureds are willing to pay. For example, outdoor trees are frequently damaged by wind, as are fences and radio and television antennas. Limited coverage is provided for some of these items under coverage extensions discussed below. All of these items are insurable either by endorsement to a BPP or in other coverage parts or policies.

Other Personal Property

All of the types of personal property in this category are insurable, except contraband. Insuring contraband is against public policy. For the remainder of excluded items, other forms of insurance are usually more appropriate.

"DEMCABS"

Money and securities and similar property are excluded in essentially the same list of excluded property that appeared in the 1943 standard fire policy. The mnemonic device traditionally used by insurance students to remember the list—**DEMCABS**—still applies:

- **D**eeds
- **E**vidences of debt
- **M**oney
- **C**urrency
- **A**ccounts
- **B**ills
- **S**ecurities and notes

To update the exclusion for the half century that has passed since the last standard fire policy revision, the BPP excludes food stamps and specifically states that lottery tickets are not securities. (However, coverage on lottery tickets is limited to $250 in the causes-of-loss forms discussed in Chapter 5.) Insurers generally prefer to cover money, securities, accounts, and so forth, under commercial crime or inland marine forms combining lower limits of insurance and specialized underwriting.

Vehicles, Watercraft, Aircraft

Most loss exposures arising out of the ownership, maintenance, or use of automobiles, watercraft, and aircraft are ordinarily insured under specialized forms. Accordingly, the BPP excludes vehicles or self-propelled machines, including aircraft or watercraft, if they are either licensed for use on public roads or principally operated away from the premises. The exclusion does *not* apply to rowboats or canoes out of the water. The BPP also covers vehicles the insured manufactures, processes, or warehouses and vehicles, other than autos, that the insured holds for sale.

Thus, the BPP covers such items as lawn mowers held for sale by a garden shop, a forklift used in a factory, an unlicensed truck that is used to move goods around the yard, and a motorized cart provided for handicapped visitors at a museum. Despite these exceptions, the BPP still excludes most autos, watercraft, and aircraft that the insured uses, as well as self-propelled machines used primarily away from the insured premises (such as a contractor's bulldozer).

Coverage may be added for some vehicles otherwise excluded by endorsing coverage to the policy. Although most insureds cover their cars and trucks under auto insurance, insureds with a large number of owned autos often retain the on-road physical damage exposure. When its autos are on the road, the organization can absorb the relatively small maximum probable loss of one or two vehicles in an incident. However, at night, the concentration of vehicles at the parking or garaging location may raise the maximum probable loss beyond the level the firm wishes to retain, so it may choose to insure this "overnight" exposure under its BPP.

Animals

The BPP specifically excludes animals owned by the insured. However, the exclusion does not apply to animals held for sale or boarded. A pet store's animals, for example, would be covered. For other animal owners, the farm coverage part or other specialized policies may be needed.

Valuable Papers and Records

The BPP does not cover the cost to research, replace, or restore the information contained in or on valuable papers and records, including electronic or magnetic media. One of the coverage extensions discussed below provides limited coverage. More complete coverage is available through inland marine coverages.

Property Otherwise Covered

Property more specifically described under the same policy or another policy is covered under the BPP only for any excess over the amount due from the other insurance. The deduction for other insurance applies whether or not the other insurance is collectible.

The meaning of "property more specifically described" is illustrated by the following examples: "stock" is more specific than "your personal property"; "electronic data processing equipment" is more specific than "machinery and equipment"; and "Bulldozer ID# 266402" is more specific than "motorized land vehicle."

Property is often "more specifically described" in another form or endorsement in the same policy that contains the BPP. For example, computers could be covered under the BPP as "your business personal property" and in an inland marine form covering only "electronic data processing equipment." A similar situation could arise if the computer were insured under a separate inland marine policy. In the case of computers, the inland marine coverage is more specific and would pay first; any remaining loss would be covered by the BPP, as long as the cause of loss was covered.

Contraband

As noted above, contraband or property in the course of illegal transportation or trade is excluded, since insuring such property is against public policy. Personal property while airborne or waterborne is also excluded. Various forms of transit insurance, discussed in Chapter 11, can be used to insure property while being transported by airplane or vessel.

Covered Locations

With only limited exceptions, the BPP restricts coverage to property located at described locations. Materials, equipment, supplies, and temporary structures used for making additions, alterations, or repairs to an insured building or structure are covered while within 100 feet of the described premises. Similarly, the insured's business personal property and personal property of others are covered in the open (or in a vehicle) within 100 feet of the described premises.

"Within 100 feet of the described premises" is ordinarily interpreted to mean within 100 feet of the nearest boundary of the land considered to be part of the insured premises, not within 100 feet of the building. If, for example, the declarations describe the insured premises as 1234 Main Street, the premises include both the building and the lot at that address. Thus, if business personal property belonging to the insured is located twenty feet from the insured's land but 200 feet away from the insured's building, the property is within 100 feet of the insured's premises and therefore covered.

Some additional coverage for property away from the described premises is provided by two coverage extensions. The "property off-premises" extension provides $5,000 of coverage at other locations within the policy territory, which consists of the United States of America (including its territories and possessions), Puerto Rico, and Canada. The "newly acquired or constructed property" extension covers property at locations the insured acquires after the beginning of the policy period. These extensions are described in more detail below.

Additional Coverages and Coverage Extensions

The BPP provides several supplemental coverages in addition to the basic building and personal property coverages described above. These supplemental coverages are set forth under two subheadings: (1) additional coverages and (2) coverage extensions. The distinction between additional coverages and coverage extensions is not readily apparent. To some degree, the additional coverages serve to define or place practical limitations on some incidental losses that might otherwise be deemed to be covered without special limitation under the BPP. In contrast, the coverage extensions provide additional amounts of insurance to cover loss exposures that are clearly not otherwise covered by the BPP.

Additional Coverages

The BPP provides four additional coverages, which are listed in Exhibit 3-3 and discussed below.

Exhibit 3-3
BPP Additional Coverages

	Coverage Limit	Payable in Addition to Policy Limit?
Debris Removal	25 percent of payment for physical loss up to $5,000 in addition to policy limit	No, except for additional $5,000
Pollution Cleanup and Removal	$10,000 per policy year	Yes
Preservation of Property	No sublimit	No
Fire Department Service Charge	$1,000	Yes

Debris Removal

It is sometimes argued that debris removal would be covered by property insurance even if it were not specifically mentioned. To avoid dispute, property forms generally spell out coverage for debris removal and place some restrictions on the coverage. The **debris removal additional coverage** specifically covers the cost of removing debris following a covered loss.

Only debris of *covered property* is covered. For example, the cost of removing downed trees or retaining walls not attached to the building is not covered debris removal expense since they are not covered property. Similarly, the cost to remove debris of damaged property belonging to a tenant that the tenant failed to remove would not be covered by the building owner's policy. (The building owner's policy would pay the expense necessary to move debris out of the way in order to commence repairs, but it would not cover other costs for the removal of the tenant's debris, such as transporting the debris to an approved dump site.)

Debris removal coverage is limited to 25 percent of the value of the physical loss before application of the deductible. The total of covered debris removal expenses and the physical loss is subject to the applicable policy limit. However, many insureds are not inclined to carry enough insurance to cover both a major loss and the additional cost of removing the debris of covered property. Accordingly, the BPP also provides up to $5,000 in addition to the policy limit when debris removal expenses exceed the amount of coverage otherwise available. (The $5,000 additional coverage is provided in the "limits of insurance" section of the BPP, not in the debris removal additional coverage.)

For example, following a $20,000 physical loss covered under a policy with a $100,000 limit and a $500 deductible, the insurer would pay no more than $10,000 (25 percent of $20,000 plus $5,000) to cover the cost of debris removal. If the direct loss equaled or exceeded the policy limit, only the $5,000 additional coverage for debris removal would be available to pay for debris removal. Subject to underwriting approval, the $5,000 additional debris removal coverage can be increased by endorsement, for an additional premium.

Although the debris removal coverage excludes the costs of extracting pollutants from land or water, cleaning up pollutants elsewhere—such as inside an insured building—is covered if the release or dispersal is caused by an insured peril and the pollutants are debris of covered property. Insureds and risk managers should carefully consider the adequacy of the debris removal coverage. In one case, a relatively small fire damaged asbestos-covered heating pipes. The burning damage amounted to $10,000; the cost to clean up and dispose of the asbestos exceeded $25,000. Only $7,500 of the debris removal expense was covered by the policy (25 percent of $10,000 plus $5,000).

Debris removal expenses must be reported within 180 days of the date of the physical loss to be covered, and the physical loss must occur during the policy period.

Pollutant Cleanup and Removal

The **pollutant cleanup and removal additional coverage** is one response to the problems insurers have had with pollution claims. Although pollution is often regarded as a problem for liability insurers, property insurers have also encountered unexpected pollution claims, in part because of the strict or absolute pollution exclusions in general liability insurance policies.

Property insurers have taken an unusual approach. Instead of totally excluding pollution cleanup, coverage is explicitly provided, but it is limited to $10,000. Insurers believe that courts are much more likely to enforce a limit of liability than an exclusion. The BPP requires the insured to report pollution incidents to the insurer within 180 days in order to eliminate the problem of "long-tail" claims (claims made long after the accident occurred), which have plagued liability insurers.

The BPP will pay up to $10,000 of the expense to extract "pollutants" from water or land at the described premises, provided that the original release, discharge, or dispersal of the pollutants was caused by a covered cause of loss that occurred during the policy period. "Pollutant" is broadly defined, using the same wording as the pollution exclusion of the commercial general liability (CGL) coverage form.

The pollutant cleanup and removal additional coverage excludes costs incurred to test for, monitor, or assess the existence, concentration, or effects of pollutants. However, the insurer will pay for testing performed in the course of extracting the pollutants from the land or water.

The $10,000 is an annual aggregate limit for each described premises. The $10,000 limit can be increased for an additional premium. Many underwriters are reluctant to provide any additional pollutant cleanup and removal coverage, and amounts in excess of $100,000 are rarely available in BPP policies.

Preservation of Property

As is typical of property insurance policies, the BPP requires the insured, in the event of a loss, to "take all reasonable steps to protect the covered property from further damage." The **preservation of property additional coverage** provides some coverage for the insured who fulfills this obligation, since moving property to a temporary location may increase the exposure to some hazards. For example, the property may be subject to the perils of transportation (such as collision or upset) while it is being moved, and it may be more susceptible to theft or other perils during and after the move.

If covered property must be moved from the described premises to preserve it from loss or damage by a covered peril, the insurer agrees to pay for any direct loss or damage to that property while it is being moved or temporarily stored. This broad protection—in effect, coverage against any accidental loss—lasts for ten days after the time the property is first moved. Before that ten-day period expires, the insured should arrange for specific coverage on the property. Otherwise, only the usual off-premises coverage—which is very limited—will apply.

The preservation of property additional coverage contains no dollar sublimit. Coverage is subject to regular policy limits.

Fire Department Service Charge

Under the **fire department service charge additional coverage**, the insurer will pay up to $1,000 if a fire department imposes a service charge that is either required by local ordinance or agreed to before the loss. However, the fire department must have been called to save or protect covered property from damage by a covered cause of loss. This additional amount of coverage is not subject to any deductible.

Coverage Extensions

The BPP provides five coverage extensions, which are listed in Exhibit 3-4 and discussed below. Coverage extensions apply only if a coinsurance percentage of at least 80 percent *or* a value reporting symbol appears on the declarations page. A coinsurance percentage is ordinarily shown even if the coinsurance clause has been suspended by the agreed value optional coverage. This is because the agreed value option is subject to an expiration date after which coinsurance is reinstated. (The agreed value optional coverage is discussed in Chapter 4; coinsurance is discussed later in this chapter.)

The coverage extensions are additional insurance—that is, they are paid in addition to the limit of insurance. Except where indicated otherwise, coverage applies to property on or in the described building and to property in the open (or in a vehicle) within 100 feet of the described premises.

Newly Acquired or Constructed Property

The **newly acquired or constructed property extension** contains two parts, one applying to buildings and the other to "your business personal property." Each part provides limited coverage for not more than thirty days. The amounts of temporary coverage can be increased by endorsement.

Exhibit 3-4
BPP Coverage Extensions

	Coverage Limit	Payable in Addition to Policy Limit?
Newly Acquired or Constructed Property:		
• Buildings	25% of building limit up to $250,000	Yes
• Personal Property	10% of personal limit or $100,000, whichever is less	Yes
Personal Effects and Property of Others	$2,500	Yes
Valuable Papers and Records—Cost of Research	$1,000	Yes
Property Off Premises	$5,000	Yes
Outdoor Property	$1,000 per occurrence, $250 per tree, shrub, or plant	Yes

Coverage applies to a new building being built on the described premises or at any other location to be used either for purposes similar to those of the building described in the declarations or as a warehouse. The most that the insured can collect under this extension is 25 percent of the indicated building limit, up to a maximum of $250,000 per building.

Personal property is covered at any newly acquired location except fairs or exhibitions. For personal property the extension is limited to 10 percent of the amount of insurance or $100,000, whichever is less.

Although the extension states that coverage is available at any location, the new location must be within the coverage territory described in the commercial property conditions. For example, a firm that acquires a new building or stores personal property at a location in Canada would have temporary coverage but, if the location were in Mexico, coverage would not apply.

The purpose of the coverage extension is to handle the named insured's coverage needs temporarily until the insured has time to arrange formal coverage. The automatic coverage is available as soon as the new building is acquired or construction begins. Coverage ends at the earliest of the following times:

1. When the policy expires
2. When the insured reports the values of the new property
3. When thirty days of automatic coverage have elapsed

A premium for the new exposure is payable from the date the exposure begins.

Personal Effects and Property of Others

The **personal effects and property of others extension** provides up to $2,500 for (1) personal effects of the insured, its officers, partners, or employees and (2) personal property of others in the insured's care, custody, or control. The personal effects coverage does not include theft, even if theft is a covered cause of loss under the policy.

Valuable Papers and Records

The **valuable papers and records—cost of research extension** provides $1,000 coverage for the cost to research, replace, or restore the information on lost or damaged valuable papers and records, including electronic or magnetic media. (These costs are otherwise excluded under "property not covered.")

Most insureds can probably retain loss that does not exceed the $1,000 limit. However, since most losses are not fully covered by insurance, the amount actually retained may be larger than intended. The valuable papers and records extension at least reduces that amount by $1,000. In addition, it serves as a reminder that the valuable papers and records exposure can be serious, so that separate coverage for it (available under inland marine forms) may be appropriate.

Property Off-Premises

The **property off-premises extension** covers property temporarily away from the named insured's premises while elsewhere in the coverage territory, subject to a $5,000 limit. The extension excludes the following types of property:

- Stock
- Property at any fair or exhibition
- Property in the care, custody, or control of salespersons

- Property in or on a vehicle
- Property at any location owned, leased, or operated by the insured

The exclusions of airborne or waterborne property and property in or on a vehicle eliminate coverage for property in transit. When the special causes-of-loss form is used with a BPP, an additional coverage extension applies to property in transit, as detailed in Chapter 5. Higher limits and broader coverage for excluded property can be provided by inland marine forms described in Chapter 11.

The extension is not limited to personal property. For example, under a policy providing building coverage, an elevator motor that was removed to a service company's shop for repairs would be covered if damaged by a covered peril while on the service company's premises.

Outdoor Property

The **outdoor property extension** provides a small amount of insurance on certain types of outdoor property that are otherwise excluded: outdoor fences; radio and television antennas; signs not attached to the building; and trees, shrubs, and plants (other than stock of trees, shrubs, or plants held in storage or for sale). The amount of insurance is $1,000, but not more than $250 for any one tree, shrub, or plant, including debris removal. Only the following perils are covered:

- Fire
- Lightning
- Explosion
- Riot or civil commotion
- Aircraft

The perils most likely to destroy outdoor property, such as motor vehicle damage, windstorm, and the weight of ice, are not covered. By use of the outdoor trees, shrubs, and plants endorsement, outdoor property can be insured for higher limits and against all covered causes of loss in the applicable causes-of-loss form. This endorsement is generally not made available to cover trees, shrubs, or plants grown for commercial purposes.

Amounts of Recovery

The BPP contains several provisions that determine how much the insurer will pay for a covered loss. These provisions address limits of insurance, the deductible, and coinsurance. (The optional coverages printed in the BPP also deal with amounts of recovery; they are discussed in Chapter 4.)

Limits of Insurance and Deductible

The limits of insurance expressed in the BPP apply separately to each occurrence. Except for the additional coverage for pollution cleanup and removal, none of the BPP coverages is subject to an aggregate limit capping the amount recoverable under that coverage each policy year.

The insurer is not obligated to pay anything to the insured unless the loss exceeds the applicable deductible; the limit of insurance then applies to the loss in excess of the deductible. In colloquial terms, the deductible comes off the loss, not off the limit of insurance. For example, payment under a policy with a $100,000 limit and a $1,000 deductible in each of the following losses would be as follows:

- $500 loss: no payment (Loss is less than the deductible.)
- $100,000 loss: $99,000 payment ($100,000–$1,000 deductible)
- $110,000 loss: $100,000 payment ($110,000–$1,000 deductible exceeds the limit of insurance.)

The **multiple deductible form endorsement** makes it possible to apply different deductibles to different buildings covered under one policy. Thus a $250 deductible might apply to a brick office building, but a $5,000 deductible might apply to a frame warehouse covered under the same policy. In addition, the **windstorm or hail percentage deductible clauses endorsement** provides the option of applying to windstorm or hail losses a deductible equal to 1 percent, 2 percent, or 5 percent of the applicable amount of insurance. If coverage is on a *blanket* basis (discussed in Chapter 4), the deductible is 1, 2, or 5 percent of the value of the property that has sustained damage. This endorsement is useful for insurers when covering property with catastrophic windstorm exposure.

A special limit of $1,000 *per sign* applies to outdoor signs *attached to the building.* Because of the outdoor property coverage extension discussed above, outdoor signs *not* attached to buildings are covered for $1,000 *per occurrence* (not per sign). However, signs attached to the building are insured against all perils covered by the policy whereas signs not attached to the building are insured against only five listed perils. In either case, the insured may need higher limits or broader perils, which can be provided under the BPP by endorsement or in an inland marine policy discussed in Chapter 11.

The amounts of insurance provided by the coverage extensions and by the additional coverages for pollution cleanup and removal and fire department charges are payable in addition to the limits of insurance. Payments under preservation of property and debris removal are not in addition to the limits except for the additional $5,000 for debris removal previously discussed.

Coinsurance

Underinsurance is a serious problem for insurance companies as well as insureds. Without some mechanism to enforce insurance to value, many insureds would purchase much lower amounts of insurance believing that the chance of a large loss is so remote that buying higher limits is unnecessary. Since most losses are partial, the insureds would collect most of their losses in full but the insurance company would not collect enough premium to pay losses and expenses. Of course, insurers could charge one rate for those who insure to 50 percent of value, another (lower) rate for those who insure to 60 percent of value, and yet another (even lower) rate for those who insure to 70 percent of value, and so forth. However, that type of rating system would be complicated and burdensome. To address this problem, the BPP, like many other property insurance forms, contains a **coinsurance clause**, which enables the insurer to charge the same rate for all insureds in the same rating class that are subject to this clause.

The effect of a coinsurance clause is that the insured agrees, in exchange for a reduced premium rate, to carry insurance at least equal to a specified percentage of the actual cash value of the covered property. The coinsurance percentages most commonly used are 80, 90, or 100 percent. If the specified amount of insurance is not carried, the loss is adjusted according to the formula:

$$\left(\frac{\text{Limit of Insurance}}{\text{Value of Covered Property} \times \text{Coinsurance Percentage}} \times \text{Total Amount of Covered Loss}\right)$$

$$- \text{Deductible} = \text{Insurer's Payment (Not to exceed limit)}$$

Insurance students often condense this formula to "Did over should times loss minus deductible," or, in formula:

$$\left(\frac{\text{Did}}{\text{Should}} \times \text{Loss}\right) - \text{Deductible}$$

"Did" is the amount of insurance carried. "Should" is the minimum amount that should have been carried to meet the coinsurance requirement. As the brackets in the formula indicate, the deductible is subtracted *after* the amount of loss is multiplied by "did over should." This is an important point, because subtracting the deductible from the loss *before* multiplying results in a slightly higher recovery. The BPP coinsurance clause clearly indicates that the deductible is subtracted after the multiplication. Another important point is that the property value used in applying the coinsurance formula is that at the time of the loss, not at the time the insurance commenced. Two examples of coinsurance applications are shown in Exhibit 3-5.

Exhibit 3-5
Coinsurance Examples

Example No. 1 (Underinsurance):

When:

The value of the property is	$250,000
The Coinsurance percentage for it is	80%
The Limit of Insurance for it is	$100,000
The Deductible is	$250
The amount of loss is	$40,000

Step (1): $250,000 x 80% = $200,000
(the minimum amount of insurance to meet Coinsurance requirements)

Step (2): $100,000 ÷ $200,000 = .50

Step (3): $40,000 x .50 = $20,000

Step (4): $20,000 – $250 = 19,750

The insurer will pay no more than $19,750.
The remaining $20,250 is not covered.

Example No. 2 (Adequate Insurance)

When:

The value of the property is	$250,000
The Coinsurance percentage for it is	80%
The Limit of Insurance for it is	$200,000
The Deductible is	$250
The amount of loss is	$40,000

Step (1): $250,000 x 80% = $200,000
(the minimum amount of insurance to meet Coinsurance requirements)

Step (2): $200,000 ÷ $200,000 = 1.00

Step (3): $40,000 x 1.00 = $40,000

Step (4): $40,000 – $250 = 39,750

The insurer will cover $39,750 in excess of the Deductible. No penalty applies.

The effect of the coinsurance clause is to penalize an insured who does not insure to at least the specified percentage of value, the penalty being proportional to the amount of underinsurance. Even when insurance meets the requirements of an 80 or 90 percent coinsurance clause, the amount paid following a loss will never exceed policy limits. It is misleading to say that a firm with enough insurance to satisfy the coinsurance clause is insured in full. Unless the amount of insurance is as great as the full value of the property plus costs of debris removal (when they exceed $5,000, as discussed earlier), the insurance is not sufficient to pay for a *total loss*, even without considering any business income loss.

When higher coinsurance percentages are used, the rate is reduced. With a 90 percent coinsurance clause on building or contents insurance, the 80 percent coinsurance rate is reduced by 5 percent; with a 100 percent coinsurance clause, the 80 percent coinsurance rate is reduced by 10 percent. Thus, the insured who "promises" to insure for 100 percent of insurable value pays a premium rate that is 10 percent lower than the organization that "promises" to insure for 80 percent. The organization with a higher coinsurance percentage must also purchase more insurance to avoid coinsurance penalties.

To illustrate, assume that Joe wishes to insure his business personal property, which has an actual cash value of $100,000. If Joe insures with an 80 percent coinsurance clause, he will have to carry at least $80,000 of insurance in order to avoid a coinsurance penalty. With a limit of $80,000 and a rate of $1.00 per $100 of insurance, the premium would be calculated as follows:

$$\$80{,}000 \times \frac{\$1.00}{\$100} = \$800$$

If, instead, Joe insured for $100,000 with a 100 percent coinsurance clause, the rate would be reduced 10 percent to $.90 and the premium would be calculated as follows:

$$\$100{,}000 \times \frac{\$.90}{\$100} = \$900$$

Although Joe would pay an extra $100 in premium with 100 percent coinsurance, he would have an additional $20,000 in coverage. (An additional $20,000 in coverage at the 80 percent coinsurance rate would cost $200.)

Failure to comply with a coinsurance requirement is usually the result of a mistake in valuation, a failure to keep up with inflation, or a misunderstanding of insurance requirements.

Valuation

In order for an insurer to determine the amount of a loss, the policy must specify some valuation basis. If the policy were silent on the valuation basis, the insured would be entitled to any reasonable valuation basis. This would undoubtedly result in numerous disputes over what is "reasonable." The BPP applies several different valuation approaches to different types of covered property. These basic valuation approaches, which apply automatically unless modified by optional provisions or endorsements, are described below. Optional alternatives to the basic valuation approaches are described in Chapter 4.

Actual Cash Value

The value of most property covered by the BPP is determined at actual cash value. **Actual cash value (ACV)** is generally defined as "replacement cost minus depreciation." Replacement cost is determined at the time and location of the loss. Thus, depreciation is subtracted from the current replacement cost, not the original cost. In some cases, such as losses involving obsolete or outdated property, calculating ACV can be problematic. (CPCU 1 discusses ACV in more detail.[3])

A simple example of an ACV loss settlement is an asphalt-shingle roof surface (not including the wood sheathing underneath) that is torn off by high winds. If the roof is ten years old at the time of loss, had an expected useful life of thirty years from the time it was installed, and would cost $9,000 to replace today, the ACV of the roof could be calculated as follows:

$$\$9{,}000 - (10/30 \times \$9{,}000) = \$6{,}000$$

Small Building Losses

If the limit of building insurance satisfies the coinsurance clause and the cost to repair or replace damaged building property is less than $2,500, the insurer will pay the full cost of repair or replacement *without any deduction for depreciation*. Since the term "building" means more than just the structure, this would also apply to the various types of personal property used to service the building or premises that are included in the building coverage. However, this provision does not apply to:

- Awnings or floor coverings
- Appliances for refrigerating, ventilating, cooking, dish washing, or laundering
- Outdoor equipment or furniture

Replacement cost coverage on both buildings and personal property, without the $2,500 limit, is available through optional replacement cost coverage, discussed in Chapter 4.

Stock Sold but Not Delivered

Stock that has been sold but not delivered is valued at selling price less any discounts or unincurred expenses. To illustrate, assume that a hardware store has sold a lawn tractor but is holding the tractor until it can deliver it to the customer's home on the next day. If the lawnmower is destroyed by a covered peril, the insurer will pay the selling price of $2,000 (less delivery expense, if any), not the $1,200 that the hardware store paid for the tractor.

Safety Glass

Many communities require the use of safety glazing materials, rather than ordinary plate glass, when replacing glass in doors, shower stalls, and similar places where people are exposed to injury by broken glass. If glass breakage is covered, payment is not limited to the ACV of the glass; the insurer will pay the increased cost for the required safety glazing.

Tenants' Improvements and Betterments

Tenants' improvements and betterments are covered for their actual cash value if the insured tenant makes repairs. If the tenant does not repair the property, he or she can recover only a proportion of the *original cost* that approximates the remaining use value of the property to the insured tenant. (This method is described in Chapter 6, along with the overall subject of insuring improvements and betterments.) If someone other than the insured tenant (such as the landlord or the landlord's insurer) pays for repair of improvements and betterments, the tenant's insurer will pay nothing.

Valuable Papers and Records

Valuable papers and records, including records on electronic or magnetic media, are valued at the cost of blank materials for reproducing the records and the cost of labor to copy the records when duplicate records exist. The "valuable papers and records—cost of research" extension described above provides up to an additional $1,000 to cover costs of recreating records when duplicates do not exist.

Other Loss Provisions

In addition to provisions that determine the *amount* of covered loss, the BPP contains several additional loss provisions that address various matters, such as the insured's duties after loss, what happens in the event of a disagreement between the insured and the insurer, and so on. These provisions (which are treated in more detail in CPCU 1) are briefly described below.

Insured's Duties in the Event of Loss

Like all other insurance policies, the BPP imposes a number of duties on the insured. These are usually held to be conditions precedent; that is, the insured must comply with these requirements before the insurance company is obligated to make any payment. Included in the insured's duties is the general requirement to cooperate with the insurer in the investigation and settlement of the claim.

Notice of Loss

The BPP requires that the insurer be given prompt notice of loss, including a description of the property involved. This language does not require written notice, only that notice in some form must be given. The period of time for giving notice is not specified, only that it must be "prompt." What constitutes "prompt" notice depends on what is reasonable under the particular circumstances. As soon as is reasonably possible, the insurer must also be given details of how, when, and where the loss occurred. This information is necessary to make an accurate determination as to whether the loss involved a covered location and a covered peril occurring during the policy period.

Police Report

If a law has been broken, the police must be notified. Thus, in situations where robbery is a covered cause of loss, notice must be given to the police if the insured expects to collect from the insurer. This provision helps to reduce fraud, since people are often more reluctant to involve the police than an insurance representative. The provision also helps to assure that questionable circumstances are promptly recorded and, where applicable, investigated. Moreover, recovery of the stolen property is sometimes possible if the criminal is apprehended.

Preservation of Property

The insured must take all reasonable steps to protect the property from further loss. For example, if the roof has been damaged by a windstorm or fire, the insured should have a temporary roof installed if doing so is reasonable under the circumstances. If installing a temporary roof is not possible, then the insured should do whatever else he or she reasonably can to prevent further loss, such as removing contents to a safe location, covering contents with plastic sheeting, or taking other reasonable measures. The insured cannot wait for the insurer's representative to arrive before taking the needed action. If the insured does not take reasonable steps to protect the property, additional damage that occurs, such as rain damage to the contents, will not be covered by the insurance policy. If feasible, the insured must separate the damaged property and keep it in the best possible order for the insurer's examination.

The costs of emergency and temporary repairs are included in the settlement of the claim, subject to the limit of insurance.

Inventory and Inspection

The insurer may require a complete inventory of damaged and undamaged goods—including quantities, costs, values, and amount of loss claimed. The insured must allow the insurer to inspect the property and to examine the records proving the loss. The inventory and record inspection requirements are useful to the insurer in determining the amount of property on hand at the time of the loss—information necessary for purposes of applying the coinsurance clause. The inspection allows the insurer to make an accurate determination of the loss and helps to reduce the number of fraudulent claims. The insurer may also take samples of damaged and undamaged property for inspection, testing, and analysis. This can be helpful in establishing the presence of accelerants, such as gasoline or kerosene, which may indicate that the loss was caused by arson. The BPP does not obligate the insurer to pay for any costs incurred by the insured in meeting the inventory and inspection requirement.

Proof of Loss

Before paying the loss, the insurer may require insureds to sign a sworn proof of loss containing information requested by the insurer. The insured is given sixty days to return the signed statement to the insurer, after the insurer provides the necessary forms. If the insurer does not request the proof of loss or does not provide the form, the insured is not obligated to file it. However once the insurer has provided the proof of loss form and requested that it be filed, failure to file the proof within sixty days may invalidate the insured's claim unless the insurer has granted an extension of time.

Examination Under Oath

The policy requires any insured to submit to questioning under oath concerning the claim. The insured's answers are to be signed by the insured and, when there is more than one insured, each insured may be examined while not in the presence of any other insured. These provisions are designed to aid in settling the claim, detecting intentional losses or fraudulent claims, and developing information for possible defense of a claim filed by an insured who does not tell the truth.

Examination under oath is an effective tool to combat insurance fraud. Although it resembles a deposition taken in connection with a lawsuit, an insurer is allowed more latitude in the areas that can be questioned in an examination under oath. Furthermore, failure to submit to an examination under oath is a defense to any policy claim since it is a condition precedent. One court has ruled that an insured's Fifth Amendment rights against self-incrimination are not violated by requiring an insured suspected of arson to undergo an examination under oath.[4]

Appraisal

If the insurer and the insured disagree about the value of the claim, either party can demand an appraisal of the loss. The **appraisal process** provides a means of resolving disputes that is less time-consuming and expensive than going to court. The appraisal clause states that each party will select a competent and impartial appraiser, and the two appraisers will select an umpire. If they cannot agree on an umpire, either one may ask a court with jurisdiction in the matter to appoint one. The appraisers then state separately the value of the property and the amount of loss. If the appraisers do not agree, they submit their differences to the umpire. The provision states that a decision agreed to by any two of the three individuals involved in the appraisal process is binding on the insurer and the insured (although state laws may provide otherwise).

The appraisal process may be used to resolve disputes over either the value of the property or the amount of the loss. In one case, the court ruled that the insured was entitled to appraisal even when the insurer claimed there was no damage at all to the covered property.[5] However, the appraisal clause does not apply to disputes as to whether or not the policy provides coverage for a given loss. For example, the appraisal process cannot be used to determine whether loss was caused by a covered cause of loss.

Insurer's Options for Loss Payment

Most losses are settled by payment from the insurer to the insured. At its own option, the insurer can pay either (1) the value of the lost or damaged property or (2) the cost of repairing or replacing it. The insurer has two other options, which are infrequently used:

- The insurer may take all or any part of the property by paying an agreed or appraised value.
- The insurer may repair, rebuild, or replace the property with other property of like kind and quality.

The insurer might use one of these options if it strongly suspects, but cannot prove, that the insured has committed arson or otherwise intentionally damaged the property.

The insurer has thirty days after receipt of the sworn proof of loss to notify the insured of its intentions. The payment by the insurer is limited to the insured's financial interest in the property.

If the covered property is owned by someone other than the insured, the insurer may adjust the losses with, and pay the losses to, the owner of the property. Payment for this property is also limited to the owner's financial interest.

The insurer must pay for a covered loss within thirty days after receiving the sworn proof of loss if (1) the insured has complied with all the terms of coverage and (2) the insured and insurer have reached agreement on the amount of loss (or an appraisal award has been made).

Recovered Property

If either the insured or the insurer recovers any property after the loss settlement, it must promptly notify the other party. The insured has the right to demand return of the recovered property, in which event the insured must refund to the insurer the amount the insurer paid for the loss. The insurer will pay for repairs and recovery expenses, subject to the limit of insurance.

Vacancy

If the building where loss occurs has been vacant for sixty consecutive days, the insurer is not obligated to pay for loss caused by vandalism, sprinkler leakage, building glass breakage, water damage, theft, or attempted theft. For all other covered perils, loss recovery is reduced by 15 percent after sixty days of vacancy. Some independently developed property policies do not provide *any* protection after sixty days of vacancy.

In the absence of a specific definition, **vacancy** has been interpreted to mean that the building does not contain any contents pertaining to the operations or activities customary to the occupancy of the building. This interpretation has led to disputes over coverage when a building contained some contents pertaining to its customary occupancy but not enough property to conduct operations. ISO has attempted to avoid these disputes by defining vacancy in the BPP. According to the BPP definition, "[a] building is vacant when it does not contain enough business personal property to conduct customary operations. Buildings under construction are not considered vacant."

Full coverage for a vacant building may be "bought back" for an additional premium by adding a **vacancy permit endorsement**. Of course, underwriters will examine the circumstances behind the vacancy and the protection of the property before granting a vacancy permit.

Lenders' Rights Under the BPP

Lenders often require their borrowers to pledge property as collateral for their loans. The lender is then said to have a security interest in the property: if the borrower defaults in repaying the loan, the lender can take possession of the pledged property to offset its credit loss. Under a mortgage loan, the borrower (mortgagor) pledges *real property* as security to the lender (mortgagee, or mortgage holder). Under other secured loans, the borrower pledges *personal property*—inventory, automobiles, mobile equipment, and so on—as collateral.

A lender with a security interest in property generally relies on the borrower's insurance for protection in the event of damage to the pledged property. Mortgage holders and insurers have long had a symbiotic relationship: insurers sell more insurance because the mortgagees insist that the borrower carry insurance; mortgage holders benefit from the special rights afforded them under the various standard mortgagee clauses, including the "mortgage holders" provision in the BPP. The **loss payable provisions endorsement** is available to extend similar, but not necessarily the same, rights to other lenders who have a security interest in covered property. Lenders with a security interest in covered personal property (as well as owners of property leased to the insured) are often insured as "loss payees" in the borrower's (or lessee's) property insurance.

Mortgage Holders' Protection

The **mortgage holders provision** of the BPP applies to covered loss to buildings or structures only. Courts have held that the mortgagee's rights under mortgagee provisions of this type are tantamount to a separate policy protecting the mortgagee.

The insurer agrees to pay mortgage holders to the extent of their financial interests in the property, and to pay them "in their order of preference." Thus, if a property has a first mortgage and a second mortgage with different mortgage holders, the insurer will pay the holder of the first mortgage first and the holder of the second mortgage second.

Although the usual practice of insurers is to issue the loss draft payable to the insured and all mortgagees, the first mortgagee can demand payment to it alone up to the amount of its interest; the second mortgagee would come next; and so forth. If the mortgagees demand payment, no payment can be made to the insured until the mortgagees' claims have been satisfied.[6]

In addition, the mortgage holders provision states that the insurer will pay covered claims to the mortgage holder even though the insurer has denied the insured's claim because of the insured's acts (such as arson) or because the insured has failed to comply with policy conditions (such as failing to file a proof of loss when requested). However, to obtain coverage in those situations, the mortgage holder (1) must pay any premiums due to the insurer, (2) must submit a proof of loss within sixty days of the insurer's request, and (3) must have notified the insurer of any change in ownership, occupancy, or substantial change in risk known to the mortgage holder.

The mortgage holders provision also gives the mortgage holder some special rights with regard to policy cancellation or nonrenewal. If the insurer cancels the policy for nonpayment of premium, it must give written notice of cancellation to the mortgage holder at least ten days before the effective date of cancellation. If the insurer cancels the policy for any other reason, it must give the mortgage holder thirty days' notice. If the insurer elects not to renew the policy, it must give the mortgage holder ten days' notice.

Loss Payees

Loss payees other than mortgage holders can be named on the declarations page or in an endorsement. Such loss payees include not only lenders with a security interest but also the owners of equipment leased to the insured and purchasers or sellers under a contract of sale. Unless these loss payees qualify as mortgage holders, they do not automatically receive the added protection granted mortgagees under the mortgage holders provision discussed above.

The rights that loss payees receive are described in the **loss payable provisions endorsement**. The endorsement includes space to describe the property in which the loss payee has an interest and contains three sets of provisions that can apply. The three sets of provisions are (1) loss payable, (2) lender's loss payable, and (3) contract of sale. An entry in the declarations or an "X" entered in the schedule indicates which set of provisions applies.

Loss Payable

The loss payable provision does not provide any right to the loss payee other than the right to have payment of any loss made jointly to the loss payee and the insured. Thus, the loss payee will not, for example, receive separate notice of cancellation or nonrenewal, nor will the loss payee be entitled to any payment if the insurer denies liability to the insured.

Lender's Loss Payable

Under the lender's loss payable provision, a loss payee whose interest in the insured property is established by written agreements such as warehouse receipts, contracts for deeds, bills of lading, and financing statements receives protection similar to that provided to mortgage holders, as discussed above. Lenders who have made a filing in accordance with the Uniform Commercial Code would be entitled to be named under this provision. It provides them with much more protection than would be available under either of the other provisions of the loss payable endorsement.

Contract of Sale

The purchaser or seller in a contract of sale can be covered under the contract of sale provision. As under the loss payable provision, payment of any loss will be made jointly to the loss payee and the named insured as their interests may appear.

Commercial Property Conditions

The **commercial property conditions** form is included in the "commercial property" coverage part, whether it includes the BPP or some other "commercial property" coverage form. Thus, the commercial property conditions apply not only to the BPP but also to the other "commercial property" coverage forms described in Chapters 6 and 8. The commercial property conditions are summarized below.

Concealment, Misrepresentation, or Fraud

The coverage part is void in case of fraud related to the insurance. In addition, intentional concealment or misrepresentation by any insured of a material fact with respect to the coverage part, covered property, or the insured's interest in the property voids the policy.

Control of Property

If the insured does not have control of the property (for example, when an entire building is rented to another firm), any act of neglect by others will not affect coverage. The insured is not held responsible for the actions of others who are not under his or her direction.

However, certain types of neglect and intentional acts of the named insured will affect coverage. When more than one location is insured, a violation of policy conditions with respect to one location will relieve the insurer of its duties to cover loss *at that location*. Coverage at other insured locations is unaffected.

Insurance Under Two or More Coverages

Some items of property might conceivably be covered by both building and personal property coverage. Similarly, theft of a building's contents might be covered by a crime coverage form, as well as a BPP in the same commercial package policy. In situations where more than one of the policy's coverages may apply to damaged property, the insurer will not pay more than the actual amount of the loss.

Legal Action Against Us

Before an insured can sue or otherwise bring legal action against the insurer under the terms of the insurance contract, he or she must comply with all the terms in the coverage part and must initiate any such action against the insurer within two years of the date of the loss.

Liberalization

Protection is automatically broadened if the insurer broadens (or "liberalizes") the coverage part (1) within forty-five days before or (2) at any time during the policy period. This condition applies only if the broadened coverage does not increase the premium of the policy.

Liberalization benefits both the insured and the insurer. The insured receives the broadened coverage, and the insurer does not have to issue a new policy or a set of endorsements to every current insured every time a liberalization is made.

No Benefit to Bailee

Sometimes property is damaged while it is in the custody of a bailee—such as a trucking company, airline, railroad, or repair service. In such circumstances, the commercial property form will pay the insured(s) for any covered loss, but will not treat the bailee as an insured. In fact the insurer may subrogate against the bailee. The bailee is supposed to be accountable for his or her own actions, and it is not the insurer's intention to protect the bailee.

The provision contains an important exception: the no benefit to bailee provision does not void coverage if the *named insured* is a bailee of property that sustains damage. In other words, the no benefit to bailee provision will not defeat whatever coverage the BPP might provide on property of others while in the named insured's care, custody, or control.

Other Insurance

The "other insurance" clause addresses two situations and offers two different solutions.

- When another policy is subject to the same terms, conditions, and provisions as the coverage part, the insurer agrees to pay its share on a pro rata basis (policy limit of the coverage part divided by the total of all applicable policy limits, times the loss).
- If the other insurance does not have the same terms, conditions, and provisions, the insurer agrees to pay on an excess basis (the other insurer exhausts its limits, and then the insurer that issued this policy pays). Courts have held that when insurers under two or more policies all try to be excess over the others, they all must share in the payment. Details of that sharing have differed from court to court.

Because other insurance can take many forms, this brief "other insurance" clause clearly does not take into account every conceivable situation. Most insurers abide by a set of principles designed to allocate liability among insurers whose policies differ and to preserve protection for insureds. These principles are expressed in a document known as the *Guiding Principles*, discussed in CPCU 1.

Policy Period and Coverage Territory

The policy period is determined by the date(s) or time period shown on the policy declarations page. It usually starts at 12:01 A.M. standard time of the address shown on the page. The coverage territory (as already noted, above) is the United States of America, Puerto Rico, and Canada. Property located in Mexico, South America, and other parts of the world is not insured under the "commercial property" coverage part.

Transfer of Rights of Recovery Against Others to Us

This condition describes the insurance company's right to recover from third parties who may be responsible for damage to the covered property. After an insurer has paid its insured for damage to covered property, the insurer has the right to seek recovery from any third party to the extent the insurer made payment to the insured. For example, if the insurer paid the insured $50,000, it may seek to recover up to $50,000 from the responsible third party (if any) through a process called **subrogation.** The insured is not permitted to take any action after the loss that will hinder the insurer's ability to recover from the third party—subject to the exceptions described below.

The named insured may waive his or her right of recovery in writing before the loss occurs. After the loss occurs, the insured can waive its recovery rights against the following:

- Someone else covered by the "commercial property" form (such as the named insured's landlord, who is named as an additional insured).

- A business firm owned or controlled by the named insured or one that owns or controls the named insured's firm. For example, if ABC owns XYZ, ABC's insurer cannot subrogate against XYZ, and XYZ's insurer cannot subrogate against ABC.
- A tenant of the named insured's. In some states, a landlord cannot subrogate against a tenant in any event.

The BPP is often subject to the **cancellation changes endorsement**. (In many states, this endorsement is superseded by a state change endorsement that brings the policy into compliance with the insurance law of the state where the property is situated.) The endorsement permits the insurer to cancel coverage with only five days' notice when the building has been vacant or unoccupied for sixty consecutive days or when certain other conditions exist. These conditions, which indicate an increased possibility of arson occurring, include the following:

1. The insured has not begun repairs to covered building damage within thirty days after receiving payment from the insurer.
2. The building has an outstanding order to be vacated or demolished or has been declared unsafe by governmental authority.
3. The building's fixtures have been stripped and are not being replaced.
4. The insured has not provided necessary heat, water, sewer service, or electricity for thirty consecutive days.
5. The insured has failed to pay property taxes for one year.

The endorsement does not apply to vacancy or unoccupancy resulting from seasonal unoccupancy or from construction or renovation. It also does not apply to buildings for which the insurer has issued a vacancy permit.

The most common commercial property policies are made up of standard forms provided by insurance advisory organizations, including Insurance Services Office, Inc. (ISO), the American Association of Insurance Services (AAIS), and the Surety Association of America (SAA).

The ISO commercial lines program can be used to produce either monoline policies or commercial package policies. A monoline policy includes only one "coverage part"; a commercial package policy (CPP) includes two or more. A coverage part consists of declarations, one or more coverage forms, endorsements (as needed), and, in some cases, a general conditions form.

The coverage parts that can be used to provide property insurance in a monoline policy or CPP include "commercial property," boiler and machinery, commercial crime, commercial inland marine, and farm. For smaller organizations, an alternative to the CPP approach of multiple coverage parts is the businessowners policy, which provides most property and liability coverages needed by eligible businesses.

The building and personal property coverage form (BPP) is widely used for providing building and contents insurance. The BPP includes separate coverage categories for (1) buildings, (2) business personal property of the insured, and (3) personal property of others in the insured's possession. Entries in the declarations indicate which categories are covered.

Although the BPP excludes several types of property, most can be covered by endorsement. With limited exceptions, the BPP covers property only while on or within 100 feet of the insured premises.

The BPP provides four additional coverages and five coverage extensions, which supplement the basic coverage for buildings and personal property. Most of the supplemental coverages are subject to a special limit of insurance. Some are payable within policy limits, others are additional insurance.

The amount recoverable for a covered loss under the BPP is determined by the limit of insurance, the deductible, the coinsurance clause, and the applicable valuation method. Various additional provisions in the BPP and the commercial property conditions form detail the procedures to be followed when settling losses covered under the BPP.

Chapter Notes

1. Treatment of leased property as a capital asset is discussed in the text for CPCU 8, James Don Edwards, Roger H. Hermanson, R.F. Salmonson, and Peter R. Kensicki, *Introduction to Accounting*, 2nd. ed. (Malvern, PA: American Institute for Property and Liability Underwriters, 1991), pp. 66-67.
2. Marshall and Swift Publication Company, *Marshall Valuation Service*, August 1980, Section 96, pp. 1-2.
3. Eric A. Wiening and Donald S. Malecki, *Insurance Contract Analysis* (Malvern, PA: American Institute for CPCU, 1992), pp. 261-266.
4. Allstate Insurance Co. v. Longwell, 1990 F&C 6140 (U.S.D.C., S.D.N.Y., 1990).
5. Louise Paris Limited v. Lloyds, 595 N.Y.S.2d 776.
6. In some states, laws require the mortgagee to pay the insurance proceeds to the insured up to the amount the insured spends to repair the covered damage.

Chapter 4

Building and Personal Property Coverage Options

The building and personal property coverage form (BPP) often must be modified in order to meet the particular needs of policyholders. Three commonly used "optional coverages" are printed in the BPP form itself; they can be activated simply by making appropriate entries on the declarations page. Other coverage options can be provided by adding endorsements to the policy. This chapter describes the more important coverage options that are available for modifying the BPP.

For ease of discussion, the BPP coverage options are presented here in logical groupings according to their purposes. The groupings consist of the following:

- Optional valuation methods
- Alternatives to coinsurance
- Blanket insurance
- Options for insuring fluctuating personal property values
- Other coverage options

Optional Valuation Methods

As discussed in Chapter 3, the BPP calls for ACV valuation of most types of covered property. Several optional methods of valuation other than actual cash value are available. These methods include replacement cost, manufacturers selling price, functional building valuation, and functional personal property valuation.

Replacement Cost Coverage

Replacement cost coverage is so popular that the provisions are printed in the BPP as an optional coverage. No endorsement is needed. Coverage is activated by marking the commercial property declarations accordingly. The basic effect of the **replacement cost optional coverage** is to pay the replacement cost of damaged property without any deduction for physical depreciation.

Historically, insurers were reluctant to provide replacement cost coverage. They feared that the potential for betterment of the insured's financial position following a loss might increase the moral hazard (the possibility that an insured will intentionally destroy property in order to profit from the insurance) or the morale hazard (the possibility that the insured will be careless about preventing insured losses).

However, in the latter half of the twentieth century, insurers came to recognize that the insured who has suffered a property loss is not truly whole after receiving a sum of money equal to the depreciated value of the damaged property; to make the insured whole, the property must be restored to working order. Therefore, a tenet of contemporary underwriting is that the potential cost to repair or replace damaged property is a loss exposure that can validly be treated with insurance even if this means providing the insured with "new" property for "old." Once underwriters adopted this philosophy, replacement cost coverage had immediate appeal to insureds and came into common use.

With replacement cost coverage, an insured recovers on the basis of replacement cost at the time and place of the loss. There is no deduction for loss of value through physical depreciation.

Replacement cost coverage is usually added at no specific additional rate. However, the coinsurance clause is then applied to the *replacement cost*, rather than the actual cash value, of property covered for replacement cost. Therefore, the insured who has replacement cost coverage must usually carry higher limits of insurance to avoid a coinsurance penalty, and the premium increases in proportion to the increased coverage.

Even when the replacement cost option is in effect, the insured has the opportunity to select loss payment on the basis of actual cash value. When that is the case, the coinsurance clause is applied to the ACV of the covered property—not the replacement cost—in order to determine whether a coinsurance penalty should apply. The circumstances in which an insured with replacement cost coverage might elect ACV recovery are examined in Exhibit 4-1.

Exhibit 4-1
Replacement Cost Versus Actual Cash Value Recovery

Here is one example of a situation in which it is advantageous to choose settlement according to actual cash value even though the policy provides replacement cost coverage.

Worth of all covered property

Actual cash value	$150,000
Replacement cost	250,000

Insurance needed to meet 80 percent coinsurance requirement

Actual cash value	$120,000
Replacement cost	200,000
Amount of insurance	$120,000

Loss

Actual cash value	$50,000
Replacement cost	75,000

In this case, the ACV of the *damaged* property was 67 percent of its replacement cost, although the ACV of *all* the property was only 60 percent of the total replacement cost. In other words, the particular property that was damaged was subject to less depreciation than the property as a whole. This is one of the conditions in which settlement on an actual cash value basis is better for the insured. Thus:

Amount payable under the policy

Actual cash value:	100% of $50,000	=	$50,000
Replacement cost:	(120/200) x $75,000	=	$45,000

Property Not Covered at Replacement Cost

Even when the replacement cost option is in effect, the following types of property are valued at ACV:

- Property of others
- Contents of a residence
- Manuscripts
- Works of arts, antiques, or rare artifacts—including etchings, pictures, statuary, marbles, bronzes, porcelains, and bric-a-brac
- Stock, unless the "including stock" option is indicated in the declarations

Actual cash value, rather than replacement cost, is used in determining compliance with coinsurance requirements on these types of property. Thus, when determining an appropriate amount of insurance and when determining compliance with coinsurance provisions, some property is valued at actual cash value and other property at replacement cost.

Each category of property in the list represents a special relationship between ACV and replacement cost. With up-to-date stock, for example, ACV and replacement cost are essentially the same, whereas with outdated stock ACV is far below replacement cost. True works of art are generally irreplaceable; the nearest thing to "replacement cost" is the price of a very similar item—which is the usual basis for deciding the "actual cash value" of a work of art. Lesser works of art can also be difficult (hence expensive) to reproduce but not nearly worth the cost of doing so.

Loss Settlement

To recover replacement cost, the insured must actually repair or replace the damaged property as soon as reasonably possible. The insurer is not obligated to pay the replacement cost claim until the replacement has been completed. An insured who wishes to collect part of the loss more quickly can make a claim on the basis of ACV. The insured then has 180 days from the date of the loss to notify the insurer of an intention to make claim on a replacement cost basis.

If the insured does not replace or rebuild the property, the claim is settled on an ACV basis. If the insured does replace or rebuild, the limit on claim payment is the smallest of the three amounts that follow:

1. The limit of insurance applicable to the lost or damaged property
2. The cost to replace the property on the same premises with other property of comparable material and quality, used for the same purpose

3. The amount *actually* spent that is *necessary* to repair or replace the property

The first condition restricts coverage to the applicable policy limits. If the policy limit is $100,000 and the replacement cost value of the loss is $105,000, the insurer will not pay more than $100,000.

The second condition limits recovery to the cost of repairing or replacing at the same location for the same occupancy, using materials of comparable quality. This clause does not require the insured to rebuild according to the specified conditions—same premises, same occupancy, same use. It merely says that the insured will not be paid more than what it would cost to reconstruct under those conditions. If the insured replaces with a more expensive building, whether at the same location or a different location, the insurer will pay no more than the amount it would have cost to replace the original building at the original location.

The third condition states that the *actual expenditure* limits recovery. The policy limit may be $200,000, and the cost to replace for the original occupancy and use at the original location may be $190,000, but if the insured builds at a different location for $150,000 or decides on a smaller building at the same location for $150,000, the insurer will pay only $150,000—the smallest of the three amounts. (If the actual cash value of the damaged property were higher than $150,000, say, $160,000, that represents another situation in which it would be advantageous to opt for an actual cash value settlement.)

Time of Replacement

Replacement cost coverage requires that the replacement be accomplished "as soon as reasonably possible after the loss or damage." As noted, the insured may choose to disregard the replacement cost coverage and make a claim on the basis of actual cash value. Even after electing an actual cash value recovery, the insured can claim the additional replacement cost by notifying the insurer of this intention during the first 180 days following the loss.

Manufacturers Selling Price (Finished Stock Only)

As discussed in Chapter 3, the BPP contains a clause valuing stock that has been *sold but not delivered* at selling price, less any discounts and expenses that the insured otherwise would have had. The **manufacturers selling price endorsement (finished stock only)** applies the same approach to the value of finished stock manufactured by the insured—whether or not it has been sold. This endorsement is important for a manufacturer that wants protection against loss of business income from an insured peril, because destruction of finished stock can reduce income and increase expenses. As will be seen in Chapter 8, business income loss resulting from destruction of finished goods is not covered by business income insurance. The endorsement, because it compensates the insured for the profit that the insured would have made on the finished goods had no loss occurred, pays the part of the business income loss that is excluded by business income insurance.

Functional Building Valuation

Many buildings have a replacement cost that is far in excess of their market value. A typical example is an older building that was constructed using designs, materials, and techniques that are now prohibitively expensive for most organizations. Insuring such buildings on a replacement cost basis would be unwise for most insureds, particularly if the building could be repaired or replaced for much less using contemporary building plans and materials.

The **functional building valuation endorsement** addresses this problem by providing modified replacement cost coverage. In the event of a total loss, the endorsement covers the cost to repair or replace the building with a less costly building that is functionally equivalent to the old one. Unlike the replacement cost option in the BPP, the endorsement requires that the replacement building be constructed at the same site unless relocation is required by an ordinance or law. For a partial loss, the insurer's payment for repair or replacement of the damaged portion of the building is calculated on the basis of using less costly material, if available, in the architectural style that existed before the loss.

For example, in the event of a total loss, an old three-story mill building in which the first floor was being used as a warehouse, with the upper floors unused and boarded up, could be replaced by a one-story cinder block building to serve the same function at a much lower cost. Or, for a partial loss, three-coat, wood-lathe plaster walls could be replaced with contemporary sheetrock construction. The loss payment cannot, in any event, exceed the amount of insurance or the amount necessarily spent to repair the damaged building with less costly material, if available.

The endorsement also deletes the BPP coinsurance clause. Therefore, if the endorsement is to be used, the insured and the insurance company should determine the cost to replace the building with a functionally equivalent structure and set the amount of insurance accordingly.

To decrease the moral and morale hazard, if the insured does not contract for repairs within 180 days after the loss occurs or otherwise chooses not to make a claim based on the cost to repair or replace, the maximum that the insured can collect is the smallest of the following amounts:

1. The limit of insurance shown in the endorsement
2. The market value of the damaged building, exclusive of the land value, at the time of the loss
3. The amount it would cost to repair or replace the building on the same site with less costly material in the same architectural style, less allowance for physical deterioration and depreciation

The endorsement defines "market value" as "the price which the property might be expected to realize if offered for sale in a fair market."

The functional building valuation endorsement automatically includes ordinance or law coverage, subject to the regular limit of insurance on the building. Basically, building or ordinance coverage insures against additional costs resulting from actions the insured must take to comply with modern building codes or laws. Ordinance or law coverage, which is also available under a separate endorsement, is discussed in Chapter 5 in connection with the ordinance or law exclusion in the "commercial property" causes-of-loss forms.

In some cases, underwriters may feel that the inclusion of ordinance or law coverage in the functional building valuation endorsement may encourage some of the moral or morale hazard that the endorsement was intended to eliminate. The buildings likely to be covered by the functional building endorsement often lack many of the items required by current building codes; a loss might result in a substantial upgrading of the building. In addition, a relatively small amount of damage might trigger a large expenditure to comply with current building codes. Thus, in some extreme cases, an underwriter may be unwilling to provide functional building valuation as configured with ordinance or law coverage.

Functional Personal Property Valuation (Other Than Stock)

The **functional personal property valuation (other than stock) endorsement** is available for providing functional valuation on personal property other than stock. The endorsement might be useful when insuring older machinery or equipment that is no longer available, such as a machine that has been superseded by a newer, more efficient, less expensive model. An example of such equipment is an older computer system that cost more than a new system that has several times the capacity of the older one. Any personal property to be affected by the endorsement must be described in the schedule.

If the insured contracts for repair or replacement of covered property within 180 days of loss by a covered peril, the insurer will pay the smallest of the following amounts:

1. The applicable limit of insurance
2. The cost to replace, on the same site, the damaged item with the most closely available equivalent property available
3. The amount necessarily spent to repair or replace the property

If claim is not made for repair or replacement, the insurance company's liability is limited to the smallest of the following amounts:

1. The applicable limit of insurance
2. The market value of the property at the time of loss
3. The amount it would cost to repair or replace the damaged property with material of like kind and quality less allowance for physical deterioration and depreciation

The functional personal property valuation endorsement also deletes the coinsurance clause of the BPP (or other "commercial property" coverage form) to which it is attached.

Alternatives to Coinsurance

The BPP coinsurance clause was discussed in Chapter 3. Establishing the exact value required to comply with the coinsurance clause is difficult. The insured is always left with the lingering doubt that a coinsurance penalty will be applied at the time of the loss; to avoid this worry, the cautious insured may decide to carry more insurance than is necessary. Although coinsurance is a standard feature of the BPP, the coinsurance clause can be (1) suspended through the agreed value optional coverage or (2) eliminated through the use of "flat insurance," whereby the insured pays a higher rate in exchange for deletion of the coinsurance clause.

Agreed Value

Before the 1986 revision of ISO policy forms, the agreed value option was available as an endorsement. The 1986 revision included agreed value as an optional coverage in the BPP form. It is triggered by an entry in the commercial property declarations. This greater prominence has undoubtedly increased the use of this option.

Suspension of Coinsurance

The **agreed value optional coverage** suspends the coinsurance clause. The ISO *Commercial Lines Manual* (CLM) requires that the insured submit a **statement of values** to the insurance company. The values must be the full actual cash value (or replacement cost if the replacement cost option has been selected) of the property to be insured. The agreed value provisions are effective for up to one year; an expiration date for the option is shown on the declarations page. Thus, on a policy issued for a term of more than one year, the agreed value option will expire before the policy expires. After the expiration date of the agreed value optional coverage, the coinsurance clause is reinstated. The agreed value optional coverage can be reactivated by submitting a new statement of values to the insurer.

Limit of Insurance

The values shown in the statement of values are also entered on the declarations page. Usually, the limit of insurance for property subject to the agreed value option equals the agreed value. When this is the case, any covered loss is paid in full, subject to deductibles—with no consideration of coinsurance—up to the applicable limit of insurance.

If, for any reason, the limit of insurance is less than the agreed amount, the insured can recover no more than the proportion of the loss that the limit of insurance bears to the agreed value. In other words, the loss is adjusted according to the following formula:

$$\left(\frac{\text{Limit of Insurance}}{\text{Agreed Value}} \times \text{Loss}\right) - \text{Deductible} = \begin{array}{c}\text{Insurer's Payment}\\ \text{(Not to exceed limit)}\end{array}$$

Thus, for example, given the following facts:

Limit of insurance	=	$750,000
Agreed value	=	$1,000,000
Amount of loss	=	$20,000
Deductible	=	$1,000

the insured's recovery is calculated as follows:

$$\left(\frac{\$750,000}{\$1,000,000} \times \$20,000\right) - \$1,000 = \$14,000$$

Although unintentional underinsurance with an agreed value provision may occasionally occur, underinsurance may sometimes be intentional. In some cases, the value of a building exceeds the amount of coverage an underwriter is able to provide, and the insured then participates in every loss in proportion to the extent of the underinsurance. In other cases, two or more insurers participate in insuring the same property; although each policy underinsures, the total amount of insurance in all policies equals the agreed value.

If, for example, the loss illustrated above were also covered under a second policy with a limit of $250,000 and an agreed value of $1,000,000, the insured would recover the balance of the loss (less the deductible) from the second policy. The second policy's share of the loss would be calculated as follows:

$$\left(\frac{\$250{,}000}{\$1{,}000{,}000} \times \$20{,}000 \right) - \$1{,}000 = \$4{,}000$$

Note that the loss payments were subject to two deductibles. The insured collected $1,000 less than it would have if one policy provided the entire amount of insurance. As stated above, the coinsurance clause is reinstated if the agreed value option expires before the policy expires. Thus, a coinsurance percentage must be selected before policy inception and shown in the declarations. The insured may elect 80 percent or higher coinsurance for specific insurance or 90 percent or higher coinsurance for blanket insurance (blanket insurance is discussed later in this chapter).

Regardless of the coinsurance percentage, if the insured wishes to be fully covered under the agreed value option, the amount of insurance must equal 100 percent of the values shown in the statement of values. It might therefore seem advisable to select 100 percent coinsurance in all cases where the agreed value option is effective in order to receive the benefit of the rate reduction for 100 percent coinsurance. However, if the agreed value clause expires, the policy will revert to 100 percent coinsurance.

Rating

The CLM calls for a 5 percent rate increase when the agreed value option is used. It also states that the agreed value option cannot be used with reporting form coverage (to be discussed in this chapter) or with builders risk insurance (which will be discussed in Chapter 6).

Agreed Value From the Insurer's Viewpoint

Submitting a statement of values does not automatically trigger the agreed value option; the insurer's consent is required. The rate structure used by most insurers assumes insurance to value. The coinsurance clause provides the insurer with some protection if the insured fails to carry insurance to value. Before eliminating this protection, insurers must be satisfied that the values shown in the statement of values are reasonably accurate.

Since a number of handbooks and guidelines are available to estimate the insurable value of buildings, insurers can usually determine the adequacy of the requested building amount. Independent appraisals are desirable in many cases to protect the insured from unintentionally underinsuring buildings. Agreed value for personal property poses a more difficult problem: an underwriter often has no way to evaluate objectively the statement of values for personal property. Occasionally an insured can provide verification to satisfy the underwriter, but more often competitive pressures dictate the use of the agreed value clause for personal property.

Insured's View of Agreed Value

Insureds generally do not understand coinsurance. To combat this problem, ISO has devoted almost a page and a half of the BPP form to explaining and illustrating the coinsurance provision. Even when they understand it, insureds seldom appreciate the insurer's need for insurance to value. Furthermore, eliminating worry is one of the reasons why insureds purchase insurance, and the insured cannot know until a loss has been adjusted whether the amount of insurance is sufficient to satisfy the coinsurance clause. The agreed value clause provides added assurance that an insured's loss will be fully covered.

Most risk managers, consultants, and experienced insurance producers regard agreed value as a key component of a property insurance program. Given the widespread use of businessowners policies, which usually do not include any coinsurance clause (see Chapter 12), it is likely that the demand for the agreed value clause in the commercial property policy will increase.

Flat Insurance

The building and personal property coverage form and some other "commercial property" forms are sometimes issued with no coinsurance requirement at all. "Commercial property" policies that do not have a coinsurance requirement are sometimes referred to as **flat insurance**. The "flat rate" charged for such policies is significantly higher than the usual 80 percent coinsurance rate. With flat insurance, the insured may purchase any amount of insurance with no penalty for underinsurance unless the loss exceeds the amount of insurance.

Under CLM rules, flat insurance is only permitted with basic form causes of loss, not with broad form or special form causes of loss. However, many insurers have independent filings permitting flat insurance with any causes-of-loss form.

The term "flat insurance" is normally reserved for describing policies in which the coinsurance clause is deleted in return for the insured's acceptance of a higher premium rate. Typically, this arrangement is used when the insured wishes to carry an amount of insurance known to be considerably less than the actual value of the covered property. "Flat insurance" is not properly used to describe *every* policy that does not contain a coinsurance clause. For example, in the businessowners policy (Chapter 13), full insurance to value is anticipated and so the rate is not surcharged. Of course, it is up to the underwriter to ascertain that the limit of insurance requested by the insured is sufficient to satisfy the insurer's insurance-to-value requirement.

Blanket Insurance

The basic approach to insuring buildings and personal property is to schedule a specific amount of insurance in the policy declarations for each building and a specific amount of insurance for personal property at each insured location, plus, if needed, a separate amount of insurance for personal property of others at each location. This basic approach is called **specific insurance**. The alternative to specific insurance is **blanket insurance**. The CLM defines blanket insurance as insurance that covers under one amount:

a. One type of property in more than one separately rated building; or
b. Two or more types of property in one or more separately rated buildings.

No endorsement or other policy modification is used to effect blanket insurance. All that is necessary is to indicate in the policy declarations that two or more types of property or locations are covered as a single item, subject to a single limit of insurance. The word "blanket" is often included in the wording used to describe covered property. Examples of blanket coverage wording are:

$400,000 on building and your business personal property at 123 Main St., Malvern, PA

$750,000 blanket limit on your business personal property at 789 Broadway, Omaha, NE and 567 First St., Lincoln, NE

Advantages of Blanket Insurance

The advantages of blanket insurance can be understood by considering the following example. Suppose Bob owns three buildings, each having an insurable value of $100,000. Bob might elect to carry $80,000 of insurance on each building to comply with an 80 percent coinsurance clause. If the coverage were on a specific basis, the covered property portion of the declarations would read, in part, as follows:

$80,000 on building located 123 Main St.

$80,000 on building located 27 Walnut St.

$80,000 on building located 999 Sycamore St.

If the building at 27 Walnut Street were destroyed by a covered cause of loss, the insured would suffer a $100,000 loss but would collect only $80,000, the limit of insurance on that building. One way to avoid this uninsured loss would be to carry $100,000 insurance on each building. Another way would be to blanket the insurance to apply the entire amount to the three buildings with no per-building limit. The limit could then be as follows:

$270,000 blanket limit on buildings located 123 Main St., 27 Walnut St., and 999 Sycamore St.

(Although the insured might like to purchase only $240,000 or even less insurance, manual rules, to be discussed below, require that a 90 percent coinsurance clause be used.)

The insured could now collect the $100,000 loss in full since the loss would be less than the limit of insurance. If all three buildings could not be damaged by any one loss, the insured would have protection against a total loss with a lower amount of insurance. These two approaches are summarized in Exhibit 4-2.

Blanket insurance can also be particularly effective for insuring contents that may be moved from one building to another, if the total contents value of all insured locations does not fluctuate widely. Firms that could benefit from blanket coverage include the following:

- An organization having a warehouse that supplies several retail outlets. The contents of the warehouse and the outlets can be blanketed.
- A firm whose stock is located in several different buildings, with an inventory control system that gives total values but does not break out values in each building.
- A manufacturing operation that moves property from one building to another in the normal course of manufacture so that total values are relatively constant, but the value in any given building may vary substantially from week to week.

Exhibit 4-2
Amounts of Insurance Needed To Protect Against a Total Loss at One Location

Building #	Insurable Value	Location
1	$100,000	123 Main St.
2	100,000	27 Walnut St.
3	100,000	999 Sycamore St.

Coverage needed to protect against a $100,000 loss at any one location if written on a specific basis:

Building #	Insurance	Location
1	$100,000	123 Main St.
2	100,000	27 Walnut St.
3	100,000	999 Sycamore St.
Total	$300,000	

Coverage needed to protect against a $100,000 loss at any one location if written on a blanket basis:

Building #	Insurance	Location
1, 2, & 3	$270,000*	123 Main St., 27 Walnut St., and 999 Sycamore St.

*Manual rules require a 90% coinsurance clause.

In general, the greater the number of locations and the smaller the proportion of total value at any one location, the greater the virtue of blanket insurance. From the insured's point of view, there may be little benefit in knowing exactly how much value is at any particular place at any given time, and it may be onerous to report insurable values by location. Blanket insurance, however, is not a substitute for good record keeping. In the event of a loss at any one location, the insured must be able to establish the values that were lost.

Coinsurance Requirement

Despite the advantages of blanket insurance, it may involve an additional cost. Except when personal property of others or tenants' improvements and betterments are the items being blanketed, the minimum coinsurance clause is 90 percent, but the rates are the same as for 80 percent coinsurance. In other words, the insured with blanket insurance must insure to 90 percent of value to avoid a coinsurance penalty but does not receive the 5 percent discount that applies to specific insurance with a 90 percent coinsurance clause. Blanket insurance with 100 percent coinsurance receives a 5 percent discount off the 80 percent coinsurance rate, in contrast with the usual 10 percent discount for specific insurance subject to 100 percent coinsurance.

The higher rate for blanket insurance is justified because, as shown in Exhibit 4-2, an insured with blanket coverage does not have to buy insurance equal to 100 percent of total values to have 100 percent coverage at each separate location (unless, of course, the policy is subject to a 100 percent coinsurance clause). This is so because the entire blanket limit applies to loss at any particular location even though most insured losses would involve only one location.

Thus (as shown in Exhibit 4-2), insuring three separate locations to 90 percent of value on a blanket basis can provide essentially the same coverage as insuring the same locations on a specific basis to 100 percent of value. Despite the difference in blanket and specific *rates*, the policy premiums will be the same if the blanket policy contains a 90 percent coinsurance clause and the specific policy contains a 100 percent coinsurance clause. If, for example, the 80 percent coinsurance rate were \$1.00 per \$100 of insured value, the rate for blanket insurance with 90 percent coinsurance would be \$1.00 and the rate for specific insurance with 100 percent coinsurance would be \$.90 (10 percent discount). Using these rates, the premiums can be calculated as follows:

$$\text{Specific:} \quad \$300{,}000 \times \frac{\$.90}{\$100} = \$2{,}700$$

$$\text{Blanket:} \quad \$270{,}000 \times \frac{\$1.00}{\$100} = \$2{,}700$$

If *both* policies had a \$270,000 limit and 90 percent coinsurance, the premium for the specific policy would be lower. Of course, the blanket policy would still provide full coverage at each location while the specific policy would pay only up to \$90,000 at each location. Hence, the higher-priced blanket policy would provide more coverage per location.

Actual Insurable Values

Another benefit of blanket insurance is obscured by the way the illustrations have been stated above. It was assumed that the insured knew the exact insurable amount with complete certainty. In reality, that is seldom the case. For most insureds, the best that can be achieved is a range of probable values with a reasonable level of certainty. For example, instead of saying that the insured knows that the replacement cost of a building will be \$1,000,000 at the time of loss, it would be more accurate to say that the insured is 95 percent certain that the insurable value at the time of loss will be between $950,000 and $1,050,000. (If three contractors estimated the cost to replace a building, the range of their estimates would in almost all cases exceed plus or minus 5 percent from the average.)

Selecting an amount of insurance is further complicated by the fact that the loss may occur as long as one year from the inception date of the policy. (Although the inflation guard option, discussed later in this chapter, offers some protection against this problem, it involves an additional cost.) Finally, the replacement cost may be greatly increased by unanticipated events. The tremendous demand for repairs following a major conflagration or hurricane can increase labor and material costs by 25 percent or more; a $1,000,000 building might then cost more than $1,250,000 to replace.

The *guaranteed* replacement cost endorsement, used in homeowners policies, will pay the cost to replace even if that cost exceeds the amount of insurance. This endorsement is not generally available for commercial property, and ISO does not include such an endorsement in its commercial lines program. With specific insurance, an insured would have to purchase a much higher limit of insurance to protect against the contingencies described above. For insureds with multiple locations not subject to the same loss, blanket insurance, *on an agreed value basis*, can solve these problems. If blanket insurance is *not* on an agreed value basis, the 90 (or 100) percent coinsurance requirement will result in a penalty if property values at the time of a loss are greater than 90 (or 100) percent of the amount of insurance.

Predicting future maximum values for contents is even more difficult than for buildings. To be properly protected, insureds can select an amount of insurance equal to the highest anticipated value or use a peak season endorsement or value reporting form (both of which are discussed below). Increased amounts of insurance or the peak season endorsement involve increased premium cost, and not all insureds can produce the timely and accurate reports required by the value reporting endorsement.

Despite the added cost in certain situations, most risk managers, consultants, and producers generally request blanket insurance for larger insureds (usually combined with the agreed value option) to achieve the most effective protection.

Rating

As discussed above, the rate for blanket insurance is higher than the rate for the same dollar amount of specific insurance. Another potential disadvantage of blanket coverage arises when more than one rate applies to property covered by the form. The CLM requires that the highest rate applicable to any one type of covered property be used on all covered property at all locations unless a blanket average rate is calculated. The blanket average rate is a weighted average based on values at each location and the premium rate at each location. The insured submits a statement of values to be used in developing the blanket average rate. A simplified example of the calculation of a blanket average rate is shown in Exhibit 4-3.

Exhibit 4-3
Simplified Calculation of Blanket Average Rate

Location	Insurable Value	Rate	Premium
123 Main St.	$100,000	$1.00	$1,000
27 Walnut St.	100,000	.35	350
999 Sycamore St.	100,000	.45	450
Total	$300,000		$1,800

$$\frac{\text{Total premium}}{\text{Total value} \div 100} = \text{Blanket Average Rate}$$

$$\frac{\$1{,}800}{\$3{,}000} = .60$$

Blanket Average Rate = .60

If no blanket average rate is computed, the $1.00 rate would be used (the highest rate for any of the properties).

Therefore, the premium for $300,000 insurance if no blanket average rate were computed would be $3,000, but with the blanket average rate the premium is $1,800.

Options for Insuring Fluctuating Personal Property Values

Fluctuating personal property values pose an insurance problem for many businesses—especially those with widely varying inventory levels. The term **fluctuating values** refers to values that rise and fall over time. For some businesses, values fluctuate in predictable cycles. A toy store, for example, may predictably double its inventory during the months preceding Christmas, with inventory values declining rapidly just before Christmas and stabilizing for the next nine months. Similarly, a seasonal business such as a nursery can be expected to have higher inventory values in spring and summer than in fall and winter. Other businesses may experience inventory fluctuations with no predictable pattern. A lumber yard's inventory, for example, may be affected by external factors such as the number of houses being built in the area. Whatever the cause or nature of the fluctuation, an insured usually wants insurance to adjust to the circumstances and give efficient, economical protection year-round.

The basic approach of a single, fixed amount of insurance, with premiums based on that policy limit, is unsatisfactory for fluctuating inventories. To fully cover temporarily large accumulations, the insured would have to purchase and pay for high limits of insurance. At times when inventory values are reduced, the organization would be paying for unneeded insurance. Conversely, the insured could choose a limit of insurance that is less than adequate to cover peak values. This keeps premiums lower but provides a coverage limit that is inadequate at times when inventory levels are high.

Two amendments to the BPP are available to meet the insured's needs in these situations: the peak season endorsement and the value reporting form.

Peak Season Endorsement

The **peak season limit of insurance endorsement** simply provides differing amounts of insurance for differing time periods during the policy term, as indicated by specific dates shown in the endorsement. For example, a toy store may have a BPP providing $100,000 coverage on personal property with a peak season endorsement increasing coverage to $200,000 during the period from October 1 to December 31. This would have exactly the same effect as endorsing the policy on October 1 to increase the coverage, and endorsing it again on December 31 to reduce the coverage; the peak season endorsement eliminates the bother of these extra transactions.

Usually, the peak season endorsement is attached when the policy is issued—although it may be added mid-term—and a pro-rata increased premium is charged for the period during which the limit is increased.

Value Reporting Form

The **value reporting form** is another way to modify the BPP to prevent over- or underinsuring personal property. Briefly, it works like this: A limit of insurance is set high enough to cover the insured's maximum expected values at any time during the policy period. The premium charged is based not on the *policy limit* but on the *values reported by the insured as exposed to loss.* The insured reports values to the insurer at periodic intervals specified in the form. As long as the insured reports property values accurately and on time, the insurer will pay the full amount of any loss that occurs (subject to the policy limit), even if the values on hand at the time of the loss are greater than those last reported to the insurer. At the end of the policy period, the insurer computes the average values that were exposed to loss and uses that average to determine the premium.

Major features of the value reporting form include the following:

- Reporting requirement
- Limit of insurance
- Penalties
- Provisional premium
- Treatment of specific (nonreporting) insurance

Reporting Requirement

The insured must submit to the insurance company a periodic report of dollar values covered by the policy. The period of time for which the reports of value are due is referred to as a reporting period. Each reporting period has a specified interval at which reports are required. Five options are available. These options and the code letters used to indicate them are as follows:

- DR—daily values reported monthly
- WR—values as of the last day of the week reported monthly
- MR—values as of the last day of the month reported monthly
- QR—values as of the last day of the month reported quarterly
- PR—values as of the last day of the month reported at the end of the policy year

Monthly reporting of monthly values is the most commonly used alternative.

The code letters DR, WR, and so forth appear in the commercial property declarations in place of the coinsurance percentage. The insured must file the required report within thirty days after the end of each reporting period and at the expiration of the policy. The reports must separately list the total value of covered property at each location as of the report dates.

Limit of Insurance

A specific limit of insurance applies to property at each location. The insurer's obligation is limited by this maximum amount per location unless coverage is written on a blanket basis, in which event the blanket limit can apply at any one location.

The insured is required to report all covered property on hand as of each report date. If $250,000 worth of property is on hand and the limit of insurance is $150,000, then the insured must still report $250,000. Since the premium is based on the *reported values*, the insured must also pay a premium based on $250,000. However, coverage is still capped by the $150,000 limit of insurance. If such a situation occurs, the insured should increase the limits or purchase specific insurance to cover the additional $100,000 of value. Insurance companies and producers may also set up systems to trigger a review in any case where values approach or exceed limits, but the ultimate burden of monitoring rests on the insured.

Penalties

In order for the value reporting form to work properly—and for the insurer to collect appropriate premiums—the insurer must have timely information that accurately reflects the values exposed to loss. To enforce this need, the form contains penalties for failure to submit reports and for inaccurate reports.

Failure To Submit Reports

If at the time of loss the *first* required report of values was due, but has not been received, the insurer will not pay more than 75 percent of the amount that would otherwise have been paid. For example, assume that the insured had made no reports of value at the time that a loss occurred under the following circumstances:

Limit of insurance	=	$100,000
Reporting period	=	MR (monthly values reported monthly)
Policy inception	=	January 1
Date of loss	=	March 12
Amount of loss	=	$40,000

Because the first report was due, but had not been received, at the time of the loss, the insured would collect only 75 percent of the amount that the insurer would otherwise have paid. Thus, ignoring any deductible, the insurer would pay $30,000 instead of the full $40,000 loss.

If at the time a loss occurs the insured has failed to submit any required report *after the first required report*, the insurer will pay no more than the values last reported for the location at which the loss occurred. This provision can result in a serious penalty for an organization whose values are rising or whose values at the loss location are higher than they were at the time of the last report. However, it has no effect on an organization whose values are the same or lower at the loss location than they were at the last report date. The following loss example illustrates the provision:

Limit of insurance	=	$100,000 (single location)
Reporting period	=	MR (monthly values reported monthly)
Date of loss	=	April 20 (second report was overdue)
Amount of loss	=	$70,000
Value last reported	=	$60,000 (first report; accurate)

Because the second report was overdue at the time of the loss, the insurer would pay no more than the value last reported for that location; thus, disregarding any deductible, the insurer would pay only $60,000, leaving the insured with a $10,000 retained loss. Had the loss been $60,000 or less, there would have been no penalty.

Inaccurate Reports

The value reporting form replaces the coinsurance provision of the BPP with a **full reporting clause,** sometimes referred to as an **honesty clause**. The full reporting clause simply stipulates that, if the last report showed less than the full value of covered property at the affected location on the report date, then the insurer will pay claims according to the following formula:

$$\left(\frac{\text{Value Reported}}{\text{Actual Value}} \times \text{Loss} \right) - \text{Deductible} = \text{Insurer's Payment (Not to exceed limit)}$$

To illustrate the consequences of underreporting values, assume that a loss occurs under the following circumstances, in which the insurer's claim representative investigating the loss discovered that actual values at the time of the last report were greater than the values reported:

Limit of insurance	=	$2,000,000 (single location)
Values shown in last report	=	$1,000,000
Actual values at time of report	=	$1,500,000
Amount of loss	=	$600,000
Deductible	=	$1,000

The insurer's payment would be calculated as follows:

$$\left(\frac{\$1,000,000}{\$1,500,000} \times \$600,000 \right) - \$1,000 = \$399,000$$

In this case, the insured's inaccurate reporting resulted in a retained loss that was $200,000 greater than if the insured had made an accurate report. The potential severity of the penalty for inaccurate reports should deter anyone who understands it from trying to save on premiums by intentionally underreporting values. Unfortunately, many insureds do not understand the consequences of inaccurate (or late) reports until they have suffered a loss.

As long as reports are accurate and on time, the penalties described above do not apply; the insurer will pay the full amount of any loss (up to the limit of insurance), even if it exceeds the amount last reported. If, for example, the amount of loss in the above example had been $1,800,000 and the last due report, totaling $1,000,000, had been accurate, the insurer would have paid the full $1,800,000 loss, minus the deductible.

Provisional Premium

Like most other types of property insurance, the value reporting form carries a limit of insurance that is the most the insurer will pay for a loss. However, unlike most other property insurance limits, the limit of insurance for property subject to the value reporting form is usually set for an amount that is higher than the maximum values that are expected at any one time during the policy term.

Because the limit does not directly reflect the exposure, the initial premium is not based on the full limit of insurance. Instead, the insured must pay, at the beginning of the policy period, a **provisional premium**. The provisional premium is typically 75 percent of the annual premium that would be required to purchase nonreporting coverage with the same limit.

The earned premium for the entire policy period depends on the average values reported during the policy term. At the end of the policy period, an additional premium may be due or a refund may be owed to the insured. Refunds and additional premiums are calculated on a pro-rata basis.

Specific Insurance

Reporting form insurance may be combined with other, nonreporting insurance covering the same property. This other insurance is then referred to as specific insurance. The terminology is confusing, since "specific" is also used as the opposite of "blanket," as discussed previously.

The value reporting form defines specific insurance as:

> . . . other insurance that:
>
> a. Covers the same Covered Property to which this endorsement applies; and
>
> b. Is not subject to the same plan, terms, conditions and provisions as this insurance, including this endorsement.

Coverage on property subject to the value reporting form is excess over the total of (1) the amount due from specific insurance plus (2) the amount of any deductible applying to the specific insurance.

If the specific insurance has a coinsurance clause, the reporting form coverage is not counted when determining whether the specific insurance's coinsurance requirement has been met. For example, suppose insured goods are valued at \$250,000. An 80 percent coinsurance clause under the specific insurance contract would require \$200,000 of coverage in order to avoid a coinsurance penalty. If the loss is \$150,000 and the amount of specific insurance is \$80,000, then, disregarding deductibles, the specific insurance coverage would pay only \$60,000, determined as follows:

$$\frac{\$\ 80{,}000}{.80 \times \$250{,}000} \times 150{,}000 = \$60{,}000$$

The reporting coverage would pay the amount of loss in excess of the specific insurance payment. In this case, the specific coverage would pay \$60,000 and the reporting coverage would pay \$90,000—again disregarding deductibles and subject, of course, to policy limits.

However, almost all policies do have deductibles. Suppose the specific insurance has a \$5,000 deductible and the reporting insurance has a \$1,000 deductible. On the \$150,000 loss described above:

- The specific insurance would pay \$55,000 (\$60,000 minus the \$5,000 deductible).
- The reporting insurance would pay \$89,000 (\$90,000 minus the \$1,000 deductible).
- The insured would retain \$6,000 (the \$5,000 deductible on the specific policy plus the \$1,000 deductible on the reporting policy).

If the specific insurance has no coinsurance clause, the specific coverage pays the loss up to its policy limit and the reporting insurance pays the balance, less any applicable deductible.

When specific coverage is combined with reporting coverage, the insured is always entitled to recovery in full (subject to deductibles) as long as the combined limits (specific plus reporting) are adequate and the reporting requirements are complied with. However if the specific insurance is uncollectible, perhaps due to insolvency of the insurer, the reporting form policy will deduct the amount due from the specific insurer in calculating its payments; it will not pay the uncollectible amount due from the specific insurer.

Since the value reporting insurance is excess over specific insurance, the premium for the reporting form is based only on the excess of covered value over the amount of specific insurance at each location. Thus, with specific insurance of $100,000 at a location and value of $250,000 in covered property, the reporting form premium rate is applied against the $150,000 difference. The insured and the insurer must be alert to any change in specific coverage. In particular, when any specific coverage expires, the change must be noted in the next report.

Advantages and Disadvantages

For some insureds, the value reporting form is an ideal way to deal with values that fluctuate substantially. As long as values do not exceed the limit of insurance, coverage is adequate to cover any loss in full, with no penalty for underinsurance. Yet, the insured does not need to pay for more insurance than is needed, since the premium directly reflects the values exposed to loss. In short, the insured can get the effect of full coverage without paying for more insurance than is necessary.

However, the value reporting form must be used with extreme care, or the cure may be worse than the disease. The penalties for late or inaccurate reports can be severe. Late reports are an all-too-common problem with reporting forms. The penalties present a compelling reason why a reporting form should not be used unless there is reason to believe that the insured can produce reports promptly and accurately.

Inaccurate reports are sometimes made because the insured knows that lower reported values will develop lower premiums. More frequently, inaccuracy reflects an inadequate system for developing the needed information. Sometimes the insured does not have an accounting system that can accurately generate reports. Other times inaccuracy stems from a misunderstanding as to the values that should be included in the report. For example, the insured might report only inventory values, when furniture, fixtures, and equipment are also among the items covered by the policy, or the insured may report book values rather than ACV or the replacement cost values called for by the policy.

Even with on-time and accurate reporting, problems sometimes arise. As noted earlier, when the value on hand exceeds the policy limit, the insured is still required to report the value and pay a premium for it, even though it is not fully covered. Such a situation is obviously undesirable and has been the source of litigation involving insureds, insurers, and producers.

In short, the value reporting form presents a sound solution to the problem of fluctuating values—but only when the insured submits on-time and accurate reports *and* care is taken to be sure that the policy limit equals or exceeds the maximum possible loss.

Other Coverage Options

Other coverage options include inflation guard coverage, the manufacturers' consequential loss assumption endorsement, and the brands and labels endorsement.

Inflation Guard

As discussed above, when a policy insuring two or more buildings is issued on a blanket basis, the entire blanket limit is available for a loss at any location. This feature of blanket insurance can be helpful in ensuring that the insurance will be adequate to cover increases in property values due to inflation. However, unless the blanket insurance is on an agreed value basis, the insured could incur a coinsurance penalty if total property values increase substantially. Moreover, the blanket approach will not help to solve the problem when the insured has only a single building.

Another coverage option that directly addresses the inflation problem is the **inflation guard optional coverage** in the BPP. To activate the inflation guard option, the insured selects a percentage equal to the expected rate of inflationary increase in property value during the coming policy term, and this percentage is inserted in the declarations. Coverage then automatically increases by the chosen percentage throughout the policy period, with the increase in coverage prorated on a daily basis.

For example, suppose the insured purchases building coverage of $100,000 and selects the inflation guard option with an annual percentage of 10 percent. Suppose the insured sustains a building loss after a one-year policy has been in force for seventy-three days. The inflation guard would increase the available amount of insurance by 2 percent, and the amount of insurance available to cover the building loss would be $102,000—determined by the three steps shown below:

1. $\frac{73 \text{ days}}{365 \text{ days}} \times .10 = .02$
2. $.02 \times \$100{,}000 = \$2{,}000$
3. $\$100{,}000 + \$2{,}000 = \$102{,}000$

The inflation guard coverage can be used for buildings or personal property or both. The additional premium for the coverage is based directly on the additional limits of coverage it provides.

Except by chance, fixed percentage increases do not exactly match inflationary increases in property values. Nor do they help much when applied to insurance that is inadequate in the first place. But they do help to address a problem imposed during periods of high rates of economic inflation. Another approach, used by some insurers, is to increase policy limits in accordance with some type of cost index, such as a construction cost index or a consumer price index.

Manufacturers' Consequential Loss Assumption

If stock in the process of manufacture is damaged or destroyed, the physical loss can decrease the value of other stock that is *undamaged.* A golf cart manufacturer, for example, could incur this type of consequential loss if the damaged property was golf cart bodies and the undamaged property was golf cart engines. If the bodies were the last lot of the current model year to be produced and the remaining engines could not be used in the new model year, their value would be considerably less than if they could have been installed in golf cart bodies and sold.

The **manufacturers' consequential loss assumption endorsement** provides coverage for this type of situation. When damage to parts of stock in the process of manufacture at the described premises causes a reduction in value to the remaining parts of the stock, coverage is provided for the reduction in value wherever the remaining, undamaged parts may be located. However, the value of portions of stock at other locations must be included when applying coinsurance.

Brands and Labels

After an insurance company pays for loss to covered property, it has the right to take any salvage, such as smoke-damaged merchandise. This can pose a problem for an insured that bases its marketing appeal on a brand name reputation for high quality. The salvaged material might be saleable but not meet the insured's quality standards.

To help protect the reputation of the insured's goods when the insurance company takes any part of the property as salvage, the **brands and labels endorsement** permits the insured, at its expense, to:

- Stamp "salvage" on the merchandise or its containers, if the stamp will not physically damage the merchandise; or
- Remove the brands or labels, if doing so will not physically damage the merchandise. The insured must relabel the merchandise or its containers to comply with the law.

The brands and labels endorsement is only available to cover the original manufacturer of the goods.

Some independently filed policies or endorsements have broader brands and labels clauses. In some cases, the insured has virtually full control over the sale of salvaged brand label merchandise.

Summary

Various coverage options are available to tailor the BPP (and other "commercial property" coverage forms) to meet the needs of a particular insured. Some coverage options are printed in the BPP and can be activated on the declarations page. Other coverage options are added by endorsement.

A widely used optional valuation method is *replacement cost coverage*, which obligates the insurer to pay for losses on the basis of current replacement cost with no deduction for depreciation, subject to several conditions. Other optional valuation methods include *manufacturer's selling price*, which values sold or unsold finished stock at its selling price; *functional building valuation*, which provides for repair or replacement using less costly materials; and *functional personal property valuation*, which covers the cost to replace property (such as an older computer) with equivalent property that is currently available.

A commonly used alternative to coinsurance is the *agreed value optional coverage*. Under this option, the coinsurance clause is suspended if the insured carries an amount of insurance at least equal to the full value of the insured property, as determined by a written statement of values submitted by the insured to the insurer. Another alternative to coinsurance under "commercial property" coverage forms is *flat insurance*, whereby the insured agrees to pay a substantially higher rate (the "flat rate") in return for deletion of the coinsurance clause.

Under *blanket insurance*, one amount of insurance applies to (a) one type of property in two or more separately rated buildings or (b) two or more types of property in one or more separately rated buildings. Because the full blanket limit can be applied to a single loss, blanket insurance is ideal for covering an insured with two or more buildings who knows what his or her total inventory value is but cannot be sure how much is in each building. When issued on an agreed value basis, blanket insurance can also be useful in making sure that the amount of insurance at one location will be adequate in spite of unintentional errors in estimating the value of covered property, inflationary increases in property values, and increased construction costs following a catastrophe.

The problem of fluctuating inventory values—the rising and falling of inventory values over time—can be addressed through either the peak season endorsement or the value reporting form. The *peak season endorsement* simply provides different amounts of insurance for different periods of the year. The *value reporting form* bases premiums on the actual values exposed to loss and reported to the insurer at regular intervals. As long as the insured makes the reports on time and accurately, the insurer agrees to pay the full amount of any loss that does not exceed the limit of insurance. Late or inaccurate reporting results in various penalties at the time of a loss. Before a reporting form is used, the insured needs to be sure that providing on-time and accurate reports is feasible.

Other coverage options include *inflation guard coverage*, which automatically increases the amount of insurance throughout the policy period in order to address inflationary increases; the *manufacturers consequential loss assumption endorsement*, which covers the decrease in value of undamaged stock due to physical damage to other stock in the course of manufacture; and the *brands and labels endorsement*, which permits the insured to remove the labels on its damaged goods if the insurer takes the goods as salvage after a covered loss.

Chapter 5

Covered Causes of Loss

The perils covered by a building and personal property coverage form (or any other "commercial property" coverage form) are determined by the causes-of-loss form that has been selected by the insured and included in the policy. Three standard causes-of-loss forms, which offer three different levels of coverage, are available. This chapter describes the causes-of-loss forms as well as several endorsements for covering additional causes of loss such as earthquake and radioactive contamination.

Evolution of Causes-of-Loss Forms

The first insurance policies on property at fixed locations covered only fire losses. Subsequently, because it was sometimes difficult to separate lightning losses from fire losses, fire policies were expanded to cover loss caused by lightning. Fire and lightning insurance was in most cases issued using a document called the **standard fire policy**. The 1943 edition of the standard fire policy remained in wide use for commercial properties until ISO and AAIS introduced simplified commercial lines forms in the late 1980s. Some states still require the 1943 standard fire policy to be attached to simplified policies so that the insured will have the benefit of whichever provisions are more favorable.

Insurance for additional perils became available over time, first as separate-peril policies and then, in the 1930s, in a package of perils known originally as "supplemental coverage" and later as **extended coverage**. Combining perils in a package reduced adverse selection against the insurance company since an insured could not select just the one peril to which he or she felt most exposed—such as windstorm—but had to purchase all the perils. By obtaining a better spread of risk, the rate needed for the package of perils was less than the sum of the rates for the individual perils. Proposals to add coverages to the various packages of perils continue to this day. For example, some people (including some insurance experts) have suggested that catastrophe perils such as earthquake and flood could be more easily insured if they were added to all policies so that all insureds would contribute premiums to pay losses.

The extended coverage perils, remembered by generations of insurance students by the name W.C. SHAVER, consist of the following:

Windstorm
Civil commotion
Smoke
Hail
Aircraft
Vehicles
Explosion
Riot, and riot attending a strike

A later development was the addition of vandalism or malicious mischief as an insured peril. For many years, the most popular set of coverages for buildings and contents was fire (provided through the standard fire policy), extended coverage (by endorsement), and vandalism or malicious mischief (by an additional endorsement)—commonly referred to as "Fire, EC, and VMM." A "sprinkler leakage" endorsement was often added when insuring a sprinkled property.

Insurance and risk management professionals still need to know the perils included in the extended coverage endorsement even though ISO withdrew its filings for the form in the late 1980s. Older leases, mortgages, and other agreements—and even some documents recently drafted by lawyers who have not adjusted to the new terminology—require the lessee, mortgagor, or other party to the contract to obtain "fire and extended coverage" on the property.

A longer list of named perils became available for dwellings and commercial properties. These "optional perils" presented a second level of coverage. A third level of coverage involved the "all-risks" approach, which had existed for many years previously in inland marine policies. In rather general terms, **"all-risks" insurance** covers loss by any accidental cause except for certain excluded perils that are uninsurable, difficult to insure, or commonly insured under other forms.

The "commercial property" causes-of-loss forms maintain the idea of three levels of coverage:

1. The **causes of loss—basic form** covers fire, lightning, the EC perils, VMM, and three others.
2. The **causes of loss—broad form** covers the basic form perils plus four others.
3. The **causes of loss—special form** covers on an "all-risks" basis.

In addition to the basic, broad, and special causes-of-loss forms, the **causes of loss—earthquake form** is available for insuring against earthquake and volcanic eruption. Various endorsements are also available for amending the causes-of-loss forms to fit insureds' or underwriters' needs.

Concurrent Causation

In the early 1980s, the emergence of the legal **doctrine of concurrent causation** threatened the concept of "all-risks" coverage as well as the effectiveness of exclusions in other causes-of-loss forms. As a result, property insurance forms were modified.

The doctrine of concurrent causation evolved, in part, from a case in which record rains broke through flood-control facilities and inundated parts of the city of Palm Desert, California. Insurers considered the resulting losses to be clearly excluded by the standard flood exclusion. However, the holders of "all-risks" homeowners policies (which covered all risks of direct loss except those specifically excluded) alleged that the cause of the loss was "negligence of the water district"—a cause of loss that the policies did not specifically exclude. The court supported the policyholders' position, on the basis that (1) the flood and (2) the negligent act of constructing flood control structures were independent, concurrent causes that interacted with each other to produce the loss.

Similar decisions were reached in other California cases. In a case involving a landslide, the policyholder successfully argued that "faulty installation of a drain by a third party" was the cause of the landslide and such negligent actions by third parties were not excluded.

The effect of the concurrent causation doctrine is that the insurer with an "all-risks" policy must pay if there is *any* cause of loss that is not specifically excluded. Stated differently, if a loss to property can be attributed to two causes—one excluded by the policy and one covered—the policy covers the loss.

In response to these decisions, policies were revised beginning in 1983. The first paragraph of the exclusions section of the basic, broad, and special causes-of-loss forms was reworded to emphasize that certain exclusions apply even if another cause is involved in the loss. The revisions also deleted the "all" from "all-risks" in the insuring agreement of the special form—a change intended to avoid representing the coverage as being broader than was ever intended. Finally, the revision modified the treatment of collapse in the broad and special forms. Collapse was excluded as a cause of loss but a new additional coverage was added to cover collapse resulting from certain named perils.

Few other jurisdictions adopted the concurrent causation doctrine, and even California has retreated from the extreme positions set out in the earliest cases.[1] However, since a court could at some time choose to accept the concurrent causation doctrine, the policy changes remain in effect.

Basic and Broad Causes-of-Loss Forms

Both the "causes of loss—basic form" and the "causes of loss—broad form" specifically list the causes of loss they cover, subject to some exclusions. Thus, if insured property is damaged by one of the listed perils, the loss is covered—unless any of the form's exclusions applies to the particular circumstances.

In most respects the basic form and the broad form are exactly the same as regards both covered perils and exclusions. The main *difference* between the two forms is simply that the broad form lists four additional perils. Consequently, the discussion that follows applies equally to both the basic and the broad form unless indicated otherwise. The causes of loss—special form takes an entirely different approach from that of the basic and broad forms and is therefore described separately in this chapter.

Specified perils forms are subject to a difficulty similar to the "concurrent causation" problem: Suppose the chain of events leading to a loss includes both a covered and an excluded peril. For example, suppose a boiler explosion (excluded) produces a fire (covered)—or, conversely, that a fire (covered) produces a boiler explosion (excluded). Or that underground water seepage (excluded) causes an electrical short that starts a fire—or that a fire weakens a wall so that underground water seepage subsequently occurs. Along with concurrent causation, this difficulty also has led to some revisions in policy wording. But not all possible situations are so treated. In the absence of any specific contractual provision, the most general rule is that once a covered peril has occurred, all subsequent damage is also covered, even when an excluded peril has meanwhile intervened. This is in accord with the general rule for contracts of adhesion, as discussed in CPCU 1: When there is ambiguity, interpretation will be against the writer of the contract, considered to be the insurer.

Perils Covered by the Basic and Broad Forms

The basic and broad forms are generally referred to as **named perils forms,** because they cover the perils specifically named in the forms. The covered causes of loss in the basic form and the broad form are shown in Exhibit 5-1. With the exceptions of fire and lightning, each of these perils is subject to provisions that serve either to define the perils or impose some conditions or limitations on coverage. The section that follows describes the perils common to both forms. The perils covered only by the broad form are discussed subsequently.

Exhibit 5-1
Covered Causes of Loss in Basic and Broad Forms

Both Forms Cover:	Broad Form Also Covers:
1. Fire	12. Breakage of glass
2. Lightning	13. Falling objects
3. Explosion	14. Weight of snow, ice, sleet
4. Windstorm or hail	15. Water damage
5. Smoke	
6. Aircraft or vehicles	
7. Riot or civil commotion	
8. Vandalism	
9. Sprinkler leakage	
10. Sinkhole collapse	
11. Volcanic action	

Fire

Protection against fire loss was the motivation for forming the first insurance companies in the United States. Fire has always been a relatively common cause of loss, and, unlike some other insured perils, fire has the potential to completely destroy a building and its contents. Despite the advances in fire safety technology in the twentieth century, fire is still a frequent and a potentially severe cause of property loss. In 1992, the number of fire losses in both residential and commercial occupancies was approximately 637,500, and the losses totaled over $12.3 billion.[2]

Although the basic and broad forms simply list fire as a covered peril without any further description or definition, the range of losses that may be considered fire losses has been interpreted in many court decisions.

Flame and Oxidation

Courts have generally held that a **fire** must involve (1) a flame or glow and (2) rapid oxidation. The flame or glow requirement may not be met when a substance merely smokes because of a buildup of heat but does not actually flame or glow.

Hostile Versus Friendly Fire

Courts have also interpreted the fire peril (in a named perils policy) to mean "hostile fire," not "friendly fire." A **hostile fire** is generally considered one that is outside an intended receptacle. In contrast, a **friendly fire** is one that is intentionally ignited and remains inside its intended receptacle.

For example, a fire in a fireplace or a wood stove is a friendly fire. Thus, when a maid accidentally threw a ring, mixed in with some trash, into a stove, the court held that a fire insurance policy did not provide coverage for the resulting loss. However, when an ember flies out of a fireplace onto a carpet and sets it on fire, the fire is considered hostile and any resulting loss is covered by fire insurance. Recent decisions, however, have blurred the distinction between hostile and friendly fire.[3]

The modern trend seems to be to categorize a fire as hostile if it burns abnormally (hotter or longer), even if the flames remain confined to the intended place. Usually such excessive heat losses involve furnaces with defective controls. The control does not work properly and the furnace overheats—and may even self destruct.

In an agricultural case, a defective thermostat failed to curtail the heating in a hog barn, the temperature rose to 120 degrees, and fifteen sows died. The Minnesota Supreme Court ruled that the loss was a fire loss under the excessive heat principle. In this case, the court actually extended the principle to include the concept of excessive time. The furnace did not actually overheat—it just operated for an excessive time and caused the barn to become too hot for the hogs.[4]

Some commentators feel that the doctrine of reasonable expectations, which has been adopted by a number of states, will spell the end of the distinction between friendly and hostile fires.[5] Essentially, the doctrine holds that insurance policies should be interpreted based on the reasonable expectations of the insured. It would be the rare insured indeed who would expect a distinction in coverage based on hostile versus friendly fire.[6]

Associated Damage

In addition to covering loss of property actually burned by fire, the fire peril also covers heat and smoke damage caused by a hostile fire, as well as water damage resulting from attempts to extinguish the fire. In addition, other damage to the property—for example, when firefighters break out windows and knock down doors in order to fight fire—is covered by the fire peril.

Lightning

Like fire, lightning is listed as a covered peril without further description. **Lightning** is an electrical discharge from cloud to cloud or between a cloud and the earth, as opposed to artificially generated electrical currents. This point is reinforced by an exclusion of loss or damage caused by artificially generated electrical current. To illustrate this difference, suppose that a surge in voltage destroyed a computer. The policyholder would have coverage if the surge was caused by lightning, but not if the surge was due to excessive voltage generated by the utility company.

Other property losses that naturally flow in an unbroken chain of events from lightning damage are considered to be caused by lightning. Hence, food spoilage due to lightning damage to refrigeration equipment has been held to be covered.

Explosion

Neither the basic nor the broad form defines **explosion**. The accepted meaning of the word includes such things as sudden combustion of gunpowder, dynamite, gasoline, and natural gas. Damage caused by a contractor's blasting would be covered within the explosion peril, as would loss due to the explosion of a container of compressed air.

The explosion peril excludes rupture or bursting due to expansion or swelling of the contents of any building or structure, caused by or resulting from water. If, for example, excess moisture in a grain storage silo or elevator causes a sudden expansion and collapse of the structure, the cause of loss will not be considered an explosion for purposes of coverage.

Another provision of the explosion peril clarifies that "rupture, bursting or operation of pressure relief devices" is not an explosion. This provision refers to the potential damage that might ensue from the operation of safety valves on steam boilers, hot-water tanks, air tanks, and so forth, which intentionally release excess pressure to avoid damage to the vessel to which the safety valve is attached.

Most furnaces are operated by the combustion of fossil fuels (such as coal, fuel oil, or natural gas), which are burned in a combustion chamber or "firebox." The resulting hot gases are routed through passageways while heating water, steam, or air and then escape from the furnace through a flue or chimney. Explosion of the fuel or gases—called **combustion explosion** or **furnace explosion**—is specifically included in the explosion peril.

Combustion explosion does not include explosion of steam boilers, even though the steam boiler is heated by the firebox. More precisely, the basic form and broad form both exclude explosion of steam boilers, steam pipes, steam engines, or steam turbines owned or leased by the insured or operated under the insured's control. (This exclusion is found in the Exclusions section of the basic and broad forms, not in the explosion peril itself.) By exception to the exclusion, loss by fire or combustion explosion that results from an excluded steam boiler explosion is covered. Because steam vessels contain steam under high pressure, they pose a severe explosion risk that insurers underwrite and insure separately under boiler and machinery insurance. The distinction between steam boiler explosion and combustion explosion will be discussed in more detail in Chapter 9.

A question sometimes heard in connection with the explosion peril is whether it covers loss (typically, glass breakage) caused by sonic boom. Sonic boom is the explosion-like sound produced when a shock wave formed at the nose of an aircraft traveling at supersonic speed reaches the ground. Prior commercial property forms specifically excluded sonic boom losses under the explosion peril. Since sonic boom is no longer specifically excluded, many people now regard it as being covered by the explosion peril.

Windstorm and Hail

Generally speaking, a **windstorm** is a wind of unusual strength that has produced general damage in an area at a particular time. Hurricanes and tornadoes are both windstorms. Less violent windstorms also can cause property damage. **Hail** consists of ice particles created by freezing atmospheric conditions. Severe hail can cause substantial damage to autos, buildings, and other property exposed to the elements.

Although tornadoes have great destructive power and can strike almost anywhere in the United States, hurricanes are a bigger threat to property owners and insurers, even though their range in the United States is generally limited to the coastal areas of the Southeast and Hawaii. Of the ten largest catastrophes since 1965 (in terms of insured losses), six were hurricanes. By far, the most severe catastrophe was Hurricane Andrew, which resulted in $15.5 billion in insured losses. It has been estimated that if Hurricane Andrew had struck Miami, a few miles north of where it did strike, the losses could have exceeded $40 billion.[7]

The perils of windstorm and hail are combined in the basic and broad forms and most other property insurance policies that insure against these perils. The basic and broad forms do not define windstorm and hail, but coverage is delineated by provisions describing what is *not* included within those perils.

The windstorm or hail peril provides no coverage for losses caused by (1) frost or cold weather, or (2) ice (other than hail), snow, or sleet—whether driven by wind or not.

The peril also does not include damage to the interior of the building or to its contents caused by rain, snow, sand, or dust unless the force of wind, or a substance driven by the wind, first causes external damage to an insured structure through which the rain, snow, sand, or dust enters. For example, damage caused by rain blown through an open window, roof vents, or cracks is not covered. But if wind breaks the window and wind-blown rain enters the structure through the broken window, the policy will cover the resulting water damage.

Windstorm damage to the interior of the building or to contents is covered even when there is no damage to the exterior. Thus, damage to expensive draperies torn by a windstorm because a window or door was left open would be covered.

Although windstorm damage caused by a hurricane is covered by the windstorm peril, much of the water damage that occurs during a hurricane is not, even though the water may have been wind driven. Damage caused by surface water or overflow from a body of water, whether wind driven or not, is excluded by the water exclusion discussed later in this chapter.

Smoke

The **smoke** peril is limited to smoke causing sudden and accidental loss or damage. Moreover, smoke from agricultural smudging or industrial operations is excluded. Agricultural smudging is the use of smudge pots to protect oranges or other crops against frost damage. No other restrictions apply to the peril. The smoke causing a covered loss may originate on or off the insured's premises.

Smoke from a hostile fire is covered by the fire peril, since the cause of the loss is fire. Hence, the value of the smoke peril is that it extends coverage to smoke resulting from *friendly* fires, such as smoke from a fireplace or furnace. The smoke peril also covers damage caused by smoke when there is insufficient flame or glow for the event to qualify as fire (such as smoldering oily rags).

Aircraft or Vehicles

The aircraft or vehicles peril includes only physical contact between (1) an aircraft (or an object falling from an aircraft), a spacecraft, a self-propelled missile, a vehicle, or an object "thrown up" by a vehicle and (2) covered property or a building or structure containing covered property. The words "vehicle" and "aircraft" are not defined in the policy. However, dictionary definitions of "vehicle" are ordinarily quite broad. For example, *Webster's New World Dictionary* (2nd ed.) defines **vehicle** as "any device or contrivance for carrying or conveying persons or objects, including land conveyances, vessels, aircraft and spacecraft."

The peril requires *physical contact* between the vehicle or other conveyance (or an object thrown up by a conveyance) and the damaged property or the building containing the property. Examples of losses in which the physical contact requirement is not literally met include the following:

- A building is damaged by the vibrations from heavily loaded logging trucks running on an adjacent road.
- A vehicle collides with a pole owned by a telephone company and the pole falls on insured property.
- A chain is attached to a loading dock and to the vehicle, and the vehicle drives away, pulling on the chain, which causes damage to the dock.

It is difficult to predict how a particular court might rule in cases such as the above, but insurers will usually deny coverage in these situations, based on a lack of physical contact between the vehicle (or thrown-up object) and the damaged property.[8]

The peril excludes damage caused by vehicles owned by the named insured or operated in the course of the named insured's business.

Riot or Civil Commotion

The basic form treats these perils together, but does not define them. **Riot** has statutory definitions, but the definitions are not the same in all states. A common definition is quoted below:

> Whenever three or more persons, having assembled for any purpose, disturb the public peace by using force or violence to any other person or to property or threaten or attempt to commit such disturbance or to do an unlawful act by the use of force or violence, accompanied with the power of immediate execution of such threat or attempt, they are guilty of riot.[9]

Some states say two people can commit an act of riot while other states require up to five people. **Civil commotion** has been described as an uprising of citizens. Civil commotion and riot are quite similar, and the two terms should include most uprisings.

The riot or civil commotion peril specifically includes acts of striking employees while occupying the described premises. An example that illustrates the potential severity of this peril occurred in 1975 when strikers at the *Washington Post* became violent and damaged many of the newspaper's printing presses.

Looting frequently accompanies riots. Although theft is not a named peril in the basic form, the riot or civil commotion peril specifically includes "looting occurring at the time and place of a riot or civil commotion." Thus, the basic form covers theft of covered property if it qualifies as looting during a riot or civil commotion.

Vandalism

The basic and broad forms define **vandalism** as "willful and malicious damage to, or destruction of, the described property." Thus, both intent ("willful") and motive ("malicious") must be established for a loss to be considered vandalism.

The vandalism peril excludes damage "to glass (other than glass building blocks) that is part of a building, structure, or an outside sign." However, damage to *other property* caused by breakage of glass by vandals is covered. For example, if vandals threw a brick through the display window of a furniture store, the glass breakage itself would not be covered, but any damage to the displayed furniture by the brick or the flying glass would be.

The vandalism peril also excludes loss caused by theft, other than building damage caused by the forcible entry or exit of burglars. Coverage for property actually taken by burglars can be purchased under either the special causes-of-loss form or under various commercial crime forms to be discussed in Chapter 10.

If a building is vacant beyond sixty consecutive days, vandalism coverage is suspended. This provision is found in the BPP vacancy clause, discussed in Chapter 3.

Sprinkler Leakage

Both forms define **sprinkler leakage** to include leakage or discharge of *any substance* from an automatic sprinkler system. Thus, the peril includes not only the discharge of water, but also accidental discharges from a system containing any other extinguishing agents, such as carbon dioxide, a dry chemical powder, or an antifreeze solution. "Automatic sprinkler system" is broadly defined in the form to include components such as sprinkler heads, piping, tanks, pumps, and stand pipes.

The definition of sprinkler leakage also includes the collapse of automatic sprinkler system tanks. System tanks are sometimes located in separate water towers, but they often stand on the roof of a building. When such a tank collapses, the weight of the collapsing tank can cause extensive damage. In addition, a tremendous amount of water may be released. For example, a 50,000 gallon tank filled to capacity contains over 200 tons of water in addition to the weight of the tank itself.

The sprinkler leakage peril also covers the cost to repair or replace damaged parts of the sprinkler system if the damage results in sprinkler leakage or is caused by freezing. The insurer will also pay for tearing out and replacing any part of the building to make these repairs. In either case, however, the building must be covered property under the policy.

Property protected by an automatic sprinkler system receives a dramatic rate reduction. Often the reduction in property insurance premiums is sufficient to pay for the sprinkler installation in only a few years. When allowing such a discount, insurers want to be sure that the protection is maintained. Accordingly, the insurer can attach to the policy the **protective safeguards endorsement**, which states that coverage is automatically suspended if the insured knows that the sprinkler system is not operational and fails to notify the insurance company. However, if the system is shut off due to breakage, leakage, freezing conditions, or the opening of sprinkler heads, no notice is necessary if full protection is restored within forty-eight hours.

The BPP vacancy clause suspends sprinkler leakage coverage when a building is vacant for more than sixty days, unless the system is protected against freezing or a vacancy permit is obtained.

Sinkhole Collapse

The peril of sinkhole collapse, formerly covered by a separate endorsement, is now included in the basic and broad forms. The forms define **sinkhole collapse** as "loss or damage caused by the sudden sinking or collapse of land into underground empty spaces created by the action of water on limestone or dolomite." Dolomite is a rock heavier than, but similar to, limestone.

Although sinkhole collapse is a covered peril, the coverage is for damage to covered property caused by sinkhole collapse—it is not intended to pay for damage to the land on which the building was situated. As noted in Chapter 3, land is not covered property under the BPP. This intention is strengthened by a statement that appears as part of the sinkhole collapse peril, specifically excluding coverage for the cost of filling sinkholes.

The peril also excludes loss caused by the sinking or collapse of land into *man-made* underground cavities. Because the sinkhole collapse peril refers to "empty spaces created by the action of water on limestone or dolomite," it would not cover mine subsidence (collapse of land into an underground mine) in any event; the exclusion merely reinforces the point. In several states with a history of mining, a mine subsidence coverage endorsement is required to be offered by insurers on certain structures.

Volcanic Action

The addition of the "volcanic action" peril can be attributed directly to the eruption of Mount St. Helens in 1980, the first volcanic eruption in the contiguous forty-eight states since 1914. Both forms define **volcanic action** as:

> direct loss or damage resulting from the eruption of a volcano when the loss or damage is caused by :
>
> a. Airborne volcanic blast or airborne shock waves;
>
> b. Ash, dust or particulate matter; or
>
> c. Lava flow.

The volcanic action peril also states that it does not cover costs to remove volcanic debris that does not cause physical loss or damage.

Volcanic action should not be confused with *volcanic eruption*. The earth movement exclusion found in the basic, broad, and special causes-of-loss forms specifically excludes coverage for "volcanic eruption, explosion or effusion" but by exception allows coverage to apply to resulting damage by volcanic action or fire. Earthquake and volcanic eruption can be insured under the causes of loss—earthquake form, described later in this chapter.

The volcanic action peril and the volcanic eruption peril do not necessarily include all causes of loss connected with volcanoes. In the Mount St. Helens eruption, much of the damage resulted from floods caused by melting of snow, displacement of mountain lake water by mudflows, and heavy rains caused by condensation of steam from the eruption. Flooding and mudflows are not covered under any of the "commercial property" causes-of-loss forms. Other forms of flood insurance are discussed later in this text. Fire damage resulting from a volcano is covered by the fire peril.

The limits and deductibles of the BPP apply separately to each occurrence. There might be some question as to whether successive eruptions of a volcano are one occurrence or multiple occurrences—subject to one set of limits and deductibles or several. This problem is avoided by the clarifying statement under the volcanic action peril that all volcanic eruptions that occur within any 168-hour period (seven days) will constitute a single occurrence.

Additional Perils Covered by Broad Form

In addition to the perils covered by both the basic form and the broad form, the broad form covers four additional perils:

1. Breakage of glass
2. Falling objects
3. Weight of snow, ice, or sleet
4. Water damage

Also added with the broad form is the "additional coverage—collapse" provision.

Breakage of Glass

Even in the absence of the glass breakage peril, the basic and broad forms both cover breakage of glass caused by an insured peril, such as fire, explosion, windstorm, or volcanic shock waves. However, glass can be broken by other perils. A common cause of glass breakage is vandalism, and the vandalism peril specifically excludes breakage of glass (other than glass building blocks).

The glass breakage peril covers breakage of building glass not covered by some other named peril and not otherwise excluded. Thus, coverage is actually for all causes of glass breakage not specifically removed by the form's exclusions. However, this coverage is limited to $100 per pane of glass and $500 in any one occurrence. The per pane and occurrence limits do not apply to glass breakage covered under any other named peril. For example, glass breakage caused by vandals is subject to the $100/$500 limitation, but glass breakage caused by a fire is not.

Coverage applies to the glass itself and also to property cut or otherwise damaged by breaking glass. The BPP vacancy clause suspends glass breakage coverage after the building has been vacant for more than sixty consecutive days.

The glass breakage peril applies only to glass that is part of a building or structure. Neon tubing, even if attached to the building, is specifically excluded. (Breakage of neon tubing attached to the building is covered, however, if caused by another covered cause of loss.)

A broader form of glass coverage, which does not impose the $100/$500 limits, is available under the glass coverage form, discussed in Chapter 6.

Falling Objects

The broad form does not define what a falling object is. Thus, it could be a branch falling from a tree or an entire tree that falls onto a building. A **falling object** could also be a rock, a meteorite, or anything else that falls.

The peril excludes damage to personal property in the open. It also excludes damage to the interior of a building or structure, or property inside a building or structure, unless the falling object first damages the roof or an outside wall. If, for example, an overhead conveyor inside a factory building dropped a heavy object, the resulting loss to both the object and any property below the object would not be covered by the falling objects peril.

Weight of Snow, Ice, or Sleet

The buildup of snow, ice, or sleet on a building's roof can exert great force on the structure, causing either roof collapse or structural damage to rafters or other building elements. Flat roofs are especially susceptible to damage by weight of snow, ice, or sleet. This peril has caused many severe building and contents losses over the years. The peril excludes gutters and downspouts and personal property outside of buildings or structures.

Water Damage

This peril might be more appropriately titled *limited* water damage; it does not cover loss caused by flooding, surface water, and other sources of water excluded by the causes-of-loss forms. In general terms, the water damage peril covers damage caused by accidental leakage from plumbing or appliances. Since sprinkler leakage is covered as a separate peril, it is excluded from coverage under the water damage peril. The broad form defines the water damage peril in part as:

> accidental discharge or leakage of water or steam as the direct result of the breaking or cracking of any part of a system or appliance containing water or steam, other than an Automatic Sprinkler System.

If the building or structure containing the system or appliance is covered property, the insurer also agrees to pay the cost to tear out and replace any part of the building or structure to repair damage to the system or appliance. The water damage peril of previous editions of property forms provided similar "tearing-out" coverage but *excluded* the cost of repairing or replacing the system or appliance itself. In place of that exclusion, the current water damage peril excludes "the cost to repair any defect that caused the loss or damage." Thus, unless the leakage was caused by a defect in the system or appliance, the cost of repairing or replacing the system itself is now covered. If, for example, a plumbing leak resulting in water damage was caused not by a defect in the system but by freezing (unless excluded, as discussed below) or by the negligence of a contractor working on the insured's building, the cost of repairing the system would be covered. Only the defect causing the loss or damage would be excluded.

In addition to the exclusion of defects, the water damage peril is subject to two other exclusions, relating to continuous seepage and freezing.

Any loss due to continuous or repeated seepage or leakage of water or steam from an insured system is excluded if it occurs over a period of more than fourteen days. This provision eliminates coverage for losses (such as rotting of flooring or structural members) that result from a gradual seepage of water down a wall or through a floor.

Freezing of plumbing can often be anticipated and prevented. The intention of insurers is to cover only those freezing losses that occur despite reasonable preventive measures. Therefore, water damage caused by freezing is excluded unless "you" (the insured) (1) "do your best" to maintain heat in the building or (2) shut off the water supply and drain the equipment if heat is not maintained. What constitutes "doing your best" to maintain heat involves a question of fact that, in borderline cases, may have to be decided by the courts.

As discussed in Chapter 3, the BPP vacancy provision eliminates all coverage for water damage that occurs after the building has been vacant for more than sixty days.

Additional Coverage—Collapse

Property policies once treated "collapse" as an insured peril. Since 1983, when ISO property forms were revised in response to the concurrent causation doctrine, collapse has been treated as an "additional coverage" rather than as a peril.

Under the **additional coverage–collapse**, the insurer agrees to pay for loss or damage caused by risks of direct loss "involving" collapse of a building or any part of a building caused by certain named perils. The named perils include all the broad form perils plus the following:

- Hidden decay
- Hidden insect or vermin damage
- Weight of people or personal property
- Weight of rain that collects on a roof
- Use of defective materials or methods in construction, remodeling, or renovation if the collapse occurs during the course of construction, remodeling, or renovation. (Collapse of a *completed* building caused by defective materials or construction methods is *not* covered.)

Certain items of property that may be excluded under the regular broad form perils are covered for collapse losses and caused by hidden decay or the other additional collapse perils listed above. These items include outdoor antennas; awnings, gutters, and downspouts; yard fixtures; outdoor swimming pools; fences; piers, wharves, and docks; beach or diving platforms or appurtenances; retaining walls; and walks, roadways, and other paved surfaces.

Collapse is not defined but is limited by a statement that it does not include settling, cracking, shrinkage, bulging, or expansion. The exact point at which settling, cracking, and so forth, ends and collapse begins has been the subject of much litigation. Insurers generally view collapse as involving a sudden substantial structural impairment but not necessarily total disintegration.

Basic and Broad Form Exclusions

In addition to the limitations and exclusions contained in the basic and broad form descriptions of covered perils, both forms have a separate section entitled "Exclusions."

Several of these exclusions are termed "special exclusions" because they apply only to certain coverage forms other than the BPP. Because these coverage forms are discussed in later chapters of this text, the special exclusions that pertain only to those forms are not described here. They will be described along with the pertinent coverage forms in later chapters.

The exclusions discussed here apply to the building and personal property coverage form or any other "commercial property" coverage form. Notice how these exclusions deal with the problem of causation involving both covered and excluded perils: They are specific about whether the presence of a covered peril does or does not create coverage. Some eliminate coverage for the excluded type of loss even if the cause of loss is one of the named perils in the form. For example, the war exclusion eliminates coverage for a building fire caused by an act of war, even though fire is a covered cause of loss. In contrast, some of the exclusions make an exception for fire (and, in some cases, other perils) that ensue from the excluded cause. For example, the earthquake exclusion states that fire or explosion loss resulting from an earthquake is *covered.* The basic and broad form exclusions are discussed in more detail below.

The lead-in paragraph to the exclusions, in response to concurrent causation claims, states that the exclusions apply to loss or damage caused directly or indirectly by any of the excluded causes and "regardless of any other cause or event that contributes concurrently or in any sequence to the loss."

Ordinance or Law

Many jurisdictions have building codes or other laws regulating building construction. Buildings already standing when such regulations are adopted are usually permitted to continue to be used and occupied even though they do not conform to the current building code or law. However, when a nonconforming building is severely damaged, the regulations often provide that it may be rebuilt only if it is made to conform to current requirements.

Where they exist, such laws increase potential loss severity. Following a loss in which the law prohibits repair of the damaged building, the insured actually loses the value of the undamaged portion of the building and also incurs the expense of demolishing the undamaged portion and removing its debris. If it is more expensive to erect a conforming building as a replacement than it would be to erect an identical building, the insured may also incur an increased cost of construction.

Ordinances and laws can increase the cost of repairs in other ways, even if demolition is not required. Building codes are constantly updated; restoration may require additional features not included in the original building. Such features might include additional fire exits; installation of a roof more resistant to fire; wiring, heating, or plumbing systems that comply with the current code; or the installation of a sprinkler system or an elevator. These upgrades do not require demolition of the building and are frequently required whenever there are any repairs or new construction. Even relatively new buildings may face an ordinance or law exposure due to the Americans with Disabilities Act of 1992, which requires improved access for the handicapped.

Because ordinance or law exposures are not anticipated by basic premium rates, the causes-of-loss forms contain an **ordinance or law exclusion**, which excludes loss resulting from:

> The enforcement of any ordinance or law:
>
> (1) Regulating the construction, use or repair of any property; or
>
> (2) Requiring the tearing down of any property, including the cost of removing its debris.

This exclusion has not been uniformly applied by the courts. When the building is physically but not legally repairable (due to an ordinance or law) some decisions have denied the insured recovery for the undamaged portion of the building. In other cases, courts have allowed the insured to collect a total loss. In states with valued policy laws (which require the insurer to pay the full policy limit in the event of a total loss), courts uniformly reject the application of the exclusion and treat the building as a constructive total loss. However, when the ordinance or law permits the building to be repaired but imposes requirements that increase the cost of repairs, the exclusion has generally been applied to eliminate payment for the increased cost.[10]

The ordinance or law exposure is excluded because some insureds do not need the coverage, not because it is too difficult to insure. The excluded loss exposures can be insured under the ordinance or law coverage endorsement, which can be added to a "commercial property" policy for an additional premium. This endorsement is described at the end of this chapter along with other "commercial property" endorsements for insuring excluded exposures.

Earth Movement

Although earthquake insurance is available under specialized forms, earthquake and other types of earth movement are excluded from almost all standard forms for insuring buildings and contents. The earthquake peril is difficult to insure, for several reasons. First, the geographic areas most likely to have earthquakes are somewhat limited, resulting in a poor spread of risk. Second, predictions regarding potential earthquake frequency and severity have been poor—making it difficult to establish a rating system that reflects loss potential. Third, and perhaps most significantly, earthquakes can cause catastrophic loss: many separate buildings and their contents are affected by a single earthquake and its aftershocks.

The 1994 earthquake centered in Northridge, California, is estimated to have caused insured property damage of $4.9 billion, which would make it one of the costliest disasters ever for the U.S. insurance industry, surpassed only by Hurricane Andrew at $15.5 billion.[11] A study by the Federal Emergency Management Agency estimated that if the 1906 San Francisco quake had occurred in 1988, it could have resulted in $38 billion in property damage.[12] Even New York City, which last experienced an earthquake in excess of 5.0 on the Richter scale in 1884, is estimated by a panel of experts from the American Society of Civil Engineers to have a 60 percent chance of an earthquake of sufficient force to result in $25 billion in property damage.[13]

The **earth movement exclusion** in the "commercial property" causes-of-loss forms eliminates coverage not only for earthquakes but also for any other type of earth movement, as well as volcanic eruption, explosion, or effusion. (See the earlier discussion of the volcanic *action* peril for the distinction between volcanic eruption and volcanic action. Volcanic *effusion* is the relatively quiet flow of lava without explosions or the ejection of fragments.) The exclusion is expressed as follows:

(1) Any earth movement (other than sinkhole collapse), such as an earthquake, landslide, mine subsidence or earth sinking, rising or shifting. But if loss or damage by fire or explosion results, we will pay for that resulting loss or damage.

(2) Volcanic eruption, explosion or effusion. But if loss or damage by fire, building glass breakage or volcanic action results, we will pay for that resulting loss or damage.

The exceptions to the exclusion are important aspects of "commercial property" coverage. Fire following earthquake is often a major source of loss, especially in congested metropolitan areas.

For those who desire coverage for damage caused by earth movement and volcanic eruption, coverage is available under the ISO causes of loss—earthquake form or under independently developed forms, such as difference in conditions (DIC) policies. The causes of loss—earthquake form is discussed at the end of this chapter. DIC insurance is discussed in Chapter 14.

Governmental Action

In some situations, police, firefighters, or other government officials must take control of an insured's property to protect the common good of the community. For example, a governmental agency might confiscate contaminated property. Since insurers do not intend to cover such intentional actions, the causes-of-loss forms contain a **governmental action exclusion**, which excludes any "seizure or destruction of property by order of governmental authority." However, the insurer agrees to pay for acts of destruction ordered by governmental authority at the time of a fire in order to prevent its spread in circumstances where fire is a covered peril.

Nuclear Hazard

The **nuclear hazard exclusion** excludes loss or damage caused by "nuclear reaction or radiation, or radioactive contamination, however caused." However, if loss or damage by fire results from the excluded events, the insurer agrees to pay for the resulting loss or damage. For example, if a nuclear reactor should go out of control and cause a fire, the fire damage would be covered, although the damage caused by the nuclear reaction—apart from the ensuing fire—would not be covered. If a fire causes the release of radioactive particles, contamination damage from them is not covered. (Coverage for fire damage in a nuclear war would still be precluded by the war exclusion, discussed below.)

Insurance for nuclear power plants is available from special pools that insurers have established. However, users of radioactive isotopes for medical, industrial, or research purposes can usually purchase radioactive contamination coverage by endorsement to their regular building and contents coverage. The radioactive contamination endorsement for use with ISO "commercial property" policies is discussed at the end of this chapter.

Off-Premises Services

The **off-premises services exclusion** eliminates coverage for loss caused by the failure of power or other utility service supplied to the described location, but only if the failure occurs away from the described location. If, for example, a fire at a public generating station causes a power outage that in turn causes spoilage of refrigerated food at the insured's store, the spoilage loss will not be covered even though it was proximately caused by fire, an insured peril. If, instead, the power outage was caused by lightning damage to equipment at the described location, the exclusion would not apply, since the cause of loss was covered and the power failure did not occur away from the described location.

The exclusion also does not apply—in other words, there is coverage—if loss or damage by a covered cause of loss results from the off-premises services failure. For example, loss of natural gas or electric service might cause a failure of a building's heating system. Water damage resulting from leaks in frozen pipes would be covered under the broad causes-of-loss form.

Loss of business income is the most common consequence of off-premises service interruptions. A fire in a power generating plant in lower Manhattan shut down dozens of firms in the Wall Street area for up to two weeks, causing millions of dollars of business income loss. However, serious physical losses can also occur. Hurricane Hugo demolished the overhead power lines serving an aluminum refining plant. Without power to continue operation, the molten aluminum in the huge electric furnace kettles hardened and had to be removed with jackhammers. The resulting loss to material, machinery, and equipment plus debris removal exceeded $1 million.

Coverage for losses resulting from failure of off-premises services can be insured under endorsements described later in this chapter.

War and Military Action

Most property insurance policies exclude loss caused by war and other hostilities, because losses caused by war are potentially highly catastrophic. Although war risk insurance is widely available on ocean vessels, aircraft, and ocean and air cargo, war risk coverage on land-based property is generally unavailable except in special circumstances. During World War II, for example, the U.S. government and a couple of commercial insurers offered coverage for continental U.S. locations.

The **war and military action exclusion** in the "commercial property" causes-of-loss forms excludes loss by insurrections, civil wars, and undeclared wars, as well as by formally declared wars. While the riots that have wracked many large cities have sometimes been colloquially referred to as insurrections or rebellions, there has never been the usurping of governmental power in the U.S. that would be necessary to trigger this exclusion. Court interpretation of the war exclusion has generally restricted its application to conflicts between entities with at least some claim to sovereignty.[14]

Unlike some other exclusions, the war exclusion contains no exception for ensuing fire. Fires resulting from war are not covered because of the potential for catastrophic loss. Some of the "fire storms" that resulted from allied bombing raids in World War II destroyed entire cities.

Water

The **water exclusion** is basically intended to exclude coverage for flood-type losses as carefully defined. Flood is generally considered a peril that is difficult to insure for two reasons: (1) floods can cause widespread catastrophic loss, and (2) the locations most susceptible to flood are low-lying areas that can be readily identified. The latter can lead to adverse selection against an insurer; that is, the entities most likely to purchase flood coverage are those who are also most likely to have a flood.

The exclusion eliminates coverage for loss caused by the following:

> (1) Flood, surface water, waves, tides, tidal waves, overflow of any body of water or their spray, all whether driven by wind or not;
>
> (2) Mudslide or mudflow;
>
> (3) Water that backs up from a sewer or drain; or
>
> (4) Water under the ground surface pressing on, or flowing or seeping through:
>
> (a) Foundations, walls, floors or paved surfaces;
>
> (b) Basements, whether paved or not; or
>
> (c) Doors, windows or other openings.
>
> But if loss or damage by fire, explosion or sprinkler leakage results, we will pay for that resulting loss or damage.

This exclusion does not eliminate coverage for all water damage. As previously noted, the basic and broad forms both cover water damage resulting from efforts to extinguish a hostile fire, as well as sprinkler leakage. Moreover, the broad form specifically covers the "water damage" peril. However, that peril deals essentially with damage caused by water that accidentally leaks from a plumbing system or an appliance, whereas the water exclusion deals with what might be considered naturally occurring water. In fact, many courts do not apply the water exclusion when the water originates from an artificial source such as a broken water main.

The water exclusion applies not only to runoff and surface water but also to underground water that seeps into a basement and water that backs up from sewers or drains. Coverage for some types of water damage is available from the National Flood Insurance Program and under difference in conditions (DIC) policies, both of which are discussed in Chapter 14. In addition, some insurers provide water damage coverage under the BPP and similar forms by either deleting part of the exclusion or adding independently developed coverage endorsements.

Additional Exclusions

In addition to the seven exclusions discussed above (and apart from the "special exclusions" that will be discussed in later chapters), the basic and broad forms each contain a second set of exclusions. These exclusions do not contain the concurrent causation lead-in language; their lead-in language simply says that the insurer "will not pay for loss or damage resulting from" any of the excluded perils.

Three additional exclusions appear in both the basic form and the broad form. Two other exclusions, dealing with water leakage, are included in the basic form only, since the broad form covers certain types of water leakage.

Artificially Generated Electrical Current

Both forms exclude loss caused by artificially generated electrical current, including arcing, that disturbs electrical devices, appliances, or wires. However, damage by an ensuing fire loss, but not any other peril, is covered. Damage caused by lightning (which is naturally—not artificially—generated electrical current) is covered under both forms and is not affected by this exclusion.

Explosion of Steam Boilers

As explained earlier in connection with the explosion peril, both the basic and the broad form exclude damage caused by explosion of "steam boilers, steam pipes, steam engines or steam turbines owned or leased by you, or operated under your control." The exclusion does not apply to combustion explosion or resulting loss by fire.

An important nuance of this exclusion is that it does not apply to steam boiler explosions when the boiler or other steam equipment is not owned or leased by the insured or operated under the insured's control. Thus, for example, a tenant's "commercial property" policy would cover damage to the tenant's personal property resulting from the explosion of a steam boiler in the landlord's building that the tenant did not own, operate, or control. In most cases, the tenant's insurer, after paying the tenant's loss, would be able to make a subrogation recovery against the landlord as long as the tenant had not waived its recovery rights against the landlord.

Mechanical Breakdown

Both the basic form and the broad form exclude loss or damage caused by mechanical breakdown, including rupture or bursting caused by centrifugal force. However, the exclusion states that the insurer will pay for resulting loss or damage by a covered cause of loss. Thus, for example, both forms would cover a fire that resulted from friction caused by the mechanical breakdown of a production machine.

Physical damage and resulting business interruption caused by the excluded perils discussed above—electrical disturbance, steam boiler explosion, and mechanical breakdown—can be insured under a boiler and machinery policy, as will be discussed in more detail in Chapter 9.

Other Basic Form Exclusions

The basic form contains two additional exclusions. These exclusions reinforce the fact that the basic form does not cover the types of damage covered by the broad form's "water damage" peril. However, the exclusions contain exceptions to clarify that breakage of plumbing systems and appliances and resulting water damage are covered if caused by a covered cause of loss. If, for example, a water pipe bursts because of a natural gas explosion (a covered cause of loss), the damage to the pipe and the resulting water damage to other insured property would be covered. However, if the water pipe bursts because of freezing, earth movement, or some other peril that is not covered, no aspect of the loss would be covered by the basic form.

Limitation on Loss of Animals

The basic and broad forms both contain a "limitation," which states that the insurer will pay for loss of animals only if they are killed or their destruction is made necessary. Thus, for example, a pet store owner is covered for death or necessary destruction of animals resulting from a covered cause of loss. The pet store owner would not be covered for decrease in value of *living* animals even though the decrease in value was caused by a covered peril.

Causes of Loss—Special Form

The broadest option for covered causes of loss is the causes of loss—special form. The special form provides what insurance professionals refer to as "all-risks" insurance. An "all-risks" form covers any accidental cause of loss unless the form specifically excludes it.

Although the word "all" no longer appears in the insuring agreement, the phrase "all-risks" remains in wide use among insurance professionals and thus is used throughout this text to describe coverages of this type. However, the term "all-risks" is almost certain to be misleading to nonprofessionals and therefore should not be used in describing the coverage to clients, claimants, or other members of the public.

Advantages of Special Form

"All-risks" insurance begins with an insuring agreement that simply provides coverage for direct physical loss to covered property. With this statement, the burden of proof as to coverage falls on the insurer—not the insured. As long as the insured can demonstrate that a direct physical loss has occurred to covered property, the cause of loss is presumed to be covered unless the insurer can prove that an exclusion applies.

In contrast, named perils forms such as the basic and broad forms place the burden of proof on the insured: unless the *insured* can prove that one of the named perils caused the loss, the insurer has no obligation to pay. Which party has the burden of proof can make a major difference when the cause of loss is not entirely clear.

Another advantage of the special form is that it does not exclude many types of theft loss, meaning that such types of theft are covered. Beyond that, since the named perils of the broad form seem to encompass most imaginable circumstances, insureds and students of insurance sometimes ask for examples of "all-risks" type losses that would not also be covered under a broad form. Some examples include:

- *Friendly fire*. The named peril "fire" is generally held to mean only *hostile* fire. No such limitation applies to the special form and most other "all-risks" forms since they do not exclude damage by friendly fire. Although court decisions are eroding the doctrine of friendly fire, an insured might have to institute a lawsuit to prevail under a named perils policy.
- *Vehicle damage*. The aircraft or vehicles peril of the basic and broad forms contains a contact requirement. As discussed earlier, vehicles can damage

property without making contact with the damaged property. The special form covers damage by vehicles whether or not there is direct physical contact. The special form also covers damage caused by vehicles regardless of whether the damage-causing vehicle is owned or operated by the insured. The basic and broad forms exclude coverage when the vehicle is owned by the insured or operated in the course of the insured's business.

- *Water damage caused by "ice dam."* When melting snow or ice backs up under roof shingles (usually because gutters are clogged with ice), the resulting water damage is covered by the special form but not by the basic or broad forms.

These examples help to illustrate the breadth of "all-risks" coverage. The key point is this: a cause of loss that is not specifically excluded is covered.

Another consideration for insureds and students is the relatively small additional premium charged for special form coverage instead of broad form coverage. The vast majority of risk managers and experienced insurance producers prefer the special form to the basic and broad forms.

Exclusions and Limitations

The special form contains the following exclusions discussed earlier in connection with the basic and broad forms:

- Ordinance or law
- Earth movement
- Governmental action
- Nuclear hazard
- Off-premises services
- War and military action
- Water damage
- Steam boiler explosion
- Disturbance by artificially generated electric current
- Mechanical breakdown

In addition, the special form contains many other exclusions and limitations. These exclusions and limitations serve various purposes, including the following:

- To duplicate some conditions attached to the broad form perils
- To restrict coverage for some exposures to "specified causes of loss" instead of "all-risks"

- To eliminate coverage for some exposures that are difficult to insure or normally insured under other policies
- To avoid application of the concurrent causation doctrine

Exclusions To Match Broad Form Conditions

The special form exclusions and limitations that duplicate broad form conditions are described below.

Windstorm or Hail

In line with a provision in the windstorm or hail peril, the special form excludes damage by rain, snow, sleet, ice, sand, or dust to the interior of a building unless the building itself is first damaged. However, an exception in the special form provides coverage for loss or damage resulting from the thawing of snow, sleet, or ice on the building or structure. This exception provides for the "ice dam" coverage noted earlier.

Smoke

Smoke from agricultural smudging or industrial operations is excluded, as under the smoke peril.

Weight of Ice, Snow, or Sleet

Like the broad form peril of this name, the special form excludes damage to gutters and downspouts caused by weight of ice, snow, or sleet; and damage by rain, snow, ice, or sleet to personal property in the open.

Water Damage

Like the broad form water damage peril, the special form excludes (1) seepage or leakage that continues over a period of fourteen days or more and (2) freezing of a plumbing system or appliance that occurs when the insured failed to take appropriate safeguards.

Collapse

The special form excludes collapse so that the only coverage provided for collapse is under the special form's additional coverage for collapse, which is identical to the collapse coverage in the broad form.

Glass Breakage

The special form applies the $100 per pane and $500 per occurrence limits of the broad-form glass breakage peril. To make these limits apply in the same manner as under the broad form, the special form states that the limits do not apply to loss or damage caused by the "specified causes of loss" other than vandalism. (The "specified causes of loss" are described below.)

Property Covered Only for "Specified Causes of Loss"

Although the "all-risks" approach applies to most property subject to coverage by the special form, some types of property are covered only for the "specified causes of loss."

The "specified causes of loss" are listed in the definitions section of the special form. The specified causes of loss are the perils listed in the broad form (other than glass breakage), but without all of the elaboration of that form. In some cases, the lack of elaboration has the effect of providing broader coverage. For example, since there is no exclusion for vehicle damage when the property owner is driving the vehicle that damages covered property, damage caused by an owner-driven vehicle would be covered.

The types of property that the special form covers for "specified causes of loss" only are valuable papers and records, animals, fragile articles, and contractors' tools and equipment.

Valuable Papers and Records

Valuable papers and records can be insured on an "all-risks" basis under an inland marine form discussed in Chapter 11. Another advantage of the inland marine form is that it can be arranged with a much higher limit than the $1,000 coverage extension under the BPP coverage form.

Animals

Loss of animals that are covered property is covered only if they are killed or their destruction is made necessary because of direct loss by one of the "specified causes of loss." This restriction prevents the insurer from covering death due to diseases or other natural causes, an exposure that can be covered under highly specialized animal mortality insurance, as described in Chapter 13.

Fragile Articles

Breakage of fragile articles—such as glassware, statuary, marbles, chinaware, and porcelain—is covered only if caused by the specified causes of loss. Building glass, photographic or scientific instrument lenses, and containers of property held for sale are exempt from this restriction. This exemption could be of considerable value to an organization that manufactures or sells a product contained in glass bottles.

It is significant that the limitation applies only to *breakage* of such articles. As long as loss is not by breakage, the insured still has the benefit of "all-risks" coverage. For example, theft of such articles would be covered even though it is not a specified cause of loss.

Builders' Equipment

Builders' machinery, tools, and equipment owned by or entrusted to the named insured while away from the described premises are covered only for specified causes of loss. "All-risks" coverage applies while such property is located on the described premises. An inalnd marine contractors equipment floater policy can be obtained to provide "all-risks" coverage on mobile equipment while located anywhere in the policy territory.

Maintenance Exclusion

A long exclusion sometimes called the **maintenance exclusion** eliminates coverage for losses that can be avoided through ordinary property maintenance or that are almost certain to occur as natural, expected consequences of the passage of time. Arguably, many of these perils, because they are certain to occur given time, are not "risks of loss" in the first place, since "risk" implies a situation in which loss may *or may not* occur. In any event, the maintenance exclusion eliminates coverage for loss or damage caused by the following:

- Wear and tear
- Rust, corrosion, fungus, decay, deterioration, hidden or latent defect
- Smog
- Settling, cracking, shrinking, or expansion
- Insects, birds, rodents, or other animals
- Mechanical breakdown (other than resulting loss caused by elevator collision)
- Dampness or dryness of atmosphere, changes in or extremes of temperature, and marring or scratching (as respects personal property only)

The maintenance exclusion contains an exception: the insurer will pay for resulting loss or damage by "specified causes of loss" or by building glass breakage. If, for example, a bird's nest causes an attic fan motor to overheat and start a fire, the resulting fire damage will be covered.

Theft-Related Exclusions and Limitations

Unlike the basic and broad forms, the special form covers theft losses. However, the special form contains several theft-related exclusions and limitations. Without these exclusions and limitations, the special form would cover an extraordinarily broad range of thefts—a scope of coverage that would make the insurance prohibitively expensive for most insureds.

Employee Dishonesty

Although commonly referred to as "employee dishonesty," the excluded exposure actually applies to a broader range of persons. The **employee dishonesty exclusion** eliminates coverage for dishonest or criminal acts of the named insured; any of the named insured's partners, employees, directors, trustees, or authorized representatives; or anyone else (such as a bailee) to whom the named insured entrusts covered property for any purpose. An exception to the exclusion provides coverage for acts of destruction by the named insured's employees. For example, arson by a disgruntled employee would be covered despite the exclusion. Theft by employees is clearly excluded, however. Employee dishonesty is insurable under commercial crime forms, as discussed in Chapter 10.

Voluntary Parting

The **voluntary parting exclusion** eliminates coverage if the insured or anyone else to whom the insured has entrusted covered property (such as an employee or a bailee) voluntarily hands the property over to another as the result of "any fraudulent scheme, trick, device, or false pretense."

This exclusion does not apply unless the property was given to the trickster *voluntarily*. In some cases, one person will use trickery—such as a feigned illness or flirtatious behavior—to distract one or more store employees while an accomplice steals money or merchandise. These types of thefts are not reached by the exclusion since the property was not *voluntarily* handed over; the duped employee usually is not even aware that property has been taken during his or her watch.

The exclusion also does not eliminate coverage when the property is handed over voluntarily in an armed robbery or any other situation in which a threat of violence is present. For the exclusion to apply, the voluntary parting must be induced by trickery or false pretenses, not a threat of violence.

An example of an excluded "voluntary parting" loss is when an antique dealer allows a customer to take home a vase or table to see how it will "fit in" with the customer's decor but the "customer" never returns. The dealer, who thought he had obtained sufficient security by holding the customer's charge card later finds that the card is bogus. An excluded trick or device loss can also occur when a storekeeper hands over sold-but-not-delivered merchandise to someone who impersonates the rightful owner.

Although insurance against trick or device losses, called false pretense coverage, is a standard option under commercial auto insurance covering auto dealers, it is not a standard "commercial property" option.

Unauthorized Instructions

Another theft-related exclusion is similar to the voluntary parting exclusion. It eliminates coverage for property transferred to a person or place outside the described premises on the basis of unauthorized instructions.

Thus, the following loss would not be covered: The insured has entrusted covered property to a repair shop. The shop, acting on an imposter's telephone message, delivers the covered property to someone other than the insured, and that person absconds with the property.

Another loss that would not be covered because of the exclusion is that which could occur if a computer hacker gained illegal access to the insured's computer system and entered unauthorized instructions to send covered property to a fictitious customer. If the covered property is subsequently delivered and thereby lost, the insured's policy will not cover the loss. This exposure is ordinarily insurable under the computer fraud coverage form that is a part of the ISO commercial crime program (Chapter 10).

Inventory Shortages and Unexplained Disappearance

The special form also excludes loss of property if the only evidence of the loss or damage is a shortage discovered on taking inventory, or if no physical evidence is available to explain the loss.

Inventory shortages, in the absence of any other signs of theft, are not conclusive evidence that a covered theft loss has occurred. Inventory shortages can be caused by employee dishonesty (which is excluded) or bookkeeping errors (in which case no physical loss has actually occurred) just as easily as by burglary, shoplifting, or some other form of theft covered by the special form. The **inventory shortage exclusion** is found in virtually all types of property insurance covering theft. The exclusion is discussed in more detail in Chapter 10 in connection with commercial crime insurance.

Similarly, an observation that property has disappeared is insufficient, in and of itself, to verify that the disappearance is attributable to a peril not otherwise excluded. Signs of a forcible entry into the building, for example, will satisfy the insurer in most cases that the loss has been caused by a burglary and is therefore covered. In the absence of physical evidence sufficient to establish that loss was by a covered cause (that is, by one that is not excluded), the insurer will ordinarily resist payment on the basis of the exclusion, which is sometimes referred to as the **unexplained disappearance exclusion**. Some policies exclude *mysterious* disappearance, with the same intent.

Disappearance of money and securities is an insurable loss exposure under a specialized crime insurance form to be discussed in Chapter 10. Most other policies covering theft of merchandise, such as various inland marine forms, typically exclude both inventory shortage and unexplained disappearance.

Theft of Building Materials

As discussed in Chapter 3, the BPP covers building materials and supplies on or within 100 feet of the described premises, to be used for making additions, alterations, or repairs to the insured building or structure. Such materials or supplies are insured against all covered causes of loss under the special form *except theft*. This limitation applies only until the materials or supplies are actually attached as part of the building or structure. The limitation also does not apply if the materials or supplies are *held for sale by the named insured*. This exception makes the special form suitable for insuring the merchandise of a lumberyard or a building supply house.

Dollar Limitations

Some types of property covered by the BPP (or another coverage form to which the special form is attached) are highly susceptible to theft. The special form therefore places special dollar limitations on recovery for certain "target commodities" when they are lost by theft. These limitations are as follows:

- $2,500 for furs, fur garments, and garments trimmed with fur
- $2,500 on patterns, dies, molds, and forms
- $2,500 on jewelry, watches, watch movements, precious and semi-precious stones, bullion, gold, silver, platinum and other precious alloys or metals. Jewelry and watches with a value of less than $100 are not subject to this $2,500 limit
- $250 for stamps, tickets, including lottery tickets held for sale, and letters of credit

Crime and inland marine policies are available to provide higher limits and broader coverage on these types of property.

Pollution

Insurance companies' concerns about pollution claims have led to the addition of a broad pollution exclusion to the special form. The exclusion eliminates coverage for loss resulting from "discharge, dispersal, seepage, migration, release or escape of pollutants unless the discharge . . . is itself caused by any of the specified causes of loss." *Pollutants* are defined (in the BPP coverage form) to include "any solid, liquid, gaseous or thermal irritant or contaminant including smoke, vapor, soot, fumes, acids, alkalis, chemicals, and waste."

This exclusion has led to the denial of coverage for many claims once thought to be covered by "all-risks" coverage. In one case, the loss was caused by an exterminator who applied the wrong pesticide to the building. The appeals court ruled that there was no coverage, holding that impurity or impairment resulting from the contact with a foreign substance was contamination and that contamination was clearly excluded.[15]

The pollution exclusion does not exclude all pollution claims, however. The escape of pollutants caused by a specified peril is covered. For example, if a fire or explosion causes the dispersal of a pollutant, coverage is provided both for repairing the damage caused and for cleaning up the debris. As discussed in Chapter 3, debris removal is limited to an amount equal to 25 percent of the loss plus $5,000, and cleaning up covered pollution from *land or water* is limited to $10,000 per policy year, per location.

Loss of Use

An exclusion unique to the special form reinforces the intention to provide coverage only against direct physical loss. The exclusion precludes coverage for loss caused by or resulting from "delay, loss of use, or loss of market." Business income insurance (discussed in Chapter 8) is available for covering income losses and extra expenses due to the inability to use property that has been damaged by a covered peril.

Additional Concurrent Causation Exclusion

Because the doctrine of concurrent causation primarily affects "all-risks" insurance, the special form contains an additional concurrent causation exclusion not found in the basic and broad forms. The exclusion provides that the insurer will not pay for loss or damage caused by or resulting from any of the following:

> a. Weather conditions. But this exclusion only applies if weather conditions contribute in any way with a cause or event excluded in paragraph 1. above to produce the loss or damage.
>
> [The reference to "paragraph 1 above" refers to the exclusions entitled ordinance or law, earth movement, governmental action, nuclear hazard, off-premises services, war and military action, and water. The weather conditions exclusion does not apply to other weather related losses, such as windstorms.]

b. Acts or decisions, including the failure to act or decide, of any person, group, organization or governmental body.

c. Faulty, inadequate or defective:

(1) Planning, zoning, development, surveying, siting;

(2) Design, specifications, workmanship, repair, construction, renovation, remodeling, grading, compaction;

(3) Materials used in repair, construction, renovation or remodeling; or

(4) Maintenance;

of part or all of any property on or off the described premises.

However, if loss or damage by a covered cause of loss results, the insurer will pay for that resulting loss or damage. If, for example, faulty design or installation of a building's electrical system results in a fire, the insurer will pay for the fire loss.

Paragraphs b and c address the "concurrent causes" of third-party negligence with respect to planning, maintenance, quality of construction materials, or poor decisions of governmental planning bodies. If a building code permits the construction of buildings that cannot withstand an earthquake, and an earthquake damages such a building, the special form will not pay the loss even if a poorly planned building code was a concurrent cause of the loss. Likewise, coverage does not apply to flood losses, whether or not faulty design or maintenance of a flood dike is a concurrent cause.

Additional Coverage Extensions

The special form contains the same additional collapse coverage as provided by the broad form. The special form also contains two "additional coverage extensions," relating to (1) property in transit and (2) damage by water, other liquids, or powder or molten material.

Property in Transit

This extension provides a modest amount of coverage on property not otherwise covered—property in transit. Specifically, the extension provides up to $1,000 of additional insurance for damage to the insured's personal property in or on a motor vehicle that is more than 100 feet from the described premises. (As discussed in Chapter 3, named insured's business personal property within 100 feet of the described premises is covered without the extension, up to the full limit of insurance.)

The extension applies only to property that is in or on a motor vehicle that the named insured owns, leases, or operates, while between points in the coverage territory. Thus, property being transported by a common or contract carrier is not covered under this extension. Moreover, the extension does not apply to property in the care, custody, or control of salespersons.

The extension does not provide "all-risks" coverage on property in transit. Property in transit is covered only against the following named perils:

- Fire, lightning, explosion, windstorm or hail, riot or civil commotion, and vandalism
- Theft, but only when an entire bale, case, or package is stolen from a securely locked body or compartment of the vehicle by a thief who leaves visible marks of the forced entry
- Collision and upset

If the insured wants a higher limit of insurance, coverage for property being transported by others, a broader scope of covered perils, a broader coverage territory, and fewer restrictions generally on property in transit, transit insurance can be obtained under inland marine or ocean marine policies, as discussed in Chapter 11.

Damage by Water, Etc.

This extension clarifies that the special form will pay the cost of tearing out and replacing any part of the building to repair damage to a system or appliance from which water or other liquid, powder, or molten material has escaped and caused damage. With respect to water, liquid, and powder, the extension duplicates the "tearing out" coverage provided by the broad form. The extension refers to molten material because the special form (for lack of an exclusion) covers damage resulting from escape of molten materials, such as molten metals at a foundry. The basic and broad forms do not cover escape of molten materials; however, an endorsement is available for adding molten materials as a covered cause of loss to either of these forms.

Optional Coverages

Optional endorsements are available for covering certain causes of loss that are not covered under the basic, broad, or special forms. These optional coverages include the following:

- Ordinance or law coverage
- Causes of loss—earthquake form
- Sprinkler leakage—earthquake extension

- Off-premises services coverage
- Spoilage coverage
- Radioactive contamination
- Pier and wharf additional covered causes of loss

Ordinance or Law Coverage

The **ordinance or law coverage endorsement** provides three coverages for losses resulting from building ordinances or laws:

- Coverage A—covers loss to the undamaged portion of the building that an ordinance or law does not permit to remain in use.
- Coverage B—covers the cost to demolish the undamaged portion of the structure and remove its debris.
- Coverage C—covers the increased cost to repair or replace the property in conformity with the ordinance or law.

Coverage A can be arranged on either an actual cash value or a replacement cost basis. If coverage is on a replacement cost basis and the building is replaced, Coverage A will pay the lowest of the following:

1. The amount the insured actually spends
2. What it would have cost to restore a building comparable to the original building
3. The limit of insurance applicable to the building

If Coverage C is chosen, replacement cost coverage must be activated. Under Coverage C, the property must be repaired or replaced as soon as reasonably possible after the loss. The insurer is not obligated to pay increased construction costs unless the reconstruction is made within two years, although the period may be extended. The replacement building may be on the same premises or elsewhere.

None of the three coverages will pay for costs associated with any ordinance or law that requires the insured in any way to respond to or assess the effects of pollutants.

Coverage A becomes part of the building coverage; no additional amount of insurance is needed. However, the *Commercial Lines Manual* (CLM) calls for a rate increase of 15 percent. Separate amounts of insurance must be shown for Coverages B and C.

An example of how to calculate the amount of coverage needed is shown in Exhibit 5-2.

Exhibit 5-2
Determining Limits for Ordinance or Law Coverage

a. Assume the following:

(1) An insured building of masonry construction has a replacement cost value of $400,000 and an actual cash value of $350,000.

(2) This building is located in an area now zoned for superior construction. The owner knows that substantial damage to the building—assume 50% destruction—will trigger the local ordinance and the entire building will have to be destroyed.

(3) Estimated cost of demolition of 50% of the structure (the undamaged portion) is $30,000.

(4) The additional cost to replace the building with a new structure to comply with the local ordinance and land use laws is $200,000.

b. For purposes of illustration, the following are possible ways of developing the limits of insurance necessary when the Ordinance or Law Coverage Endorsement is attached.

Example 1. Replacement Cost Coverage Option Applies.

To provide coverage for:

(1) Replacement cost value of the current building (including loss of value of the undamaged portion), choose a Building limit of $400,000.

(2) Additional cost to replace the building to comply with an ordinance or law, choose an Increased Cost of Construction limit of $200,000.

(3) Cost to demolish the undamaged part of the existing building, choose a Demolition Cost limit of $30,000.

Example 2. Replacement Cost Coverage Option Does **NOT** Apply.

To provide coverage for:

(1) Actual cash value of the current building (including loss of value of undamaged portion), choose a Building limit of $350,000.

(2) Cost to demolish the undamaged part of the existing building, choose a Demolition Cost limit of $30,000.

Setting the proper amount of insurance requires a knowledge of the pertinent ordinances and laws, a worst-case debris removal estimate, and, if Coverage C is included, an estimate of the cost to replace with a building that meets the requirements of the ordinance or law.

In addition to increasing the severity of the direct loss, the operation of ordinances and laws can increase the severity of business income losses. This is because the length of time the building is unusable is increased by the extra time needed to demolish and rebuild the undamaged portion of the building. Rebuilding to the updated code can also increase the time required to return the building to service. The additional business income loss can be covered by attaching the "ordinance or law—increased period of restoration" endorsement to the insured's business income coverage form, as explained further in Chapter 8.

Causes of Loss—Earthquake Form

For an additional premium, the earthquake form extends "commercial property" coverage to include earthquake and volcanic eruption ("eruption, explosion or effusion of a volcano") as covered causes of loss.

The term "earthquake" is not defined. However, to clarify the application of the per-occurrence limit and deductible, the form makes it clear that all earthquake shocks or volcanic eruptions within a 168-hour (seven-day) period will be considered a single earthquake or volcanic eruption. This means that most aftershocks will be considered part of the original event for insurance purposes.

Exclusions

The earthquake form contains the standard exclusions pertaining to ordinance or law, governmental action, nuclear hazard, off-premises services, and war and military action. More importantly, the form excludes loss caused by landslide, mine subsidence, tidal wave, flood, mudslide, or mudflow, even if attributable to an earthquake or volcanic eruption. Fire and explosion losses resulting from earthquake or volcanic eruption are also excluded, but such losses are covered under the basic, broad, and special causes-of-loss forms. Also excluded is an earthquake or volcanic eruption that begins before inception of the insurance.

Underground Foundations

As discussed in Chapter 3, underground foundations, excavations, and similar types of property not normally susceptible to damage by fire or other basic causes of loss are excluded from coverage in the BPP in order to reduce the amount of insurance needed to meet coinsurance requirements. These property items are highly susceptible to earthquake damage. Therefore, when earthquake coverage is purchased, the insured should carefully consider using the additional covered property endorsement to restore coverage on such excluded property items, if that step has not already been taken. Adding the excluded items insures them against damage by any covered peril, not just earthquake. Appropriate adjustments in policy limits should be made in order to avoid a coinsurance penalty.

Masonry Veneer

Masonry veneer (such as brick facing on a frame structure) is particularly vulnerable to earthquake. The earthquake form excludes coverage for loss to masonry veneer, unless the veneer is limited to 10 percent or less of the exterior wall area. Masonry veneer coverage can be added by placing the words "including masonry veneer" in the premises description in the declarations and paying an appropriate additional premium.

Earthquake Deductible

For purposes of earthquake losses, a **percentage deductible** in the earthquake form replaces the dollar deductible in the BPP or other coverage form to which it is attached. The applicable percentage, which appears in the declarations, is a percentage of the *value* of the property (not the limit of insurance). So, for example, if a policy had a 5 percent earthquake deductible, a $5,000 deductible would apply to a building valued at $100,000 and insured for $80,000. If the deductible were applied to the limit of insurance instead of the property value, it could discourage insurance to value because a lower limit would result in a lower dollar deductible.

Sprinkler Leakage—Earthquake Extension

The **sprinkler leakage—earthquake extension endorsement** can be used to cover sprinkler leakage loss or damage resulting from an earthquake or volcanic eruption. Such losses are covered (and thus the endorsement is not needed) if the insured has purchased the earthquake form described above. However, some insureds who do not wish to purchase full earthquake coverage may still want to insure, for a considerably lower premium, against the considerable sprinkler leakage losses that can result from quake, even when the building is not seriously damaged. The endorsement does not impose the percentage deductible of the earthquake form.

Off-Premises Services Coverage

Coverage for physical losses excluded by the off-premises services exclusion can be provided through the **off-premises services—direct damage endorsement**. The endorsement extends coverage to include damage to property described in the endorsement schedule, caused by the interruption of service to the described premises. The interruption must result from damage by a covered peril to any of the following types of property not on the described premises:

1. Water supply services
2. Communication supply services
3. Power supply services

Each of the three types of services is described in more detail in the endorsement. The insured can select coverage for any or all of the services. The insured's choices as to covered property and locations, type of service, and causes of loss applicable are indicated in the endorsement schedule, which is reproduced in Exhibit 5-3.

Exhibit 5-3
Schedule for Off-Premises Services—Direct Damage Endorsement

SCHEDULE*

Water Supply	Communication Supply (**not** including overhead transmission lines)	Communication Supply (including overhead transmission lines)	Power Supply (**not** including overhead transmission lines)	Power Supply (including overhead transmission lines)
☒	☐	☒	☐	☒

Prem. No.	Bldg. No.	Covered Property	Causes of Loss Form Applicable
1	1	Office Building and Contents	Special
	2	Factory Building and Contents	Special
		1250 Industrial Parkway Workingtown, PA 19380	

*Information required to complete this Schedule, if not shown on this endorsement, will be shown in the Declarations.

Coverage for business income losses resulting from interruption of off-premises services can be added to the business income coverage form with the off-premises services—time element endorsement.

Spoilage Coverage

Power or equipment failure can cause spoilage of perishable stock such as food and cut flowers. Although spoilage losses can be covered under the off-premises services endorsement, they can also be covered by the **spoilage coverage endorsement**. Coverage under the off-premises services endorsement applies only if the loss of power is caused by damage to off-premises power supply services by an insured peril. The spoilage coverage endorsement provides broader coverage. It covers spoilage of perishable stock resulting from change in temperature or humidity caused by either mechanical breakdown or power outage.

Mechanical breakdown also includes loss caused by contamination by the refrigerant used in cooling equipment. Power outage coverage applies whether the outage occurs on or off the premises, and there is no requirement that the outage be caused by another insured peril. However, the power outage must be due to conditions beyond the insured's control.

The insured can select either mechanical breakdown or power outage or both. The BPP optional coverages (agreed value, inflation guard, and replacement cost) do not apply, nor does coinsurance.

According to the CLM, the maximum amount of insurance available under this endorsement is $50,000. For a smaller firm, perhaps a small food store, the spoilage endorsement may provide sufficient coverage. The $50,000 limit, however, would probably be inadequate for a business with a potentially large spoilage loss, such as a milk bottling plant. Boiler and machinery insurance, discussed in Chapter 9, can provide higher coverage limits for spoilage.

The spoilage endorsement contains a selling price valuation option. If the selling price option is chosen, the damaged property will be valued at the selling price as if no loss had occurred—less any discounts and unincurred expenses.

A rate credit is allowed for a refrigeration maintenance agreement. If a refrigeration maintenance agreement is specified, the insured must notify the insurance company if the agreement is voluntarily terminated. Failure to give notice suspends the breakdown coverage.

Radioactive Contamination Endorsement

The **radioactive contamination endorsement** is available to meet the needs of organizations that have a radioactive contamination exposure on their premises, other than a nuclear reactor. (Facilities with nuclear reactors are insured only under special nuclear energy policies, available from specialized insurers.) Hospitals, medical clinics, and educational and research institutions frequently use radioactive materials. Some manufacturers, contractors, and engineers may also use radioactive materials, principally in measuring devices. The endorsement provides some coverage that would otherwise be eliminated by the nuclear hazard exclusion. Overall, the number of organizations that could benefit from this coverage is much greater than the number needing a nuclear energy property policy.

The endorsement covers "radioactive contamination," which it defines as follows:

> direct physical loss or damage caused by:
>
> a. Sudden and accidental radioactive contamination; or
>
> b. Resultant radiation damage to the described property.

Two coverage alternatives are possible—the first treats radioactive contamination as a consequence; the second, as a peril.

- *Limited radioactive contamination* means "Radioactive Contamination that directly results from any other Covered Cause of Loss." For example, if a tornado causes radiation to be released from its container, with resulting contamination, the loss would be covered.
- *Broad radioactive contamination* treats radioactive contamination as a free-standing peril, without the requirement that the contamination must result from another covered peril. Contamination caused by the negligence of a laboratory technician would be covered by the broad coverage in addition to contamination resulting from tornado damage.

Neither basic nor broad radioactive contamination coverage applies if the described premises contain a nuclear reactor or new or used nuclear fuel. Losses arising from radioactive material off premises are also excluded. CLM rules do not permit the limited radioactive contamination option to be used with the special causes-of-loss form.

Pier and Wharf Additional Covered Causes of Loss

As discussed in Chapter 3, the BPP coverage form excludes piers and wharfs. Although piers and wharfs (and all other "instrumentalities of transportation") can be, and often are, insured under marine insurance policies, they can also be covered under the BPP by the "additional covered property" endorsement. When that is done, the insured may also want to add the **pier and wharf additional covered causes of loss endorsement**. The endorsement adds two additional covered perils:

1. Floating ice
2. Collision of any vessel or floating object

The endorsement is not used with the special causes-of-loss form. Although the special form does not exclude either of the additional perils, CLM rules state that all policies on waterfront properties to which the special form applies must be endorsed with the **watercraft exclusion endorsement**. This endorsement excludes damage caused by watercraft to retaining walls, bulkheads, piers, wharves, or docks. If the insured wants coverage for the excluded exposure, the endorsement can be eliminated for an additional charge.

Summary

Three causes-of-loss forms are available for expressing the perils covered in a "commercial property" policy: the basic form, the broad form, and the special form.

The basic form covers fire, lightning, explosion, windstorm, hail, smoke, aircraft, vehicles, riot, civil commotion, vandalism, sprinkler leakage, sinkhole collapse, and volcanic action. The broad form covers the same exclusions plus breakage of glass; falling objects; weight of ice, snow, or sleet; and water damage. These perils are subject to various limitations and exclusions.

The special form provides "all-risks" insurance, covering risks of loss except those that are specifically excluded. This approach encompasses the broad form perils, theft, and other perils that are not excluded. Another advantage of the special form is that it shifts the "burden of proof" to the insurer. That is, under an "all-risks" policy, if the insurer wants to deny coverage for a loss, it must be able to prove that the loss was caused by an excluded peril. Under named perils forms, the insurer is not obligated to pay for a loss unless the insured can prove that loss was caused by an insured peril.

All three causes-of-loss forms exclude building ordinance or law requirements, earth movement, governmental action, interruption of off-premises utility services, war, flood, electrical disturbances, steam boiler explosion, and mechanical breakdown.

The special form contains those and several additional exclusions. The additional exclusions duplicate conditions expressed within the broad form perils; restrict coverage to "specified causes" for some exposures; place limitations on theft and other perils; and guard against the concurrent causation doctrine.

Optional endorsements are available to cover ordinance or law exposures; earthquake; interruption of off-premises services; spoilage resulting from breakdown or power outage; radioactive contamination; and additional perils affecting piers and wharves.

Chapter Notes

1. Douglas Houser and Christopher Kent, "Concurrent Causation in First Party Claims," *Tort and Insurance Law Journal*, vol. 21, p. 58.
2. Insurance Information Institute, *Fact Book 1994*, pp. 69, 73.
3. Kenneth H. York and John W. Whelan, *Insurance Law* (St. Paul, MN: West Publishing Co., 1982), pp. 195-199.
4. Engel v. Redwood County Farmers Mutual Insurance Co., 1979 CCH (Fire & Casualty) 466.
5. For a comprehensive discussion of the hostile fire issue, see *FC&S Bulletins*, Fire & Marine Volume, Misc. Property Ba-1 through 6 (July 1993).
6. The doctrine of reasonable expectations is discussed in more detail in the text for CPCU 1, Eric A. Wiening and Donald S. Malecki, *Insurance Contract Analysis* (Malvern, PA: American Institute for CPCU, 1992), p. 379.
7. Insurance Services Office, Inc., "The Impact of Catastrophes on Property Insurance," ISO Insurance Issues Series, 1994, pp. 1, 4.
8. *FC&S Bulletins*, Fire & Marine Volume, Misc. Property Exe-2 (June 1990).
9. Philip Gordis, ed., *Property and Casualty Insurance*, 23rd ed. (Indianapolis: The Rough Notes Co., 1974), p. 75.
10. Thomas W. Mallin, "Pollution and Contamination: How Will Property Insurers Respond?" Tort and Insurance Practice Section, American Bar Association, pp. 78-79.
11. E. Scott Reckard, "California Quake Claims Seen at Twice Original Estimate," *The Journal of Commerce*, March 30, 1994, p. 13A.
12. The FEMA study is cited in Insurance Services Office, Inc., "The Impact of Catastrophes on Property Insurance," p. 12.
13. "Coast-to-Coast News Roundup," *Insurance Review*, October, 1992, p. 8.
14. *FC&S Bulletins*, Fire & Marine Volume, Misc. Property Ea-2 (August 1993).
15. Auten v. Employers National Ins. Co., 722 SW2d 468 (Texas Court of Appeals, 1986), cited in *FC&S Bulletins*, Personal Lines Volume, Dwellings Pol-4 (May 1992). Although the case involved a homeowners policy, the exclusion wording was almost identical to that used in commercial property forms.

Chapter 6

Other "Commercial Property" Forms

In addition to the building and personal property coverage form (BPP), several other "commercial property" coverage forms are available for covering special situations and exposures. This chapter describes several of these additional forms, as listed below.

- Condominium association coverage form
- Condominium commercial unit-owners coverage form
- Builders risk coverage form
- Standard property policy
- Legal liability coverage form
- Glass coverage form
- Leasehold interest coverage form

This chapter also examines insurance for tenants' improvements and betterments.

Condominiums

Because condominium ownership interests differ from other ownership interests, specially designed forms are used to insure condominium buildings and contents. The discussion that follows describes the nature of condominium ownership and the forms that have been tailored to insure condominiums.

Nature of Condominium Ownership

Condominiums involve the separate ownership of individual units in a multiple-unit building or buildings. In a condominium, each unit owner is the owner of that condominium unit and has an undivided interest with all other unit owners in the jointly owned "common elements" of the building.

A **condominium association** is formed by unit owners to manage the condominium and to own the common elements. A **condominium unit** can be thought of as the "box of air" enclosed by the unfinished surfaces of perimeter walls, floors, and ceilings. Property of any kind within the condominium unit, except (1) common building elements and (2) pipes, wires, conduits, and other utilities specified in easements, is considered to be solely owned by the unit owner. In addition, the unit owner may be the sole owner of some property normally considered as "building" (such as a wall) that is located within the unit but is not a common building element or building utility.

The **common elements**, which are jointly owned by all unit owners, generally include the foundations; exterior walls; interior walls except those contained within individual units; structural columns and beams; roofs; corridors; lobbies; stairs; parking and storage areas; central power, light, heating, and air conditioning systems; and often other property items. Some of these items may be located within, or may pass through, the unit owner's "box of air." The condominium association agreement, discussed below, specifically designates what is considered part of the condominium unit and what is considered to be a common element.

Pertinent Documents

All fifty states, Puerto Rico, and the District of Columbia have enabling legislation or statutory law for condominiums. These laws vary substantially among jurisdictions. Many of the laws have some provisions relating to ownership interests and the purchase of insurance. Producers, underwriters, and persons with risk management responsibility for condominium exposures must familiarize themselves with applicable state law.

The other essential document for evaluating the exposures of any particular condominium is the **condominium association agreement**, also referred to as the master deed, declarations, or bylaws. This formidable document, prepared by the developer who first established the condominium association, usually describes what each unit owner has purchased and clarifies unit owners' rights and responsibilities. The master deed should describe the land, the building, and the common elements and identify each individual unit. It should establish a method of collecting and paying for such expenses as maintenance, upkeep of common areas, and insurance. The master deed should also specify the governing procedures, the powers of the association, and the procedures for modifying the bylaws.

Under condominium statutes or master deeds, the condominium association is usually obliged to maintain insurance coverage for the benefit of unit owners. Unit owners are also permitted to purchase insurance at their own expense for their own benefit.

Condominium agreements are individually drawn and can vary in important respects. Therefore, in addition to having a working knowledge of the condominium law in the jurisdiction, those responsible for arranging insurance coverage for a condominium association must also review the condominium association agreement.

Bare-Walls Concept Versus Single-Entity Concept

When dealing with condominium exposures, an important issue involves the dividing line between the unit owners' property interests and the association's property interests. Two general approaches appearing in law or in a master deed or declaration are the bare-wall concept and the single-entity concept.

Under the **bare-walls concept**, the association has no ownership interest within the unit's bare walls. All paint and wall coverings, carpet and floor coverings, drapes, cabinets, appliances, nonload-bearing interior walls, interior doors, plumbing, and electrical fixtures are considered to be owned by the individual unit owner, but the association may be required to insure these elements on behalf of the individual unit owners (by statute, declarations, or bylaws). In that event, the association's insurable interest in the unit owner's property is that of a trustee.

Under the **single-entity concept**, also known as the "all-in" concept, the condominium association is considered to be the owner of all property contained in the unit as sold to the original purchaser. Normally, at the time of sale, carpets, cabinets, electrical fixtures, and appliances have been installed. Consequently, the association would be responsible for insuring these items.

In practice, the master deed is often not clear with respect to how to insure all items exposed to loss. To illustrate the problems of applying these concepts, consider the exterior doors, the windows, air conditioner compressors, sinks, or balcony railings associated with individual units of a residential condominium building. Should they be insured by the unit owners or by the association?

In any areas where there is doubt, the problem can be addressed by having the association obtain insurance with the broadest possible description of covered property, with a policy limit set accordingly. However, if unit owners adopt a similar strategy and insure as broadly as possible, they may be obtaining expensive and unnecessary duplicate coverage. Then again, if the wrong entity insures a given property item, that entity may not be able to collect due to lack of an insurable interest and the entity with an insurable interest will not collect because it has no insurance. If neither the association nor the unit owner insures some property items, there may be no source of recovery following a loss.

The problem is not merely one of describing covered property. More difficult is the problem of measuring insurable values and purchasing appropriate amounts of insurance. It can be especially difficult for the directors of a condominium association to value items located within the various units, particularly if they have been modified by the unit owners. Failure to properly evaluate property items exposed to loss could leave a commercial unit owner or a condominium association with a coinsurance penalty following a partial loss, or with inadequate coverage to pay for a substantial loss. The agreed value option can eliminate the possibility of a coinsurance penalty, and, for associations composed of separate structures spread over several acres, blanket insurance can reduce the possibility of inadequate coverage for a substantial loss.

Insurance Requirements

Faced with these difficulties, one would hope that the condominium association agreement, if not the statutes, would be clear enough to indicate what insurance should be carried by the association. Unfortunately, these documents are often drafted by attorneys who have little understanding of insurance practice and terminology. Consider, for example, the following excerpt from a master deed:

> The Board of Directors shall be required to obtain and maintain...the following insurance: fire insurance with extended coverage, water damage, vandalism and malicious mischief endorsements....

This clause causes several problems. The extended coverage endorsement, as discussed in Chapter 5, is no longer in use. In addition, what does "water damage" mean? Does it include flood? seepage? backup of sewers and drains? Many standard policies exclude these types of water damage. The association in this case had not been carrying flood insurance. Would the directors have been liable for mismanagement in the event of an uninsured flood loss? This clause is not the exception. Most agreements raise as many questions as they answer with regard to insurance.

When analyzing condominium loss exposures, one must consider the particular situation. The requirements vary substantially from one jurisdiction to another, and often from one association to another within the same jurisdiction. Ambiguities should be resolved by action of the board of directors, or of the entire membership if necessary, so that exact insurance requirements can be established. It may be necessary for the association to consult an attorney familiar with condominium law.

Condominium Property Insurance

In oversimplified terms, the insurance needs of a condominium association can be said to be similar to the building insurance needs of a building owner/landlord, and the needs of a condominium unit owner are similar to the personal property insurance needs of a tenant. Two ISO commercial property forms have been designed especially for condominium property exposures:

1. Condominium association coverage form
2. Condominium commercial unit-owners coverage form

Like the building and personal property coverage form (BPP), each of these forms can be combined with causes-of-loss forms and other component documents to form a monoline policy or a commercial package policy.

The condominium commercial property forms resemble the BPP in many ways; much of the language is identical. Discussion here emphasizes the distinctive features of the condominium forms rather than repeating points of similarity that have already been discussed in previous chapters.

Condominium Association Coverage Form

Like the BPP, the **condominium association coverage form** provides coverage for property in three categories:

1. Building
2. Business personal property of the named insured
3. Personal property of others

Each coverage applies only if a limit of insurance for that coverage is shown in the declarations. The condominium association coverage form also provides the same additional coverages and coverage extensions as the BPP.

Building Coverage

The building coverage of the condominium association coverage form closely resembles the building coverage of the BPP. However, a significant difference relates to the following types of property contained within individual units: (1) fixtures, improvements, and alterations, and (2) appliances including (but not limited to) those used for refrigerating, ventilating, cooking, dishwashing, laundering, or housekeeping.

The condominium building coverage applies to the above items only if the condominium association agreement requires the association to insure them. Otherwise, such property items are not included in the association's building coverage. As will be explained in more detail below, the unit owner's coverage picks up where the association's coverage leaves off, and vice versa.

This provision underscores the importance of examining the condominium association agreement when establishing insurance requirements. The agreement affects the amount of insurance required to comply with the coinsurance provision as well as the coverage to be carried by the unit owner.

Because of the ambiguities present in most of the insurance requirements set out in condominium association agreements, some independently developed forms do not tie coverage to the agreement. One such policy offers three options, as described in Exhibit 6-1.

Exhibit 6-1
Non-ISO Condominium Coverage Options

Bare-Walls Coverage

Under the bare-walls concept the association has no ownership interest in property within the unit's bare walls. Accordingly, bare-walls coverage does not insure any of the property contained within the bare walls.

Original Specifications

The original specifications coverage option insures (1) property within units that was originally installed in accordance with the condominium's plans and specifications and (2) replacements of like kind and quality.

Additional Installations

The additional installations option covers improvements or additions to the units, including the following: fixtures; wall, floor, and ceiling coverings; refrigerating, heating, and cooling systems; cooking ranges and ovens; dishwashers; clothes washers; and fire protection and security systems.

The association may choose bare-walls coverage, original specifications, or both original specifications and additional installations. Unless both "original specifications" and "additional installations" are chosen, the association must still be certain that it has not omitted coverage that it is required to carry.

The ISO condominium association coverage form can be amended to provide coverage similar to any of the options described in Exhibit 6-1. That is done by careful use of the ISO *additional covered property* or *additional property not covered* endorsements.

Coverage for the Named Insured's Business Personal Property

A condominium association might need personal property insurance to cover personal property that does not already fall within the scope of building coverage. For example, many condominiums have community clubhouses, recreation halls, health clubs, and the like. The furnishings and equipment of these facilities can be covered as business personal property.

Here, again, the condominium association coverage form clarifies the dividing line between personal property insured by the association and that insured by individual unit owners:

- Business personal property is covered if it is owned by the association or if it is indivisibly owned by all unit owners.
- Business personal property is not covered if it is owned only by a unit owner.

Coverage for Personal Property of Others

The condominium association coverage form's coverage for personal property of others is the same as that of the BPP. If an 80 percent or higher coinsurance clause is in effect, the form automatically includes a coverage extension for property of others up to $2,500 at each described location. If this extension is not adequate to meet exposures, an additional amount of insurance can be purchased under the personal property of others coverage.

This coverage may take on special significance in some condominiums where individual unit owners allow their personal property to be used in the building's common areas for decorative purposes or for specific building maintenance and repair projects. Subject to other terms of the policy, the condominium association coverage form would cover such items, provided a limit for this coverage is shown in the declarations or under the coverage extension.

Conditions

Most of the conditions of the condominium association form are the same as those of the BPP. The important variations from the BPP are described below.

Loss Payment to an Insurance Trustee The loss payment condition of the condominium association form contains an additional provision stating that if the association has designated an insurance trustee, the insurer may pay covered claims to the insurance trustee. The board of trustees of a condominium generally serves in this capacity, receiving all loss proceeds "in trust" for the individual unit owners. The board then acts on behalf of all unit owners. Sometimes, however, a financial institution serves as trustee. Designating an insurance trustee can avoid unnecessary complications in the event of a loss since some insurers feel that otherwise the names of all the unit owners and their mortgagees must appear on a loss draft.

Coordination With Unit Owner's Insurance If a unit owner has coverage applying to the same property covered by the association's policy, the association's policy is primary.

Waiver of Rights of Recovery The insurance company agrees not to subrogate against any unit owner of an insured condominium.

Condominium Additional Provisions Endorsement

Other provisions not contained in the condominium association form are often either required by the condominium agreement or requested by the condominium association and its mortgagee. For example, a condominium agreement might include the following provision:

> All policies...shall contain waivers...of invalidity arising from any acts of the insureds or any Unit Owner....

The **condominium additional provisions endorsement**, a mandatory policy amendment in a dozen or more states, includes several provisions to meet special needs. In states that do not require the endorsement, a manuscript endorsement could be used in order to delete or modify the onerous cancellation clause in the amendatory endorsement. Independently developed condominium association forms often include some of these provisions as standard. The provisions of the endorsement are described below.

Act or Omission No act or omission by any unit owner will void the policy or bar recovery, but this waiver does not apply to acts by unit owners on behalf of the association. Thus, a fire intentionally set by a unit owner would not bar recovery by the association unless the unit owner were acting on behalf of the association.

Expanded Waiver of Right of Recovery The endorsement replaces the waiver of rights of recovery provision of the condominium form with an expanded clause waiving rights of recovery against any unit owner, including the developer, members of his or her household, the association, and members of the board of directors when acting within the scope of their duties. However, the insurance company retains any rights it might have against the developer in his or her capacity as developer.

Notice of Cancellation or Nonrenewal The insurance company will provide written notice at least thirty days in advance of any cancellation or nonrenewal to the first named insured and to each unit owner to whom a certificate or memorandum of insurance has been issued. (In large condominium developments, this provision can present an administrative nightmare for the insurer.)

Additional Protection for Mortgage Holders The insurer will also give thirty days' advance notice of cancellation or nonrenewal to each of the mortgage holders. If the condominium is terminated, the insurance company will pay covered loss to buildings or structures to each mortgage holder shown in the declarations in their order of precedence, as their interests may appear.

Condominium Commercial Unit-Owners Coverage Form

Condominium association coverage can apply to either residential or nonresidential condominiums. In contrast, only nonresidential condominium unit-owners are eligible for coverage under the **condominium commercial unit-owners coverage form.** Unit owners in residential condominiums can insure their personal property, liability, and related exposures with a homeowners form HO-6 policy, as discussed in CPCU 2. Not all condominiums are residential. Some are used for offices, stores, or other business activities. The condominium commercial unit-owners coverage form provides the coverages needed by unit owners in *commercial* condominiums.

Covered Property

A condominium unit owner generally has no need for building insurance in its own name, so the form includes coverage only for "your business personal property" and personal property of others.

These coverages are generally the same as in the BPP. However, "your business personal property" in the unit-owners form includes fixtures, improvements, and alterations that are part of the building and owned by the unit owner. The BPP personal property coverage includes improvements and alterations only to the extent of a tenant's *use interest* in them, since the tenant does not own improvements and betterments. A unit owner, in contrast, can actually own fixtures, improvements, and alterations to his or her unit.

Coordination with Association Coverage

An exclusion of the unit-owners form coordinates the unit owner's coverage with the condominium association's coverage. Fixtures, improvements, alterations, and appliances (such as those used for refrigerating, cooking, and so on) are *not* covered by the unit owner's policy if the condominium association agreement requires the association to insure them. If the agreement requires the association to insure such property but the association fails to do so, the unit owner's policy still does not apply.

Another policy provision makes unit-owners coverage excess over the coverage of any association insurance covering the same property.

Optional Coverages

Two optional coverages often needed by condominium unit owners are available in a single endorsement that can be attached to the unit-owners coverage form. Either or both of these optional coverages may be purchased; they are included in a single endorsement for the sake of convenience.

Loss Assessment Coverage Typically, condominium associations have the right to assess all unit owners for uninsured losses that the association incurs. Under the optional **loss assessment coverage**, the insurer agrees to pay the unit owner's share of any assessment charged to all unit owners by the condominium association when the assessment is made as a result of direct physical loss or damage caused by an insured peril to property in which each unit owner has an undivided interest.

The form allows payment for each assessment up to the limit of insurance shown for the endorsement, subject to a $250 deductible. However, if the assessment is a result of a deductible in the insurance purchased by the condominium association, the insurer's payment is limited to $1,000. Coverage is provided by the policy in force when the assessment is made, not when the loss occurred.

Miscellaneous Real Property Coverage The unit-owners coverage form normally covers only personal property, fixtures, improvements, and alterations. The **miscellaneous real property coverage** extends the form to include real property items when:

1. the property pertains to the named insured's condominium unit only, or
2. the named insured has a duty to insure the real property according to the condominium association agreement.

Should the condominium association have other insurance covering the same property, the unit owner's insurance will be excess coverage.

A variety of situations may suggest a need for this coverage. Examples include the following:

- A storage building erected by a unit owner for use in its business operations

- A separate garage structure owned by the association but used solely by the unit owner
- An attached addition to the external walls, such as a balcony that benefits only the unit owner

Cooperative Corporations and Planned Unit Developments

Two additional forms of combined ownership of real property by the occupants—cooperative corporations and planned unit developments—are similar to condominiums. The distinguishing characteristics of cooperative corporations and planned unit developments are discussed below and summarized in Exhibit 6-2.

Exhibit 6-2
Comparison of Condominiums, Cooperatives, and Planned Unit Developments

	Condominium Unit Owners	Cooperative Shareholders	Planned Unit Development Homeowners
Own an identifiable portion of the property?	Yes	No	Yes
Own common elements jointly with others?	Yes	No*	Yes
Own stock in the corporation that owns the property?	No	Yes	No
Have "fee simple" title to the structure which they occupy (or have the right to occupy)?	No	No	Yes
Insurance requirements are usually spelled out in the governing agreements or bylaws?	Yes	Yes	Yes

*Shareholders do not directly own corporate property.

Cooperative Corporations

In **cooperative corporations,** the real property is owned by a corporation rather than jointly by the unit owners. However, the tenants of the property are the shareholders of the corporation.

Unlike condominium unit owners, the shareholder-tenants of a cooperative corporation do not have the ownership of the "box-of-air" contained within their units. However, the proprietary lease that gives occupancy rights to the shareholder-tenants often makes each shareholder-tenant responsible for the maintenance and repair of all fixtures and appliances within the leased unit. Some agreements even adopt the bare-walls approach discussed in connection with condominiums.

Usually, the lease or the cooperative agreement makes the cooperative corporation responsible for insuring these items; however, sometimes this responsibility is left to the shareholder-tenants. Again, only by examining the pertinent documents—the cooperative agreement, the proprietary lease, and local real property law—can the insurance be properly arranged.

Most insurers use the same forms to insure condominiums and cooperatives. Careful drafting would suggest that the policy be endorsed to indicate that "cooperative corporation" be substituted for "condominium" wherever the policy reads "condominium." However, if it can be shown that the insurer was informed during the application process that the owner was a cooperative corporation and not a condominium association, a court of law would certainly make that substitution if a dispute later arose.

Planned Unit Developments

A **planned unit development** (PUD), also referred to as a **homeowners' association**, resembles individual home ownership more than it does a condominium or a cooperative corporation. In a PUD, the occupants have exclusive ownership of their own units, in exactly the same way that individual homeowners own their property. However, a PUD differs from individual home ownership in that the only land that a PUD occupant owns is the land that the structure occupies and not the surrounding land. The surrounding land, including lawns, ponds, private roads, swimming pools, tennis courts, recreational or service buildings, and the like, is owned in common by a homeowners association composed of all the unit owners.

No standard insurance specifications exist for PUDs. In some cases, each unit owner is required to insure his or her own unit and the association is responsible only for the insurance on the commonly owned property. In other cases, the homeowners association has the duty to insure all real property whether owned by the association or an individual unit owner. Only examination of the pertinent documents can indicate how the insurance should be arranged.

When the association is responsible for insuring all the real property, insurers often use condominium policy forms. Associations sometimes have difficulty in obtaining coverage when only the common property is to be insured by the association, since the liability coverage of the policy will then apply to high-risk liability exposures such as swimming pool accidents, assault and battery in public areas, and the like, with little property coverage to balance the account.

Builders Risk Insurance

Buildings under construction—referred to in insurance jargon as **builders risks**—present several special problems. One problem is the changing values as the work progresses; another is the variety of interests involved—such as owner(s), contractor(s), and subcontractor(s).

Buildings under construction also face some special hazards. Building materials are especially susceptible to loss by theft, since it can be difficult to secure a building under construction. Moreover, because fire protection (sprinkler systems, stand pipes, and so on) may not be fully installed or operational and fire walls may not be in place, builders risks can be especially susceptible to fire damage. Collapse is also more likely during construction. These hazards may require special policy treatment and are reflected in the premium rates.

Because builders risk insurance forms are designed to cover buildings or structures *under construction*, they attempt to specify clearly the point at which construction is deemed to be completed and coverage ceases. At that point, the building owner needs to obtain a BPP or other comparable form to replace the builders risk policy.

A basic approach to insuring buildings under construction is the "commercial property" **builders risk coverage form.** Although builders risk policies providing broader coverage can be obtained under inland marine forms (Chapter 11), the "commercial property" builders risk form is often used for smaller projects and by producers who may not have access to the more specialized inland marine markets.

Builders Risk Coverage Form

The ISO builders risk coverage form is similar to the BPP in many respects. The significant differences between the BPP and the builders risk form are described below.

Eligible Property and Insureds

Under *Commercial Lines Manual* (CLM) rules, the builders risk coverage form may be used to insure any building in the course of construction, including buildings such as farm buildings and dwellings that will not be eligible for coverage under the BPP when construction is completed.

The builders risk coverage form may also be used for additions or alterations to existing buildings. Rules in the CLM explain how to go about (1) using the builders risk renovations endorsement to exclude the value of the existing property from the builders risk coverage form, and (2) excluding the value of the renovation from the BPP or other insurance form covering existing property.

The builders risk coverage form may be used to insure the interests of the building owner, the contractor, or the owner and the contractor jointly, as their interests may appear. When appropriate, subcontractors' interests may be excluded or specifically insured using special endorsements.

Covered Property

In general terms, the builders risk form covers the building or structure being built, building materials and supplies intended to become a permanent part of the building, and temporary structures such as scaffolding and forms. The precise definition of covered property is shown in Exhibit 6-3.

Exhibit 6-3
Covered Property Under Builders Risk Form

Covered Property

Covered Property, as used in this Coverage Part, means the following type of property for which a Limit of Insurance is shown in the Declarations:

Building Under Construction, meaning the building or structure described in the Declarations while in the in the course of construction, including:

a. Foundations;

b. If intended to become a permanent part of the building or structure described in the Declarations, the following property located in or on the building or structure or within 100 feet of its premises:

 (1) Fixtures, machinery and equipment used to service the building; and

 (2) Your building materials and supplies used for construction;

c. If not covered by other insurance, temporary structures built or assembled on site, including cribbing, scaffolding and construction forms.

Coverage applies to building supplies and other covered personal property—such as uninstalled windows, doors, sinks, and furnaces—only if they are located in or on the building or structure or within 100 feet of its premises. This restriction eliminates coverage for building materials and supplies while in transit to the work site or in storage at other locations. If the insured is exposed to loss of property in transit to the site and wishes to insure the exposure, separate transit insurance is needed. One advantage of inland marine builders risk policies is that they include coverage for property in transit and property being stored at locations away from the construction site.

The list of "property not covered" by the builders risk form is short. Like the BPP, it excludes land or water. The only other excluded types of property are outdoor (1) lawns, trees, shrubs, or plants, (2) antennas, and (3) signs not attached to the building. Unlike the BPP, the builders risk form does not exclude foundations; they are specifically covered.

Additional Coverages

The builders risk form contains the same four additional coverages as the BPP, relating to debris removal, preservation of property, fire department service charges, and pollutant cleanup and removal. However, the builders risk form does not provide any of the five coverage extensions included in the BPP. Instead, the builders risk form contains only one coverage extension, which is unique to that form.

The extension provides up to $2,500 to cover building materials and supplies owned by others, such as a plumbing or roofing subcontractor that has brought building materials onto the work site. The materials and supplies must be in the named insured's care, custody, or control; located in or on the building or within 100 feet of its premises; and intended to become a permanent part of the building.

In some cases, the insured may be required to insure materials and supplies owned by others. When the value of such property exceeds the limit of the extension, special arrangements are needed to cover the additional values.

Covered Causes of Loss

Like the BPP, the builders risk form must be combined with a basic, broad, or special (and possibly also an earthquake) causes-of-loss form and any necessary endorsements to form a complete policy. Two especially important points about the causes-of-loss forms, as they apply to builders risks, are described below.

Collapse During Construction

As discussed in Chapter 5, the broad and special causes-of-loss forms cover collapse of a building due to certain named perils, including "use of defective materials or methods in construction, remodeling or renovation if the collapse occurs during the course of the construction, remodeling or renovation." The builders risk form specifically excludes collapse caused by this peril, which leaves a serious loss exposure uninsured.

Collapse occurs all too frequently during construction, with tragic financial and human consequences. One of the most notorious collapses of a building under construction was reported by *The New York Times* on April 24, 1987, as follows:

> A $17 million high-rise apartment building under construction in downtown Bridgeport, Conn., collapsed in a thundering roar of concrete slabs and twisted steel beams yesterday afternoon, trapping dozens of construction workers under tons of rubble.

Collapse damage to a building in the course of construction can be insured by adding the **builders risk—collapse during construction endorsement** to the builders risk policy. The endorsement reinstates the coverage described above, and it extends the coverage to also cover collapse caused by faulty design, plans, specifications, or workmanship.

Collapse of a building during construction frequently results from errors committed by one or more of the parties involved in the project, such as architects, engineers, or contractors. If, at the insured's request, such parties are added as additional insureds (which ordinarily shields them from subrogation) or granted waivers of subrogation, the CLM calls for the rate for the endorsement to be multiplied by a factor of five times.

Theft

Building sites are often targeted by thieves. Before burglar alarm systems and doors and windows are installed, burglars can enter the open building at will. Materials that have not yet been installed are an easy target, but burglars will also tear out items that have been installed, such as appliances, lighting fixtures, and copper pipes. Even after doors and windows have been installed, an unoccupied, unguarded, unlighted building is still highly attractive to thieves. Naturally, many risk control measures can and should be taken, including guards, security patrols, and exterior lighting.

As discussed in Chapter 5, the basic and broad causes-of-loss forms do not cover theft. The special form covers theft, subject to various exclusions. One of these exclusions eliminates coverage for loss of "building materials and supplies not attached as part of the building or structure." Thus, even when it includes the special form, a builders risk policy does not cover theft of uninstalled building materials. To obtain coverage for this exposure is another reason why many builders are insured under inland marine builders risk forms.

Completed Value Approach

The inception date of a builders risk policy should be no later than the date construction starts above the lowest level of the basement floor or, if there is no basement, the date construction starts. At that point, the dollar values exposed to loss are little more than zero, and they progressively increase until the building reaches its full completed value.

Unless the reporting form endorsement is chosen (see below), the builders risk coverage form is designed to be issued, at policy inception, for an amount of insurance equal to the *full completed value* of the building. Builders risk rates (which are applied to the full limit of insurance) are lower than regular building rates in consideration of the fact that actual values at risk are substantially lower than the limit of insurance for part of the policy period.

Although builders risk policies are issued for a minimum term of one year, many buildings are completed in a shorter period of time. When coverage ceases, the insured is given a pro-rata refund of the unearned premium.

When Coverage Ceases

The builders risk coverage form is intended to cover buildings during the course of construction only. When they are completed, another policy such as the BPP or a homeowners policy should be used. The builders risk form therefore contains an explicit statement of when coverage comes to an end. This statement is contained in the **"when coverage ceases" provision.**

Unless the insurer specifies otherwise, coverage ceases when an insured building is occupied, in whole or in part, or put to its intended use. Some buildings or structures—water towers, for example—are not literally "occupied." Even if no occupancy or use takes place—as, for example, if the building remains vacant while the owner tries to sell it—coverage ceases ninety days after the construction is completed or abandoned. Coverage ceases immediately when the named insured's interest in the property ceases or the property is accepted by the purchaser. Obviously, coverage also ceases when the policy expires or is canceled. Despite the apparent precision of these policy provisions, the date and time that one of these conditions occurs are sometimes difficult to determine.

Valuation

The builders risk coverage form contains a standard valuation condition, providing coverage on the basis of actual cash value. Because there is usually little practical difference between the actual cash value and the replacement cost of a building under construction, the builders risk coverage form does not contain the optional replacement cost coverage provisions of the BPP.

Need for Adequate Insurance

The policy condition titled "need for adequate insurance" is, in effect, a 100 percent coinsurance clause in which the amount of insurance that should be carried is based on the value of the building on the date it will be completed. The formula is as follows:

$$\left(\frac{\text{Limit of Insurance}}{\text{Completed Value}} \times \text{Loss}\right) - \text{Deductible} = \text{Amount Payable}$$

No underinsurance penalty is involved if, at the time of the loss, the limit of insurance equals or exceeds the building's completed value. The CLM points out that the value of all permanent fixtures and decorations that constitute a part of the building should be included in setting the completed value.

Although complying with this requirement might appear to be a simple matter, the completed value of a building is not necessarily firmly fixed before construction begins. Changes in design, increases in labor or material costs, or accidents during the course of construction can increase the final cost of the building—and can result in a potential penalty for underinsurance if a loss occurs.

To avoid this problem, the builders risk limit should be reviewed whenever changes occur that will increase the completed value of the building. (The agreed value option is not available for builders risk insurance.) If the policy limit is increased at some point in the policy period, CLM rules call for the additional premium to be calculated from the time of policy inception regardless of when the increase becomes effective.

Builders Risk Reporting Form

Through use of the **builders risk reporting form endorsement**, the builders risk form can be arranged on a value reporting basis instead of the completed value approach described above. The endorsement requires the insured to report to the insurer the actual cash value of covered property as of a specified date each month during the policy period. The insurer charges an initial premium and adjusts the premium during the policy period based on the values reported by the insured. Reports are overdue if not received by the insurer within thirty days after the effective date of each required report of value.

To illustrate, assume that the insured selects the tenth of the month as the effective date of reports, and the policy period began on May 20. Thus, the first report would show the value of the property as of June 10, and this report must be made to the insurer by no later than July 10 (thirty days after the *effective date* of the report).

As with the value reporting form used with the BPP, serious penalties apply if reports are late or inaccurate.

First Report Overdue

If at the time of a loss no report has been made as required, the insurer will not pay more than the actual cash value as of the policy inception date. Using the reporting dates stated above, this penalty would apply if a loss occurred after July 10 and no report had been received by the insurer.

Subsequent Report Overdue

If at least one report has been made but a later required report is overdue, the insurer will not pay more than the value stated in the last report actually filed. In the above example, this penalty would apply if a loss occurred on November 26 and no report had been made since one filed on September 20 for the period ending September 10. In this case, the report for the period ending October 10 was overdue, so the insured would not be able to collect more than the amount reported on September 20. Had the next report been submitted on time (that is, within thirty days after October 10) and accurately, the insured would have been able to collect the full amount of loss occurring on November 26, even if it exceeded the amount last reported.

Inaccurate Reports

The builders risk reporting form contains the same type of full reporting clause as in the value reporting form used with the BPP. That is, if actual values at the time of the last report were greater than the values reported, the insurer's payment will not exceed that proportion of the loss that the value reported bears to the actual value of covered property. For example, if the value reported was $100,000 and the insurer could show that the actual value at the time of that report was $150,000, the insured would be able to collect only $100,000/$150,000 (two-thirds) of the loss, minus the deductible.

Most Insureds Prefer Completed Value

Given the potential penalties for late or inaccurate reports, it is not surprising that most insureds prefer their builders risk policies to apply on a completed value basis. The potential savings that can result from using the reporting form are usually too small to justify the added effort required to comply with the reporting requirements.

Limitations on Waiver of Subrogation

The builders risk form modifies the commercial property condition that grants the insured much leeway in waiving subrogation against others. The builders risk form provides that the insured may not waive its rights to recover damages from an architect, engineer, or building trades contractor or subcontractor unless agreed to in writing by the insurance company. Since many construction agreements do contain such waivers, the risk manager must either obtain permission from the insurance company or amend the construction contract to provide that the waiver is effective only to the extent permitted by insurance.

Other Coverage for Builders Risks

Alternatives to the ISO builders risk form include the following:

- The BPP coverage form
- Inland marine builders risk policies
- Highly protected risk (HPR) and other independently developed policies

BPP Coverage

As discussed in Chapter 3, the BPP provides some coverage for new construction.

Coverage for *additions or renovations* is available under the BPP as part of "building" coverage, provided there is no other insurance in effect. The amount of insurance would have to be increased to reflect the added value. This could be done either at the inception of the project based on the estimated completed value or periodically as the work progressed to reflect the value increase expected before the next adjustment is to be made. For smaller renovation or addition projects, the BPP is often the most effective alternative.

The BPP also provides a coverage extension for thirty days for up to 25 percent of the amount of building insurance or $250,000, whichever is less, for *new buildings* at the described premises. No coverage is provided for new construction away from the premises. The $250,000 limit for the extension can be increased by endorsement if needed.

Inland Marine Policies

Many builders risks are insured on inland marine forms, as noted above. Rating under inland marine forms is often more flexible than under commercial property forms, and inland marine underwriters can tailor forms to create specialized insurance contracts for large or complex projects. Flood and earthquake coverage, transit coverage, and theft coverage for property that has not been attached to the building can often be obtained in an inland marine builders risk policy. Inland marine policies for insuring builders risks and related loss exposures (such as contractors' mobile equipment) will be discussed in Chapter 11.

HPR and Independent Forms

HPR forms, discussed in Chapter 14, and other independent property forms sometimes include automatic coverage for new construction during the policy period with no time limit other than policy expiration and with no premium adjustment required. (Values are adjusted on renewal.) Since these policies are frequently written for blanket limits of insurance, if the total values exposed to any one loss do not exceed the limit of insurance, no increase in amount and no additional premium are necessary.

Standard Property Policy

The **standard property policy** (SPP) was developed by ISO for use when insurers are reluctant to grant the broader coverage of the BPP and related causes-of-loss forms. The SPP is used by the FAIR plans, which function as the residual markets for property insurance in many states.

The SPP is a self-contained monoline policy containing all necessary coverages, conditions, exclusions, and causes-of-loss descriptions in a single document. Only a completed declarations page is needed to complete the contract. As a result, the SPP cannot be a part of a package policy. Any additional coverages wanted by an insured with the SPP—such as general liability coverage—must be obtained in a separate policy.

In most respects, property coverage under the SPP is similar to that under the BPP. It can also be endorsed to cover condominium associations, condominium unit owners, or builders risks. The discussion that follows summarizes the differences, which are also illustrated in Exhibit 6-4.

Covered Property

The declarations indicate what limits of insurance, if any, apply to buildings, business personal property, or property of others. The additional coverages and coverage extensions are the same as those of the BPP, except that the coverage extensions apply only to property located in the same state as the described premises.

Exhibit 6-4
Comparison of SPP and BPP

Standard Property Policy	BPP With Basic Perils
Policy is self-contained. Form includes: • Common policy conditions • Commercial property conditions • Causes of loss (and exclusions)	Separate forms must be attached to provide these.
Coverage may be purchased separately for the following incremental groupings of causes of loss: • Fire, lightning, & explosion (mandatory) • Windstorm and hail (may be excluded), smoke, aircraft or vehicles, riot or civil commotion, sinkhole collapse, volcanic action • Vandalism and/or sprinkler leakage	All perils included automatically in basic causes-of-loss form, with options to exclude: • Windstorm and hail • Vandalism • Sprinkler leakage
Coverage extensions apply only in state where described premises are located.	No such limitation.
5 days' notice of cancellation permitted—10 days for mortgage holders.	30 days' notice of cancellation, except 10 days for nonpayment of premium.
No coverage for buildings vacant or unoccupied after: • 30 days for vandalism • 60 days for any other peril	Unlimited unoccupancy permitted. No coverage for vacancy after 60 days for losses due to vandalism or sprinkler leakage.
No replacement cost coverage.	$2,500 replacement cost coverage built in for building losses if coinsurance is complied with. Full replacement cost coverage is optional.
Coverage is suspended during any increase in hazard.	No such condition.
No optional coverages.	Optional coverages available in form for inflation guard and agreed value.

Adapted from ISO handout at Commercial Lines Seminar, 1986.

Coverage applies on an actual cash value basis. There is no replacement cost option, nor are the inflation guard and agreed value options offered.

Covered Perils

All the perils covered by the basic causes-of-loss form are available in the SPP. Considering the nature of the exposures insured with the SPP, flexibility in limiting the covered perils is an important feature of the policy. Some of the possible combinations of perils include the following:

- Fire, lightning, and explosion (all are mandatory).
- Windstorm, hail, smoke, aircraft, vehicles, riot, civil commotion, sinkhole collapse, and volcanic action can be added by making an appropriate entry in the declarations (windstorm and hail can be omitted).
- Vandalism and sprinkler leakage can also be triggered by marking the declarations page.

Conditions

The SPP contains three conditions that result in more restrictive coverage than under the BPP.

Vacancy and Unoccupancy

The insurer will not pay for loss or damage by any peril if the building has been vacant *or unoccupied* for more than sixty days. After thirty days of vacancy or unoccupancy, coverage for vandalism ceases. Vacancy is defined to mean containing no contents pertaining to the operations or activities customary to occupancy of the building, rather than the stricter definition that appears in the BPP. This does not liberalize coverage in the SPP since it, unlike the BPP, also excludes coverage when the premises are unoccupied.

Increase in Hazard

Coverage is suspended during any period in which the hazard has been increased by means within the knowledge and control of the named insured. This clause, which was a provision of the standard fire policy, is not included in the BPP.

Cancellation

The insurer may cancel the policy by providing only five days' advance notice to the insured. This difference from the BPP is not significant since most state laws require longer notification periods.

Legal Liability Coverage Form

The **legal liability coverage form** is an unusual commercial property form since it actually provides liability coverage on property of others in the insured's care, custody, or control. The logic of including a liability form in the "commercial property" division is based on the nature of the underlying exposure: Fire is the major cause of property loss for which a bailee is held liable. When this coverage was first developed, underwriting functions were split into property and liability departments; it was the property underwriters (then called "fire underwriters") who had the expertise needed to evaluate the fire and other property perils involved in this exposure.

The commercial general liability (CGL) coverage form, which is used to insure most of an organization's general liability exposures, excludes coverage for damage to property of others in the insured's care, custody, or control. However, by exception to the exclusions, it does provide limited coverage for liability arising out of damage to *real property* rented to or temporarily used by the insured. This so-called fire legal liability coverage of the CGL form insures property damage liability arising out of fire damage (but not damage by other perils) to the portion of the building occupied by the insured. A minimum of $25,000 fire legal liability coverage is provided by the standard CGL form, and this amount can be increased.

As discussed in Chapter 3, the building and personal property coverage form (BPP) can be used to insure personal property of others in the insured's care, custody, or control. The BPP coverage for personal property of others applies regardless of whether the insured is legally liable to pay the customer for the damage. Inland marine bailees customers policies, discussed in Chapter 11, provide similar coverage.

The legal liability coverage form takes a different approach. It covers loss by an insured peril to property of others in the insured's care, custody, or control, but *only if the insured is legally liable for the loss*. Because the legal liability coverage form covers only legal liability losses, and not all losses, the rate is lower than the usual "contents" or "building" rate.

The legal liability coverage form can be used to cover either real property or personal property. The property covered must be described in the declarations or a coverage schedule.

Insuring Agreement

The insuring agreement of the legal liability coverage form states that the insurer agrees to pay those sums that the named insured becomes legally obligated to pay as damages because of direct physical loss or damage, including loss of use, to covered property caused by accident and arising out of any covered cause of loss.

The fact that "loss of use" is included means that the insurer will pay for time element losses that the owner of the property incurs as a result of the physical damage. Such time element losses include loss of income or rental of replacement property. This is an important advantage of the legal liability form. Although the BPP pays for direct damage to property of others regardless of fault, the BPP does not cover claims for loss of use of the damaged property.

The causes of loss covered by the legal liability coverage form are determined by whichever causes-of-loss form is attached to it. The basic, broad, and special causes-of-loss forms all cover a much broader scope of perils than the fire legal liability coverage of the CGL.

Besides paying for damages up to the limit of insurance, the insurer agrees to pay related defense costs and other supplementary benefits in addition to the limit. As is common with liability insurance, the form contains no deductible.

Exclusions

In addition to the provisions discussed in Chapter 5, the causes-of-loss forms contain an exclusion that applies only to the legal liability coverage form. The exclusion applies to damages that the insured is legally liable to pay solely by reason of the insured's assumption of liability in a contract or agreement. The test for applying this exclusion is: Would the insured have been liable in absence of the assumption of liability? If so, the exclusion does not apply even though the insured may have made some assumption of liability. When the insured has assumed responsibility for property regardless of negligence, the exposure should be insured by the "property of others" portion of the BPP, which provides coverage on a direct basis.

All of the other exclusions of the causes-of-loss forms apply to the legal liability coverage form except the following:

- Ordinance or law
- Governmental action
- Nuclear hazard
- Off-premises services
- War and military action

The nuclear hazard exclusion is replaced with an exclusion of defense costs or damages for all loss resulting from nuclear reaction or radiation or radioactive contamination, however caused.

Premium Rates

Legal liability coverage is less costly than direct property insurance. The legal liability rate is lower because the insurer pays only when the insured is responsible for the damage. The rate for real property is 25 percent of the 80 percent coinsurance building rate that would otherwise apply. For personal property, the rate is 50 percent of the 80 percent coinsurance contents rate. Thus, for example, if the 80 percent coinsurance contents rate is $.50 per $100 of coverage, the legal liability rate for contents at the same location is $.25 per $100.

Insurance to Value

There is no coinsurance clause in the legal liability coverage form and therefore no requirement that the insured purchase insurance in an amount equal to the value of the covered property. This is another advantage of using the legal liability form instead of the BPP; the insured frequently does not know the value of property of others in his or her care, custody, or control.

Despite the omission of coinsurance, insurance buyers and advisers should carefully estimate the severity of the exposure when establishing insurance limits. The maximum possible loss that could be sustained under this form would include loss of all covered property of others in the care, custody, or control of the insured—including damages for loss of use—that might be sustained in a single loss.

As noted earlier, the legal liability coverage form can also be used to cover the insured's liability for damage to *building* property in the insured's care, custody, or control. If the insured occupies the entire building, the limit of insurance should reflect the full value of the building, including projected damages for loss of use. If the tenant occupies only a portion of the building, the limit should reflect the value of that portion only (plus loss of use). Damage to portions of the building not in the insured's care, custody, or control, if caused by the insured's negligence, would normally be covered by the insured's CGL insurance.

Glass Coverage Form

The **glass coverage form** is available for supplementing the glass coverage provided by the BPP, condominium forms, or builders risk form in connection with the basic, broad, or special causes-of-loss forms. To help you understand when the glass coverage form is needed, we will describe some of the characteristics of glass loss exposures and review the coverage that other forms provide for glass.

Glass Loss Exposures

Exterior glass is normally considered part of the building. Glass may also be part of the contents of a building—for example, glass in movable showcases or merchandise made of glass or glass bottles used as containers. In still other cases, glass may be considered improvements and betterments, such as tenant's glass office partitions.

Glass of many different types is subject to breakage or other damage by a variety of causes. While glass exposures represent a relatively minor portion of property values for most insureds, some buildings have exterior walls composed almost entirely of glass, with glass values in the millions of dollars.

An exposure to additional loss results from laws and ordinances in some localities that require glass in some cases to be replaced with "safety glazing material." This requirement generally applies to glass in doors or display windows that pedestrians might inadvertently walk or run into. A merchant whose windows are of ordinary glass may be required by law to install the more expensive safety glazing materials if the windows are broken.

Glass Coverage Under the BPP and Other Forms

The BPP, the condominium coverage forms, and the builders risk coverage form do not exclude glass, but the causes-of-loss forms impose substantial coverage restrictions.

The basic causes-of-loss form covers glass breakage only when it is caused by one of the named perils, with the exception of the vandalism peril, which excludes breakage of building glass (other than glass building blocks) by vandals.

The broad form includes a glass breakage peril, subject to limits of $100 per item and $500 per occurrence. These limits apply only to glass breakage—such as glass breakage by vandalism—that is not caused by another covered peril.

The special form covers glass breakage by any cause of loss not specifically excluded. The $100 per item and $500 per occurrence limits apply to glass breakage caused by perils *other than* the "specified causes of loss" (the broad form perils other than glass breakage).

The main reason for purchasing the glass coverage form is to eliminate the $100/$500 limitations on glass breakage caused by perils other than the basic and broad form perils or the "specified causes of loss" in the special form. Moreover, the glass coverage form does not contain some of the exclusions—such as flood and earthquake—found in the causes-of-loss forms. Other advantages of the glass form will be apparent as it is described below.

Covered Property

Certain types of glass, which can usually be insured under inland marine forms, are ineligible for the glass coverage form. These ineligible types include art glass, halftone screens, lenses, memorial windows, mosaic art, rotogravure screens, stained glass, and stained glass in leaded sections. Virtually all other "glass" is eligible, including such diversified categories as burglar alarm foil, glass blocks, mirrors, and plastic substitutes for glass such as Plexiglas and Lucite.

Under the glass form, the insurer agrees to pay for direct physical loss of or damage to the described glass. The location of the building is listed, along with individual descriptions of covered glass or wording such as "all glass of the type described." The description may appear in the declarations or, more usually, in a glass coverage schedule that describes the kind of glass and its size, along with a description of any lettering, ornamentation, or other covered decorations.

Glass that is broken or cracked at the inception of the policy period can be covered by using a **broken or cracked glass exclusion endorsement,** which describes (by diagram or verbally) the current extent of the damage and excludes coverage for any extension of current breaks or cracks. This approach might be feasible when, for example, a large plate glass window has a rock chip, a small bullet hole, or a cracked corner which, by itself, does not warrant replacement of the window.

Covered Perils

Two causes of loss are covered in the glass coverage form: (1) breakage of glass and (2) chemicals accidentally or maliciously applied to glass. Other than scratches or abrasions, these two perils encompass virtually every cause of damage to or destruction of glass.

Only three causes of loss are excluded: nuclear hazard, war, and fire. Glass breakage caused by flood or earthquake is therefore covered, as is any increase in replacement cost resulting from building ordinances or laws. Glass breakage by fire is covered under the BPP (or other building and contents form) only.

The insurer will not pay for loss or damage when the building has been vacant for more than sixty consecutive days before the loss. Coverage for vacant buildings may be added for an additional premium—subject, of course, to the insurer's approval.

Additional Coverages

The glass coverage form includes four additional coverages relating to debris removal, temporary plates, frames, and removal of obstructions. The form also provides a coverage extension for newly acquired glass. These features are described below.

Debris Removal

When glass breaks, its debris may be blown into the street or sidewalks or get enmeshed in carpets, furniture, or other personal property. Accordingly, the glass coverage form pays the expenses of removing debris of covered property following damage by a covered peril.

Temporary Plates

The insurer agrees to pay the cost of installing temporary plates in, or boarding up, openings containing insured glass when necessary because of delay in repairing or replacing such damaged glass.

Frames

The insurer agrees to pay the necessary cost of repairing or replacing frames encasing the damaged glass.

Removal of Obstructions

Also covered is the cost incurred to remove or replace any obstructions, other than window displays, when repairing or replacing covered glass. A certain amount of clear space is required to maneuver a large pane of glass. However, there is no coverage for removing or replacing window displays.

Newly Acquired Glass

An extension similar to the newly acquired property extension of the BPP provides thirty days' automatic coverage for newly acquired glass at the described location or glass at newly acquired locations. Within thirty days the insured must report the new location to the insurer and pay a premium from the date the exposure was originally acquired.

Limits, Deductible

An unusual feature of the glass coverage form is that it usually has no dollar limit of coverage on glass. Premiums are calculated based on the type, size, and location of the glass rather than by applying rates to a limit of insurance. Since there is no overall limit, there is also no coinsurance clause.

However, a dollar limit is usually specified in the glass coverage schedule for lettering and ornamentation. Some types of glass in special installations may also be insured for a specified dollar limit.

The glass coverage form can be issued with no deductible or with a per-occurrence deductible—not a per-item deductible. CLM rules require a minimum deductible of $50 when the deductible option is selected.

Replacement Service

In many glass losses, the replacement is arranged directly by the insurance company. In fact, one important reason for the purchase of glass insurance is to secure the replacement service of the insurer. Replacement service can be especially important when a storm results in heavy breakage in a neighborhood. The volume of business an insurance company gives to a glass dealer may secure preferred service for replacements ordered by the insurance company.

Large Plates Replacement Option

An "optional coverage" printed in the policy is actually an optional *reduction* in coverage in exchange for a premium credit. Large plates of glass over 100 square feet are costly to repair or replace. The **loss payment for large plates option** gives the insurer the right to replace such large plates with two or more smaller plates of glass and to pay for the necessary alterations to accomplish this. The total cost for smaller plates is often less than the cost of the larger plate even with the added cost for the alterations to the frames.

Leasehold Interest Coverage Form

The **leasehold interest coverage form** is available for insuring a tenant's financial losses resulting from the cancellation of the tenant's lease because of damage to the premises by an insured peril. Some leases of premises permit the lessor (landlord) to terminate the lease if (1) the building or premises are damaged by fire or other perils to a stipulated percentage of the value of the building or premises or (2) the amount of time required to repair or replace the damaged property exceeds a stipulated period. A typical cancellation clause in a lease reads as follows:

> If the building or premises are damaged by fire or other cause to the extent of 25 percent of the value thereof, the lease may be terminated by the lessor.

Cancellation of a lease may cause a lessee (tenant) to suffer a financial loss in any of the following circumstances:

1. The lessee has a lease at a rental rate much lower than the current rental value of comparable premises. If, as is likely the case, the lessee would be unable to obtain as favorable a lease upon cancellation, the loss would be the additional cost to rent equivalent premises for the duration of the current lease.
2. The lessee has sublet the premises to another at a profit. The loss would be the loss of the profit margin for the duration of the lease.
3. The lessee paid a bonus to acquire the lease. The loss would be the unamortized value of the bonus. If, for example, the bonus was $5,000 for a five-year lease and the lease was canceled with three years remaining on the lease, the unamortized value would be 3/5 of the $5,000, or $3,000.
4. The lessee has paid advance rent that is not recoverable under the terms of the lease in the event of cancellation. The loss would be the value of the advance rent.
5. The lessee has installed improvements and betterments. The tenant's use value of the improvements and betterments would be lost as a result of the cancellation of the lease. This exposure is distinct from the improvements and betterments exposure covered by the BPP. The BPP exposure involves physical damage to the improvements by a covered cause of loss. In contrast, a leasehold interest loss involving improvements and betterments is caused by cancellation of the lease because of damage by an insured peril at the insured premises; the improvements and betterments themselves need not be damaged at all.

Leasehold interest insurance covers the total amount of net leasehold interest of the insured for the unexpired period of the lease. The amount of insurance is automatically reduced during the life of the lease in much the same way that some mortgage life insurance policies reduce in amount each month.

For some organizations, leasehold interest insurance fills a valuable need. As a practical matter, however, little insurance of this type is actually used. This may be because many risk managers and producers are unaware of its existence. Leasehold interest is also a relatively small exposure for most tenants, one that they may choose to retain. However, in some instances, such as long-term leases in areas where rents have risen sharply, the cancellation of a lease can pose a substantial loss exposure.

Tenants' Improvements and Betterments

As discussed in Chapter 3, the description of "your business personal property" includes the insured's use interest as a tenant in improvements and betterments. Because the subject of insuring improvements and betterments involves several important considerations and bears some relationship to leasehold interest insurance, it is revisited in additional detail here.

The specific description in the BPP of the covered exposure reads as follows:

> Your use interest as tenant in improvements and betterments.
>
> Improvements and betterments are fixtures, alterations, installations or additions:
>
> (a) Made a part of the building or structure you occupy but do not own; and
>
> (b) You acquired or made at your expense but cannot legally remove.

Improvements and betterments are fixtures to real property that generally change the property and enhance its value—that is, they improve or better the property. However, improvements and betterments do not include "trade fixtures."

Trade Fixtures Versus Improvements and Betterments

The question often arises whether an item is a trade fixture or an improvement or betterment. Ideally, such questions are settled in the lease agreement, but often they are not. As discussed in Chapter 3, fixtures are part of the realty and are the property of the building owner. **Trade fixtures**, however, are characterized by the right (or obligation) of the tenant to remove them when the premises are vacated. They may include counters, machinery, and appliances.

Whether an item is a trade fixture or an improvement and betterment cannot always be established by looking at it—not even by examining the apparent firmness of its attachment to the structure. Many cases are determined by trade customs. Thus, for example, walk-in freezers and refrigerators in a restaurant and the stage machinery in a theater may be completely built-in and firmly attached to the structure. However, by custom they are trade fixtures subject to removal by the tenant and not building improvements.

The BPP covers a tenant's trade fixtures under the "furniture and fixtures" category of the business personal property coverage, and a tenant's improvements and betterments are covered under another category of the coverage. Thus, both trade fixtures and improvements and betterments are covered. However, the valuation basis in the event of a loss differs, thus making the distinction important.

Trade fixtures are valued at actual cash value (ACV) or replacement cost, depending on which option the insured has purchased. Improvements and betterments, as discussed below, can sometimes be valued on a basis that reflects neither ACV nor replacement cost.

Repairs and Maintenance

Another question about the definition of improvements and betterments concerns the status of maintenance performed by the tenant, such as painting or minor repairs. One school of thought holds that improvements and betterments must be more substantial, such as a new store front, partitions, acoustical insulation, elevators, floor coverings, and central air conditioning systems. Another school of thought holds that anything a tenant does that upgrades the building or structure and cannot be removed qualifies as improvements and betterments. Under the second theory, painting done by the tenant would be covered as an improvement and betterment. Local usage differs and the exact facts in any particular case would have to be considered.[1]

If a tenant has a significant exposure in this area—for example, he or she is responsible for all repairs to the building under the terms of a long-term lease—coverage should be clarified with the underwriter when the policy is issued.

Building Owner's Coverage

Under the BPP, a landlord's interest in any improvements and betterments is insured by the landlord's building coverage. The amount of building insurance carried by the landlord should therefore reflect any values that tenants have added to the structure. Since the landlord and the tenant have simultaneous but separate insurable interests in the same property, each may buy insurance. In order to avoid a coinsurance penalty, the landlord should include the value of improvements and betterments when selecting a building insurance limit. Such coexistent insurance on separate interests is enforceable: the landlord can collect for the loss of owned property, and the tenant can collect on the basis of loss of use of the property for the remainder of the rental or lease period.

The most common arrangement is for the landlord to carry insurance on the building, including the landlord's interest in the improvements, while the tenant insures its use interest in the improvements. This is why most standard forms, including the BPP, provide automatic coverage on a tenant's interest in improvements when the tenant buys contents coverage.

Tenant's Coverage

Since the tenant's interest in the improvements lies in the right to use them, measurement of the tenant's loss requires special attention. The BPP specifies three different ways of determining the amount the tenant can recover for loss to improvements and betterments.

When Owner Repairs Without Charge

When the owner repairs or replaces the improvements without charge to the tenant, the tenant's insurance pays nothing.

When Tenant Repairs

When the tenant makes prompt repairs or replacement, the improvements and betterments coverage pays based on the actual cash value (or replacement cost, if that option has been chosen) of the improvements just as though the tenant owned the improvements.

When Not Repaired or Replaced

When the improvements are not repaired or replaced, payment is based on unamortized cost. An example will clarify the unamortized cost approach. Suppose improvements costing $60,000 were installed on June 1, 1994. On June 1, 1999, the improvements are destroyed, and they are not replaced. At the time of the loss, the tenant has a lease running to June 1, 2009. The tenant invested $60,000, expecting to use the improvements for a period of fifteen years (1994 to 2009). However, only five of those fifteen years had passed at the time of the loss. Since five-fifteenths (one-third) of the original cost has been "used up" at the time of the loss, the insurer will pay two-thirds of the original $60,000, or $40,000, to cover the tenant's loss.

The following points about the third method of valuation are especially noteworthy:

1. The dollar figure used as the basis is the *original* cost, including necessary cost to prepare the premises before the improvements could be installed. Neither actual cash value nor replacement cost is relevant in this situation.

2. The lease whose expiration date is considered is the one in effect *at the time of loss*. If the lease contains a renewal option, then the expiration of the renewal option period is used.

Alternatives to Both the Landlord and the Tenant Carrying Insurance

One alternative is for the owner and tenant to be named as insureds in a single policy. A drawback to this approach is that owners and tenants do not always favor the idea of sharing a policy. When owner and tenant are jointly insured, the acts of one may affect the coverage of the other. For example, contracts are voidable in the event of fraud by an insured.

Another problem is that since the first named insured would have the right to cancel the policy, that named insured may have more control over the coverage than the other. These problems do not exist when each party has its own insurance.

A second alternative is for the lease to require one party to make repairs in the event of damage. In that manner, the other party is protected to the extent the obligor (the party with the obligation) can fulfill its duty. A common arrangement to assure the financial ability to make the repairs is to require that the obligor carry adequate insurance on the property. One premium, in effect, pays for protection for both parties. To avoid coinsurance problems, the other party can exclude the improvements and betterments from its insurance coverage. There is, of course, the possibility that the coverage may be voided by acts or omissions of the insured party.

Summary

In addition to the BPP, several other "commercial property" forms are available for insuring special situations and exposures.

The *condominium association coverage form* can be used to insure a condominium association against loss to its buildings, personal property, and personal property of others. However, the form covers fixtures, improvements, alterations, and appliances *within condominium units* only if the condominium association agreement requires the association to insure them.

The *condominium commercial unit-owners coverage form* provides business personal property coverage for commercial (not residential) unit owners. The form provides essentially the same coverage for the insured's business personal property as the BPP. To dovetail with the condominium association form, the unit-owners form covers fixtures, improvements, alterations, and appliances owned by the insured unless the condominium association agreement requires the association to insure them. Loss assessment coverage and miscellaneous real property coverage can be added to the unit-owners form by endorsement.

The *builders risk coverage form* is designed to insure the interests of owners and/or contractors in buildings or other structures during the course of construction. The form covers the building under construction, building materials in or on the building or within 100 feet of the premises, and temporary structures at the construction site. The builders risk form is normally issued with a limit equal to the completed value of the building. An alternative approach is for the insured to report actual values to the insurer monthly.

The *standard property policy* (SPP) is designed for use in situations (such as FAIR plans) when insurers are reluctant to grant the broader coverage of the BPP and related causes-of-loss forms. The SPP covers fire, lightning, and explosion; other basic perils can be added. Some SPP conditions are more restrictive than under the BPP, and none of the BPP optional coverages are available under the SPP.

The *legal liability coverage form* insures damage to real or personal property of others in the insured's care, custody, or control—*but only if the insured is legally liable for the loss*. Advantages of the legal liability approach include lower premiums and coverage for the owner's loss of use of the property.

The *glass coverage form* provides extremely broad coverage on glass and eliminates the $100 per pane and $500 per occurrence limits that apply to glass breakage by some perils under the broad and special causes-of-loss forms. The form covers glass breakage and damage by chemicals, subject to exclusions of nuclear hazard, war, and fire.

The *leasehold interest coverage form* covers a tenant against losses resulting from cancellation of the tenant's lease because of damage by an insured peril at the insured location.

A tenant's use interest in improvements and betterments is covered under the BPP. When insuring this exposure, several questions may arise: the distinction between "improvements and betterments" and "trade fixtures"; the status of maintenance and repairs performed by a tenant; and avoiding coverage overlaps in the landlord's and tenant's property policies.

Chapter Note

1. Paul I. Thomas and Prentiss B. Reed, Sr., *Adjustment of Property Losses*, 4th ed. (New York: McGraw-Hill Book Company, 1977), pp. 202-203.

Chapter 7

Business Income Loss Exposures

The "commercial property" forms discussed in preceding chapters are mainly concerned with insuring two financial effects of property loss: (1) reduction in value of the property and (2) increased costs to repair or replace the property. Business income insurance, although part of the "commercial property" line, covers two other financial effects:

1. Reduction of the insured's revenues because of physical damage to covered property by a covered cause of loss
2. Extra expenses that the insured incurs to avoid or minimize loss of income following a physical loss

Business income exposures are often referred to as **time element** or **business interruption exposures**. Both of these phrases emphasize important attributes of the overall exposure. The phrase "time element" emphasizes the fact that the severity of a business income loss usually increases with the length of time required to restore the damaged property. "Business interruption" emphasizes the operational effect of a physical loss that leads to either reduction in revenues or the incurring of extra expenses. The phrases "business income," "time element," and "business interruption" are used interchangeably in practice and in this text.

Despite the presence of the word "business" in two of the phrases, the exposure is not unique to for-profit organizations. Not-for-profit entities such as universities, museums, and governmental units can all lose revenues and incur extra expenses following a physical loss to their properties. For example, following destruction of its administration building, a college may be unable to collect tuitions; following extensive fire damage to its galleries, a museum may be unable for several months to admit visitors and collect admissions; and following earthquake damage to a bridge, a transit authority may be unable to collect bridge tolls until repairs are made. In each of these situations, the potential loss of revenue may be just as serious as for a "business" whose operations have been slowed down or suspended because of property loss.

This chapter examines business income loss exposures; business income insurance is examined in Chapter 8.

Financial Elements of Business Income Loss

Business income losses can be quantified in terms of net income. **Net income** is the difference between **revenues** (assets received, such as money from sales of goods or services) and **expenses** (reductions in net assets, such as money paid for merchandise, rent, and insurance). The definition of net income can be expressed by the simple formula that follows:

Revenues – Expenses = Net Income

As discussed in Chapter 1 and above, two adverse financial effects of a business interruption are (1) decrease in revenues and (2) the incurring of extra expenses. Net income reflects both of these financial effects, as well as a third, more subtle, effect: some normal expenses may actually *decrease* during a shutdown or a slowdown. Any decrease in expenses during a business interruption reduces the loss of net income by an equal amount.

A simple example of a business interruption loss experienced by a fictitious business—an individual proprietorship called Pete's Auto Repair—will help to illustrate how these components interact in a business income loss. Assume that most of Pete's business personal property, and parts of his building, were damaged by fire and ensuing smoke and water damage and that the resulting business interruption lasted for two months.

Loss of Net Income

To measure Pete's loss of net income, we can compare (1) his net income if no loss had occurred with (2) his actual income during the two months that the store was being repaired. In Pete's case, all revenues are in the form of sales of auto repair labor and parts.

By examining income statements from previous months and years, the figures in the left column below were determined to be a reasonable projection of what Pete's financial results would have been for the two months if no loss had occurred. The figures in the right column show what actually happened for the same period.

	Normal	Actual
Sales	$60,000	–0–
Expenses	50,000	8,000
Net Income (Loss)	$10,000	($8,000)

During the shutdown, Pete had no revenue from sales. However, Pete incurred $8,000 of expenses, since he continued the salary for a key employee and paid some other normal expenses. Other expenses were curtailed or below normal. For example, hourly employees were not paid during the shutdown, utility charges were reduced, and no shop supplies were consumed.

As a result of these changes in revenues and expenses, Pete's actual net income during the shutdown was a net loss of $8,000, meaning that expenses exceeded sales by $8,000. In financial statements, losses are expressed by placing the amount of loss inside parentheses, as above. In mathematical notation, the loss could also be expressed as –$8,000.

Under normal circumstances, if no loss had occurred, Pete would have experienced a net profit of $10,000, meaning that sales would have exceeded expenses by $10,000. Pete's loss of net income attributable to the shutdown is therefore the difference between what would have occurred had there been no loss and what actually occurred. The amount of the loss can be calculated by subtracting the actual net income from the projected normal net income, as shown below:

$$\$10,000 - (-\$8,000) = \$18,000$$

The difference between the net profit that would have occurred and the net loss that did occur can also be visualized as the amount of dollars between two points on a number line, as shown below:

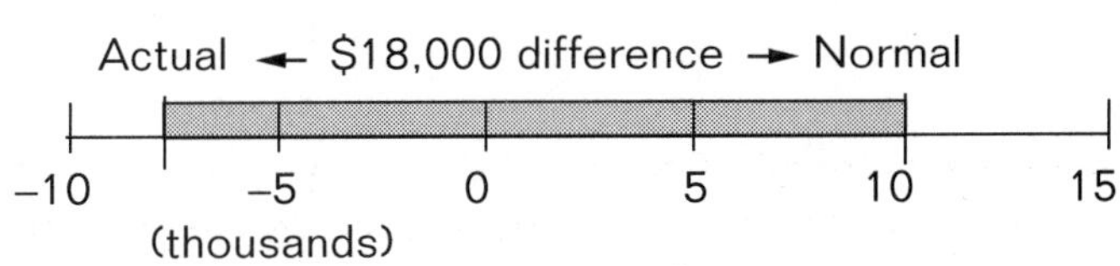

In other words, Pete's net income was reduced by $18,000 during the shutdown. This $18,000 reduction in net income is the "business income" loss that is insurable under business income insurance. (Note that property-related repair or replacement expenses—such as paying the contractor handling repairs—would not be taken into consideration for purposes of calculating the *income* loss.)

"Net Loss" Versus Business Income Loss

Looking only at Pete's actual net income during the shutdown, we can say that Pete experienced a net loss of $8,000 for that period. Although that is an accurate statement, it does not address the business income loss.

As explained above, Pete's business income loss for purposes of risk management treatment is not the $8,000 net loss for that period but the *difference* between the net income that would have been earned under normal circumstances and the net profit or loss that actually occurred. In evaluating business income losses that have occurred, one must always compare what *did* occur during the period with what *would have* occurred during the same period. Similarly, in analyzing business income exposures (losses that may occur), one must compare what *could* occur during the shutdown or slowdown with what *would* occur during the same period under normal circumstances.

Using a similar analysis, it can be seen that an organization that is not operating profitably under normal circumstances (in other words, it is operating at a net loss) can also suffer a business income loss. In the case of an unprofitable business, a slowdown or shutdown may *increase* the net loss. This situation is illustrated below. As in the case of Pete's Auto Repair, "normal" is what would have occurred had there been no loss, and "actual" is what did occur during the period of interruption.

	Normal	Actual
Revenues	$100,000	$ 30,000
Expenses	150,000	100,000
Net Income (Loss)	($ 50,000)	($ 70,000)

In this case, the company has suffered a $20,000 business income loss. That is, its net loss was $20,000 greater than would have been expected if an interruption had not occurred. This $20,000 business income loss is insurable; the remainder of the $70,000 net loss ($50,000) is not. The business would have incurred a $50,000 net loss if no business interruption had occurred.

Continuing and Noncontinuing Expenses

As noted above, an important aspect of business income losses is the extent to which normal expenses continue during a shutdown. If the expenses that continued during Pete's shutdown had been $20,000 instead of $8,000, the loss of net income would have been $12,000 greater than it was. Expenses for a particular period are paid out of revenues for the same period. Thus, each dollar of expense decreases the net income by one dollar. By the same token, each dollar of expense that does *not* continue during the shutdown *reduces* the net income loss by the same amount.

Hence, an important part of estimating potential business income losses is deciding which normal expenses will continue and which will not in the event of a shutdown of a particular length. A later section of this chapter examines this important question in more detail.

Extra Expenses

The only expenses considered in the case of Pete's Auto Repair are ordinary expenses, some of which continued during the shutdown and some of which did not. In evaluating business income exposures, we also need to consider any additional expenses incurred to mitigate the effects of a business interruption. In insurance and risk management, these additional expenses are usually referred to simply as extra expenses.

In real life, Pete's Auto Repair probably would have incurred some extra expenses. For example, Pete might have rented some office space to provide a base of operations for ordering new tools and stock, communicating with contractors and the insurance adjuster, collecting accounts receivable from customers, paying creditors, and performing other essential activities. By doing so, Pete might actually have reduced the length of time needed to reopen the garage and therefore reduced the amount of revenue lost.

Incurring extra expenses can sometimes prevent a complete shutdown of revenue-earning activities and thus reduce the business income loss. To illustrate this situation, assume that you are the owner and manager of a medium-sized insurance agency. One evening, while you are eating dinner, the phone rings and the caller tells you that the building housing your office is on fire. When you arrive at your office building you see it engulfed in flames and it soon becomes obvious that the building will be unusable for weeks if not months while repairs are made. In addition, you realize that much of your agency's equipment and records will be destroyed or damaged.

Perhaps you had the foresight to have compiled a disaster plan prior to such an occurrence that you can immediately activate. In any event, you would probably try to find another office location; obtain temporary telephone, computer, and other equipment; notify employees where to report; advise clients how to contact you; obtain duplicate records; and do other tasks so that you could continue operations with as little disruption as possible. Obviously, you would incur substantial additional expense even if you were able to avoid a loss of commission income.

Depending on their objectives, some organizations are willing to incur extra expenses irrespective of whether they reduce the current loss of net income. For example, a hospital may incur considerable extra expenses to maintain essential services for its patients even though such expenses currently increase the net income loss. Similarly, many other businesses may be willing to incur large extra expenses in order to avoid a shutdown that could impair their good relations with customers or their long-term market share. Try to imagine the financial consequences if the insurance agency described above had simply ceased operations for six months while its office was being rebuilt!

The distinction between extra expenses that reduce the immediate business income loss and those that do not reduce it is important both in analyzing loss exposures and in arranging appropriate insurance coverage. As will be discussed in more detail in Chapter 8, one form of business income insurance covers both types of extra expenses, and another form covers extra expenses only to the extent that they reduce the current loss. To select the appropriate form of insurance, the risk analyst must first determine what types of extra expenses would likely be incurred in response to a possible business interruption.

Analyzing Business Income Exposures

The discussion above is based on an analysis of a business income *loss*. Risk management and insurance professionals are often confronted with a more difficult problem: *pre-loss* analysis of business income exposures to serve as the basis for selection of appropriate risk control and risk financing measures. The section that follows examines several factors that should be considered when identifying and analyzing business income loss exposures.

The material covered in this section is presented under the following major subheadings:

- Events That Could Cause a Business Income Loss
- Timing of a Business Income Loss
- Distinguishing Between Continuing and Noncontinuing Expenses
- Estimating Maximum Probable Loss

Events That Could Cause a Business Income Loss

In a very broad sense, "business income loss" can encompass any situation in which an organization suffers a decrease in net income, for whatever reason. In the context of insurance and risk management, however, business income loss ordinarily refers to loss of net income that results from accidental damage to property, rather than from poor business management, market conditions, competitive forces, or other so-called "business risks." Loss of business income resulting from the death or disability of key employees is a loss exposure that can be treated with life insurance and disability insurance. (This use of life and disability insurance is examined in CPCU 2.)

In the insurance and risk management context, most business income losses arise as a consequence of physical damage to property at the organization's own premises, preventing the organization from operating or reducing its capacity to operate. Thus, identifying an organization's physical damage loss exposures also identifies potential sources of business income loss. By the same token, any risk control measure taken to reduce the frequency or severity of *physical* losses affecting the organization can also reduce the frequency or severity of *business income* losses.

However, an organization can also suffer a business income loss because of physical damage to property at locations not owned or controlled by the organization but on which the insured depends in some way. This situation is called a **dependency exposure**. Four basic situations in which dependency exposures occur are when the organization is highly dependent on (1) one supplier, (2) one buyer, (3) a manufacturer that makes a product sold by the organization, or (4) a "leader" or "magnet" business, such as a department store in a mall.

Dependency on One Supplier

For a business that is highly dependent on a single supplier for key materials, shutdown of that supplier's operation, whether by fire, windstorm, or other cause, will at some point reduce or stop entirely the customer's operations as well. How soon or for how long will depend on various factors: what stockpile the customer has when the loss occurs; how available are alternative suppliers of the same product; and what alternatives the supplier has to continue or resume supply, to name only a few.

Dependency on One Buyer

A similar business income exposure exists when a supplier or producer is highly dependent on one buyer. For example, more than half of a small manufacturer's output of machinery parts may be sold exclusively to a larger manufacturer that uses the parts in assembling machines. If the large manufacturer's plant is shut down by a major property loss, the supplier will suffer a loss of business income because the manufactured parts will not be needed again until production is resumed.

Dependency on a Manufacturer

Rather than produce a particular product line itself, Manufacturer A may contract with Manufacturer B to have B produce the line according to A's specifications. The usual motivation for such arrangements is that the other manufacturer can produce the goods less expensively. If B sustains a physical loss at its factory and experiences a resulting shutdown for six months, A will sustain a business income loss unless it has a large stockpile of the manufactured goods or can produce the product line by using its own factory or contracting with another manufacturer.

Dependency on a "Leader Property"

Another type of dependency exists for many small businesses in or near a shopping mall. Such businesses, typically stores, gain customers that are drawn to the mall by a major department or discount store, sometimes referred to as a "leader property" or "magnet store." If the magnet store is shut down by a property loss, the customers shop elsewhere and the small "satellite stores" will also lose customers and business income even though the satellite stores themselves have suffered no physical loss.

Controlling Dependency Exposures

An obvious, but in many cases impractical, way of controlling such dependency exposures is to lessen the dependency. A manufacturer who is highly dependent on one or two suppliers might increase the number of its suppliers and reduce the amount purchased from any one of them. Likewise, a company that depends highly on one buyer might try to diversify its markets.

However, in many cases, the "dependency" is an important source of funds and perhaps even defines the company's marketing niche. For example, a small specialty store in a mall may operate profitably only *because* it is adjacent to a large department store. Reducing the dependency (by relocating outside the mall) would probably reduce profits. The flexibility of business income insurance to address dependency exposures allows businesses with dependency exposures to achieve some certainty against risk. However, to treat this exposure, the risk analyst must of course be able to recognize the dependency exposure in the first place.

Organization's Own Property Off Premises

The dependency exposures described above result from damage to property of others away from the dependent organization's premises. A similar situation, but not necessarily involving dependency on another organization's property, involves damage to an organization's *own* property while off premises, perhaps while in transit or while being stored or worked on at the premises of a bailee.

For example, the damaged property could be essential components in a manufacturing process. Without those components, production might be curtailed until the components can be replaced.

Acts of Civil Authority

Another instance when an organization can suffer a business income loss because of damage to property at some location other than its own involves acts of civil authorities. In some cases, damage to nearby property creates a sufficiently hazardous exposure to a wider area to cause the police or fire department to prohibit access to the area. Even though a particular business in the affected area may have sustained no damage within its own premises, the act of the civil authority will prevent occupancy, resulting in a loss of business income.

Off-Premises Power Failure

Physical damage to power transmission lines or generating stations is another source of business interruption caused by off-premises occurrences. The resulting loss of power or other utilities (such as telephone service or water) can shut down almost any organization that uses those services.

Timing of a Business Income Loss

In order to develop a pre-loss assessment of business income exposures and their loss potential, it is necessary to estimate the probable duration of any interruption. The answer to the question "How much could a business interruption cost?" depends not only on revenue and expense figures but also on the following:

1. *How long* business income could be reduced.
2. *When* during the year the interruption could occur.

How Long Business Income Is Reduced

The duration of a reduction in business income is directly related to the time required to replace damaged property plus the time that may be required to restore the normal rate of income. Under various circumstances, a relatively small physical loss can result in a severe business income loss.

Time Required To Replace Damaged Property

As a practical matter, it is not necessary to determine a replacement period for each and every property item exposed to loss. Rather, the effort can be placed on identifying critical items—those that take a long time to replace.

For example, a giant turbine for an electric generating plant might require a year or more to manufacture and deliver. Firms that use highly specialized machinery or equipment or depend on overseas manufacturers for parts or repairs can face long interruption exposures.

When critical items are identified, the exposures can be evaluated by asking the manufacturer, dealer, or servicer of the particular item to determine how expeditiously a replacement could be obtained under the worst possible circumstances.

This aspect of the business income exposure is often responsive to risk control. Advance planning can sometimes reduce the amount of time needed to repair or replace critical items. For example, spare critical parts might be kept in inventory, and replacement machinery might be kept on hand. Other measures that might be effective include safeguarding building and machinery plans to simplify reconstruction, keeping a current list of capable contractors and suppliers, investigating alternative facilities before any loss occurs, and maintaining duplicate records at a second location for both electronic and other data.[1] The availability of replacement parts and emergency repair service might also be used as a decision criterion when buying new equipment or machinery.

In many cases, the time required to resume operations will depend on the time needed to repair or rebuild a building. The most reliable method of estimating the rebuilding time for a building is to obtain an estimate from a reputable contractor. If that is impractical, reference books or services are available for determining rebuilding times.

The enforcement of building or zoning codes following damage to the premises can sometimes cause a considerable delay in rebuilding or repair before business can be resumed. The extra cost of complying with these laws (see Chapter 5) is not considered part of the business income loss exposure, but the delay caused by having to meet these requirements is an additional part of the business income loss and must be taken into account when estimating the maximum probable business income loss.

The possible length of an interruption is also affected by the presence of time-consuming production processes. Some manufacturers have production processes that require a long time to complete, perhaps because drying, seasoning, or "aging" processes are involved. The aging of wines and liquors is one example, and the making of some varieties of cheese is another. When goods in process sustain physical loss, the severity of the resulting business income loss depends on the amount of time required to bring new raw materials to the same stage of production the destroyed goods had reached before the physical damage occurred. The longer the production process takes, the more severe the loss exposure.

Another possibility is illustrated by the problems that have followed major hurricanes and earthquakes: Whenever there is extensive damage over a considerable area, transportation and communication are disrupted, and the people and materials needed for repair and replacement are in short supply. Under such circumstances, interruption can be extended for many weeks or even several months.

Time Required To Restore Normal Rate of Income

Not all business income losses cease when the damaged property has been restored. In some cases, businesses lose their customers after a long shutdown and must win them back, which can take time. In other cases, businesses lose important licenses, leases, or contracts as the result of a business interruption. A shutdown can also lead to loss of customer goodwill and market share.

Loss of Customers Besides employees, building, equipment, and stock, businesses also need customers. This point is particularly important for some types of businesses. For example, a bowling alley might be entirely restored and ready for business following a shutdown, but might have few customers because all leagues for the season have already formed at other bowling alleys. Special circumstances affect schools and colleges, which may lose tuition for an entire academic year or longer if the campus is unusable when students are enrolling or committing themselves financially to that school year.

Many other businesses also lose customers during a shutdown, though not necessarily to the same degree. For example, when a restaurant or store is closed, its customers develop the habit of eating or shopping elsewhere and may not return to those establishments as soon as they are restored. Similarly, a beauty parlor's patrons may have transferred their loyalties to other hairdressers, or an office equipment firm's customers may have found other suppliers. Added time will be need to recapture lost business even after the property has been completely restored.

Traditionally, business income insurance has only covered reduction of net income during the "period of restoration"—that is, the time between when the physical damage occurred and when the property is restored to use. Modern business income insurance provides an automatic extension to the period of restoration to cover decreases in business income during the thirty days following the restoration of the property, and longer extensions are available for an additional premium. (This subject is discussed further in Chapter 8.)

Loss of Licenses, Leases, Contracts, Goodwill, Market Share Another aspect of loss that may continue after the restoration of the physical premises involves loss arising from the cancellation of a license, lease, or contract. For example, a license as the exclusive distributor of a product may be contingent upon the licensee's selling a certain minimum quantity. Loss of the license because of failure to meet this requirement might adversely impact a firm's profitability long after its facilities are restored if it is unable to obtain a replacement product to sell.

Similarly, the interruption of business may reduce a firm's market share or erode carefully developed customer goodwill. Market share and goodwill are valuable in their own right; the selling price of many businesses exceeds the value of their tangible assets primarily because of the value of market share or goodwill.

Losses caused by the cancellation of a license, lease, or contract or the loss of market share or goodwill are not insured by standard business income forms. (However, loss of a favorable lease because of a fire or other covered peril is insurable under leasehold interest insurance, as discussed in Chapter 6.)

Although they are often not insurable, these losses should not be overlooked during exposure analysis. If such losses are important to a firm, other risk management techniques might be appropriate. For example, if minimizing the loss of market share or goodwill that might result from an interruption of production is of critical importance, several manufacturing facilities might be used to produce a product even though a single facility would be more economical.

Small Physical Damage Loss, Long Interruption

Business income loss exposures would be easier to deal with if physical damage losses and business income losses always occurred simultaneously and in proportionate amounts. Because they do not, risk management professionals should be alert to situations in which relatively small physical damage could cause a long interruption and therefore a large business income loss. Losses involving "bottlenecks" and losses resulting from pollution incidents are two examples of situations when a long interruption can result from a relatively small physical damage loss.

Bottlenecks Just as blockage in the neck of a catsup bottle can stop the flow of catsup, blockage or "bottlenecks" in a business operation can cause the business process to slow down or stop. The term **bottleneck** is often applied to situations where work from several assembly lines or processes must flow through (or depend on continued operation at) a single job site or position. A relatively small physical loss at this bottleneck position could shut down several assembly lines. Production bottlenecks are easiest to imagine, but bottlenecks can also exist in purchasing and selling.

Some companies manufacture a product assembled in a long series of steps that must be performed in sequence. Autos, for example, are assembled in the sequence dictated by the assembly line, which usually has many bottlenecks. Other companies manufacture a product that can be completed in steps that have no necessary sequence. These companies are less prone to production bottlenecks, because no one position has an extraordinary impact on operations at other positions.

Flowcharts (discussed in Chapter 1) are often effective in identifying bottlenecks. However, bottlenecks can be difficult to identify before a loss occurs. For example, suppose that a large plant is not permitted to operate without adequate pollution control devices. A small fire in the pollution control system could shut down the entire plant. This is an important exposure but one that most flowcharts would not identify.

Pollution Losses Relatively small fires in buildings have caused significant pollution and contamination problems that took a lot of money *and time* to clean up. In one case, the smoke and fumes from a fire in an outside underground vault entered a fresh air intake duct and contaminated six floors of an adjacent office building. The affected areas were uninhabitable for ten months while cleanup costing in excess of $20 million was in process.[2]

Horror stories concerning contamination losses abound. Polychlorinated biphenyls (PCBs) have been a particular culprit. Thought to be harmless, and used for many years in electrical transformers and elsewhere as a "safe" nonflammable substitute for flammable petroleum products, PCBs subsequently were found to be a carcinogen, capable of inducing human cancer with prolonged exposure. Because their use was "grandfathered" in most environmental laws, many PCB-filled transformers are still in active use.

When involved in even a small fire or explosion, smoke contaminated with PCBs can spread throughout the building with disastrous results, requiring long and costly decontamination, during which time the premises cannot be occupied. Severe business income loss results, including the need to relocate the business elsewhere while decontamination proceeds. Interruptions of nine to twelve months are not uncommon, and in the case of one modern eight-story office building, contaminated as a result of a small electrical fire in the basement, decontamination took more than three and one-half years. Buildings insulated with asbestos can also require lengthy cleanup after being damaged by fire, explosion, or other perils.

Another contamination exposure of relatively recent origin is nuclear isotopes, now in widespread use not only in production of energy and weapons of war but in hospitals and research laboratories throughout the country. Because of the long "half-life" of nuclear isotopes (the time needed for the isotope to lose one-half of its radioactivity), nuclear contamination does not dissipate quickly, but requires elaborate and time-consuming decontamination and disposal procedures before the facility can be used again.

Effect of Seasonal Fluctuations

Some organizations earn significantly different amounts of income at different times of the year. For example, retail jewelers and fur dealers may transact as much as half their annual business during their peak three months, and perhaps three-fourths of their annual business during the six consecutive months of highest business activity. Businesses with an even more seasonal pattern (such as vegetable and fruit packers, canneries, and ski resorts) might gain their entire annual income in a three-month period.

For such organizations, the business income loss resulting from a shutdown could vary considerably depending on when during the year it occurred. To address this problem, seasonal income differences need to be considered when business income exposures are being analyzed.

Suppose a maximum shutdown of six months is projected for a particular company. Which six months of the year would the company be shut down? It is impossible to foretell when an interruption will occur, but the question is important unless the company has an earnings pattern that does not vary substantially from month to month. If a seasonal pattern exists, the pattern of fluctuation in earnings should be identified—either by studying the past seasonal figures of the business in question or through the use of figures that show typical seasonal patterns for the same type of business as that being analyzed. (Such information can sometimes be obtained from trade associations for the company's industry.)

Distinguishing Between Continuing and Noncontinuing Expenses

Not all expenses will continue during a period of interruption. As discussed earlier, expenses that do not continue reduce the loss that the business would otherwise suffer. Estimating which expenses will continue and which will not is a difficult task, but if done carefully it can help to develop a more accurate estimate of probable maximum loss than by simply assuming that all expenses will continue during a shutdown.

The following paragraphs describe the degree to which expenses in various categories may continue during a business interruption.

Payroll Expense

The extent to which payroll expenses continue during a business interruption depends on many factors, such as the duration of the shutdown, the number of employees who have special value to the company, conditions in the local labor market, union contracts, severance pay policies, and obligations to continue providing employee benefits.

Some employees are paid by the hour, and when they do not work they are not paid. Other employees are promised, or have some reason to expect, regular paychecks. How long the latter would be kept on the payroll during a shutdown depends on several factors, including the expected length of closure. If a long period is expected, the organization will probably discontinue payroll expense for many employees. But in few cases would all employees be dismissed, even during a prolonged interruption. Some employees usually are necessary (or desirable) to assure a smooth transition back to business, and new employees will have to be hired and trained before operations can resume. In addition, many businesses have employees with special skills, such as designers or tool and die makers, who could not be easily replaced and who may find other jobs if they are eliminated from the payroll.

Some personnel are usually required to manage the process of repair and construction and to prepare for successful operations after reopening. In practice, officers' salaries are usually continued regardless of the duration of an interruption. Salaries may or may not be continued for department managers and supervisors.

Employees such as retail clerks and assembly-line workers who have no special skills and would be easy to replace usually are not retained unless the period of interruption is brief. How easily unskilled employees can be replaced varies with local labor market conditions at the time of the loss.

The payroll for office employees might also be discontinued in the event of a long interruption if rehiring and retraining could be accomplished in a short period of time before reopening. One exception would be employees involved in processing accounts receivable and accounts payable. Assuming the records have not been destroyed, these functions might continue for sixty, ninety, or more days after the date of the loss, depending on the speed with which a firm collects its receivables and pays its creditors.

Heat, Light, and Power Expense

The cost of heat, light, and power would probably be only minimally affected during short periods of shutdown. During longer periods, the expense might be discontinued entirely until shortly before reopening. However, sometimes a minimum charge has to be paid to the utility companies. Organizations that normally have small utility bills will see little difference in their utility expenses during a period of interruption. However, those that normally use a large amount of electricity, such as an aluminum manufacturer, or otherwise run up large utility bills will see a substantial drop.

Expenses for Services Performed by Others

Many companies hire independent contractors to perform some functions or services. Part of a manufacturing process, such as chrome plating or application of plastic coatings, may be performed by independent job shops. And many retailers, such as hardware, appliance, or jewelry stores have alteration, installation, or repair work performed by outsiders. Restaurants and bars often hire musical groups and other entertainers. These services, performed by others, may be under contract—that is, guaranteed; if so, a company may be obligated to make payments to the other companies even during a business interruption. More often, services performed by outside companies will not be continued and payments will not be required.

Lease or Rental Expense

In any particular situation, whether or not lease or rental expense for buildings and equipment would continue during a business shutdown depends on the terms of the rental or lease agreement. Continuing rental expense is not necessarily bad. A less desirable long-range outcome might be cancellation of a favorable lease. (This exposure can be insured by leasehold interest coverage, as described in Chapter 6.)

Generally, if the lease agreement provides for abatement of rent, it does so only when the rented property itself is damaged and made unusable. Thus, rent on branch offices, warehouses, and storage facilities normally continues during a business interruption at the main location. Likewise, suspension of business normally does not free a lessee from rental payments for autos and trucks rented on a long-term basis.

Interest Expense

Interest payments generally are a continuing expense, but there are some exceptions. If a building is totally destroyed, the mortgage debt probably will be retired from property insurance proceeds. Although new loans are likely to be used to finance a new building, mortgage interest expense will be reduced until borrowing reaches the previous level. Interest on other loans, and mortgages on property away from the undamaged premises, are not affected by a business suspension, and therefore will necessarily continue.

Taxes

A conservative assumption is that property taxes will be a continuing expense. Depending on the situation, major losses may reduce taxable real property values. However, in many areas taxes are assessed as of a given date, say January 1. If a firm has a loss immediately after that date, it could be a year before any property tax relief is given. If the insured rebuilds before the next January 1, reduction in assessments will usually not be made. Similarly, partial losses may cause a business interruption in which there is only a small reduction in taxable property values.

The same reasoning applies to personal property taxes based on inventory. These taxes may continue at the same level (or at virtually the same level) even though business is suspended.

Sales tax, however, is not an expense for a business. The business is merely an agent of government for the collection of the tax—sales taxes paid to the government are offset by the sales taxes collected from customers. However, the decrease in sales tax collections may be a loss of income for the governmental unit. A municipality that receives substantial sales tax revenue from a large shopping mall may suffer a severe loss of income when a fire closes the mall.

Employer contributions for Social Security and unemployment compensation only continue for those employees who are paid during the interruption.

Advertising Expense

To determine whether advertising expense would be continued during a business suspension, the company's advertising policy must be considered. Some advertising is intended to stimulate sales in the short run; other advertising is intended to enhance the image of the company, and no short-run benefits are expected.

If advertising has been contracted in advance and cannot be canceled, it would be a continuing expense. Otherwise, advertising to stimulate sales would not be necessary except perhaps shortly before the business reopens. However, companies will often choose to maintain their image-enhancing advertisements even during a long shutdown. Such expenses may help to reduce the residual loss of business income once the business reopens.

Firms that relocate to temporary locations while repairs are being made at the damaged location usually advertise their temporary location. In so doing, they may incur advertising expense greater than normal.

Franchise and License Fees, Royalties

If based on sales or production, payment to others of royalties, franchise fees, and license fees would cease upon suspension of operations. These expenses may continue, however, if there is a guaranteed minimum level or a flat fee.

Postage and Telephone Expense

Communication expenses would probably continue in full during a short period of suspension. In fact, some extraordinary expenses might be incurred because of the necessity to use long-distance telephone service more extensively than usual. During a prolonged period of suspension, these expenses probably would be discontinued immediately but resumed sometime before the business reopens.

Professional Fees

Fees for accounting and legal services normally are continuing expenses if paid on a retainer basis. If not on a retainer, it may be reasonable to assume one or two months' expenditure as a continuing expense. Although the need for the usual services may abate, extraordinary legal and accounting services may become necessary as a result of the loss.

Insurance Expense

Some insurance premiums may be reduced during a business interruption. The premium for property insurance arranged on a reporting form basis will be reduced as lower values are reported because of the loss. Workers compensation premiums based on payroll and liability premiums based on payroll or sales will be reduced with any reduction in payroll or sales due to the interruption.

Maintenance Expense

In most instances, maintenance costs would not continue during a business shutdown. However, if the property consists of more than one building or fire division, the property not affected by the loss would probably require at least a minimum amount of maintenance—even if no operations are taking place.

Depreciation Expense

In accounting, **depreciation expense** is the current allocation of a capital expense, as reflected in an organization's accounting and tax records. Although it does not represent a current outflow of cash, depreciation expense does reduce the net income of an ongoing business. Thus, it is necessary to examine the extent to which depreciation expense is affected by a business interruption.

Property Totally Destroyed

Depreciation ceases with respect to property that has been totally destroyed. The value of the property has suddenly dropped to zero, and no further depreciation is possible. Some commentators make the analogy to the sale of property. Once property is sold no further depreciation can be taken; in a sense, they say, property destroyed by an insured peril has been sold to the insurance company and therefore the depreciation expense does not continue.

There are, however, those who argue that depreciation should not be regarded as a noncontinuing expense. In their opinion, depreciation is an arbitrary accounting charge related to calculating taxable income. There have been a few court decisions agreeing with this position, but the predominant opinion in the insurance industry is that for property that is totally destroyed, depreciation should be regarded as a noncontinuing expense.[3] Depreciation of totally destroyed property is addressed by insurance covering the physical loss of the property.

Property Not Totally Destroyed

The situation is different when property that has not been totally destroyed is rendered unusable during a business interruption. Depreciation can be caused by numerous factors. Wear and tear is one element in depreciation; technological innovation and just the passage of time can cause a reduction in value even if property is not used. Personal computers that a firm purchased three years ago would have a greatly reduced value today even if they had never been taken out of their original cartons. A building will continue to depreciate (the roof will wear, the paint will age, and so forth) even if operations are suspended.

On the other hand, the depreciation of some equipment is clearly related to usage. Motors that must be rebuilt after a stated number of hours of usage or stamping dies that are useful for a certain number of stampings may suffer little depreciation during a period of interruption, and the depreciation charges for such equipment would be a noncontinuing expense.

Treatment of Depreciation When Estimating MPL

For many insureds the conservative procedure when estimating maximum probable loss would be to assume that depreciation will be a continuing expense. This is especially true when the worst possible case scenario involves the time necessary to replace key machinery or age stock such as cheese or wine—that is, a business interruption that may not involve extensive damage to buildings and other depreciable property.

Profit-Sharing Payments

Payments to the owners of a business as owners are not an expense of the business but a share of the profits. In a corporation these payments are called "dividends"; in an unincorporated business (sole proprietorship or partnership) they are called "distributions" (of profits). Either way, they are not expenses. Indeed, in the equation, "revenues – expenses = net income," "profit" is another name for "net income." So payment or nonpayment of profit shares does not affect the amount of profits lost. However, in most unincorporated businesses, part of the payment received by the owners is salary for services rendered; this part is, of course, an item of "payroll expense," and is included in the computation of "net income."

Corporations must consider the effect that cessation of dividend payments might have on its stockholders and on the price of its stock. Similarly, profit-sharing payments to some or all of the owners of an unincorporated business may need to be continued to protect those owners and the organization's relations with them. Since profit shares can be paid from prior earnings, a business may want to continue payments even if its profits have been reduced or eliminated by the interruption of its operations. In that case, the organization must plan to have the necessary funds available to continue profit-sharing payments when the cash flow from its usual activities is interrupted. Of course, if the organization has business income insurance, it will provide a source of income replacement, out of which dividends can be paid.

Estimating Maximum Probable Loss

A conservative approach to estimating maximum probable business income loss is to assume a complete shutdown at the worst possible time of the year, lasting for the maximum amount of time that can be foreseen to replace a destroyed building, replace critical machinery, and restore inventory and personnel to their pre-loss status.

A conservative approach would also suggest an assumption that all expenses would continue throughout the interruption period. However, as discussed above, analysis of conditions affecting the organization can lead to some basis for estimating the degree to which expenses will continue.

In estimating maximum probable business income loss, the objective is to estimate the largest loss likely to occur *in the future*. Past income and expense figures must therefore be analyzed and updated in order to project them into the future. How far they must be projected depends on the potential duration of a business interruption.

If net sales figures for the past several years are known, if the figures seem to indicate a definite trend without too much yearly variation from that trend, and if there is reason to assume that net sales will increase at approximately the same rate in the future, the business interruption exposure can be projected by using a simple trend factor. For example, if the average rate of increase in net sales for the past four years has been 10 percent per year and there are no unusual circumstances, it is reasonable to assume that net sales next year will increase by 10 percent and that the year after next will show an increase of 10 percent over next year.

In some instances, more sophisticated methods of forecasting sales and income may be desirable. In larger companies, the accounting or finance department may already have made sales and income projections.

The Business Income Worksheet

Insurance Services Office publishes a "business income report/worksheet." It is called a "report/worksheet" because it is used both to calculate the amount of insurance necessary to comply with the coinsurance clause of business income insurance and to report business income values to the insurance company when the agreed amount option or provisional amount endorsement applies. (The details of the agreed amount option and the provisional amount endorsement discussed in Chapter 8.) For the sake of simplicity, the business income report/worksheet will be referred to here as the **business income worksheet**.

The material that follows shows how the business income worksheet can be used to analyze an organization's business income loss exposure and (if insurance is wanted) to determine an appropriate limit of insurance. Although the discussion that follows necessarily involves explanation of some accounting practices, accounting is not the primary focus of the discussion, nor does the discussion presume that readers have any prior knowledge of accounting.

In most cases, the business income worksheet is prepared by the insured's accountant or financial officer, perhaps with some assistance from the insured's insurance agent, broker, or consultant. Thus, the insurance or risk management professional should be prepared to assist someone knowledgeable in accounting in completing the worksheet. As a general rule, producers should not prepare the business income worksheet on behalf of the client.

As noted above, one of the principal purposes of the worksheet is to determine the amount of insurance needed to comply with the coinsurance clause in the business income coverage form. The coinsurance clause requires the insured to carry an amount of insurance equal to the chosen coinsurance percentage times the sum of (1) the insured's net income, and (2) all operating expenses for the twelve months following policy inception (including those that would not continue if a business interruption occurred). The worksheet refers to this sum as the business income basis for coinsurance.

In other words, the coinsurance basis times the applicable coinsurance percentage equals the amount of insurance required to avoid a coinsurance penalty. The worksheet elicits income and expense figures for the insured that, with appropriate calculations, enable the insured's accountant or financial officer to determine the coinsurance basis.

The coinsurance basis, although often referred to as the "business income exposure," is not necessarily a reasonable approximation of maximum probable loss. As discussed earlier, the maximum probable interruption period for most organizations is ordinarily other than twelve months. (This explains why the available coinsurance percentages for business income insurance are 50, 60, 70, 80, 90, 100, and 125 percent.) In addition, some expenses may not continue during a business interruption, thereby reducing the loss of net income actually sustained. However, the business income worksheet does not deduct any expenses unless they are specifically excluded from coverage by using optional exclusionary endorsements. Thus, as will be explained in more detail below, several adjustments must be made to the worksheet coinsurance basis when it is being used to estimate maximum probable loss.

As long as the differences between the coinsurance basis and the maximum probable loss are understood, the worksheet can be a useful tool for analyzing the actual loss exposure and selecting an appropriate amount of insurance.

Relationship Between Income Statements and the Business Income Worksheet

The source of most information entered in the business income worksheet is the organization's income statement. The **income statement** (sometimes called an earnings statement or a profit and loss statement) reports on the organization's profitability for a stated period of time by comparing the revenues generated in the period with the expenses incurred to produce those revenues.[4] Exhibit 7-1 shows condensed income statements for a service business, a merchandising business, and a manufacturing business.

Income Statement for a Service Business

A service business, such as an insurance agency or an accounting firm, has the simplest income statement. Revenues are generated by fees or commissions, and

Exhibit 7-1
Sample Condensed Income Statements

For a Service Business	
Commissions and fees	$ 1,000,000
Operating expenses	800,000
Operating income	200,000
Other income	25,000
Net income before tax	225,000
Provision for income tax	65,000
Net income after income tax	$ 160,000

For a Merchandising Firm	
Net sales	10,000,000
Cost of goods sold	6,500,000
Gross profit (also called "gross margin")	3,500,000
Operating expenses	3,000,000
Operating income	500,000
Other income	50,000
Net income before provision for income tax	550,000
Provision for income tax	165,000
Net income after income tax	$ 385,000

For a Manufacturing Firm		
Gross income		$10,000,000
Cost of goods sold		
Materials	$5,700,000	
Direct labor	800,000	
Factory overhead	1,000,000	7,500,000
Gross profit (also called "gross margin")		2,500,000
Operating expenses		2,000,000
Operating income		500,000
Other income		50,000
Net income before provision for income tax		550,000
Provision for income tax		165,000
Net income after income tax		$ 385,000

expenses are incurred to earn those fees or commissions. The difference between revenues and expenses is operating income. Other income may be derived from other sources, such as investments or the sale of unneeded equipment.

Income Statement for a Merchandising Business

The income statement for a merchandising business (any wholesale or retail selling business) introduces an additional element—cost of goods sold. **Cost of goods sold** is the cost to the firm of the products that it sells. In an income statement, the cost of goods sold is usually subtracted from net sales to yield the gross margin (or gross profit). Operating expenses are then subtracted from the gross margin to arrive at operating income.

Some firms calculate cost of goods sold by keeping track of the cost of the specific items, such as diamond rings sold by a jeweler. Other firms calculate cost of goods sold by adding the cost of purchases during the period to the cost of the merchandise inventory on hand at the beginning of the period to determine the total cost of goods available for sale during the period and then deducting the merchandise inventory at the end of the period. This yields the cost of goods sold during the period. Purchases and inventories are valued at cost. An example of a cost-of-goods-sold calculation for a merchandising firm using this method is shown below:

Merchandise inventory, at cost, as of 1/1/94	$100,000
Plus purchases during the year 1994	300,000
Total goods available for sale during 1994	400,000
Minus merchandise inventory, at cost, as of 12/31/94	90,000
Cost of good sold during 1994	$310,000

Various methods are used in valuing inventory, such as first-in, first-out (FIFO) and last-in, first-out (LIFO). The details of these methods are not important for purposes of using the business income worksheet. However, the same method must be used at the beginning and the end of the period covered by the worksheet. Changing the method during the period may misstate the income generated. If the inventory valuation method has been changed, the firm's financial officer or accountant must recalculate the statement to show what the results would have been if the same valuation method had been used for the opening and closing inventories.

Income Statement for a Manufacturing Business

The income statement for a manufacturing business resembles that of a merchandising business. However, the method of calculating cost of goods sold is different. First, the cost of raw materials is calculated by methods similar to those used for the inventory of a merchandising business. Then the cost of labor directly involved in manufacturing the product and the portion of the overhead expense (rent, insurance, maintenance, depreciation, and so forth) attributable to the manufacturing operation are added to arrive at the cost of goods sold. (The exact method of apportioning overhead expenses, a sometimes complex cost-accounting problem, is not significant for present purposes since all overhead expenses, both factory and non-factory, are treated the same in the business income worksheet.)

Completing the Business Income Worksheet

To illustrate how the business income worksheet should be completed, figures will be extracted from the detailed income statement for a fictitious manufacturing firm—Manufacturer, Inc.—shown in Exhibit 7-4. The statement for a manufacturing firm presents all of the problems that may be posed by statements for service or merchandising firms plus some that are specific to manufacturing firms.

The worksheet consists of four pages. Each page is discussed in sequence below. The four pages of the worksheet, filled in with the relevant information for Manufacturer, Inc., are displayed in four separate exhibits located in proximity to the applicable textbook explanations.

Page 1—Identification, Instructions, and Signatures

Page 1 of the worksheet (shown in Exhibit 7-2) calls for the name and location of the insured. The insured's signature is required when the worksheet is being used in connection with the agreed value coverage option or the premium adjustment form.

The instructions state that the form must be completed on an accrual basis in conformity with generally accepted accounting principles. This may pose a problem for firms that do not prepare financial statements in adherence with generally accepted accounting principles (GAAP). Many firms, particularly smaller ones, receive only compilation statements from their accountants. A compilation statement records only the information appearing in the firm's books and records. The accountant does not perform the tests that GAAP require and therefore cannot render an opinion about the statements. Due to the added expense, few firms will be willing to change to GAAP accounting if the only purpose is to complete a business income worksheet.

It has been proposed to drop this requirement in the next revision of the worksheet. If the worksheet is to be filed with the insurer, the insurer should be

Exhibit 7-2
Worksheet Page 1

POLICY NUMBER: COMMERCIAL PROPERTY

BUSINESS INCOME REPORT/WORK SHEET

Your Name ______________________ Date ____________

Location ______________________

____

This work sheet must be completed on an accrual basis in conformity with generally accepted accounting principles.

Indicate the inventory valuation method used by your company:

_____ Specific Identification Method
_____ Average-Cost Method
_____ First-In, First-Out (FIFO) Method
_____ Last-In, First-Out (LIFO) Method
_____ Other (specify):
____

APPLICABLE WHEN THE AGREED VALUE COVERAGE OPTION APPLIES:

I certify that this is a true and correct report of values as required under this policy for the periods indicated and that the Agreed Value for the period of coverage is $ __________ , based on a Co-insurance percentage of _________%.

Signature ______________________
Official Title ______________________

APPLICABLE WHEN THE PREMIUM ADJUSTMENT FORM APPLIES:

I certify that this is a true and correct report of values as required under this policy for the 12 months ended __________

Signature ______________________

Official Title ______________________

Agent or Broker ______________________

Mailing Address ______________________

advised that the firm does not follow GAAP in preparing its statements. For smaller firms the distortion, if any, is usually not significant.

However, the **accrual basis** must be used to estimate accurately a firm's business income exposure. Under the accrual basis, revenues are recorded as they are earned and expenses are charged as they are incurred. This basis provides a better match of income and expense and a more accurate report of the firm's profit or loss. The alternative, the **cash basis**, records revenues and expenses only when payments are actually received or made. It does not match income with expense as accurately as the accrual basis. Although most businesses use the accrual basis, the cash basis is used by some firms, particularly smaller ones.

The insurance industry provides a good example of the contrast between accrual and cash basis accounting. Insurance companies use accrual basis accounting for losses and loss adjustment expense: The expected amount of loss and expense is entered when losses are incurred, not when they are paid. If an insurance company used cash basis accounting and recorded loss expenses only when losses were *paid*, their accounting statements would not provide a true picture of their profitability. Many liability and workers compensation policies, for example, would appear to be generating large profits at the end of the policy year when evaluated by cash basis accounting. In reality, the policies may be very unprofitable. Incurred losses (based on payments made during the year and estimates of future payments) might far outstrip premium income since most of the claims under such policies are not paid until after policy expiration, in some cases years later.

The worksheet also asks for the *inventory* method used. The inventory method is requested for informational purposes only; it has no effect on the later calculations. The important point is that the method must not have changed during the year. As noted above, using a different inventory method for opening and closing inventories may distort the profit and loss calculation. If the accounting method has changed, accounting statements will have to be restated so that the same basis is used for opening and closing inventories. Fortunately, firms do not usually change their method of inventory valuation.

Page 2—Calculating Total Revenues

As shown in Exhibit 7-3, page 2 of the worksheet begins with gross sales (item A) and, after a series of calculations, ends with total revenues (item H).

Page 2 contains two sets of identical double columns for purposes of filling in relevant financial data. The set of columns on the left-hand side is captioned as follows:

Exhibit 7-3
Worksheet Page 2

BUSINESS INCOME REPORT/WORK SHEET
FINANCIAL ANALYSIS
(000 omitted)

Income and Expenses		12 Month Period Ending 12/31/94 Manufacturing	12 Month Period Ending 12/31/94 Non-Manufacturing	Estimated for 12 Month Period Beginning 4/1/95 Manufacturing	Estimated for 12 Month Period Beginning 4/1/95 Non-Manufacturing
A. Gross Sales		$ 10,050	$	$ 10,350	$
B. DEDUCT: Finished Stock Inventory (at sales value) at Beginning		− 500		− 550	
		9,550		9,800	
C. ADD: Finished Stock Inventory (at sales value) at End		+ 533		+ 480	
D. Gross Sales Value of Production		$ 10,083		$ 10,280	
E. DEDUCT:					
Prepaid Freight	0				
Returns & Allowances	+ 20				
Discounts	+ 30				
Bad Debts	+ 25				
Collection Expenses	+ 0				
Total		− 75	−	− 80	−
F. Net Sales			$		$
Net Sales Value of Production		$ 10,008		$ 10,200	
G. ADD: Other Earnings from your business operations (not investment income or rents from other properties):					
Commissions or Rents	0				
Cash Discounts Received	+ 0				
Other	+ 10				
Total Other Earnings		+ 10	+	+ 15	+
H. Total Revenues		$ 10,018	$	$ 10,215	$

Exhibit 7-4
Manufacturer, Inc.
Income Statement for the Year Ended December 31, 1994

Gross sales			$10,050,000
Less: Sales discounts	$ 30,000		
Returns and allowances	20,000		50,000
Net sales			10,000,000
Cost of goods sold *			
Inventory 1/1/94:			
Raw materials	$800,000		
Work-in-process	250,000		
Finished stock	375,000	$1,425,000	
Purchases		5,700,000	
Freight-in		15,000	
Supplies		25,000	
Direct labor		800,000	
Factory overhead:			
Indirect labor	$406,000		
Depreciation	125,000		
Insurance & taxes	84,000		
Repairs & maintenance	63,000		
Rent	300,000		
Other	22,000	1,000,000	
Total		8,965,000	
Less: Inventory 12/31/X4:			
Raw Materials	$820,000		
Work-in-process	245,000		
Finished stock	400,000	1,465,000	
Cost of goods sold and manufactured			7,500,000
Gross profit (also called "gross margin")			2,500,000
Operating expenses:			
Officers' salaries		$ 660,000	
Clerical salaries		340,000	
Sales salaries		757,000	
Depreciation		44,000	
Insurance & taxes		48,000	
Travel, entertainment, and advertising		40,000	
Uncollectible accounts		25,000	
Professional services		36,000	
Other		40,000	2,000,000
Operating income			500,000
Other Income:			
Interest income		$ 40,000	
Gain on sale of equipment		10,000	50,000
Net Income before income tax			550,000
Provision for income tax			165,000
Net income after provision for income tax			$385,000

*To facilitate this presentation, the detail of the cost-of-goods-sold computation has been included in the income statement. It is often shown in a separate cost-of-goods-sold schedule with only the total appearing in the income statement. In that event, the information would be obtained from the cost-of-goods-sold schedule.

12-month period ending ...19__

The right-hand set of columns is captioned as follows:

Estimated for 12-month period beginning ...19__

The left-hand set of columns is completed using the latest actual financial data available for the organization being analyzed. In the case of Manufacturer, Inc., whose income statement is shown in Exhibit 7-4, the date used would be that for the twelve-month period ending December 31, 1994. The right-hand set of columns is completed based on the estimate for the twelve-month period beginning with the policy inception or anniversary date—April 1, 1995, for Manufacturer, Inc.

Note the gap between the end of the period for the actual figures and the start of the policy period. Since actual figures are never available until after the end of the accounting period, this gap is inevitable—in some cases it may amount to almost a full year. It also complicates the task of estimating the amounts to be used in the right-hand columns.

The first step is to complete the left-hand column with past financial data. Then, projections for the twelve-month period commencing with policy inception or anniversary can be made and entered in the right-hand column. The twelve-month period starting with policy inception is used because that is the base period for the coinsurance calculation.

Manufacturing Versus Nonmanufacturing Operations

Each set of columns has one column for manufacturing operations and another for nonmanufacturing operations. This division is necessary because the business income exposure for nonmanufacturing firms is based on loss of *sales*, whereas the business income exposure for a manufacturer is based on the loss of *production* or, as stated in the worksheet, the "net sales value of production."

In order to calculate the net sales value of production, additional computations are necessary. These additional computations, performed in items B, C, and D, modify the amount shown in item A as gross sales. When the worksheet is being completed for a nonmanufacturing firm, items B, C, and D do not apply. Certain deductions from gross sales are made in item E for both manufacturing and nonmanufacturing firms. The result of these calculations (item F) is labeled "net sales value of production" for a manufacturer, and "net sales" for a nonmanufacturing firm. The various calculations made on page 2 of the worksheet are described in more detail below.

Gross Sales

The first entry on page 2 is item A, gross sales. **Gross sales** is the total of all sales at the invoiced price. In the case of Manufacturer, Inc., gross sales were $10,050,000.

Some income statements start off with *net sales*. **Net sales** is calculated by subtracting sales discounts, returns, and allowances from gross sales. If the insured's income statement begins with net sales, the net sales figure can be entered in item A, gross sales. In that case, no entry would be made in item E for sales discounts, returns, and allowances, and the end result on line F would be the same.

Finished Stock Inventory

Item B of the worksheet (which, remember, applies only to manufacturers) calls for the deduction of the sales value of finished stock inventory at the beginning of the period, since this inventory was produced in a prior period. The *sales* value of inventory does not appear in the income statement—the finished stock inventory shown in a manufacturer's financial statements is valued at *cost*, not sales value.

The sales value of finished stock can be estimated using the **cost-of-goods-sold ratio**. The cost-of-goods-sold ratio equals 1 minus the **gross-profit ratio**. The gross-profit ratio is gross profit divided by sales. Thus, if the gross profit is $100,000 and the sales are $400,000, the gross-profit ratio is .25. These calculations are part of what accountants call the **gross-profit method**. The gross-profit method estimates the inventory value at the end of a period by multiplying sales for the period by the ratio of cost of goods sold to selling price.[5] The following example illustrates the method for a firm that has a gross-profit ratio of .30 and therefore a cost-of-goods-sold ratio of .70 (that is, 1 – .30 = .70), a beginning inventory of $30,000, purchases of $70,000, and sales of $90,000:

Beginning inventory	$ 30,000
Purchases	70,000
Goods available for sale	100,000
Less estimated cost of goods sold:	
$90,000 sales x .70	63,000
Estimated ending inventory	$ 37,000

The gross-profit method is generally used for interim financial statements when an inventory value must be calculated without a physical inventory. It is also used in property loss adjustments to estimate the value of inventory that has been burnt beyond identification (so-called "burnt out of sight" losses). It can be adapted to the problem of converting inventory values from cost to sales value.

In the above example, sales were multiplied by the cost-of-goods-sold ratio to obtain the cost of goods sold. Thus, if we know the cost of goods sold, we can obtain the sales value by *dividing* the cost of goods sold by the cost-of-goods-sold ratio. (Using the data given in the example, that would be $63,000 ÷ .70 = $90,000.) In the same way, inventory valued at cost can be converted to sales value by dividing by the cost-of-goods-sold ratio.

Manufacturer's gross-profit ratio is .25 (gross profit of $2,500,000 divided by net sales of $10,000,000). The cost-of-goods-sold ratio, therefore, is .75 (calculated as 1 – .25). Dividing the finished stock inventory by the cost-of-goods-sold percentage changes the value of finished stock inventory from cost to sales basis. Manufacturer's income statement shows an opening inventory of $375,000, which if divided by .75 equals $500,000. Therefore, $500,000 is deducted in item B.

In item C, the finished stock inventory at the end of the period, at sales value, is added since this inventory was produced during the current period. It is calculated by the same method used in item B. The income statement shows a finished stock inventory on 12/31/94 of $400,000 at cost. Dividing by .75 gives a finished stock inventory on 12/31/94, at sales value, of $533,333.

The financial statements for some firms may combine raw materials, work-in-process, and finished stock into one item, just called "inventory." In that event, the separate amount for finished stock will have to be determined from the firm's books and records. Only finished stock is treated in worksheet items B and C.

Gross Sales Value of Production

Item D is the **gross sales value of production** during the period. This value is calculated by deducting item B from gross sales and adding item C. For Manufacturer, the gross sales value of production is $10,083,000. Again, item D applies only to manufacturers.

Deductions

Item E (which applies to both manufacturing and nonmanufacturing firms) lists certain sums that reduce the value of a firm's gross sales: prepaid freight, returns and allowances, discounts, bad debts, and collection expenses. Discounts and returns and allowances were discussed above in connection with gross sales. Prepaid freight is the freight charges on shipments to customers paid for by the seller.

Prepaid freight does not appear on Manufacturer's income statement. Many firms do not prepay freight on shipments to customers and in that case no entry would be made on the "prepaid freight" line. The "freight-in" item that appears in the cost of goods sold represents the freight paid by Manufacturer on shipments it received from its suppliers. It is not separately deducted; freight-in, just like the purchases to which it relates, is included as part of the cost-of-goods-sold calculation.

Bad debts—that is, accounts that cannot be collected from customers who are either unwilling or unable to pay—are also deducted in item E since they are really a reduction in the amount the insured received for selling its products. In Manufacturer's income statement, bad debts are called "uncollectible accounts" and amount to $25,000.

Collection expense refers to fees paid when outside collection agencies or attorneys are used to collect past-due accounts. No deduction is made for payroll of the insured's employees who work in a collection department. No separate item for "collection expenses" appears in Manufacturer's income statement.

We would have to check with Manufacturer's financial officer to see if collection expense or prepaid (outgoing) freight were included in some other account, such as miscellaneous. In that event, they would be entered in item E. To simplify this illustration, we have assumed that Manufacturer had no collection expense or prepaid outgoing freight during the period.

The sum of the deductions in item E is subtracted from either the amount shown for item D (in the case of a manufacturer) or from item A (in the case of a nonmanufacturing firm). The result, shown as item F, is the net sales value of production (for a manufacturer) or net sales (for a nonmanufacturing firm). In Manufacturer's case, the net sales value of production is $10,008,000.

Other Earnings

Other earnings from the insured's operations are added in item G. This includes, for example, investment income or rents from locations not covered by the worksheet.

In most cases, investment income is independent of the operations of the business. A portfolio of stocks and bonds will continue to yield income whether the business is operating or not. In some unusual cases, the funds for investment are generated by the business operations rather than capital or retained earnings, and therefore the earnings on such funds should be viewed as a business income exposure.

An insurance agency is an example of a business that derives income from the use of customers' funds. Agencies often have forty-five days or more after the inception of the policy to remit payment to the insurance company. Another example is a gambling casino. Gambling casinos realize substantial investment income on the "float" from the sale of chips, that is, the use of customers' funds for the time between the sale and redemption of chips.

In Manufacturer's case, the gain on sale of equipment amounting to $10,000 would be included as "other income" in item G; the interest income would not be included. Manufacturer's income statement shows no items for commission or rents or cash discounts received. If there were any such items, they would also be included in item G.

Total Revenues

Item H, "total revenues," is (for the purposes of the business income worksheet) the total of items F and G. In Manufacturer's case, item H amounts to $10,018,000.

Page 3—Calculating "Net Income and Expenses"

On page 3, the cost of goods sold is calculated and subtracted from "total revenues." The resulting figure, "net income and expenses," is used in determining the necessary amount of insurance to satisfy coinsurance requirements.

As will be discussed in more detail below, the possible coinsurance percentages for business income insurance range from 50 percent to 125 percent, reflecting the fact that some businesses, under a worst-case scenario, may expect only a relatively short interruption, whereas others may face an interruption exceeding one year.

Cost of Goods Sold

For nonmanufacturing firms the accounting and business income meanings of "cost of goods sold" are very similar. However, cost of goods sold as calculated in the business income worksheet does not correspond to what accountants call "cost of goods sold" for a manufacturing firm. Income statements for manufacturing firms include direct labor and factory overhead in the calculation of cost of goods sold. Neither labor nor overhead is included in cost of goods sold in the business income worksheet. (This problem does not exist for nonmanufacturing firms since they do not have direct labor and factory overhead categories.)

The first figure needed to calculate the worksheet "cost of goods sold" is inventory at the beginning of the year including, for manufacturing risks, stock-in-process (often called "work-in-process" in accounting statements)

Exhibit 7-5
Worksheet Page 3

	12 Month Period Ending 12/31/94			Estimated for 12 Month Period Beginning 4/1/95		
I. DEDUCT: The cost of the following (net of any cash discounts received):						
1. Cost of Goods Sold: Inventory (including stock in process) at beginning of year	$ 1,050			$1,110		
ADD: Cost of the following purchased during the year: Manufacturing risks only:						
Raw Stock Consumed	5,715			5,820		
Factory Supplies Consumed	+ 25			+ 20		
Merchandise Sold	+ 0			+ 0		
Other Supplies Consumed (including transportation charges)	+ 0			+ 0		
Total Purchase Costs	+ 5,740			+5,840		
Cost of Goods Available for Sale	$ 6,790			$6,950		
DEDUCT: Inventory (including stock in process) at end of year	− 1,065			−1,050		
Cost of Goods Sold	$ 5,725			$5,900		
2. Services purchased from outsiders (not your employees) to resell, that do not continue under contract	+ 0					
Total (Mining Properties – see next page)		− 5,725	−		− 5,900	−
J.1. Net Income and Expenses (Business Income Basis for Coinsurance if a Coverage Modification does not apply)		$ 4,293	$		$ 4,315	$
J.2. Combined (for firms engaged in both manufacturing and non-manufacturing operations)		$			$	
K. Business Income Basis for Coinsurance if a Coverage Modification does apply – see reverse side		$			$	
L. Amount of Insurance Required (Multiply the amount in J.1., J.2. or K. by the coinsurance percentage specified in the Declarations)					$	

and raw stock, but not including finished stock; the adjustment for finished stock inventory for manufacturing firms was made in items B and C. Thus, in Manufacturer's case, the income statement figures for raw materials ($800,000) and work-in-process ($250,000) are added, and the resulting sum ($1,050,000) is entered for "inventory at beginning of year." The "cost-of-goods-sold" portion of the worksheet, as filled in for Manufacturer, is shown in Exhibit 7-5.

The worksheet is somewhat unclear on the entries that follow at this point. Some of this confusion will be clarified in proposed future editions of the worksheet. The entries that should be made are as follows:

For a manufacturing firm:

- The cost of raw stock consumed. (All purchases of raw stock should be included since raw stock is included in the inventory at the beginning and the end of the year.) In Manufacturer's case, the cost of raw stock consumed is the sum of the following figures from the income statement: $5,700,000 (purchases) + $15,000 (freight-in).
- Factory supplies consumed. Manufacturer's income statement has a $25,000 entry for "supplies" (such as lubricating liquids, filters, and cleaning rags), which is entered on the worksheet line for "factory supplies consumed," as shown in Exhibit 7-5.

For both manufacturing and nonmanufacturing firms:

- The purchase cost of merchandise sold. For a manufacturer, this would be the purchase cost of goods sold that are not manufactured by the insured but are purchased from others. An example would be specialty items purchased from other manufacturers in order to complete the firm's product line. Manufacturer had no sales of merchandise manufactured by others.
- The cost of other supplies consumed. Manufacturer had no cost for other supplies consumed.

The items listed above are added. The sum, "total purchase costs," is added to "inventory (including stock in process) at beginning of year" to determine the "cost of goods available for sale." Inventory at the end of the year (comprising stock-in-process and raw stock but, again, not finished stock for a manufacturer) is then subtracted from the cost of goods available for sale, and the result is "cost of goods sold." These calculations are shown in Exhibit 7-5.

In the case of Manufacturer, the "cost of goods sold" for the purposes of the business income worksheet is $5,725,000 rather than $7,500,000, the amount that appears as cost of goods sold in Manufacturer's income statement. If the higher figure from the income statement were used in the worksheet without the preparer having performed the required calculations, the "cost of goods sold" for worksheet purposes would be overstated, and the business income exposure would be substantially understated. (The exposure would be *understated* because, as you will see below, determining the exposure involves subtracting the "cost of goods" sold from total revenues, thus resulting in a lower value than if the lower, correct figure had been subtracted.)

Services Purchased From Outsiders

After the "cost of goods sold" is determined, the cost of services purchased from others (not employees of the insured) that do not continue under contract is added to the cost of goods sold. The sum of the two is then subtracted from the total revenues calculated on page 2.

Manufacturers often use the services of independent contractors in the course of manufacturing their products. For example, a printer (manufacturer of books, etc.) might use the services of an independent bindery. Or a manufacturer of machinery parts might use an independent metallurgical contractor to perform annealing (heat treating) processes. Nonmanufacturing firms also use the services of independent contractors. For example, an appliance store may use independent contractors to deliver and install appliances in customers' homes.

Business Income Basis for Coinsurance

The difference between "total revenues" ($10,018,000) and the sum of "cost of goods sold" and "services purchased from outsiders" ($5,725,000) is shown in item J.1 as "net income and expenses." When adjusted in the second set of columns to the twelve months following policy inception, the amount shown for item J.1 is the basis for calculating the amount of insurance needed to comply with coinsurance—unless a coverage modification applies. For Manufacturer, the entry for "net income and expenses" is $4,293,000.

If the insured has both manufacturing and nonmanufacturing operations, the cost of goods sold for nonmanufacturing must be separately calculated and subtracted from the total revenues for nonmanufacturing operations shown on page 2. The remainder is added to the manufacturing net income and expenses shown in J.1 to arrive at *combined* net income and expenses in item J.2. Manufacturer did not have any nonmanufacturing operations.

Page 4—Coverage Modifications

Net income and expenses are adjusted on page 4 if either of two endorsements is attached to the policy: (1) ordinary payroll limitation or (2) power, heat, and refrigeration deduction. These endorsements, which eliminate business

Exhibit 7-6
Worksheet Page 4

BUSINESS INCOME REPORT/WORK SHEET
COVERAGE MODIFICATION

	12 Month Period Ending . . .19___	Estimated for 12 Month Period Ending . . .19___
NET INCOME and EXPENSES (item J.1. or J.2.)	$ ______	______
1. If Ordinary Payroll Limitation form is attached:		
DEDUCT: All Ordinary Payroll Expenses	– ______	– ______
	______	______
If "90 days" or "180 days" is indicated for Ordinary Payroll Limitation: ADD: The largest amount of Ordinary Payroll Expense incurred during the specified number of days	+ ______	+ ______
Total	______	______
2. If Power, Heat and Refrigeration Deduction form is attached: DEDUCT: Power, heat and refrigeration expenses that do not continue under contract	– ______	– ______
BUSINESS INCOME BASIS FOR COINSURANCE (Transfer to Line K. on previous page)	$ ______	$ ______
MINING PROPERTIES: In the Total for Line I include the following:		
Royalties, unless specifically included in coverage	$ ______	
Actual depletion, commonly known as unit or cost depletion (not percentage depletion)	+ ______	
Welfare and retirement fund charges based on tonnage	+ ______	
Hired Trucks	+ ______	
Subtotal	$ ______	

income coverage for the described items and therefore reduce the amount of insurance needed to comply with coinsurance, will be discussed in Chapter 8. These endorsements are not attached to Manufacturer Inc.'s policy.

Page 4, shown in Exhibit 7-6, also provides space to calculate special deductions that apply to mining properties. Manufacturer did not have any mining operations.

Provision for Income Tax

You may have noticed that income tax is not deducted in calculating the business income exposure. That is the proper procedure; any amount collected from the insurance company to replace business income will itself be subject to income tax. To restore the insured to its position before the loss, insurance must replace the income *before* income tax.

Projections for the Twelve-Month Period Beginning With the Policy Inception

After completing the first set of columns, the insured is ready to estimate figures for the twelve months beginning with the policy inception date. Each item should be considered individually. A change in one item may not be accompanied by a change of exactly the same magnitude in another item. For example, year-to-year increases or decreases in sales might not be accompanied by any change in depreciation or rent. Scheduled increases in salaries may occur even if sales and profits decrease.

In the case of a manufacturer, it is particularly important to estimate the beginning and ending finished stock inventory since business income insurance is linked to production. If an increase in sales is expected but it will be accompanied by a reduction in finished stock inventory at the end of the period, the business income exposure may actually be reduced despite increased sales and profitability.

For example, Bob Jones, Manufacturer's vice-president for production, feels that, with the aid of a new computer system, he can more accurately match inventory to sales. In the current year, Manufacturer produced and sold 100,000 units. It forecasts sales of 103,000 units for the coming twelve months, an increase of 3 percent over the current year. However, instead of maintaining a finished stock inventory of 10,000 units, it plans to have only 5,000 units on hand at the end of the year. Thus it will only have to produce 98,000 units in the coming twelve months, a reduction of 2 percent despite a projected 3 percent increase in sales. The calculation would be as follows:

Inventory planned for the end of the period	5,000 units
Units to be sold during the period	103,000
Total units needed	108,000
Inventory on hand at beginning of the period	10,000 units
Units to be produced during the period	98,000

If the forecast is accurate and price levels stay the same, sales will increase but the value of production will decrease.

The worksheet suggests multiplying the projected values in items J.1, J.2, or K by the applicable coinsurance percentage to arrive at an amount of insurance. This overlooks a number of important considerations. A more accurate procedure is to estimate the maximum probable loss first and then select a coinsurance percentage. The business income worksheet can be used in estimating maximum probable loss.

Using the Business Income Worksheet To Estimate Maximum Probable Loss

The starting point in estimating maximum probable loss (MPL) is the business income exposure for the twelve-month period beginning with policy inception, as calculated in the right-hand columns of the business income worksheet.

Projected figures for Manufacturer, Inc. are shown in Exhibits 7-4 and 7-5. The exact process by which such figures would be determined, other than the general comments in the preceding section, is beyond the scope of this text. Most firms prepare projections of future income and expenses. This is not generally a risk management activity, and it certainly is not an activity that an insurance producer should undertake unless he or she has specialized accounting or financial expertise. The job of the risk manager or insurance producer is to take the projections that the firm's financial officers have prepared and help them fit the numbers into the business income worksheet.

Starting with the amount in J.1 in the right-hand column ($4,315,000 for Manufacturer), some adjustments are necessary to arrive at total exposure. The items that should be considered are described below.

Noncontinuing Expenses

Firms that have not eliminated ordinary payroll or power, heat, and refrigeration by endorsement should consider whether any adjustment is necessary for these items in calculating MPL. Even if ordinary payroll and power, heat and refrigeration exclusion or limitation endorsements are attached to the policy and those items have therefore been eliminated from the worksheet, there are other expenses that may not continue that are not eliminated from the worksheet. These might be telephone, rent, advertising, and the other items discussed earlier in this chapter.

Maximum Length of Time Required To Restore Damaged Property

The business income worksheet is focused on the coinsurance requirement, which is based on twelve months beginning with the policy inception. Few organizations will have a period of restoration that is exactly equal to twelve months. Some may have a shorter period; for others the period may be longer. Thus, after noncontinuing expenses are eliminated, the values have to be extrapolated for the maximum period of restoration anticipated under a worst-case scenario.

Anticipated Changes in Expenses and Profits During the Period of Restoration

The worksheet is based on the period of twelve months that begins with the policy inception. Although it is sometimes recommended that firms review their business income values at least quarterly,[6] few firms examine their business income exposure more than once a year. Therefore, they must consider how conditions may have changed if the period of restoration commences on the last day of the policy period rather than at inception.

If a firm projects an increase in sales of 15 percent a year and a maximum restoration period of two years, its projected sales volume in the final year of a loss that began on the last day of the policy period would be over 32 percent higher than the sales value projected for the policy period.[7] Even a firm that estimates only a six-month period of restoration must consider the six months beginning on the last day of the policy period, or the last day of the quarter if the firm reviews its figures quarterly. This may yield a very different estimate of the maximum probable loss if the firm's operations are rapidly changing.

Peak Periods

The business income exposure also has to be adjusted for peak periods. As discussed earlier, many organizations have sharp variations in business from month to month.

For example, Peg's Toy Store has four peak months, September through December, which account for 60 percent of sales. The remaining 40 percent of sales are divided equally over the other eight months. The estimated maximum restoration period is six months. If the interruption began on September 1, the store would lose 70 percent of a year's sales rather than 50 percent (60 percent during September through December and 5 percent in each of the next two months). Thus, Peg's maximum probable loss would be 70 percent of the annual estimate rather than the 50 percent that a six-month restoration period would seem, at first glance, to indicate.

Extended Business Income Loss

As discussed earlier, net income does not always return to normal levels as soon as the damaged property is rebuilt or repaired. When calculating MPL for insurance purposes, only those losses that will be covered by insurance should be included. Business income insurance can be extended, on an optional basis, to cover reductions in net income that continue more than thirty days after the damaged property is restored to use. This coverage will be examined in Chapter 8.

Extra Expense

As already discussed, many organizations can continue operations at close to normal levels by renting temporary quarters and equipment. The extra expenses incurred for these items are not included in the worksheet but would be part of the MPL.

Compensating for Possible Errors

Errors are inevitable in any estimate. Since the consequences of underestimating the loss exposure (a potentially uninsured loss) are greater than the consequences of overestimating the loss exposure (the waste of a portion of the premium), a factor to allow for possible underestimates can be added to the maximum probable loss. Such a practice is also justified by the tendency of insureds to be overly optimistic about the length of time it would take to restore operations in the event of a devastating loss.

Selecting a Coinsurance Percentage

Once MPL has been estimated, the amount of insurance can be set and a coinsurance percentage selected. The general rule is: The amount of insurance should equal the MPL or the amount necessary to satisfy the coinsurance requirement, whichever is higher. There are three general possibilities, as described below.

1. *The MPL is less than or equal to 50 percent of the business income exposure shown in the worksheet for the policy period.* In this case, 50 percent coinsurance would be selected since it is the lowest available coinsurance percentage. The amount of insurance would be set equal to 50 percent of the amount shown in the worksheet for the policy period even though this is more than the estimated MPL.
2. *The MPL is greater than 50 percent but less than 125 percent of the business income exposure shown in the worksheet for the policy period.* In this case, the maximum probable loss should be divided by the business income exposure and the next higher coinsurance percentage should be selected. The amount of insurance should be equal to the business income exposure multiplied by the coinsurance percentage.

   For example, the coinsurance basis for Manufacturer is $4,315,000 (the amount shown in item J.1 in the right-hand column in Exhibit 7-5). If Manufacturer estimated its MPL to be $2,850,000, it would select 70 percent coinsurance since $2,850,000 divided by $4,315,000 is approximately 66 percent; 70 percent is the next higher coinsurance percentage. The amount of insurance carried would be at least $3,020,500 (70 percent of $4,315,000). As an alternative, Manufacturer could select the next lower coinsurance percentage, in this case 60 percent coinsurance, and carry $2,850,000 insurance. (If they carried only the $2,589,600 needed to comply with the coinsurance requirement, they would not have enough coverage in the worst-case scenario of a $2,850,000 loss.) However, since the rate for 60 percent coinsurance is higher than for 70 percent coinsurance, the additional coverage provided by the 70 percent coinsurance option would cost little more and might even cost less. Most firms are best served by electing the higher coinsurance percentage. The added insurance provides another cushion against the possibility that the MPL was underestimated.
3. *The MPL is equal to or more than 125 percent of the business income exposure shown in the worksheet for the policy period.* In this case 125 percent coinsurance would be selected since it is the highest available coinsurance percentage (and carries the lowest *rate*). The amount of insurance would be equal to the MPL.

Given the great difficulty of accurately estimating the amount of insurance needed to comply with the coinsurance clause in a business income policy, many experienced risk managers, producers, and consultants advocate eliminating coinsurance from the business income policy. The methods by which coinsurance can be eliminated from the policy is discussed in Chapter 8.

Summary

When an organization loses partial or total use of its property because the property has been physically damaged, the organization will likely suffer a reduction in net income. The possibility of such loss is the business income exposure, also known as the business interruption or time element exposure.

Business income loss can result not only from damage to an organization's own property but also from damage to property of another organization whose relationship to the first organization is that of supplier, buyer, or magnet business. Moreover, an organization that has sustained no physical damage itself can experience a business income loss when public access to its property is prevented by acts of civil authority.

The severity of a business income loss depends on how long business income could be reduced and when during the year the interruption could occur. For example, a three-month interruption that coincided with a retailer's peak selling season would cause a more severe business income loss than a three-month interruption during the slower months of the year.

The duration of a business interruption depends largely on the time required to replace or repair damaged property. Factors that can seriously affect the time required to replace property include critical items (such as a foreign-built, custom-made machine), building or zoning laws, and time-consuming production processes. After the property is restored to use, net income may continue to be reduced. A business may need to "win back" its old customers. During the interruption, it may also have lost important licenses, leases, contracts, and market share.

In some cases, a relatively small physical damage loss can cause a large business income loss. For example, damage that occurs only at a "bottleneck" can shut down an entire process or operation. And a fire, explosion, or other occurrence that releases contaminants throughout a building can result in a long shutdown while the building is being decontaminated.

Some operating expenses do not continue at their normal levels during a business interruption. To the extent that normal expenses do not continue in full, they offset some part of the reduction in revenues during the interruption. Thus, in analyzing business income loss severity, one should try to determine which expenses would be reduced during an interruption. The probable size of extra expenses to continue operations also needs to be considered.

The business income worksheet provides a means of analyzing a firm's income statement in order to determine the maximum probable loss and the amount of insurance needed to comply with the coinsurance clause in business income insurance. These two figures are unlikely to be the same.

The original source of figures in the business income worksheet is the organization's income or earnings statement, but it must not be simply copied. Even where the two have entries with the same names (such as "cost of goods sold"), they are unlikely to mean exactly the same thing. And there are significant differences according to whether the organization is engaged in manufacturing, in selling products produced by others, or in providing services.

The worksheet relies on generally accepted accounting principles (GAAP); and it is based on accrual accounting, which most but not all organizations use.

The first column of the worksheet is historical: It contains the amounts from the most recent fiscal year for which the organization's figures are available. The second column contains estimates, *line by line*, for the coming policy year; these are for determining how much insurance will be needed to meet the coinsurance requirement. From the worksheet figures, the organization's management then needs to estimate the figures applicable to the most significant period of interruption to which the policy will apply.

The amount of business income insurance purchased needs to cover the maximum probable loss and meet the coinsurance requirement. Because of possible errors in estimates, it is wise to settle on a figure somewhat higher than the directly estimated maximum probable loss, and set the coinsurance percentage accordingly.

Chapter Notes

1. See "Limiting Business Interruption," in *Handling a Loss* (Norwood, MA: Factory Mutual Engineering Corporation, 1981), pp. 10-13.
2. Industrial Risk Insurers, "PCB Contamination: Shutdown Facilities, Expensive Cleanup, A Lingering Threat," *The Sentinel*, vol. 16, no. 4, 4th qtr., 1984.
3. One court decision holding that depreciation should not be treated as a noncontinuing expense in calculating the loss of earnings when property is completely destroyed is Grevas v. United States Fidelity and Guarantee Company (CCH 1993 Fire and Casualty 3986). A case holding the opposite position is Cohen Furniture Company v. St. Paul Insurance Company of Illinois, IL Appellate Court, 3rd District, No. 3-90-0241 (CCH 1991-92 Fire and Casualty 3320).

   The management consulting division of the accounting firm Deloite & Touche, in a white paper published in the Fall 1992 issue of *The M&E Appraiser* (Washington, D.C.: American Society of Appraisers, 1992), argued that depreciation should not be deducted as a discontinued expense even in the event of total destruction. This, however, is not a generally accepted insurance industry opinion. A rebuttal written by Chris Campos, of the accounting firm Campos & Stratis, appeared in the Winter 1992/93 issue of *The M&E Appraiser*.

4. For more information concerning the income statement and accounting in general, see the CPCU 8 text, James Don Edwards, et al., *Introduction to Accounting*, 2nd ed. (Malvern, PA: American Institute for Chartered Property Casualty Underwriters, 1991).
5. See Lee J. Seidler and D. R. Carmichael, editors, *Accountants' Handbook* (New York, NY: John Wiley & Sons, 1981), Chapter 8, p. 6, and Chapter 18, p. 77; and Kermit D. Larson and William W. Pyle, *Fundamental Accounting Principles*, 11th ed. (Homewood, IL: Richard D. Irwin, Inc., 1987), pp. 340-341. Larson and Pyle provide an example of the gross-profit method used to value inventory totally destroyed by fire.
6. Robert B. Edgar, *Business Income* (Warren, NJ: Chubb & Son, Inc., 1987), p. 8.
7. The increase is 32.25 percent, not 30 percent, because the 15 percent increases are cumulative. Thus, the first year is 100 percent, the next year is 115 percent (100 percent plus 15 percent of 100 percent) and the final year is 132.25 percent (115 percent plus 15 percent of 115 percent).

Chapter 8

Business Income Insurance

The ISO "commercial property" program includes three coverage forms for insuring time element loss exposures:

1. Business income coverage form (and extra expense)
2. Business income coverage form (without extra expense)
3. Extra expense coverage form

These forms and the coverage options available for modifying the forms to meet particular coverage needs are the main subjects of this chapter.

Business Income Coverage Form

The two versions of the business income coverage form (1 and 2 above) are identical except with regard to their treatment of coverage for extra expense. Although this difference will be discussed in greater detail below, it can be summarized as follows:

- The **business income coverage form (and extra expense)** covers extra expenses regardless of whether they reduce the loss of business income.
- The **business income coverage form (without extra expense)** covers extra expenses only to the extent that they reduce the income loss.

Because the two versions of the form differ in this respect only, the discussion that follows describes both forms equally except where indicated otherwise. The abbreviation BIC refers to both forms.

Insuring Agreement

In the main insuring agreement of the BIC, the insurer agrees to pay for actual loss of "business income" that the named insured sustains due to the necessary suspension of "operations" during the "period of restoration." In order for the loss to be covered, the operations must be suspended because of physical loss of or damage to property at the described premises caused by a covered cause of loss. The terms in quotation marks above, as well as several other aspects of the insuring agreement, are explained below.

Actual Loss

The BIC covers only *actual loss sustained* by the named insured. Thus, the insurer is obligated to pay nothing unless the insured has actually sustained a business income loss, and the extent of the insurer's obligation is limited to the dollar amount of loss actually sustained (or, if less, the limit of insurance). In contrast with the BIC, some forms of business income insurance simply pay an agreed upon amount for each day or week that the business is shut down. Such forms are called **valued business income coverage.** Valued business income coverage is discussed in more detail later in this chapter.

The "actual loss sustained" approach does not mean that the insured must have been earning a net profit before the loss occurred in order to receive any benefit. As was illustrated in Chapter 7, a business already operating at a net loss can sustain a business income loss if a partial or total shutdown *increases* the net loss beyond what was expected. Business income insurance responds to such losses of net income.

In some extreme cases, an organization operating at a net loss might sustain no actual business income loss during a shutdown. For example, say that LSR Company would have had a net loss of $1.2 million if no physical loss and resulting shutdown had occurred. However, because of the shutdown, expenses were reduced to the point that LSR did not suffer a reduction in net income and therefore could not collect for loss of business income under its BIC. (If LSR had the BIC *with extra expense* form, it could collect for extra expense.)

Business income insurance is also used to provide coverage on buildings under construction that are not yet earning revenue. If property damage delays the date on which the building begins to earn rental income or income from operations, business income insurance will pay the owner for the resulting reduction in net income commencing from the date when the building would have been occupied. It will pay extra expenses (if covered) beginning immediately after the physical loss occurs.

"Business Income"

The BIC form covers loss of "business income"— in other words, the reduction in net income that results from suspension of operations due to a physical loss at the insured premises. The definition of **business income** is intended to clarify what sums can be included when calculating the amount of loss. The definition reads as follows:

> Business Income means the:
>
> a. Net Income (Net Profit or Loss before income taxes) that would have been earned or incurred; and
>
> b. Continuing normal operating expenses incurred, including payroll.

Calculating the difference between the net income that could have been expected for the period of restoration (had no physical loss occurred) and the actual net income during that period takes into consideration all of the elements of the "business income" definition. Recall from Chapter 7 the example of Pete's Auto Repair, which suffered an $18,000 reduction in net income because of a shutdown following a fire. If Pete's had had a BIC policy, the $18,000 reduction in net income would have been covered under that policy. The $18,000 payment from Pete's insurer would have covered the $10,000 net profit that Pete would have realized had no loss occurred, and it would have covered the $8,000 in continuing expenses during the shutdown.

Period of Restoration

In determining the actual loss sustained, the time element is measured by the **period of restoration**—essentially the length of time required to rebuild, repair, or replace the damaged or destroyed property "with reasonable speed and similar quality." According to the BIC definition of this phrase, the period of restoration begins when the physical loss or damage occurs; it ends when the property should, with reasonable speed, be repaired or replaced. The period of restoration does not include any increased time required because of the enforcement of any ordinance or law that regulates construction, use, repair, or demolition; or that requires testing for pollutants or cleaning them up.

Expiration of the policy does not end the period of restoration. As long as the physical loss occurs during the policy period, the BIC will cover for the duration of the period of restoration even though the policy expires before the period of restoration ends.

The reference to "reasonable speed" is important. If the insured causes unreasonable delay in obtaining estimates and doing whatever else is necessary to get repairs made, the insurer will not be liable for loss sustained beyond the reasonably expected repair period. However, courts have held that delays in reconstruction due to acts of persons other than the insured, or even reasonable disputes between the insured and others, are reimbursable. Similarly, if unusually severe weather or delay in shipping causes delay in rebuilding, the period of restoration is extended. These latter delays are beyond the insured's control, and it would be "unreasonable" to handle a loss as though construction could have continued during a period when weather conditions made construction impossible.

The restoration period does not cease the instant a damaged or destroyed building is repaired or rebuilt. Time is permitted for the insured to refurnish supplies and restock merchandise. For a manufacturer, time is allowed to bring the production process to the same point where it was before the loss.

An exclusion in the causes-of-loss forms specifically addresses "finished stock." The BIC defines **finished stock** as stock manufactured by the insured, other than stock manufactured by the insured and held for sale at a retail outlet insured under the policy. This exclusion eliminates coverage for loss caused by (1) damage to or destruction of finished stock and (2) the time required to reproduce finished stock. The building and personal property form (or some other type of personal property coverage) is required to cover the values represented by finished stock in the hands of its manufacturer. Adding the *manufacturers selling price endorsement* (see Chapter 4) to the BPP (and arranging limits to reflect that valuation basis) will assure that the insured can collect for loss to finished stock on the basis of selling price.

Net income often does not return to the normal level as soon as the suspension of operations ends. One of the BIC additional coverages, titled "extended business income," covers business income loss for up to thirty days after the period of restoration ends. In many cases, returning to normal income levels takes more than thirty days. Accordingly, one of the optional coverages included in the BIC, titled "extended period of indemnity," can be used to increase the number of additional days covered under the "extended business income" provision from thirty to whatever higher number is inserted in the declarations. This extension is discussed in more detail later in this chapter.

Damage to Property at the Insured Premises

A common misconception about business income insurance is that the physical loss or damage must be to property covered under the insured's BPP or other building and contents form. In reality, the BIC requires that the suspension of operations must be caused by loss of or damage to "property at the premises described in the Declarations." The property can be real or personal property, owned by the insured or by others.

To illustrate, say that a hailstorm damages almost the entire stock of new and used autos on an auto dealer's lot, and obtaining replacement stock will take two to three weeks. Automobiles are not covered property under the dealer's building and personal property coverage form. However, the resulting business income loss would nevertheless be covered under the dealer's BIC if the damaged autos on the lot were "property at the premises described in the Declarations." If the autos had been stored on a lot at a location not shown in the policy, the loss would not have been covered.

The BIC also covers suspension of operations caused by damage by a covered peril to personal property in the open (or in a vehicle) within 100 feet of the described premises.

The BIC contains both an additional coverage ("civil authority" clause) and a coverage extension ("newly acquired locations") that provide some coverage for business income resulting from physical damage occurring away from the described premises. Those provisions will be discussed below. If the insured has an off-premises business income exposure because of dependency on a particular supplier, buyer, manufacturer, or "magnet" property, it can be insured under a separate endorsement to be discussed later in this chapter.

Covered Causes of Loss

Any of the causes-of-loss forms described in Chapter 5—basic, broad, or special—can be used to designate the perils covered by the BIC. Earthquake coverage can be added by endorsement. The perils insured against do not need to be the same ones covered under the insured's building and contents coverage. Usually, however, the same perils are covered on both forms.

Standard business income insurance forms do not cover such perils as flood, landslide, or subsidence. However, coverage is available in some difference in conditions (DIC) policies, and many insurers are willing to cover such exposures using nonstandard forms or endorsements.

Some perils are particularly important as causes of business shutdowns but are generally uninsurable. For example, many businesses are shut down when workers go on strike demanding higher wages or other concessions, and loss of business income caused by strike is not generally insurable. If a strike turns into a riot, business interruption attributable to property damaged by rioters would be covered by all three ISO causes-of-loss forms.

In addition to the exclusions and limitations discussed in Chapter 5, the basic, broad, and special causes-of-loss forms contain some exclusions that apply *only* to the BIC forms and the extra expense coverage form. These exclusions are described below.

Finished Stock

The finished stock exclusion applies to both (1) damage or destruction of finished stock and (2) the time required to reproduce finished stock. As noted above, a manufacturer can insure its finished stock at the selling price through the building and personal property coverage form and manufacturers selling price endorsement.

The finished stock exclusion does not apply to extra expense coverage, however. If, for example, a manufacturer's finished stock warehouse and contents were destroyed by a fire, the manufacturer's extra expense coverage would pay for overtime wages and other extra expenses incurred for the purpose of increasing production in order to replenish the finished stock as quickly as possible.

Interference by Strikers

Neither the BIC nor the extra expense form covers any increase in loss resulting from delay in rebuilding, repairing, or replacing the property because of interference by strikers or other persons *at the location of the rebuilding, repair, or replacement*. The exclusion does not apply to delay resulting from interference by strikers or others at locations *away from the work site*. If, for example, reconstruction of the building at the insured's premises is delayed because of picketing at the general contractor's office and warehouse, such delay would not be excluded. The additional time caused by the strike would be included in the period of restoration. If the strike were at the repair location—even if it did not involve the insured's employees—the delay would not extend the covered period of restoration.

Loss of License, Lease, or Contract

Also excluded is any increase in loss resulting from the suspension, lapse, or cancellation of any license, lease, or contract. However, if a suspension, lapse, or cancellation is caused by the suspension of operations, the insurer will pay such loss that affects the insured's business income *during the period of restoration*.

To illustrate, say that all tenants in an office building cancel their leases after the building is badly damaged by a fire. The building owner's BIC policy will cover the resulting loss of rental income, but only during the period of restoration. Once the period of restoration has ended, the insurer will not continue to pay for loss of rents due to unoccupancy of the building.

Any extra expense resulting from suspension, lapse, or cancellation of any license, lease, or contract beyond the period of restoration is also excluded. Thus, additional advertising costs to find new tenants after the building was restored would not be covered.

Antennas

Another exclusion eliminates coverage for loss resulting from physical damage to radio or television antennas. If, for example, a radio station's transmitting antenna collapsed as a result of freezing rain and high wind, the station's business income and extra expense coverage would not apply to either resulting loss of business income or extra expenses to get back on the air.

Although the exclusion can be deleted by endorsement, radio and television stations often insure their antennas and other communications equipment under specially designed inland marine policies that cover both physical damage and resulting business income and extra expense.

Any Other Consequential Loss

The final special exclusion reads simply "any other consequential loss." This is to make clear that the policy does not cover loss of market share, loss of goodwill, and similar losses. Firms spend large sums of money to obtain market share and to develop brand loyalty. Interruption of production can cause a reduction in market share or brand loyalty and thus a reduction in the value of the firm apart from any loss of income.

"Operations" and Related Coverage Options

The BIC covers loss of business income sustained because of the necessary suspension of the insured's "operations." Operations are defined in the BIC as (1) the named insured's business operations at the described premises and (2) the tenantability of the premises—but only if the policy covers "rental value."

The BIC defines "rental value" to include anticipated rental income from tenants, as well as all charges that are the legal obligation of the tenants and would otherwise be the insured's obligation (such as real-estate taxes and charges for electrical service). "Rental value" also includes the fair rental value of any portion of the described premises occupied by the insured.

Whether a BIC policy covers rental value is shown in the policy declarations. Three options are available:

1. Business income including "rental value"
2. Business income other than "rental value"
3. "Rental value" only

Option 1 covers both loss of rental value and loss of other business income. A real estate brokerage that owns, and operates out of, a multi-tenant office building that it rents in part to other tenants might choose option 1. If the building became physically damaged and untenantable, the insurer would pay for both the insured's loss of rental income from tenants and the insured's loss of business income from (or extra expenses for) its own real estate brokerage business.

Option 2 covers business income *other than* rental value. This option could be chosen by a business that has rental income to lose but does not wish to insure it. Either option 1 or 2 could be chosen by a business that has no rental income to lose. However, such a business might be better served by option 1 since it might sublet a portion of its premises in the future and thus have a need for rental value coverage.

Option 3 covers rental value only. This option might be purchased by a landlord whose only income is derived from renting property to others.

Additional Coverages and Coverage Extension

The two versions of the BIC each contain four additional coverages. In the "BIC (and extra expense)" form, the additional coverages are titled as follows:

- Extra expense
- Extended business income
- Civil authority
- Alterations and new buildings

The BIC (without extra expense) form contains the same additional coverages except extra expense. Instead of extra expense, the BIC (without extra expense) form provides what is called "expenses to reduce loss."

Both versions of the BIC also provide a coverage extension for newly acquired locations.

Extra Expense

The BIC (and extra expense) form defines **extra expense** as necessary expenses the insured incurs during the period of restoration that would not have been incurred if there had been no physical loss caused by a covered peril. The form then describes, in three categories, the types of extra expenses that are covered. These categories of covered extra expenses are summarized below, along with some examples of what is covered by each.

The first category covers extra expenses incurred to avoid or minimize the suspension of business and to continue operations, at either the described premises or at temporary or replacement premises. For example, this category would cover the extra expense of renting, moving to, and equipping a temporary location while the original premises are being repaired.

The second category covers extra expenses incurred to minimize the suspension of business if the insured cannot continue operations. For example, a printer whose plant has been totally destroyed might have contract obligations to print a certain number of books or magazines by a certain date. Although the printer would be unable to do the printing itself, it might hire another printer (as a subcontractor) to fulfill the contract. The extra expense involved in doing so (to the extent it exceeds the printer's normal costs) would be covered by the BIC and extra expense form.

The third category covers extra expense incurred for the following purposes:

- Repairing or replacing any property
- Researching, replacing, or restoring the lost information on damaged valuable papers and records

An example of extra expense covered under this provision is payment of overtime wages to expedite building repairs; or payment of above-market prices to obtain replacement merchandise so that sales activities can be resumed more quickly. Extra expenses to restore lost information might include the cost of buying customer prospect mailing lists from an outside vendor, or hiring telephone operators to call the firm's known customers and request information that was contained on the destroyed records.

The third category will also cover extra expenses incurred to pay for a shortfall of property insurance. For example, the amount of insurance on business personal property may have been insufficient to pay for replacement of all merchandise lost. Extra expense coverage may be used to replace the property if the BIC limit is sufficient and such payment will reduce the business income loss by the amount spent. If the amount spent, in this category, is more than the business income saved, it will only pay up to the amount of business income saved by such action (subject, of course, to the limit of insurance).

The extra expenses described in the first and second categories above are covered regardless of the extent to which they reduce the business income loss. They are covered even if they do not reduce the loss at all. Thus, they provide the type of extra expense coverage appropriate for organizations that have a strong need to continue operations or deliver their services, even if that would cost more than suspending operations.

However, extra expenses in the third category are covered only to the extent that they reduce the amount of loss that otherwise would have been payable under the policy. Thus, returning to the earlier example of an extra expense under the third category, if the additional cost paid to obtain merchandise was greater than the reduction in the business income loss, the insurer would not be obligated to pay more than the amount it would have paid for business income if extra expenses had not been incurred.

Expenses To Reduce Loss

Instead of extra expense coverage, the BIC (without extra expense) form contains an additional coverage titled **expenses to reduce loss.**

Under this coverage, the insurer agrees to pay any necessary expenses incurred by the named insured (except the cost of extinguishing a fire) to reduce the business income loss. Thus, the insured can incur the same *types* of expenses as covered under the extra expense coverage, but they are covered only to the extent that they reduce the business income loss, in the same manner as the third category of extra expense discussed above.

A danger of the BIC *without extra expense* form is that the insured can incur more extra expenses than the resulting reduction in the business income loss. A large *uninsured* extra expense loss can result. The BIC (and extra expense) from greatly reduces the possibility of that occurring.

Extended Business Income Coverage

Extended business income coverage is an addition to the business income coverage provided by both versions of the BIC. To prevent confusion, the concepts of *extended business income* and *business income* must be distinguished from one another.

Business income coverage replaces income lost during the "period of restoration," which ends when property at the described premises is repaired, rebuilt, or replaced. If the restoration is delayed, the "period of restoration" ends on the date when property should have been restored "with reasonable speed and similar quality." In many cases, this time runs out before the insured's business volume has completely returned to normal. A business that has been shut down for a while does not immediately regain all its customers when its doors reopen. The damaged property may be restored, but business activity may still be depressed.

The *extended business income* additional coverage extends for thirty days the time period for which the insured will be reimbursed for loss of business income. The period of extended business income coverage begins on the date the property is actually repaired, rebuilt, or replaced and operations are restored.

The beginning date of extended business income coverage is not necessarily the same as the date on which the "period of restoration" ends. A gap can occur if the restoration is not completed "with reasonable speed." A gap can also occur if operations do not resume until some time after the property is restored. Business income coverage ends when the property should have been repaired, rebuilt, or replaced—but extended business income coverage does not begin until the property is restored *and* operations are resumed.

Extended business income coverage lasts for thirty days if normal business income cannot be completely restored within that time period. However, if the insured could (not "does," but "could") restore the business in a shorter period of time, extended business income coverage ceases.

The 30-day limitation in the extended business income coverage can be lengthened in 30-day increments to as long as 360 days through use of the BIC optional coverage titled **extended period of indemnity**. This optional coverage, which is printed in the BIC form and requires an additional premium, is activated when the applicable number of days is entered in an appropriate place on the declarations page.

Civil Authority

The **civil authority additional coverage**, contained in both versions of the BIC, extends the BIC to cover business income losses incurred by the insured because civil authorities have cut off access to the insured's premises. Occasionally a fire or other peril will cause an interruption at a number of businesses that, themselves, sustain no direct damage. For example, the police or fire department may deny access to an entire city block when a serious fire occurs.

For civil authority coverage to apply, three criteria must be met:

1. Access to the insured's premises must be denied by the order of civil authority.
2. The denial of access must be caused by damage or destruction of property that is not on the described premises.
3. The direct property damage must result from a cause of loss covered by the insured's BIC policy.

Standard forms at one time limited this coverage to damage at adjacent properties—some nonstandard forms still do. Under the current ISO wording, the damage could be at a location far removed from the insured's premises, perhaps an explosion on the other side of town. If the damage caused by the explosion results in access being denied by civil authorities, coverage applies.

Civil authority coverage applies for a period of up to two consecutive weeks after the date of the civil authority's action.

Alterations and New Buildings

Business income losses do not result only from property damage to existing buildings and disruption of operations currently in progress. Business income can also be lost if completion of a new building is delayed because the building is damaged during the course of its construction. Similarly, if alterations to an existing building are not completed on schedule, operations will not begin when planned and a loss of income may result.

The additional coverage titled **alterations and new buildings** insures loss of business income sustained due to physical damage to new buildings or structures or alterations or additions to existing buildings or structures. The coverage also applies to business income losses resulting from damage to machinery, equipment, supplies, or building materials located on or within 100 feet of the described premises and used in the construction or incidental to the occupancy of new buildings.

Coverage applies only if the physical loss or damage delays the start of operations. The "period of restoration" begins on the date operations would have begun if the direct physical loss or damage had not occurred. However, under the business income form *with extra expense*, extra expense payments may be used immediately to try to rush repairs so that the property may be used by its scheduled date.

Newly Acquired Locations

Unlike the "additional coverages" discussed above, the "coverage extension" titled **newly acquired locations** applies only when a coinsurance percentage of 50 or more is shown in the declarations. As a practical matter, this requirement is met in the majority of policies, but it would not apply when the "maximum period of indemnity" or "extended period of indemnity" options are chosen. (These options are discussed below.)

The extension provides up to thirty days' temporary coverage at a new location, which should give the insured ample time to report the added exposure to the insurance company. Coverage under the extension ceases when the policy expires, when the new location is reported to the insurer, or thirty days after the exposure begins, whichever comes first. This is automatic insurance—not free insurance. The insurer is entitled to charge a premium from the date the exposure begins.

Coverage for newly acquired locations does not apply to property at fairs and exhibitions. The limit of insurance for this coverage is 10 percent of the business income limit subject to a maximum of $100,000 at each location. The coinsurance provision does not apply to this coverage extension.

Application of Limits to Additional Coverages and Extension

Business income coverage is ordinarily issued with a single limit of insurance that applies to each occurrence. Payments under the additional coverages do not increase the limit. However, the coverage extension for newly acquired locations is an additional amount of insurance.

Conditions

The BIC contains various conditions, some of which are similar to conditions found in the building and personal property coverage form (BPP). The BIC conditions are described below.

Appraisal

The BIC contains an appraisal clause that calls for essentially the same appraisal procedures as in the BPP appraisal clause. The difference, of course, is that the objective of the BIC appraisal clause is to reach agreement on the amount of income loss rather than the value of damaged property.

Duties in the Event of Loss

The duties that the BIC insured must perform following loss are virtually identical to those under the BPP. However, the BIC contains one additional duty: If the insured organization intends to continue its operations, it must resume all or part of its operations as quickly as possible. If the insured does not resume operations or does not resume operations as quickly as possible, the insurer will calculate the loss based on the length of time it would have taken to resume operations as quickly as possible.

Limitation—Electronic Media and Records

If business income loss results from damage by an insured peril to electronic data processing (EDP) media or programming records, *and if no other property has been damaged*, coverage is limited to a period of sixty days. If other property has been damaged along with the EDP media, the time limit is the time required to repair or replace the property other than EDP, if longer than sixty days. These limitations do not affect extra expense coverage.

For an additional premium, the EDP media limitation can be changed to 180 days or eliminated entirely. Alternatively, the exposure can be insured with an EDP equipment policy, described in Chapter 11.

Loss Determination

The loss determination condition contains several parts. The first part lists the various things that will be taken into account in determining the amount of business income loss:

- The insured's net income before the loss occurred
- The likely net income if no loss had occurred
- Operating expenses, including payroll, necessary to resume operations at the same level of service that existed just before the loss occurred
- Other relevant sources of information, including (but not limited to) the insured's financial records, bills, invoices, and so on

The loss determination condition in the BIC (and extra expense) form also contains an explanation of how the amount of extra expense coverage will be determined. The covered extra expense loss consists of all expenses in excess of normal operating expenses that would have been incurred if the physical loss had not taken place. The covered loss also includes all necessary expenses that reduce the business income loss that would otherwise have been incurred. The insurer will deduct from this total the salvage value of any property bought for temporary use during the period of restoration, as well as extra expenses covered by other insurance.

To illustrate the clause relating to salvage value, the insured might have bought a mobile home to be placed outside the damaged building for use as a temporary office and a command post for reconstruction efforts. Although the purchase price is includable extra expense, the insurer will have the right to deduct the salvage value of the trailer once operations are resumed. Without this provision, the remaining value of property purchased to expedite recovery would become a "gift" to the insured.

Under both versions of the BIC, the insurer reserves the right to reduce its payment for business income loss to the extent that the insured can resume operations in whole or in part using damaged or undamaged property at the described premises or elsewhere. In other words, the insured organization must do what it can to minimize the loss, even if that means setting up temporary operations at another location. If the insured does not resume operations, or does not resume operations as quickly as possible, the insurer will only pay on the basis of what the loss would have been had the insured resumed operations as quickly as possible. This points to the desirability of the business income form *with extra expense*, which covers the extra expenses paid to resume operations quickly.

Loss Payment

The insurer will pay for covered loss within thirty days after receiving the insured's sworn proof of loss, if two conditions are met: (1) The insured has complied with all policy terms and (2) the amount of loss has been determined either by agreement between the insurance company and the insured or by an appraisal award.

Coinsurance

In order to encourage insurance to value and to simplify ratemaking, the BIC form contains a coinsurance clause that operates essentially the same as the coinsurance clause in property insurance policies covering physical loss. However, *the value of property is not the value against which the coinsurance percentage is applied; instead, it is the total of net income and operating expenses that would have been earned or incurred (had no loss occurred) for the twelve months beginning with policy inception* (or policy anniversary, for a multi-year policy). The coinsurance clause does not apply to extra expense coverage or to the newly acquired locations extension.

As discussed in Chapter 7, the insured may choose coinsurance of 50, 60, 70, 80, 90, 100, or 125 percent. As in direct damage property insurance, the rates charged for business income insurance *decrease* as the coinsurance percentage *increases*. The chosen percentage generally corresponds roughly to the expected duration of a business interruption. An organization expecting a maximum interruption of six months might purchase coverage with a 50 percent coinsurance clause, since six months is 50 percent of one year. At the other extreme, an organization facing a potential interruption of more than one year might elect coverage with 125 percent coinsurance. However, relating the coinsurance percentage solely to the expected period of interruption would be a gross oversimplification. As explained in Chapter 7, the maximum probable loss must be analyzed and compared with business income coverage provisions in order to determine the limit of insurance to purchase.

Three points about the BIC coinsurance clause must be emphasized:

1. The amount reflecting the potential business income loss is not necessarily the amount of insurance that will meet coinsurance requirements.
2. To comply with the coinsurance clause, an insured may be required to purchase more business income insurance than seems necessary.
3. What looks like overinsurance is justified, in part, by the additional coverages, which provide for recovery in excess of the loss of business income. And, as pointed out in Chapter 7, the amount actually needed is often underestimated (especially by being too optimistic about the time required for replacement and repair).

Business income insurance can also be purchased without coinsurance, on a "flat rate" basis. However, the rate is approximately 250 percent of the rate for 50 percent coinsurance.

Business Income Exposure Versus Coinsurance Requirement

The BIC coinsurance percentage does not apply to the exposure. Business income is defined as net income plus *continuing* expenses incurred during the interruption, but the coinsurance clause applies to net income plus *all operating expenses* that probably would have developed during the twelve month period following the inception date of the policy. *In determining compliance with the coinsurance provision, both continuing and noncontinuing expenses are taken into account.* A simplified business income coinsurance calculation is shown in Exhibit 8-1.

Exhibit 8-1
Business Income Coinsurance Example

Young's Book Store has suffered a fire loss that will result in a one-month period of restoration and a corresponding business income loss of $50,000. In cooperation with Young's accountant, the insurer determines that Young's net income and operating expenses for the twelve months following policy inception would have been $500,000. Young's BIC has a limit of $200,000 with a 50 percent coinsurance clause and no deductible. The amount of covered loss is calculated as follows:

$$\frac{\$200{,}000}{\$500{,}000 \times .50} \times \$50{,}000 = \$40{,}000$$

By using standard endorsements, certain operating expenses can be excluded from both business income coverage and the coinsurance calculation. The result is that the insured can purchase a lower amount of insurance and still meet coinsurance requirements. The expenses that can be excluded are (1) payroll and (2) power, heat, and refrigeration expenses. (The latter exclusion is available to manufacturing and mining risks only.) These endorsements are discussed in more detail later in this chapter.

The usual practice when buying business income insurance is to project income and expense figures for one year. The limit of insurance should be reviewed at least once during the policy period to see whether any major changes have occurred that could affect the projection. As the policy period progresses and earnings and expenses are booked, there is less and less uncertainty over the amount of insurance required to comply with coinsurance provisions.

More Insurance Than Seems Necessary

It might seem more logical for the coinsurance percentage to apply to the exposure insured—net income plus expenses that would continue during a shutdown. However, those who drafted the contract language recognized that it is difficult, if not impossible, to distinguish continuing from noncontinuing expenses before any loss occurs. Requiring such a distinction might make it extremely difficult to comply with a coinsurance provision (and even more difficult for an insurer to prove noncompliance).

Another reason for having more insurance than seems necessary is that the "extra" limits may actually be needed, because the BIC covers more than loss of business income. Automatically included in the BIC are the four additional coverages and the coverage extension discussed earlier in this chapter.

The BIC coinsurance clause, like that of the building and personal property coverage form, can be replaced with alternative provisions. These provisions are discussed along with other "BIC coverage options" in the section that follows.

BIC Coverage Options

The unmodified business income coverage form represents a basic approach to insuring time element loss exposures. Various coverage options are available to modify the BIC to meet particular coverage needs. These options can be grouped according to the following purposes:

- To exclude certain expenses from coverage and from coinsurance calculations
- To eliminate or suspend coinsurance
- To adjust the premium at the end of the policy period
- To provide blanket insurance
- To cover certain special cases: dependent properties, school tuition, off-premises utilities, and building law exposures.

Some of these options are printed in the BIC form itself, and others can be added by endorsement or (in the case of blanket insurance) by indication on the declarations page.

Excluding Certain Expenses

By endorsement, the BIC can be modified to exclude either or both of the following:

- Ordinary payroll expense
- Power, heat, and refrigeration expense

The purpose of excluding either item is to enable the insured to buy a smaller amount of insurance than would otherwise be required to comply with the coinsurance clause. In many cases, the excludable expenses actually do not continue during a business interruption and thus are not part of the loss. And yet, unless they are excluded, the insured must include such expenses when calculating the amount of insurance necessary to avoid a coinsurance penalty.

Payroll Coverage Options

As discussed in Chapter 7, some payroll expenses do not normally continue during an extended period of interruption. The noncontinuing payroll expenses generally fall within the definition of ordinary payroll. **Ordinary payroll** (as defined in the endorsement to be described below) includes the entire payroll expense (including employee benefits, FICA payments, union dues paid by the employer, and workers compensation premiums) for all employees of the named insured except officers, executives, department managers, and employees under contract.

Ordinary payroll may be treated in any of the following ways:

1. *Ordinary payroll may be covered in full.* The unmodified BIC covers all necessary payroll expense, including ordinary payroll. Payroll cost is treated as an operating expense, and thus is included when determining the amount of insurance necessary to meet the coinsurance requirement.
2. *Ordinary payroll may be excluded.* This is accomplished by using the **payroll limitation or exclusion endorsement.**
3. *Ordinary payroll may be limited.* The third approach, which also uses the payroll limitation or exclusion endorsement, covers ordinary payroll for a limited period of time. Coverage may be provided for 90 or 180 days.

The choice among the three approaches to ordinary payroll depends on the insured's situation, the possible length of an interruption, and the extent to which payroll expenses would continue. Full coverage of ordinary payroll is appropriate for many insureds, especially if the maximum duration of a shutdown is brief, if union or other contracts require salary continuation, or if employees generally would be difficult to replace and would not be laid off during a shutdown.

Ordinary payroll should be excluded entirely only after considering the variables that might enter into post-loss handling of ordinary payroll. For example:

- The labor market might be tight in the insured's locale at the time of a loss, and there may be some difficulty in hiring employees. It may thus be prudent to retain existing employees.

- There may be more expense than anticipated in training new employees. Existing employees are already trained.
- Disputes in loss adjustments may develop over which employees should be classified in the ordinary payroll category. The issue is not raised when the entire payroll expense is covered.

The CLM calls for an increase in rate for all options to limit or exclude ordinary payroll, with the exception of the 180-day limitation. Thus, the insured must decide whether there will be any savings in premium by eliminating ordinary payroll and, if so, whether the savings are of sufficient amount to be worthwhile.

Power, Heat, and Refrigeration Deduction

As discussed in Chapter 7, power, heat, and refrigeration expenses are relatively large for some manufacturing operations. Yet, if the power, heat, or refrigeration is consumed in the manufacturing process, most such expenses do not continue when the process is shut down. When these "energy" expenses are unlikely to continue, they can create a sizable gap between the business income loss exposure and the amount of business income coverage that must be purchased to meet coinsurance requirements.

The **power, heat, and refrigeration deduction endorsement** provides some relief for manufacturers who have recognized this problem. With the endorsement, the cost of such "energy" used in production operations is not included in either the definition of business income or in coinsurance computations, as long as such expenses do not continue under contract. When energy expenses are excluded, the insured can purchase a lower limit of insurance. However, the CLM calls for an increase in rate when the endorsement is used. Unless energy expense is a significant part of the insured's total operating expenses, there may be no advantage gained by using the endorsement.

The energy expense of some larger users of electricity consists of two elements: (1) a "demand" charge and (2) a charge for electricity actually used. The demand charge is made in consideration of the electric company's obligation to maintain the capacity to meet the user's needs. The user must pay the demand charge even if the user's operations and energy usage are curtailed. Thus, demand charges are not excluded by the power, heat, and refrigeration limitation endorsement. They are a continuing expense that would be covered under the BIC. The existence and size of a demand charge can usually be determined by reviewing the insured's electrical service invoices.

Alternatives to Coinsurance

The BIC contains three "optional coverages" that can be used to eliminate or suspend the coinsurance clause. These alternatives to coinsurance are known by the following names:

- Maximum period of indemnity
- Monthly limit of indemnity
- Agreed value

Each of these optional coverages is printed in the BIC form and can be activated by an appropriate entry in the declarations.

Maximum Period of Indemnity

The optional coverage titled **maximum period of indemnity** is a reasonable alternative for organizations that are unlikely to sustain a business interruption of more than four months. The chief advantage of the optional coverage is that it is uncomplicated.

The coinsurance condition does not apply. Instead, the insurer promises to pay whatever business income loss is sustained for up to 120 days following the physical damage loss or until the limit of insurance is exhausted, whichever comes first. Premium rates are substantially higher with this option, but lower limits of insurance may be chosen to cover the maximum probable loss.

Monthly Limit of Indemnity

The **monthly limit of indemnity** option also suspends the coinsurance clause. With this option, the most the insurer will pay for each period of thirty consecutive days is the actual business income loss sustained, not to exceed the limit of insurance times the fraction shown in the declarations. The fractions ordinarily used are $^1/_3$, $^1/_4$, and $^1/_6$, corresponding to expected interruption periods of three, four, and six months, respectively. (In this discussion of the monthly limit of indemnity option, "month" means a period of thirty consecutive days, not a calendar month.)

After selecting an appropriate percentage limitation, based on the maximum duration of a shutdown, the highest net income and continuing expense for any single month should be determined. This is necessary because no one knows in which month a loss will occur. The amount of insurance that will cover the maximum anticipated loss is simply the maximum number of months multiplied by the highest monthly exposure. This simple approach to calculating an amount of insurance makes the monthly limit approach attractive to smaller businesses for which forecasting is difficult.

Coverage and Loss Illustration

To illustrate, assume the following facts about the RST Company:

- It conducts a seasonal business with its best month in December.
- In December, net profits and continuing expenses are expected to be $8,000.
- The maximum duration of a shutdown is estimated to be four months.

Based on these facts, the 1/4 monthly limit is selected and the amount of insurance purchased is four times $8,000, or $32,000.

Now, assume that RST Company is shut down for two weeks and incurs a business income loss of $5,000. The loss will be paid in full because the 1/4 of $32,000, an $8,000 monthly limit, is not allocated evenly over the month. In other words, the $8,000 monthly limit is not further subdivided into $4,000 for two weeks. The full $8,000 is available for any loss lasting less than one month. This is important because it often is not possible to cut continuing expenses quickly or to cut them as much in short shutdowns as in long ones. For example, when the interruption will be short, it may be best to keep on paying all payroll to assure the availability of the full workforce at reopening.

Suppose the actual loss turns out to be $6,000 in the first month and $9,000 in the second month (despite the *expected* maximum of $8,000). The insurer will pay the full $6,000 for the first month, but only $8,000 of the second month's loss. The total reimbursement is $14,000. If the full limit is not used in a month, the "unused" insurance is not added to the limit for future months. *The limit applies separately to each month.*

Suppose RST Company suffers a business interruption lasting four and one-half months (the four-month estimate was inaccurate) with monthly losses of $6,000, $9,000, $8,000, $8,000, and $4,000. The insurer will pay as shown in Exhibit 8-2. There is no limitation on the number of months during which losses will be paid, but there are limits on the amount payable (1) in any thirty-day period and (2) for the entire period of interruption.

Comparative Cost

Premium *rates* for the monthly limit of indemnity option are higher than the rates for the basic BIC. However, there are situations when the *premium* for an appropriate monthly limit of indemnity is less than that for an unmodified BIC covering the maximum expected loss with no penalty for underinsurance.

These situations often develop when the period of restoration is less than six months, the exposure is small, and earnings do not vary month to month. The

Exhibit 8-2
RST Company Recovery for 4 1/2 Month Loss

Month	Loss	Payment	Basis
1	$ 6,000	$ 6,000	Actual Loss Sustained
2	9,000	8,000	Monthly Maximum
3	8,000	8,000	Actual Loss Sustained
4	8,000	8,000	Actual Loss Sustained
5	4,000	2,000	Limited by $32,000 Policy Limit
Totals	$35,000	$32,000	

basic BIC has a 50 percent minimum coinsurance clause, which implicitly assumes a minimum six-month restoration period and an amount of insurance equal to at least half the firm's net income and expenses. By contrast, the 1/3, 1/4, and 1/6 monthly limitation options implicitly assume interruptions of three, four, or six months, respectively. Furthermore, since the coinsurance requirement is eliminated, the insured may purchase a much lower amount of insurance with no fear of a coinsurance penalty.

In any case, the coverage and cost of both approaches must be compared to determine which produces the better insurance value.

Agreed Value

The **agreed value** option of the BIC is comparable to the agreed value option of the building and personal property coverage form. In both cases, the coinsurance clause is suspended and the insured and insurance company agree to a set of values reported in a written statement. If the limit of insurance agrees with the values in the statement at the time of the loss, the insured's loss will be covered in full, subject to the policy limit.

The agreed value option of the BIC differs from that of the BPP in some ways. First, the values reported are not property values, but projected business income values. The business income report/worksheet discussed in Chapter 7 is made a part of the policy.

The second difference is that a coinsurance percentage is used in determining the amount of insurance, even though the coinsurance provision has been suspended for purposes of loss settlement. For example, if the insured elects a limit of insurance based on 50 percent coinsurance, a coinsurance percentage of 50 percent would be shown in the declarations, and the insured would carry a limit of insurance equal to 50 percent of the annual values subject to loss.

A third difference is that many insurers make a 10 percent premium surcharge for this option in the BIC. In the BPP the charge is usually 5 percent.

Adjusting the Premium to Reflect Actual Exposures

The basic rating procedure for business income coverage is to calculate the policy premium at the beginning of the policy period based on the selected limit of insurance, which in turn is based on anticipated values and the expected period of interruption. Unless the policy is canceled mid-term, the calculated premium is the premium earned by the insurer. In contrast, the **business income premium adjustment endorsement** bases the earned premium on the actual exposure as reported by the insured at twelve-month intervals. Thus, the endorsement serves essentially the same purpose as the value reporting form used with the BPP—to base the premium on actual values. However, unlike the value reporting form, the business income premium adjustment endorsement does not suspend the coinsurance clause.

When the endorsement is used, the BIC covers business income losses subject to the stated limit of insurance, which should be set high enough to cover any anticipated loss. An initial premium is collected based on the limit. At the time the endorsement becomes effective, the insured must submit a business income worksheet to the insurer showing business income values for the insured's *latest available* twelve months' operating experience. Within 120 days following each successive period of twelve months, the insured must submit a report of actual business income values for each period. On the basis of the reports, the earned premium is calculated to reflect actual business income values.

The insured receives a return premium if the earned premium is less than the premium charged at inception. However, *no* additional premium is charged if the earned premium exceeds the original premium. This is proper because the coinsurance clause is not suspended by the business income premium adjustment endorsement. Had a loss occurred and the amount of insurance required to satisfy the coinsurance clause exceeded the amount of insurance carried, the insured would have received exactly the same loss payment whether the policy included the premium adjustment endorsement or not.

If the insured fails to submit reports as required, the insurer is released from the obligation to adjust the premium. Thus, the insured would lose any refund otherwise due. As will be seen below, *inaccurate* reports can also cause problems on later claims.

In addition to the stated limit of insurance, any of three other limitations, if smaller, will cap the insurer's loss payment.

- One of these limitations operates like the "honesty clause" discussed in Chapter 4 in connection with the value reporting form. The limitation would be derived in the following example as shown below.

  Net income and operating expenses reported in last report = $800,000
  Actual net income and operating expenses for that period = $900,000
  Amount of loss = $180,000
  Stated limit of insurance = $600,000

  Amount of limitation: $\frac{\$800,000}{\$900,000} \times \$180,000 = \$160,000$

- The second of the three limitations takes into consideration the net income and operating expenses that the insured would have experienced, had no loss occurred, during the twelve months *following the date of the physical loss or damage.* That sum is multiplied by the coinsurance limit shown in the declarations. If the result is smaller than the stated limit of insurance or the "honesty clause" limitation, that smaller result is the most that the insurer will pay. Returning to the above loss example, assume that the applicable net income and expense figure (for the twelve months following the physical loss) would have been $1,400,000. If the coinsurance percentage was 50 percent, the limitation amount would be calculated as follows:

  $$\$1,400,000 \times .50 = \$700,000$$

  Since $700,000 is greater than both the stated limit and the amount determined by the "honesty clause," it would have no effect on recovery.

- The third possible limitation in addition to the stated limit is simply the amount resulting from the application of the coinsurance clause. Remember that the "coinsurance basis" (the amount used in applying the BIC coinsurance clause) is net income and operating expenses that would have been earned in the twelve months following *policy inception* (not the twelve months following the *physical loss*). Thus, returning to the example above, if the "coinsurance basis" was $1,200,000, the applicable limitation would be calculated as follows:

  $$\frac{\$600,000}{\$1,200,000 \times .50} \times \$180,000 = \$180,000$$

In the case described above, the $160,000 calculated under the "honesty clause" is lower than the stated limit of insurance and the other two limitations. Thus, the insurer would pay $160,000 of the $180,000 loss. This example demonstrates the importance of making accurate reports.

Blanket Insurance

Many organizations conduct operations at more than one location and face the problem of interdependency among locations. In other words, if one of an organization's locations is damaged or destroyed, its other locations may also suffer a reduction in output, sales, or other revenue-earning activity.

If its operations are highly interdependent, an organization may be poorly served by insuring each building or location separately. In such cases, blanket coverage may be preferred. With blanket coverage, several locations are shown as a single item with a single amount of insurance. Blanket coverage is indicated on the declarations page of the policy, and blanket rates are usually used. (Blanket business income rates are usually computed on a weighted average based on floor areas at the various locations.)

Under ISO advisory rules, a major requirement for blanket business income insurance is that all premises must be substantially owned, managed, or controlled by the insured. Thus, a dependent property under separate ownership or management, such as an important supplier, cannot be added to the blanket description. ISO advisory rules also do not permit blanket insurance to be used for BIC policies in which the *maximum period of indemnity* or *monthly limit of indemnity* options are in effect.

When operations of the same insured at two or more locations are completely independent (that is, there is no interdependency), either specific or blanket coverage may be appropriate. As with blanket building and contents coverage, there is more flexibility in the application of blanket policy limits.

Dependent Property Exposures

Chapter 7 discussed dependent property exposures. To recap briefly, dependent property exposures arise when an organization could suffer a business income loss because of damage occurring at the premises of some other organization that the first organization does not own or control. The other organization might be an important supplier, an important buyer, a manufacturer of a product sold by the insured, or a "leader property" such as a large department store in a mall that includes several smaller stores. The unmodified BIC provides no coverage for dependent property exposures, because it covers business income loss only if it results from physical loss to property at the insured's premises.

Two endorsements to the BIC are available for insuring dependent property exposures:

- **Business income from dependent properties—broad form.** This endorsement is used when the insured wants the same limit that applies to business income loss resulting from damage at its own premises to apply to business income loss resulting from damage to other properties as well.
- **Business income from dependent properties—limited form.** This endorsement is used when *separate* limits are wanted. It is also used when coverage is wanted for income dependent on others' properties only.

Insurance Provisions

The insurance covers business income losses resulting from suspension of the insured's operations because of physical loss of or damage to property described in the endorsement schedule. This property must not be owned, controlled, or operated by the insured. If it is, the unmodified BIC form, perhaps arranged on a blanket basis, is appropriate.

For coverage to apply, a covered peril must cause the physical loss or damage of the *described other property*, causing a shutdown or reduction of the *insured's* operations. There is no requirement that operations at the specified location must be shut down. A peril might destroy a machine used to make a component for the insured at a contributing property, causing a shutdown of the insured's operations but not shutting down the other company at all. Conversely, it is possible for a total shutdown at a contributing property not to affect the insured's business. This could happen, for example, if the recipient had a large inventory when the loss occurred.

The endorsement limits compensation to the actual loss of business income necessarily sustained during the period of restoration. The period of restoration is the amount of time required, with reasonable speed and similar materials, to repair or replace *the damaged dependent property*. This provision focuses not on the insured's resumption of operations but on conditions at the dependent property location. However, the "resumption of operations" condition reduces the insured's recovery to the extent the insured can resume operations by using other sources of materials or other outlets for its products.

Normally, the physical loss must occur at a location specified in the endorsement schedule. However, an additional coverage applies to unscheduled locations not operated by the insured. This miscellaneous locations coverage is limited to an amount not exceeding 0.03 percent of the sum of all limits for scheduled locations for any one day of interruption of the insured's business. A policy with $400,000 in limits would therefore provide up to $120 per day ($400,000 x .0003 = $120).

Amount of Insurance To Purchase

The dependent properties *broad form* endorsement does not add any additional limits but extends coverage to apply to interruptions resulting from losses at scheduled locations. The *limited form* endorsement requires a scheduled limit of insurance for each scheduled location. Limits should be selected based on an analysis of the business income that is dependent on each contributing location—giving due consideration to the possibility of using materials from a substitute source or selling through an alternative outlet.

Tuition and Fees Coverage

Schools and colleges have a business income loss exposure that differs, to some extent, from that of the typical merchandising or manufacturing organization. If, for example, school property is damaged during the summer recess, the school may be unable to open its doors at the beginning of the fall session. Even if the school is able to open by October or so, it will find that most students have already enrolled elsewhere. Thus, if property is unusable during a fairly short, but critical, time period, it could cause the school to lose an entire year's tuition.

To insure this type of exposure, the **tuition and fees endorsement** can be added to the BIC form. The endorsement defines business income in a way that clearly includes a school's sources of revenue. It also addresses the issue of critical time periods, by providing a specialized version of extended business income coverage.

Covered Sources of Revenue

The tuition and fees endorsement may be used to provide either broad or limited coverage. The difference is that the broad coverage defines business income in a way that includes more revenue sources.

- With *broad coverage*, business income specifically includes tuition, fees, and other income from educational services and related activities including laboratory fees, bookstores, athletic events, and research grants.
- With *limited coverage*, business income specifically includes tuition and fees from students, including fees from room, board, laboratories, and other similar sources. However, it does not include income from other sources, such as bookstores, athletic events, and research grants.

Extended Business Income

Whether broad or limited coverage is provided, the extended business income provision of the BIC is replaced by a provision in the endorsement. This provision states that if damaged property is actually repaired, rebuilt, or replaced within thirty days or less before the scheduled opening of the next school term, the BIC covers the actual loss of business income sustained during that entire school term.

Off-Premises Services—Time Element

A business interruption is likely to occur when utilities supplying electrical, water, or telephone services to the insured's premises are cut off for a significant period of time. Even businesses that do not use water in their operations may find it necessary to send employees home if a loss of water service makes toilets unusable.

The **off-premises services—time element endorsement** can be used to cover this business income exposure. (It can also be added to the extra expense coverage form, described later in this chapter.) The endorsement modifies the BIC to include loss of business income or extra expense at the described premises resulting from an interruption of service provided to the described premises. The interruption of service must be caused by direct physical loss or damage by a covered peril to off-premises property of one or more of the following types, as indicated in the endorsement schedule:

- Water supply
- Communication supply (not including overhead transmission lines)
- Communication supply (including overhead transmission lines)
- Power supply (not including overhead transmission lines)
- Power supply (including overhead transmission lines)

Although most time element insurance does not involve a deductible, the off-premises utilities endorsement carries a twelve-hour deductible. Temporary utility outages can be expected on occasion. The role of insurance is to deal with more serious, unexpected losses. The twelve-hour deductible (or "waiting period") effectively accomplishes this goal.

Ordinance or Law Coverage

The ordinance or law exclusion in the causes-of-loss forms eliminates coverage for any extra loss resulting from the operation of building ordinances or laws—for example, when the undamaged portion of a building must be torn down, following an insured loss, in order for the entire building to be reconstructed in compliance with current building codes. The exclusion also applies to business income and extra expense coverage.

The endorsement that can be used to insure the "direct loss" aspects of ordinance or law exposures was discussed in Chapter 5. Another endorsement, titled **ordinance or law—increased period of restoration**, is available for modifying the BIC to cover the business income aspects of such losses. (The endorsement can also be added to the extra expense coverage form, described later in this chapter.) The operation of building laws can increase the length of a business interruption to the extent that additional time is required to demolish the undamaged structure, remove its debris, and rebuild the entire structure to conform to code.

The time element endorsement extends business income coverage to encompass the increased period of suspension of operations brought about by the operation of building laws. Moreover, the period of restoration is redefined to include the added time necessary to replace damaged property with replacement property that complies with the minimum standards of the law.

The ordinance or law exposure is often overlooked, particularly with regard to its time element implications. The limit of insurance chosen for business income coverage that includes the ordinance or law endorsement should reflect the additional rebuilding time required to comply with the law.

Extra Expense Coverage Form

The **extra expense coverage form** provides no business income coverage and is thus intended for organizations that place a high priority on continuing their operations after sustaining physical loss, even though that alternative may be more costly in the short run than just shutting down and losing income until the property is restored to use.

A bank, for example, may not be able under any circumstances to survive an interruption of business activities. The flow of money cannot come to a grinding halt simply because a bank has been damaged or destroyed. It must remain in operation "at all costs." Schools and hospitals and other organizations serving a community may be unable simply to drop out of operation without providing some continuity of service. Newspapers must continue publishing after a physical loss, particularly so that public notices may appear at appropriate times, advertising contracts can be fulfilled, and readers' habits can be sustained.

To remain in operation despite property damage to buildings or equipment, these organizations will incur substantial extra expenses. Extra expenses are covered as an additional coverage in the BIC, but the primary emphasis of that form is on the replacement of business income. The extra expense coverage form, in contrast, is designed for organizations whose business interruption exposure is primarily one of extra expenses rather than lost income.

For insureds whose primary objective is remaining in operation, complying with even a 50 percent coinsurance requirement of a BIC may require a much larger amount of insurance than the extra expense form. However, even insureds who want to remain in operation at all costs and who therefore do not anticipate having a business income loss may find that certain situations make that impossible. For example, a devastating hurricane may make alternative facilities impossible to obtain.

Some insureds may find that the lower amounts of insurance permitted by the "maximum limit of indemnity" or the "maximum period of indemnity" options in the BIC will provide both the needed extra expense coverage and business income coverage at little, if any, additional premium. The BIC has the added advantage of not limiting the amount of coverage for extra expense to a certain percentage per month of the amount of insurance, as discussed below.

Insurance Provisions

The extra expense coverage form provides essentially the same coverage as the extra expense additional coverage in the BIC form. The principal difference between the two results from the "limits on loss payment" condition found only in the extra expense coverage form. This condition encourages insurance to value by limiting recovery for certain time periods to stipulated percentages of the overall limit of insurance. The percentages that apply to a particular extra expense policy are listed on the declarations page, along with the overall limit of insurance.

The application of these percentages is best clarified by using an illustration. A popular combination of percentages is 40%-80%-100%. (Many other combinations of percentages are shown in the *Commercial Lines Manual.*) With this combination, and a policy with a $100,000 limit of insurance, loss payments would be limited as follows:

- If the period of restoration is thirty days or less, extra expenses up to $40,000 would be covered.
- If the period of restoration is between thirty and sixty days, extra expenses up to $80,000 would be covered.
- If the period of restoration is longer than sixty days, extra expenses up to $100,000 would be covered.

In the example above, suppose an interruption lasted thirty days and the insured incurred $50,000 of extra expense. The insured would recover only 40 percent of the overall limit: $40,000. If the insured incurred less than $40,000, the insurer would pay the actual loss sustained.

As another example, suppose an interruption lasted forty-five days and the insured incurred extra expenses of $50,000 the first month and $10,000 the second month. The full $60,000 would be covered. Recovery would not be limited to $40,000 for the first month, because the period of restoration extended into the second month.

Determining the Extra Expense Limit

There is often little relationship between the normal cost of doing business and the extra expenses necessarily incurred in order to maintain a normal volume of business after loss or damage. This makes it difficult to determine how much insurance to purchase.

Assuming that a firm anticipates that it will be able to continue operations using emergency measures, consideration should be given to the cost of such emergency measures. There is no principle or rule of thumb on which to base anticipated extra expense of maintaining a normal volume of business during an interruption, but much consideration should be given to an estimate of how long it would take to rebuild or repair the principal building or equipment or both.

By using a worksheet like the one illustrated in Exhibit 8-3, one can tabulate the greatest amount of expense that might reasonably be anticipated. The worksheet shown here is designed to record only the first, second, and third months following a loss. Of course, it could be extended for a longer period.

One way to determine the amount of extra expense insurance required is to determine from the worksheet the probable extra expense for *two* periods of restoration:

1. A period of one month
2. A period covering the maximum number of months that could reasonably be anticipated for resumption of normal operations

The *minimum* amount of insurance that should be carried is determined by dividing the estimated extra expense for the one-month period by the percentage reimbursement when the period of restoration is one month or less. This amount of insurance, however, might not be enough to cover the total extra expense estimated for the maximum possible interruption. In this case, the estimate for the longer period should be used.

For example, using the extra expense coverage form with monthly percentage limits of 40-80-100, the insured might estimate that extra expense indemnification of $20,000 for a one-month period of restoration would be sufficient. The minimum required insurance is $20,000 divided by 40 percent (.40), or $50,000.

Exhibit 8-3
Extra Expense Worksheet

Expenses Necessary to Continue Business	First Month		Second Month		Third Month	
Rent of temporary premises						
Cleaning temporary premises						
Labor equipping temporary premises						
Rent of temporary machinery, equipment, etc.						
Net cost of equipment, purchased						
Expense of moving equipment, etc.						
Light, power, and heat at temporary premises						
Labor at temporary premises						
Insurance expense at temporary premises						
Janitor and watchman at temporary premises						
Other expenses at or because of temporary premises (advertising, telephone, telegraph, legal, etc.)						
Total due to temporary premises						
Add payments to others for manufacturing or processing						
Add necessarily continuing expenses at original location after a loss						
Add bonuses for quick services, etc.						
Total expenses after a loss						
Deduct total of expenses which would have been incurred at the original location for the corresponding period had no loss incurred						
Extra expense insurance to be carried						

Reprinted, with permission, from Henry C. Klein, *Business Interruption Insurance* (Indianapolis: The Rough Notes Co., 1964), p. 253

The $50,000 total amount will assure recovery of up to $20,000 (40 percent) during the first-month period, up to $40,000 (80 percent) during a two-month period, and up to $50,000 (100 percent of the amount of insurance) for any period in excess of two months. However, the total amount might not be sufficient to cover estimated expenses for a longer period of time.

If $80,000 of total coverage is needed, the insured could obtain that amount for the overall limit and arrange the coverage for 40 percent recovery for the first month, and so on, as previously described. It is also possible to arrange an alternative combination of cumulative percentages of recovery, such as 35, 70, and 100 percent, or 30, 60, 90, and 100 percent. As can be seen, a considerable amount of judgment must be used in determining the amount of insurance for extra expense coverage.

Extra Expense Coverage Options

As with business income coverage, extra expenses can be incurred due to direct loss or damage at other properties such as those of key suppliers, major customers, or "leader" properties. For example, a manufacturer that depends heavily on one supplier may be able to obtain needed materials from other suppliers while the regular supplier's business is interrupted by a physical loss. However, the new suppliers may charge a higher price, which would be an extra expense loss for the manufacturer. Similarly, if a major *customer* of the manufacturer suffered a business interruption, the manufacturer might sustain extra expenses in promotion and advertising in order to find new buyers for its products.

The **extra expense from dependent properties endorsement** can be attached to the extra expense coverage form to cover this loss exposure. The endorsement states that the insurer will pay extra expense incurred by the insured because of physical loss of or damage to property at the premises of a "dependent property" described in the schedule. The physical loss or damage must result from a covered cause of loss.

Two other optional coverages have already been discussed in connection with business income coverage. The *off-premises services—time element* and the *ordinance or law—increased period of restoration* endorsements can also be added to the extra expense coverage form.

Other Types of Business Income Insurance

In addition to the standard forms described above, many other forms are available for insuring business income and extra expense losses. These include (1) valued policies and (2) time element coverages provided for other lines of insurance, such as boiler and machinery, inland and ocean marine, and businessowners.

Valued Policies

The BIC and extra expense coverage forms apply on an actual loss sustained basis. Business income and extra expense coverage is also available on *valued forms*. Most valued business income and extra expense coverage is on non-standard forms. The only standard forms of valued business income insurance are those provided in connection with the ISO boiler and machinery program.

How Valued Policies Work

The valued approach is uncomplicated. In some valued business income policies, the insured is paid a specified amount for each day the business is interrupted, up to a specified number of days. These policies are called *per diem* ("per day") forms. In other plans, the amount of reimbursement may be on a weekly or monthly basis. With any type, the policy may be subject to a time deductible (waiting period) of an agreed number of days.

Valued policies contain no coinsurance provision and thus cannot result in a coinsurance penalty. That does not mean that the insured will necessarily be reimbursed fully for any loss. The amount of insurance may be inadequate either in the daily, weekly, or monthly amount or in regard to the maximum period benefits will be paid.

A business need not be totally shut down to receive valued business income benefits. Partial interruptions are also covered according to the percentage that the business is reduced. Suppose, for example, that a company is entitled to receive $50,000 each week it is totally inoperative. If the company suffers a 60 percent reduction in production or sales during a partial interruption lasting one week, the insured will receive 60 percent of the $50,000 weekly limit, or $30,000. For manufacturers, the percentage of activity is determined by the percentage reduction in production or output. For merchants, partial suspensions are measured by various methods. The reduction in gross sales probably is most common.

Advantages and Disadvantages of Valued Approach

Valued forms have several advantages. One is their simplicity. With no coinsurance and a daily, weekly, or monthly benefit, the coverage is easy to understand. Second, loss adjustments are much simpler with the valued forms. It is not necessary to project earnings and expenses for a twelve-month period. Apart from determining that operations have been suspended because of physical loss caused by a covered peril, the insurer only needs to ascertain the number of days of the interruption and the percentage of the shutdown.

The valued policy approach has some possible disadvantages. The simplicity of the form may be an illusion. If the insured does not accurately estimate the loss exposure, the amount of insurance purchased is likely to be inadequate. If the amount of insurance is excessive, a moral hazard may arise.

The speed of recovery may not be a genuine advantage of the valued forms. Recovery under a valued policy may be prompt, but even with the other policies, most insurers will advance payments, at least for serious losses.

Business Income Coverage for Other Lines of Insurance

Business income and extra expense coverage is not unique to the "commercial property" line. Other varieties of time element insurance are provided by boiler and machinery policies, inland and ocean marine policies, and businessowners policies.

Boiler and Machinery Forms

Recall that the forms described in this chapter respond only to suspension of operations resulting from physical loss caused by a peril covered under one of the "commercial property" causes-of-loss forms. As discussed in Chapter 5, the causes-of-loss forms exclude steam boiler explosion, mechanical breakdown, and other perils that are separately insured under boiler and machinery policies. Because business interruption can result from physical damage covered under boiler and machinery policies (such as loss of heat or damage to buildings or contents resulting from a boiler explosion or other accident), insurers offer boiler and machinery business income and extra expense coverages. These coverages will be discussed in Chapter 9.

Inland and Ocean Marine Forms

Damage to property insured under various inland marine and ocean marine policies can cause business income and extra expense loss. Accordingly, inland and ocean marine policies are often configured to include coverage for such time element losses. Inland and ocean marine insurance are the subjects of Chapter 11.

Businessowners Policies

The simplified package policies known as businessowners policies and widely used for small to medium-sized businesses ordinarily include business income and extra expense coverage. Although the business income and extra expense coverage provided by the ISO businessowners policy is similar to that provided by the BIC, it has some important differences. These differences are discussed in Chapter 12, along with the rest of the businessowners program.

Case Study

The following case study illustrates much of the material in Chapters 7 and 8 using a hypothetical firm, Gardener Company. The case examines the questions of how much insurance to buy, whether or not to include coverage for ordinary payroll, and what endorsements may be needed.

Analyzing the Exposure

Assume that the business income exposures of Gardener Company (GC) are being evaluated in August in preparation for an October 1 renewal of GC's commercial property insurance. After identifying what property damage could occur and estimating the effect of such damage on GC's operations, the next step in analyzing the exposure is to determine the effect of the physical damage on GC's revenues and expenses.

Description of Operations

A wholesale distributor of specialty home gardening equipment, GC is located in a suburb of Chicago in a one-story noncombustible building under a ten-year lease. The lease contains a "rent abatement" clause providing that if the building is damaged more than 50 percent, GC's obligation to pay rent will be suspended until the building is restored and able to be occupied by GC. GC sells to garden supply stores and hardware stores throughout the Midwest.

The officers of GC head up the key functions: sales, purchasing, distribution, and finance. Most of the other employees are unskilled warehouse and delivery personnel or low-skilled clerical employees. In the current labor market, these employees could be easily replaced. However, GC also employs a skilled graphic designer (who handles all of GC's advertising and package design) and a computer manager. GC's computer system controls both inventory and billing; loss of computer capability would seriously interfere with operations. The designer and the computer manager would be difficult to replace and their replacements would require extensive training.

Although GC has exclusive distributorship for some of the products it sells, most of GC's products are also available to customers from competing firms. The exclusive products, which account for approximately 25 percent of GC's annual sales, are manufactured by one firm in Cleveland, Ohio.

Financial Analysis

In preparation for the renewal of their property insurance, GC's chief financial officer, working with GC's insurance producer, has completed an ISO business income worksheet of the same type as discussed in Chapter 7. The worksheet estimates of financial data for the policy year commencing October 1 are summarized in Exhibit 8-4. Other key financial estimates for the coming policy year, not contained in the worksheet, are shown in Exhibit 8-5.

Exhibit 8-4
Gardener Company: Summary of Worksheet Estimates

F. Net sales		$15,000,000
G. Other earnings		50,000
H. Total revenues		15,050,000
I. Deduct:		
1. Cost of goods sold	$10,500,000	
2. Services purchased from outsiders	700,000	11,200,000
J. Business income basis for coinsurance		$ 3,850,000

Exhibit 8-5
Gardener Company: Summary of Non-Worksheet Estimates

Salaries of executives and officers*	$ 540,000
Salaries of designer and computer manager*	120,000
Wages of other employees*	1,200,000
Power, heat, and refrigeration	150,000
Rent	300,000
Other expense	2,600,000
Interest income	75,000
Net income before income tax	386,000
Income tax	120,000
Net income after income tax	266,000

*Salaries and wages include fringe benefit costs, payroll taxes, and workers compensation premiums.

Determining the Business Income Exposure

The figures shown are annual figures, but it is unlikely that GC would be shut down for exactly one year. Therefore, it is necessary to develop an estimate of the longest time GC could be out of operation. Since GC's operations do not involve any specialized equipment or lengthy production process, the longest interruption would be caused by a severe direct loss requiring the complete reconstruction of the building.

A reliable local contractor has estimated it would take five months to rebuild the entire building. The contractor has pointed out, however, that should the loss occur in the winter, severe weather conditions could add as many as forty-five days to the period required for restoration. Another month would be needed to install trade fixtures and equipment and an additional half month would be needed to restock merchandise and staff the operation with trained employees. The maximum length of a possible shutdown for GC, under a "worst-case scenario," therefore, is approximately eight months.

Which eight months of the year would the company be shut down? It is impossible to foretell when an interruption will occur. The safest assumption, therefore, is that the shutdown will occur during the months of greatest earnings. The net profits and continuing expenses during the highest eight consecutive months should be used. GC's seasonal pattern is shown in Exhibit 8-6. For GC, the highest eight months of activity are November through June. In this period the company typically generates 75 percent of its total volume. The maximum probable loss of profit would be $233,250, calculated as follows:

$386,000	(annual net income before income tax)
– 75,000	(interest income)
$311,000	
x .75	
$233,250	

Interest income, earned from investments, would not be lost during a shutdown at GC's premises and is therefore subtracted from the annual net income when determining maximum probable business income loss.

If GC were shut down from November through June, how much expense would continue during the period? Based on a careful assessment of the various types of expense involved in GC's operation and the degree to which each would continue or abate, GC's financial officer has calculated that $1,280,000 of payroll and other normal operating expenses would probably continue during the shutdown.

In addition, the financial officer estimates that $50,000 of extra expense would be incurred during the shutdown and that $40,000 of income would be lost during the 30 days following restoration before business returned to normal. The financial officer assumes, because of the rent abatement clause in GC's lease, that GC would not incur rental expense for the six and one-half months that might be needed to rebuild. Rent would not be abated for the six weeks following building completion, during which GC would be installing equipment, restocking merchandise, and training employees.

Exhibit 8-6
Gardener Company: Monthly Sales as a Percentage of Annual Sales

January	9.3%
February	10.4%
March	10.1%
April	9.4%
May	9.3%
June	9.0%
July	6.9%
August	7.0%
September	5.7%
October	5.4%
November	8.2%
December	9.3%
Total	100.0%

The estimates developed by the financial officer and the insurance producer suggest a maximum probable loss of $1,610,000, calculated as follows:

Lost Profit	$ 233,250
Continuing Expenses	1,280,000
Extra expense	50,000
Business income loss during 30 days following restoration	40,000
Total	$1,603,250

$1,603,250 is rounded up to $1,610,000. Using an exact figure would imply a greater accuracy than is possible with any estimating procedure.

Determining How Much Insurance to Purchase

Determining the amount of insurance requires coordinating the maximum probable business income loss with available coinsurance percentages. (See the discussion of selecting a coinsurance percentage in Chapter 7.)

The lowest coinsurance percentage ordinarily available is 50 percent. Fifty percent of GC's coinsurance basis of $3,850,000 is $1,925,000. Since this is greater than the maximum probable loss of $1,610,000, a coinsurance percentage of 50 percent could be used with a limit of $1,925,000, the minimum amount needed to comply with that percentage.

Suppose, instead, that GC purchases $1,610,000 of business income coverage with 50 percent coinsurance. This limit matches GC's business income exposure, but according to the BIC coinsurance clause, GC needs a limit of $1,925,000 (50 percent of $3,850,000—the business income basis for coinsurance calculated in the business income worksheet). If the policy limit were $1,610,000, GC would only be able to recover approximately 84 percent of any covered loss, calculated as follows:

$$\frac{\$1,610,000}{\$1,925,000} \times \text{Loss} = \text{Insurer's Payment}$$

Thus, GC should purchase at least $1,925,000 of coverage to avoid a coinsurance penalty even though it has calculated its exposure to be $1,610,000. Although this limit may appear to provide $315,000 of excess insurance, it is not coverage that could never be used. It would be available if the period of restoration were longer than estimated or if the lost profits and continuing expenses, extra expense, or business income lost during restoration or in the thirty days following restoration exceeded expectations.

Payroll or Power Coverage Options

The amount of insurance that will meet BIC coinsurance requirements can be reduced if the insured chooses to limit or exclude coverage for ordinary payroll. Likewise, power, heat, and refrigeration expenses may be excluded for manufacturing or mining risks.

GC does not incur substantial power, heat, and refrigeration expenses and, as a nonmanufacturing firm, it is not eligible to use the endorsement anyway. However, GC anticipates $1,320,000 in payroll for employees other than officers and executives. (Recall that the salaries of officers and executives are not included in the definition of "ordinary payroll.")

Excluding ordinary payroll seems to pose a problem for GC. The salaries of the designer and the computer manager are included in the definition of ordinary payroll. Even if GC were unable to operate, it would probably want to continue paying these two employees since they are critical to GC's business and could not be easily replaced. However, GC could limit or exclude ordinary payroll without eliminating coverage for the salary of these two employees by amending the payroll limitation or exclusion endorsement to eliminate their salaries from the definition of ordinary payroll. That would reduce the annual ordinary payroll for GC to $1,200,000.

Although GC's revenues have peak seasons, the financial officer advises that payrolls are nearly constant throughout the year. Thus, approximately one-quarter of the year's payroll expense, or $300,000, is incurred in any given ninety-day period. The calculations used to arrive at the minimum limits needed to comply with a 50 percent coinsurance clause for each of the payroll exclusion/limitation options are shown in Exhibit 8-7. The calculations assume that the salaries for the designer and the computer manager have been eliminated from the definition of ordinary payroll.

- With full coverage of ordinary payroll, GC needs at least $1,925,000 of business income coverage to avoid a coinsurance penalty.
- With no coverage of ordinary payroll, GC needs at least $1,325,000 of coverage.
- With ninety days' ordinary payroll coverage, GC needs at least $1,475,000 of coverage.
- With one hundred eighty days' ordinary payroll coverage, GC needs at least $1,625,000 of coverage.

Exhibit 8-7
Gardener Company: Limits Needed To Comply With Coinsurance When Payroll Options Used

Estimated for 12-month period beginning at policy inception:		
Business income basis for coinsurance	$3,850,000	
x 50%		$1,925,000
If ordinary payroll is excluded:		
Deduct all ordinary payroll expense	1,200,000	
Revised coinsurance basis	2,650,000	
x 50%		$1,325,000
If ordinary payroll is limited to 90 days:		
Add the largest amount of ordinary payroll expense incurred during any 90-day period	300,000	
Revised coinsurance basis	2,950,000	
x 50%		$1,475,000
If ordinary payroll is limited to 180 days:		
Add the largest amount of ordinary payroll expense incurred during any 180-day period	600,000	
Revised coinsurance basis	3,250,000	
x 50%		$1,625,000

Remember, however, that GC's maximum probable loss is $1,610,000. GC should not purchase less than this amount of insurance unless it wishes to retain part of the exposure. If GC eliminated ordinary payroll or covered it for only ninety days, GC should still carry at least $1,610,000 insurance even though the coinsurance formula requires a lower limit. Under those conditions, GC could change the coinsurance percentage to 60 percent, which would reduce the rate. (With the ninety-day limitation GC would have to carry $1,770,000 insurance to satisfy a 60 percent coinsurance clause, but the lower rate for 60 percent coinsurance would still produce a lower premium.)

In deciding how to insure ordinary payroll expense, GC needs to consider whether or not it would continue to pay those employees who fall into the "ordinary payroll" category in the event of a business interruption. For example, if GC would furlough all employees without pay in the event of any interruption, then the ordinary payroll *exclusion* would be a viable option. If, instead, GC would keep all employees on the payroll during a brief interruption of, say, one or two months, but not if the interruption were longer, then the ninety-day option might be the most logical choice.

Before making a final decision, GC needs to consider the relative cost of the alternatives. According to the *Commercial Lines Manual*, the ninety-day payroll limitation increases the rate by 6 percent, and the complete payroll exclusion increases the rate by 12 percent. The 180-day payroll limitation does not change the rate. Differences in premiums for the various coverage alternatives are not emphasized in this text. However, this example underscores the fact that many coverage decisions can logically be made only after considering the cost of the various alternatives.

Other Coverage Options and Endorsements

GC should consider the other coverage options and endorsements described earlier in this chapter. However, two endorsements are particularly apt for GC based on the information presented in this case study: the endorsement for insuring dependent properties and the endorsement for deleting the limitation on electronic media and records.

Business Income From Dependent Properties

If not modified by endorsement, business income coverage applies only when a covered peril damages property at the insured's described location. The products sold exclusively by GC, which account for 25 percent of GC's sales, are manufactured by one firm in Cleveland. Destruction of this firm's facilities might seriously impair GC's business. Accordingly, GC should consider business income from dependent properties coverage. An alternative might be for GC to develop other sources of supply so that it would not be completely dependent on one supplier.

Electronic Media or Records Limitation

Unless modified by endorsement, the BIC provides only sixty days' coverage for interruption caused by damage to the insured's electronic media or records (unless other property sustains damage that requires more than sixty days to restore). GC's computer system is important to GC's operations. If restoring GC's media or records would take more than sixty days, the electronic media or records limitation can be extended or deleted by endorsement.

GC should also follow proper backup procedures and store backup tapes in a secure location off-premises. In addition, many firms arrange for off-premises "hot-site" facilities—that is, a computer-equipped location at another location where computer operations can be performed if the insured's computers are incapacitated.

Summary

The ISO "commercial property" program includes two versions of the business income coverage form (BIC). Both versions of the BIC cover actual loss of business income that the named insured sustains due to necessary suspension of operations during the period of restoration. The suspension must have occurred because of physical loss to property at the described premises by a covered cause of loss.

The only difference between the two BIC forms is that one—*business income coverage form (and extra expense)*—covers certain extra expenses regardless of the extent to which they reduce the business income loss. The other version—*business income coverage form (without extra expense)*—covers extra expenses only to the extent that they reduce the business income loss.

Both BIC forms also cover the following:

- Business income losses that occur during the thirty days after the damaged property is restored to use
- Business income losses incurred because access to the insured premises is cut off by order of civil authorities
- Business income losses resulting from damage to alterations and new buildings at the described premises

- Up to thirty days' coverage for business income losses resulting from damage to property at newly acquired locations

The percentages that may be used for the BIC coinsurance clause range from 50 to 125 percent, reflecting the wide range of restoration periods that different organizations may experience. The chosen percentage is applied to the total of net income and all operating expenses for the twelve-month period beginning with policy inception. Because some expenses usually do not continue during a business interruption, the amount of insurance required is usually greater than the maximum probable loss.

Various coverage options are available to modify the BIC to meet particular needs. These options may be used to exclude payroll or other expenses; eliminate or suspend the coinsurance clause; provide blanket insurance; or cover special exposures such as dependent properties, school tuition, or building law exposures.

A third "commercial property" time element form is the extra expense coverage form, which covers extra expense only. It is intended for organizations that must continue their operations "at any cost." The coverage provided is essentially the same as the extra expense coverage under the BIC (and extra expense) form. One important difference is that the extra expense coverage form is subject to percentage limitations that correspond to different periods of restoration.

An alternative to the "actual loss sustained" forms described above is the valued coverage approach. Under this approach, the insurer pays an agreed amount for each day (or week or month) that the insured is shut down.

Apart from "commercial property" forms, business income insurance is also provided in boiler and machinery policies, marine policies, and businessowners policies.

Index

A

AAIS (American Association of Insurance Services), 103
Access controls, against employee dishonesty, 96
Accounting controls, against employee dishonesty, 96
Accrual basis, business income exposure and, 279
Acts of civil authority, business income loss and, 261
Actual cash value (ACV), BPP, 132
Actual insurable values, blanket insurance and, 159
Actual loss sustained, BIC, 300
Additional concurrent causation exclusion, in the causes of loss–special form, 205
Additional coverage–collapse, in the causes of loss–broad form, 188
Additional coverage and coverage extension, in the BIC, 306
Additional coverage extension, in the causes of loss–special form, 206
Additional coverages and coverage extensions, BPP, 121
Advertising expense, during a business interruption, 269
After the fire is out, 78
Agreed value, BPP, 152
Agreed value option, in the BIC, 320
Agreed value optional coverage, BPP, 153
Agreement, condominium association, 218
Alarm systems, approved, 90
burglary and robbery, 83
deficiencies of, 90
insured's view of, 155
insurer's view of, 154
selection of, 90
Alarms, auxiliary, 73
central station, 73
local, 73
proprietary, 73
remote, 73
"All-in" concept, 219
"All-risks" insurance, 174
in the causes of loss–special form, 197
Alterations and new buildings coverage, in the BIC, 310
Alternatives to coinsurance, in the BPP, 152
American Association of Insurance Services (AAIS), 103
Americans with Disabilities Act, 18
Amount subject, 20
Amounts of recovery, BPP, 127
Analysis, loss, 18
Analyzing business income exposures, 258
Animal exclusion, under the BPP, 119

Animals, in the causes of loss–special form, 200
  limitation on loss of, in the causes of loss–basic form and broad forms, 196
Antennas exclusion, BIC, 305
Anti-theft devices, 93
Any other consequential loss exclusion, BIC, 305
Application of limits to additional coverages and extension, BIC, 311
Appraisal condition, in the BIC, 311
Appraisal process, BPP, 136
Approved alarm systems, 90
Area protection or space protection, 86
Arson, controlling loss from, 66
Artificially generated electrical current exclusion, in the causes of loss–basic form and broad form, 195
Association, condominium, 218
  homeowners' (planned unit development), 228
Automatic fire detection/suppression systems, 67
Automatic fire doors, 64
Auxiliary alarms, 73
Avoidance, 42

B

Balance sheet, 12
Bare-walls concept versus single entity concept, 219
Basic causes-of-loss form, 176 (*see also* Causes of loss-basic form)
BIC (*See* business income coverage form, 299)
Blanket insurance, actual insurable values under, 159
  advantages of, 156
  BIC, 323
  BPP, 156
    coinsurance requirement under, 158
    rating for, 160
Boiler and machinery business income and extra expense coverages, 333
Boiler and machinery insurance, 107
Bottlenecks, 264
"Box of air," 218
BPP (*See* Building and personal property coverage form, 109)
BPP additional coverages, 121
BPP building description, 111
BPP and SPP, comparison of, 238
Brands and labels endorsement, BPP, 170
Breakage of glass (*See* Glass breakage)
Brick construction, 55
Brick joisted construction, 55
Brigades, fire, 76
Broad causes-of-loss form, 176 (*see also* Causes of loss–broad form)
Builders risk–collapse during construction endorsement, 232
Builders risk coverage form, 229
  additional coverages under, 231
  completed value approach to, 233
  completed value basis, 235
  covered causes of loss in, 231
  covered property under, 230
  limitations on waiver of subrogation in, 236
  need for adequate insurance in, 234
  property and insureds eligible under, 229
  valuation condition in, 233
Builders risk insurance, 229
Builders risk reporting form endorsement, 234
  penalties applying under, 235
Builders risks, other coverage for, in inland marine policies, 236
  other coverage for, 236
    in the BPP, 236
    in HPR and independent forms, 237
Builders' equipment, in the causes of loss–special form, 201
Building, under the CPP, 110
Building construction, types of, 54
    fire-resistive, 58

frame, 54
heavy timber, 56
joisted masonry, 55
masonry noncombustible, ,58
mill construction, 56
modified fire resistive, 58
noncombustible, 57
wood frame, 54
Building contents as fuel, 53
Building and contents insurance, 105
Building coverage, in the condominium association coverage form, 221
Building owner's coverage, for improvements and betterments, 249
Building and personal property coverage, 103
Building and personal property coverage form (BPP), 109
actual cash value (ACV) and, 132
additional coverages and coverage extensions under, 121
agreed value coverage in, 152
agreed value from the insurer's viewpoint, 154
alternatives to coinsurance in, 152
amounts of recovery under, 127
appraisal process under, 136
brands and labels endorsement in, 170
builders risks coverages in, 236
buildings and other real property not covered under, 116
coinsurance under, 129
examples of, 130
coverage extensions under, 124
covered locations under, 120
covered property under, 100
debris removal under, 121
examination under oath and, 135
fire department service charge additional coverage under, 124
functional personal property valuation endorsement (other than stock), 151
glass coverage under, 243
improvements and betterments under, 144
inflation guard optional coverage in, 169
insured's duties in the event of loss under, 134
insurer's options for loss payment under, 136
inventory and inspection in the event of a loss under, 135
labor, materials, or services furnished on property of others, 114
leased personal property under, 115
lender's loss payable provision under, 140
lenders' rights under, 138
limit of insurance in, 153
limits of insurance and deductible under, 128
loss payable provision under, 139
loss payable provisions endorsement, 139
loss settlement under, 148
manufacturers selling price endorsement (finished stock only), 149
manufacturers' consequential loss assumption endorsement in, 170
mortgage holders provision in, 138
newly acquired or constructed property extension under, 124
notice of loss under, 135
optional valuation methods in, 146
other coverage options in, 169
other loss provisions in, 133
other personal property not covered under, 118
outdoor property extension under, 127
personal effects and property of others extension under, 126
personal property of others under, 115
plants and outdoor property not covered under, 116
police report in the event of a loss under, 134
pollutant cleanup and removal additional coverage under, 123
preservation of property additional coverage under, 123

preservation of property in the event of a loss under, 134
proof of loss under, 135
property not covered at replacement cost under, 148
property not covered under, 116
property off-premises extension under, 126
property owned by the insured under, 113
rating for, 154
recovered property under, 137
replacement cost optional coverage under, 146
safety glass coverage under, 133
small building losses under, 132
stock sold but not delivered under, 133
tenants improvements and betterments coverage under, 133
time of replacement under, 149
vacancy permit endorsement to, 138
vacancy under, 137
valuable papers and records under, 133
cost of research extension under, 126
valuation under, 132
value reporting form and, 162
"your business personal property" under, 112
Building and personal property coverage options, 145
Buildings as fuel, 54
Buildings and other real property, not covered under the BPP, 116
Burglar alarm detection devices, 87
Burglary, 81
Burglary and robbery, physical protection against, 82
Burglary and robbery losses, controlling, 81
Business income, definition of, 301
time required to restore normal rate of, 261
Business income coverage, extended, 308
Business income coverage form (and extra expense), 299
Business income coverage form (without extra expense), 299
Business income coverage forms (BIC), 299
actual loss sustained, 300
additional coverages and coverage extension in, 306
alterations and new buildings coverage in, 310
alternatives to coinsurance in, 317
application of limits to additional coverages and extension, 311
blanket insurance, 323
"business income" defined in, 301
business income exposure versus coinsurance requirement in, 314
business income premium adjustment endorsement in, 321
civil authority additional coverage in, 309
conditions in, 311
appraisal, 311
coinsurance, 313
duties in the event of loss, 311
limitation–electronic media and records, 311
loss determination, 311
loss payment, 312
coverage options, 315
covered causes of loss under, 303
damage to property at the insured premises and, 302
dependent property exposures and, 323
exclusions applying to, 304
expenses to reduce loss coverage in, 308
extra expense defined in, 306
finished stock in, 302
insuring agreement in, 300
newly acquired locations coverage extension in, 310
"operations" and related coverage options in, 305

period of restoration under, 301
tuition and fees endorsement for, 325
Business income coverage for other lines of insurance, 333
Business income from dependent properties–broad form, 324
Business income from dependent properties–limited form, 324
Business income exposure versus coinsurance requirement, in the BIC, 314
Business income exposures, pre-loss analysis of, 258
Business income insurance, 299
other types of, 331
Business income loss, 8, 253
effect of seasonal fluctuations on, 266
events that could cause, 258
acts of civil authority, 261
dependency on a "leader property," 260
dependency on a manufacturer, 260
dependency on one buyer, 259
dependency on one supplier, 259
organization's own property off premises, 260
extended, 294
financial elements of, 254
length of, 261
loss of customers and, 263
"net loss" versus, 256
physical damage losses and, 264
timing of, 261
Business income loss exposures, 253
analyzing, 258
Business income premium adjustment endorsement, BIC, 321
Business income worksheet (business income report/worksheet), 273
completing, 277
estimating maximum probable loss (MPL) using, 292
page 1–identification, instructions, and signatures, 277
page 2–calculating total revenues, 279
deductions, 284
finished stock inventory, 283
gross sales, 283
gross sales value of production, 284
manufacturing versus nonmanufacturing operations, 279
other earnings, 285
total revenues, 286
page 3–calculating "net income and expenses," 286
business income basis for coinsurance, 289
cost of goods sold, 286
services purchased from outsiders, 289
page 4–coverage modifications, 289
projections for the twelve-month period beginning with the policy inception, 291
provision for income tax, 291
relationship of, to income statements, 274
Business interruption exposures (*see also* Business income loss exposures), 253
Business interruption loss, 8
Business personal property, named insured's, coverage of, in the condominium association coverage form, 223
Businessowners policies, 109
business income and extra expense coverage under, 333

C

Calorific content, 54
Cameras, surveillance, 91
Cancellation changes endorsement, commercial property conditions, 143
in the SPP, 239
Captive insurer, 31
group, 35
multi-parent, 35
Carbon dioxide systems, 70
Case study, for business income loss exposures and insurance, 334

for applying the risk management process, 39
Cash basis, business income exposure and, 279
Cause of loss, 6
Causes of loss—basic form, 175
aircraft or vehicle coverage under, 182
exclusions in, 189
explosion coverage under, 179
fire coverage under, 177
lightning coverage under, 179
other exclusions in, 196
perils covered by, 177
riot or civil commotion coverage under, 182
sinkhole collapse coverage under, 184
smoke coverage under, 181
sprinkler leakage coverage under, 183
vandalism coverage under, 183
volcanic action coverage under, 185
windstorm and hail coverage under, 180
Causes of loss–basic form and broad forms, additional exclusions in, 195
difference between, 176
Causes of loss—broad form, 175
additional coverage–collapse, 188
additional perils covered by, 186
aircraft or vehicle coverage under, 182
breakage of glass coverage under, 186
exclusions in, 189
explosion coverage under, 179
falling objects coverage under, 187
fire coverage under, 177
lightning coverage under, 179
perils covered by, 177
riot or civil commotion coverage under, 182
sinkhole collapse coverage under, 184
smoke coverage under, 181
sprinkler leakage coverage under, 183
vandalism coverage under, 183
volcanic action coverage under, 185
weight of snow, ice, or sleet coverage under, 187
windstorm and hail coverage under, 180
Causes of loss—earthquake form, 175, 210
exclusions to, 210
masonry veneer coverage in, 211
underground foundations coverage in, 210
percentage deductible in, 211
Causes of loss–special form, 175, 197
additional coverage extensions in, 206
advantages of, 197
exclusion and limitations in, 198
exclusions in, that duplicate causes of loss–broad form conditions, 199
maintenance exclusion in, 201
property covered only for "specified causes of loss" in, 200
Causes-of-loss forms, 173
Central station alarms, 73
Chemical heat energy, 51
Civil authority additional coverage, in the BIC, 309
Civil commotion, 183
Clause, full reporting, in the value reporting form, 165
honesty, in the value reporting form, 165
CLM (*Commercial Lines Manual*), 104
Coinsurance, alternatives to, in the BIC, 317
in the BPP, 129, 152
suspension of, 153
Coinsurance clause, in the BIC, 313
Coinsurance percentage, selecting, MPL and, 295
Coinsurance requirement, with blanket insurance, in the BPP, 158
Collapse, in the causes of loss–special form, 199
Collapse during construction, in the builders risk coverage form, 231
Combustible gas/vapor detectors, 73
Combustion explosion, 189
Commercial crime insurance, 108
Commercial inland marine insurance, 108

Commercial Lines Manual (CLM), 104, 328
Commercial lines program, ISO, 104
Commercial package policy, (CPP), 104
  components of, 106
"Commercial property" causes of loss forms, 175
Commercial property conditions, 140
  cancellation changes endorsement, 143
  concealment, misrepresentation, or fraud, 140
  control of property, 140
  insurance under two or more coverages, 141
  legal actions against us, 141
  liberalization, 141
  no benefit to bailee, 141
  other insurance in, 141
  policy period and coverage territory, 142
  transfer of rights of recovery against other to us, 142
"Commercial property" forms, other, 217
"Commercial property" insurance, 105
Commercial property insurance, overview of, 103
Common elements, in a condominium, 218
Completed value approach, to the builders risk coverage form, 233
Concealment, misrepresentation, or fraud, commercial property conditions, 140
Concurrent causation, doctrine of, 175
Conditions, BIC, 311
  commercial property, 140
  in the condominium association coverage form, 223
  in the SPP, 239
Condominium additional provisions endorsement, 224
  act or omission, 224
  additional protection for mortgage holders, 225
  expanded waiver of right of recovery, 224
  notice of cancellation or nonrenewal, 225
Condominium association, 218
Condominium association agreement, 218
Condominium association coverage form, 221
  building coverage in, 221
  conditions in, 223
    coordination with unit owner's insurance, 224
    loss payment to an insurance trustee, 223
    waiver of rights of recovery, 224
  coverage for personal property of others in, 223
  coverage for the named insured's business personal property in, 223
Condominium association's coverage, coordination of, with the condominium commercial unit-owners coverage form, 225
Condominium commercial unit-owners coverage form, 225
  coordination of, with association coverage, 225
  covered property under, 225
  optional coverages for, 226
Condominium coverage options, non-ISO, 222
Condominium ownership, nature of, 218
Condominium property insurance, 221
Condominium statutes, 219
Condominium unit, 218
Condominiums, 217, 218
  cooperatives, and planned unit developments, comparison of, 227
  insurance requirements for, 220
  pertinent documents regarding, 219
Consequential loss, 9
Contingent business interruption loss, 8
Continuing and noncontinuing expenses, 256
  distinguishing between, 266
Contraband exclusion, under the BPP, 120

Control, risk, 25
Control of property, commercial property conditions, 140
Controlling burglary and robbery losses, 81
Controlling dependency exposures, 260
Controlling employee dishonesty losses, 94
Controlling explosion losses, 97
Controlling fire losses, 49
Controlling heat sources, 60
Controlling loss from arson, 66
Controlling other losses, 97
Controlling shoplifting losses, 92
Controlling theft losses, 80
Controlling water damage, 77
Controlling windstorm damage, 98
Cooperative corporations, 227
Coordination with unit owner's insurance, in the condominium association coverage form, 224
Corporations, cooperative, 227
Cost of goods sold, 286
Cost-of-goods-sold ratio, 283
Coverage, building and personal property, 103
  extended, 173
Coverage extensions, BPP, 124
Coverage form, builders risk, 229
  glass, 242
  leasehold interest, 246
  legal liability, 240
Coverage options, BIC, 315
  building and personal property, 145
  for the extra expense coverage form, 331
  other, in the BPP, 169
  payroll, in the BIC, 316
Coverage parts, ISO, 104
Covered causes of loss, 173
  BIC, 303
  in the builders risk coverage form, 231
Covered locations, under the BPP, 120
Covered perils, in the SPP, 239
  under the glass coverage form, 244
Covered property, under the BPP, 110
  under the builders risk coverage form, 230
  under the condominium commercial unit-owners coverage form, 225
  under the glass coverage form, 244
  under the SPP, 237
CPP (commercial package policy), 104
Credibility, of data, 23
Crime insurance, commercial, 108
Crisis management, 79
Current funding, for paying losses, 30
Customers, loss of, 263

D

Damage by water extension, in the causes of loss–special form, 207
Damage to property at the insured premises, BIC, 302
Dampers, fire, 63
Debris removal, under the BPP, 121
Deductible, percentage, in the causes of loss–earthquake form, 211
  under the BPP, 128
Deluge sprinkler system, 69
DEMCABS, 118
Dependency exposure, business income loss and, 259
  controlling, 260
Dependency on a "leader property," 260
Dependency on a manufacturer, 260
Dependency on one buyer, 259
Dependency on one supplier, 259
Dependent property exposures, BIC and, 323
Depreciation expense, during a business interruption, 270
  for property not totally destroyed, 271
  for property totally destroyed, 271
  treatment of, when estimating MPL, 271
Detection devices, burglar alarm, 87
  fire, 72

Detection and signaling systems, 72
Detectors, combustible gas/vapor, 73
flame, 73
smoke, 73
Determining the extra expense limit, for the extra expense coverage form, 329
Difference in conditions (DIC) policies, 303
Direct loss, 9
Disaster planning, 79\
Dishonesty, employee, 81
Divisions, fire, 65
Doctrine of concurrent causation, 175
Dollar limitations, in the causes of loss–special form, 204
Door switches (contacts), 87
Doors, self-closing, 54
Dry chemical systems, 69
Dry-pipe sprinkler system, 68
Duties, separation of 96
Duties in the event of loss condition, in the BIC, 311

E

Earth movement, losses caused by, 100
Earth movement exclusion, in the causes of loss–basic form and broad form, 191
Electrical current, artificially generated, exclusion of, in the causes of loss–basic form and broad form, 195
Electrical heat energy, 51, 60
Elements of fire loss, 50
Employee dishonesty, 81
Employee dishonesty exclusion, in the causes of loss–special form, 202
Employee dishonesty losses, controlling, 94
Endorsement, brands and labels, in the BPP, 170
builders risk–collapse during construction, 232
builders risk reporting form, 234
condominium additional provisions, 224
extra expense from dependent properties, 331
functional building valuation , BPP, 150
functional personal property valuation (other than stock), BPP, 151
manufacturers selling price (finished stock only), BPP, 149
manufacturers' consequential loss assumption, 170
off-premises services–direct damage, 212
off-premises services–time element, 326
ordinance or law–increased period of restoration, 326
ordinance or law, to the causes of loss–basic, broad, and special forms, 208
payroll limitation or exclusion, 316
peak season limit of insurance, 162
pier and wharf additional covered causes of loss, 215
power, heat, and refrigeration deduction, 317
radioactive contamination, 214
spoilage coverage, 213
sprinkler leakage–earthquake extension, 211
tuition and fees coverage, 325
Energy, types of, 51
Engineering approach, to risk control, 50
Entry, restraints to, 82
Events that could cause a business income loss, 258
Examination under oath, BPP
Exclusion, additional concurrent causation, in the causes of loss–special form, 205
antennas, in the BIC, 305
any other consequential loss, 305
artificially generated electrical current, in the causes of loss–basic form and broad form, 195

earth movement, in the causes of loss–basic form and broad form, 191
employee dishonesty, in the causes of loss–special form, 202
explosion of steam boilers, in the causes of loss–basic form and broad form, 195
finished stock, BIC, 304
governmental action, in the causes of loss–basic form and broad form, 192
interference by strikers, BIC, 204
inventory shortage, in the causes of loss–special form, 203
loss of license, lease or contract, BIC, 304
loss of use, in the causes of loss–special form, 205
maintenance, in the causes of loss–special form, 201
mechanical breakdown, in the causes of loss–basic form and broad form, 196
nuclear hazard, in the causes of loss–basic form and broad form, 192
off-premises, in the causes of loss–basic form and broad form, 193
ordinance or law, in the causes of loss–basic form and broad form, 190
pollution, in the causes of loss–special form, 204
unauthorized instructions, in the causes of loss–special form, 203
unexplained disappearance, in the causes of loss–special form, 203
voluntary parting, in the causes of loss–special form, 202
war and military action, in the causes of loss–basic form and broad form, 193
water, in the causes of loss–basic form and broad form, 194
Exclusions, additional, in the causes of loss–basic form and broad form, 195
in the causes of loss–basic form and broad forms, 189
in the causes of loss–earthquake form, 210
in the causes of loss–special form, 198
in the legal liability coverage form, 241
Exclusions and limitation, theft-related, in the causes of loss–special form, 201
Expense, depreciation, 270
extra, 8
Expenses, business, 254
continuing and noncontinuing, 256
distinguishing between, 266
extra, 257
Expenses to reduce loss, in the BIC (without extra expense) form, 308
Expenses for services performed by others, during a business interruption, 268
Explosion, 179
combustion, 180
furnace, 180
Explosion control, 97
Explosion of steam boilers exclusion, in the causes of loss–basic form and broad form, 195
Exposure, dependency, 259
loss, 2
Extended business income coverage, 308
Extended business income loss, 294
Extended coverage perils, 174
Extended period of indemnity, in the BIC, 309
Extensions, coverage, BPP, 124
External fire protection, 76
Extinguishers, fire, 73
Extinguishment of fires, 67
Extra expense, 8
definition of, in the BIC (and extra expense) form, 306
MPL and, 294
Extra expense coverage form, 299, 327
coverage options for, 331
determining the extra expense limit for, 329
insurance provisions in, 328
Extra expense from dependent properties endorsement, 331

Extra expense worksheet, 330
Extra expenses, 257

F

Failure to submit reports, under the value reporting form, 164
Falling objects coverage, under the causes of loss–broad form, 187
Farm insurance, 109
Financial elements of business income loss, 254
Financial statement, 12
Financial statement analysis, for exposure identification, 12
Finished stock, in the BIC, 302
Finished stock exclusion, in the BIC, 304
Fire, associated damage, coverage of, 179
 definition of, 178
 friendly, 178
 hostile, 178
 loss control following, 78
 oxygen, air flow, and related factors involved in, 59
Fire brigades, 76
Fire control measures, pre-loss, 59
Fire coverage, under basic causes-of-loss forms, 177
 under broad causes-of-loss forms, 177
Fire dampers, 63
Fire department service charge additional coverage, BPP, 124
Fire detection devices, 72
Fire detection/suppression systems, automatic, 67
 carbon dioxide, 70
 detection and signaling, 72
 dry chemical, 69
 Halon, 70
 water, 68
Fire divisions, 65
Fire doors, automatic, 64
Fire extinguishers, 73
 types of, 75
Fire load, 54
Fire loss, elements of, 50
Fire losses, controlling, 49
Fire partition, 65
Fire protection, external, 76
 internal, 67
Fire salvage, 79
Fire spread, horizontal, limiting, 64
 vertical, limiting, 62
Fire wall, 65
Fire-resistive construction, 58
Fires, extinguishment of, 67
 life safety in, 79
First report overdue, under the builders risk reporting form endorsement, 235
Fixed location planned heat sources, 61
Fixed temperature heat detectors, 72
Fixed temperature rate-of-rise detectors, 72
Fixed versus mobile heat sources, 52
Fixture, under the BPP, 110
Flame and oxidation, in a fire, 178
Flame detectors, 73
Flash point, of liquids, 52
Flat insurance, 155
Flood and high water damage, 98
Flow chart analysis, for exposure identification, 15
Fluctuating values, personal property, options for insuring, 161
Form, business income coverage, 299
Form of the material, 53
Forms, causes-of-loss, 173
Fragile articles, in the causes of loss–special form, 200
Frame construction, 54
Franchise and license fees and royalties, during a business interruption, 267
Friendly fire, in the causes of loss–special form, 197
Friendly fires or heat sources, separation and, 61
Fuel, buildings as, 54
 building contents as, 53
Fuels, 52

Full reporting clause, in the value reporting form, 165
Full separation, in fire risk control, 65
Functional building valuation endorsement, BPP, 150
Functional personal property valuation (other than stock) endorsement, BPP, 151
Funding, current, 30
Furnace explosion, 180

G

Gardener Company case study, 334
Glass, breakage of,
  loss exposures of, 243
Glass breakage, in the causes of loss–broad form, 186
  in the causes of loss–special form, 199
Glass coverage form, 242
  additional coverages under, debris removal, 245
    frames, 245
    newly acquired glass, 245
    removal of obstructions, 245
    temporary plates, 245
  covered property under, 244
  limits and deductible in, 245
  loss payment for large plates option in, 246
  replacement service for, 246
Glass coverage under the BPP and other forms, 243
Governmental action exclusion, in the causes of loss–basic form and broad form, 192
Gross sales value of production, 284
Gross-profit method, 283
Gross-profit ratio, 283
Group captive, 35
Guard services, 75

H

Hail, 180
Halon systems, 70
Heat as a by-product, 60
Heat detectors, fixed temperature, 72
  rate-of-rise, 72
Heat energy, electrical, 60
Heat sources, 51
  controlling, 60
  mobile versus fixed, 52
  planned, 60
  planned versus unplanned, 51
  unplanned, 62
Heat, light, and power expense, during a business interruption, 267
Heavy timber construction, 56
"Hold-harmless" agreement, 33
Homeowners' association (planned unit development), 228
Honesty clause, in the value reporting form, 165
Horizontal fire spread, limiting, 64
Hostile fires, separation and, 62
Hostile versus friendly fire, 178
HPR (highly protected risks) and independent forms, builders risks coverage in, 237
Human behavior approach, to risk control, 50

I

Identifying and analyzing loss exposures, 3
Improvements and betterments, tenants', 248
  trade fixtures versus, 248
  under the BPP, 114
Inaccurate reports, under the builders risk reporting form endorsement, 235
  under the value reporting form, 165
Income, business, definition of, 301
  net, 254
Income statement, 14
  for a manufacturing business, 276
  for a merchandising business, 276
  sample, 275
  for a service business, 274

Income statements, relationship of, to the business income worksheet, 274
Income tax, provision for, business income exposure and, 291
Increase in hazard, in the SPP, 239
Indirect loss, 9
Inflation guard optional coverage, in the BPP, 169
Infrared detectors, 89
Inland marine insurance, commercial, 108
Inland marine policies, builders risks coverage in, 236
Inland and ocean marine business income and extra expense coverages, 333
Inspections, property, 10
Insurance, 32
  "all-risks," 174
  blanket, 156
  "commercial property," 105
  boiler and machinery, 107
  builders risk, 229
  building and contents, 105
  business income, 299
    other types of, 331
  commercial crime, 108
  commercial inland marine, 108
  definition of, 32
  farm, 109
  flat, 155
  retrospectively rated, 35
    specific, 15
    reporting form insurance and, 166
Insurance advisory organizations, role of, 103
Insurance expense, during a business interruption, 270
Insurance provisions, for dependent property exposures, 324
  in the extra expense coverage form, 328
Insurance requirements for condominiums, 220
Insurance Services Office, Inc. (ISO), 103
Insurance survey questionnaire, 11
Insurance to value, in the legal liability coverage form, 242
Insurance under two or more coverages, commercial property conditions, 141
Insured's duties in the event of loss, BPP, 134
Insured's view of agreed value, 155
Insurer, captive, 31
Insurer's options for loss payment, BPP, 136
Insuring agreement, business income coverage form, 300
  in the legal liability coverage form, 240
Interest expense, during a business interruption, 268
Interference by strikers exclusion, BIC, 204
Internal fire protection, 67
Internal theft prevention system, 95
Interviews, for exposure identification, 11
Inventory and inspection, BPP, 135
Inventory method, business income worksheet and, 27 9
Inventory shortage exclusion, in the causes of loss–special form, 203
ISO (Insurance Services Office, Inc.), 103
ISO *Commercial Lines Manual* (CLM), 104
  statement of values in, 153
ISO commercial lines program, 104
ISO coverage parts, 105
Item exposed to loss, 4

J

Joisted masonry construction, 55

L

Labor, materials, or services furnished on property of others, under the BPP, 114
Lacing (paneling), 88
Leader property, 8, 323
Lease or rental expense, during a business interruption, 268
Leased personal property, under the BPP, 115

Leasehold interest coverage form, 246
Legal action against us, commercial property conditions under, 141
Legal liability coverage form, 240
  exclusions in, 241
  insurance to value in, 242
  insuring agreement in, 240
  premium rates in, 242
Lender's loss payable provision, BPP, 140
Lenders' rights under the BPP, 138
Liability loss, 1
Liberalization, commercial property conditions, 141
Licenses, leases, contracts, goodwill, market share, loss of, 265
Life Safety Code, 79
  goals of, 80
Life safety in fires, 79
Lightning, 179
Limit of insurance, BPP, 153
  value reporting form and, 163
Limitation–electronic media and records, in the BIC, 311
Limitation on loss of animals, in the causes of loss–basic form and broad form, 196
Limitations, in the causes of loss–special form, 198
Limitations on waiver of subrogation, in the builders risk coverage form, 236
Limiting access, to control shoplifting, 93
Limiting horizontal fire spread, 64
Limiting vertical fire spread, 62
Limits and deductible, in the glass coverage form, 246
Limits of insurance and deductible, BPP, 128
Liquids, flash point of, 52
Load, fire, 54
Local alarms, 73
Looping, of a fire, 62
Loss, business income, 8
  business interruption, 8
  cause of, 6
  consequential, 9
  contingent business interruption, 8
  covered causes of, 173
  direct, 9
  effects of, 6
  fire, elements of, 50
  indirect, 9
  item exposed to, 4
  liability, 1
  maximum possible, 20
  maximum probable, 21
  property, 1
Loss analysis, 18
Loss assessment coverage, for the condominium commercial unit-owners coverage form, 226
Loss control, 25
  following a fire, 78
Loss determination condition, in the BIC, 311
Loss exposure, 2
Loss exposures, analysis of, 18
  business income, 253
  glass, 243
  identifying and analyzing, 3
  property, 3
    methods for identifying, 9
Loss frequency, potential, 19
Loss of license, lease, or contract exclusion, BIC, 304
Loss of licenses, leases, contracts, goodwill, market share, 264
Loss payable provision, BPP, 139
Loss payable provisions endorsement, BPP, 139
Loss payees, under the BPP, 139
Loss payment, insurer's options for, under the BPP, 136
Loss payment condition, in the BIC, 312
Loss payment for large plates option, in the glass coverage form, 246
Loss payment to an insurance payee, in the condominium association coverage form, 223
Loss prevention and reduction, 42
Loss provisions, other, in the BPP, 133

Loss settlement, under the BPP, 148
Loss severity, potential, 209
Loss of use exclusion, in the causes of loss–special form, 205
Losses, burglary and robbery, controlling, 81
  employee dishonesty, controlling, 94
  retained, methods of paying, 30
  shoplifting, controlling, 92
  theft, controlling, 80
Losses caused by earth movement, 100

M

Maintenance exclusion, in the causes of loss–special form, 201
Maintenance expense, during a business interruption, 270
Management, crisis, 79
Manufacturers selling price endorsement (finished stock only), BPP, 149
Manufacturers' consequential loss assumption endorsement, BPP, 170
Manufacturing business, income statement for, 276
Manufacturing versus nonmanufacturing operations, 282
Masonry noncombustible construction, 58
Masonry veneer, coverage of, in the causes of loss–earthquake form, 211
Master deed, condominium, 219
Maximum length of time required to restore damaged property, MPL and, 293
Maximum period of indemnity option, BIC, 318
Maximum possible loss, 20
Maximum probable loss (MPL), 21
  estimating, for business income, 272
    using the business income worksheet, 292
McCormick Place fire, 49
Mechanical breakdown exclusion, in the causes of loss–basic form and broad form, 196
Mechanical or frictional heat energy, 51
Merchandising business, income statement for, 276
Metallic foil (window tape), 87
Microwave detectors, 89
Mill construction, 56
Miscellaneous real property coverage, for the condominium commercial unit-owners coverage form, 226
MNO Corporation case study, 40
Mobile planned heat sources, 61
Modified fire-resistive construction, 58
Money safes, 83
Monitoring a risk management program, 39
Monoline policy, 104
Monthly limit of indemnity option, BIC, 318
  illustration of, 319
Mortgage holders' provision, BPP, 138
Multi-parent captive, 35

N

Named perils forms (causes of loss–basic and broad forms), 177
National Fire Protection Association (NFPA), 61, 79
Need for adequate insurance condition, in the builders risk coverage form, 234
Net income, business 254
  loss of, 254
"Net loss" versus business income loss, 256
Newly acquired locations coverage extension, in the BIC, 310
Newly acquired or constructed property extension, BPP, 124
No benefit to bailee, commercial property conditions, 141
Non-ISO Condominium coverage options, 222
Noncombustible construction, 57
Noncontinuing expenses, calculating MPL and, 292
Noninsurance transfer, 43

for risk financing, 33
Notice of loss, under the BPP, 134
Nuclear hazard exclusion, in the causes of loss–basic form and broad form, 192
Nuclear heat energy, 51

O

Object protection, 89
Off-premises services–direct damage endorsement, 212
Off-premises services–time element endorsement, 326
Off-premises services exclusion, in the causes of loss–basic form and broad form, 193
Operations, definition of, in the BIC, 305
"Operations" and related coverage options, 305
Optional coverages available for the causes of loss–basic, broad, and special forms, 207
Optional valuation methods, BPP, 146
Ordinance or law–increased period of restoration endorsement, BIC, 326
Ordinance or law coverage endorsement, to the causes of loss–basic, broad, and special forms, 208
Ordinance or law exclusion, in the causes of loss–basic form and broad form, 190
Ordinary construction, 55
Ordinary masonry construction, 55
Ordinary payroll, definition of, 316
Organization's own property off premises, 260
Other "commercial property" forms, 217
Other insurance, commercial property conditions, 141
Other personal property not covered under the BPP, 118
Outdoor property extension, BPP, 127
Oxygen, air flow, and related factors, 59

P

Package policy, 104
Partition, fire, 65
Payroll, ordinary, definition of, 316
Payroll coverage options, in the BIC, 316
Payroll expense, during a business interruption, 267
Payroll limitation or exclusion endorsement, BIC, 316
PCB losses, 265
Peak periods, 293
Peak season limit of insurance endorsement, 162
Penalties, under the value reporting form, 164
Percentage deductible, in the causes of loss–earthquake form, 211
Perils, covered, by the causes of loss–basic form and broad forms, 177
  in the SPP, 239
    under the glass coverage form, 244
  extended coverage, 174
Perimeter system, 86
Period of restoration, under the BIC, 301
Personal effects and property of others extension, BPP, 126
Personal property, 4
  building and, coverage options for, 145
  leased, under the BPP, 115
Personal property of others, coverage of, in the condominium association coverage form, 223
  under the BPP, 115
"Personal property of others," under the BPP, 113
Personal property values, fluctuating, options for insuring, 161
Personnel screening, to control employee dishonesty, 96
Pete's Auto Repair (example of a business interruption loss), 254
Photoelectric (eyes, beams), 88

Physical protection, against burglary and robbery, 82
Pier and wharf additional covered causes of loss endorsement, 215
Planned heat sources, 60
  fixed location, 61
  mobile, 61
Planned unit development (PUD), 228
Planned versus unplanned sources of heat, 51
Planning, disaster, 79
Plants and outdoor property, not covered under the BPP, 116
Police report, BPP, 134
Policies, businessowners, 109
  valued, 331
Policy, monoline, 104
  package, 104
Policy period and coverage territory, Commercial property conditions, 142
Pollutant cleanup and removal additional coverage, BPP, 123
Pollution exclusion, in the causes of loss–special form, 204
Pollution losses, business income losses and, 265
Postage and telephone expense, during a business interruption, 270
Post-funding, for paying losses, 30
Potential loss frequency, 19
Potential loss severity, 20
Power, heat, and refrigeration deduction endorsement, BIC, 317
Preaction sprinkler system, 69
Pre-funding, for paying losses, 30
Pre-loss fire control measures, 59
Premium, provisional, in the value reporting form, 166
Premium rates, in the legal liability coverage form, 242
Preservation of property, BPP, 134
Preservation of property additional coverage, BPP, 123
Process, risk management, 2
Production, gross sales value of, 284
Professional fees, during a business interruption, 270
Profit-sharing payments, during a business interruption, 272
Projections for the twelve-month period beginning with the policy inception, 291
Proof of loss, BPP, 135
Property, classification of, for risk management purposes, 5
  covered, under the glass coverage form, 244
  damaged, time required to replace, 261
  increased cost to repair or replace, 8
  loss of revenue from, 8
  personal, 4
  real
  reduction in value of, 7
Property covered only for "specified causes of loss," in the causes of loss–special form, 200
Property insurance, commercial, overview of, 103
  condominium, 221
Property loss, 1
Property loss exposures, identifying and analyzing, 3
  methods for identifying, 9
Property not covered, under the BPP, 116
Property not covered at replacement cost, under the BPP, 148
Property off premises, organization's own, 260
Property off-premises extension, BPP, 126
Property otherwise covered exclusion, under the BPP, 119
Property owned by others, under the BPP, 113
Property owned by the insured, under the BPP, 113
Property perils, examples of, 7
Property risk control, 49
Property risk management, 1
Property totally destroyed, depreciation expense and, 271

Property in transit extension, in the causes of loss–special form, 206
Proprietary alarms, 73
Protective procedures, 92
against shoplifting, 94
Provisional premium, in the value reporting form, 166
Proximity (capacitance or electrostatic), 89

Q

Questionnaire, insurance survey, 11
risk management survey, 12
Questionnaires, for exposure identification, 11

R

Radioactive contamination endorsement, 214
Rate of rise heat detectors, fixed temperature, 72
Rating, for blanket insurance, 160
for the BPP, 152
Ratio, cost-of-goods-sold, 283
gross-profit, 283
Real property, 4
"Reasonable speed," in the BIC, 301
Recovered property, BPP, 137
Reducing damageability, in fire control, 66
Reduction value of property, 7
Remote alarms, 73
Rental value, in the BIC, 305
Repairs and maintenance, for improvements and betterments, 249
Replace cost optional coverage, in the BPP, 146
Replacement, time of, under the BPP, 149
Replacement cost versus actual cash value recovery, 147
Replacement service, in the glass coverage form, 246
Reporting form endorsement, builders risk, 234
Reporting requirement, under the value reporting form, 162
Reports, failure to submit, under the value reporting form, 164
Restraints to entry, 82
Retained losses, methods of paying, 30
Retention and transfer, techniques for combining, 34
Retrospectively rated insurance, 35
Revenue, 8
business 254
Riot, 182
Risk control, 25
engineering approach to, 50
human behavior approach to, 50
property, 49
Risk financing, noninsurance transfer for, 33
Risk management, property, 1
Risk management decisions, effect of size on, 36
Risk management process, 2
Risk management process at work, 39
Risk management program, monitoring, 39
Risk management survey questionnaires, 12
Risk management techniques, alternative, examining the feasibility of, 25
implementing, 38
selecting the best, 35
selection methods for, 37
Robbery, 81

S

Safe and vault classifications, 84
Safes, 83
money, 83
Safety glass coverage, BPP
Salvage, fire, 79
Seasonal fluctuations, effect of, on business income losses, 266

Security patrols, watchman or, 91
Segregation of exposures, 43
Self-closing doors, 64
Self-insurance, 31
Separation, friendly fires or heat sources, 61
full, 65
hostile fires, 62
Separation of duties, 96
Service business, income statement form 274
Services purchased from outsiders, 289
Shoplifting, 81
Shoplifting losses, controlling, 92
Signaling systems, 73
Single-entity concept, 219
Sinkhole collapse, 184
Small building losses, BPP, 132
Small physical damage loss, long interruption, 264
Smoke, 181
in the in the causes of loss–special form, 199
Smoke detectors, 73
Snow, ice, or sleet, weight of, 187
Special causes-of-loss forms, 197 (*see also* Causes of loss–special form)
Special multi-peril (SMP) package policy, 104
Specific insurance, 156
reporting form insurance and, 166
Spoilage coverage endorsement, 213
Sprinkler leakage–earthquake extension endorsement, 211
Sprinkler systems, 67
water, 68
Standard fire policy, 173
Standard property policy (SPP), 237
and BPP, comparison of, 238
conditions in, 239
cancellation, 239
increase in hazard, 239
vacancy and unoccupancy, 239
covered perils in, 239
covered property under, 237
Standpipe systems, 75
Statement, financial, 12
Statement of values, BPP, 153
Statutes, condominium, 219
Steam boilers, explosion of, in the causes of loss–basic form and broad form, 195
Stock sold but not delivered, BPP, 133
Subsequent report overdue, under the builders risk reporting form endorsement, 235
"Supplemental coverage," 173
Surveillance, to control shoplifting, 93
Surveillance cameras, 91
Suspension of coinsurance, in the BPP, 153

T

Taxes, during a business interruption, 269
Temperatures at which substances vaporize, 52
Tenants' improvements and betterments, 248
alternatives to both building owner and tenant carrying insurance for, 251
BPP, 133
building owner's coverage of, 249
repairs of and maintenance for, 249
tenant's coverage of, 250
Theft, in the builders risk coverage form, 232
Theft of building materials limitation, in the causes of loss–special form, 204
Theft losses, controlling, 80
Theft prevention system, internal, 95
Theft-related exclusions and limitations, in the causes of loss–special form, 201
Time element exposures (*see also* business loss income exposures), p. 253
Time of replacement , under the BPP, 149
Time required to replace damaged property, 261

Time required to restore normal rate of income, 261
Timing of a business income loss, 261
Total loss concept, 23
Trade fixtures, under the BPP, 113
Trade fixtures versus improvements and betterments, 248
Transfer, 32
  noninsurance, 43
  noninsurance, for risk financing, 33
  retention and, techniques for combining, 34
Transfer of rights of recovery against others to us, 142
Tuition and fees endorsement, BIC, covered sources of revenue, 325

U

Ultrasonic detectors, 88
Unauthorized instructions exclusion, in the causes of loss–special form, 203
Underground foundations, coverage of, in the causes of loss–earthquake form, 210
Unexplained disappearance exclusion, in the causes of loss–special form, 203
Unit, condominium, 218
Unplanned heat sources, 62

V

Vacancy, in the BPP, 137
Vacancy permit endorsement, BPP, 138
Vacancy and unoccupancy, in the SPP, 239
Valuable papers and records, cost of research extension, BPP, 126
  in the causes of loss–special form, 200
  under the BPP, 133
Valuable papers and records exclusion, under the BPP, 119
Valuation, BPP, 132
Valuation condition, in the builders risk coverage form, 233
Value reporting form, advantages and disadvantages of, 168
  BPP, 162
  limit of insurance under, 163
  penalties under, 164
  reporting requirement under, 163
Valued business income coverage, 300
Valued policies, 331
  advantages and disadvantages of, 332
Values, fluctuating, options for insuring, 161
  statement of, 153
Vandalism, 183
Vaults, 83
Vehicle damage, in the causes of loss–special form, 198
Vehicle, 182
Vehicles, watercraft, aircraft exclusion, under the BPP, 118
Vertical fire spread, limiting, 62
Vibration detectors (seismic), 90
Volcanic action, 185
Voluntary parting exclusion, in the causes of loss–special form, 202

W

Waiver of rights of recovery, in the condominium association coverage form, 224
Wall, fire, 65
War and military action exclusion, in the causes of loss–basic form and broad form, 193
Watchman or security patrols, 91
Water damage, in the causes of loss–special form, 199
  controlling, 77
Water damage caused by "ice dam," in the causes of loss–special form, 198
Water exclusion, in the causes of loss–basic form and broad form, 194
Water spray sprinkler system, 69
Water systems, 68
W. C. SHAVER, 174

Weight of ice, snow, or sleet, in the causes of loss–special form, 199
Weight of snow, ice, or sleet, coverage of, under the causes of loss–broad form, 187
Wet-pipe sprinkler system, 68
Windstorm damage, controlling, 98
Windstorm or hail, in the causes of loss–special form, 199
Windstorm, 180
Wood frame construction, 54
Wood joisted construction, 55
Wooden screens, 87
Worksheet, business income, 273
  extra expense, 330

Y

"Your business personal property," under the BPP, 112